Soviet
Military
Doctrine

Soviet Military Doctrine

Continuity, Formulation, and Dissemination

Harriet Fast Scott
and William F. Scott

Westview Press / Boulder and London

Copyright © 1988 by Westview Press, Inc.

Published in 1988 in the United States of America by Westview Press, Inc., 5500 Central Avenue, Boulder, Colorado 80301, and in the United Kingdom by Westview Press, Inc., 13 Brunswick Centre, London WC1N 1AF, England

Library of Congress Cataloging-in-Publication Data
Scott, Harriet Fast.
    Soviet military doctrine : continuity, formulation, and
dissemination / Harriet Fast Scott, William F. Scott.
    p. cm.
    Bibliography: p.
    Includes indexes.
    ISBN 0-8133-0656-6   ISBN 0-8133-0671-X (if published as a pbk.)
    1. Soviet Union—Military policy.   2. Communism—Soviet Union.
3. Communist strategy.   I. Scott, William Fontaine, 1919–
II. Title.
UA770.S355 1988
355′.0335′47—dc19   88-11102
                                                                          CIP

Printed and bound in the United States of America

The paper used in this publication meets the requirements of the American National Standard for Permanence of Paper for Printed Library Materials Z39.48-1984.

10   9   8   7   6   5   4   3   2

Contents

Tables and Figures

ix

Preface

The purpose of this book is to document from basic Soviet sources the development of Soviet military doctrine and its impact upon the Soviet Armed Forces.

Soviet military doctrine is defined as the military policy of the Communist Party. In one way or another, this policy affects the lives of all of us—as a possible threat to free institutions and political processes as well as to our economic life and well-being. Generally we approach Soviet military policy in terms of military balances and weapons: comparisons in the number of men under arms, the speed of aircraft of the Soviet bloc versus that of NATO aircraft, the number of ballistic missiles and their throw-weights. Studying such balances is of critical importance in defining, to some degree, existing forces. But it is only through a deep and thorough study of the military policy of the Communist Party, which translates directly into military doctrine, that we can obtain the background that might aid in negotiating with the Soviets on arms control matters or in making decisions that will enable those nations outside of the Soviet bloc to deter future Kremlin military moves.

Since there is no commonly held ideology in the United States, there is a tendency to assume that Marxist-Leninist ideology, from which Soviet military doctrine stems, is of no consequence to the Kremlin leadership. In like manner, since we do not have a military doctrine in the Soviet sense, we generally consider Soviet military doctrine to be unimportant or overlook it entirely.

The various aspects of Soviet military doctrine are found in many Soviet books, from those for young children to those for teenagers getting ready for compulsory military service, and philosophical treatises for officers, generals, and admirals. This should not be surprising, because the purpose of military doctrine is to prepare the entire nation for the possibility of future war.

Soviet military theorists frequently paraphrase V. I. Lenin: "To determine the direction in which a known process will develop further, it is necessary to detect in it the remnants of the past, the basis of the present, and the embryo of the future." In order to understand what the future might hold for a certain concept, "one must start with an examination of how the concept arose and what actual conditions gave birth to it." Similarly, to understand Soviet military doctrine and its possible changes at any specified time, we must start with the early days of the Soviet state when the concept of a military doctrine was first formulated and trace the development of that doctrine up to the present. We also should investigate where, how, and by whom the doctrine is formulated and how it is disseminated.

In the first part of this book, we will examine the content of Soviet military doctrine. We will begin our examination with the earliest formulations made after the 1917 October Revolution and trace the emerging doctrine through the noisy debates of the 1920s and through the long silence of the Stalin years to its reemergence in 1960. The military doctrine of Khrushchev will be contrasted and compared with the military doctrine of Brezhnev. We will then look closely at Soviet military doctrine as it passed through the short regimes of Andropov and Chernenko and describe its development in the Gorbachev era.

It is difficult to examine military doctrine without also looking at a very closely connected subject, the laws of war. After giving a short analysis of that subject, we will turn to the question of how military doctrine is formulated, what role the Communist Party and the government play, and what input is made by the military and by the Soviet military-industrial complex. Once military doctrine is formulated, the Party must disseminate selected elements of the doctrine both to the military and to the population at large. The Party also makes known certain portions of doctrine to potential enemies. In some periods the doctrine is made to appear threatening; at other times, as in the late 1980s, to appear benign.

We recognize the danger of concluding a work about Soviet military doctrine when significant changes may be taking place in the Soviet Union. But at some point research must stop and conclusions must be drawn. Whatever may be the outcome of the *perestroika* undertaken by General Secretary Mikhail S. Gorbachev in the latter half of the 1980s, we hope other analysts will build on the research we have completed.

Assistance from the Earhart Foundation has made it possible to devote time to research. John H. Morse, as in the past, continued to provide encouragement. The pioneering work of John Sloan and Allan Rehm in investigating the laws of war was of major assistance. One of our sons, Christopher Scott, was most helpful in final editing and in rechecking sources.

Harriet Fast Scott   *William F. Scott*

Acronyms

CPSU	Communist Party of the Soviet Union
DOSAAF	Volunteer Society for Cooperation with the Army, Aviation, and Fleet
GKNT	State Committee on Science and Technology
GKO	State Committee of Defense
GOSSNAB	State Committee for Material and Technical Supplies
GOSPLAN	State Planning Committee
GOSSTROI	State Construction Committee
GRU	Main Intelligence Directorate of the Ministry of Defense
ICBM	intercontinental ballistic missile
IMEMO	Institute of World Economy and International Relations
IUSA	Institute of the United States of America ("and Canada" added in 1974)
KGB	Committee of State Security
MIRV	multiple independently targeted reentry vehicle
MPA	Main Political Administration
MVD	Ministry of Internal Affairs
NKVD	People's Commissariat of Internal Affairs
OGPU	Combined State Political Directorate (forerunner of the KGB)
OSO	Society for Cooperation with the Defense of the Country
PKK	Political Consultative Committee of the Warsaw Pact
PKO	antispace defense
PRO	antimissile defense
PVO	antiair defense
RKKA	Workers' and Peasants' Red Army
RVSR	Revolutionary Council of the Republic
STO	Council of Labor and Defense
SVE	*Soviet Military Encyclopedia*
TPK	territorial-production complexes
TVDs	theaters of military actions
TVs	theaters of war
VGK	Supreme High Command
VNO	Military Science Society
VPK	Military-Industrial Committee

Part 1
Continuity and Change in Soviet Military Doctrine

1
The Background of
Soviet Military Doctrine

War has been the constant companion of humanity for all of recorded history. Many people fatalistically assume that wars will continue. Others, more idealistic, sincerely believe that eternal peace could be achieved if only nations of the world would do this or that. Some attribute the cause of war to the territorial instinct to defend one's turf with blood if necessary. Others feel that fighting in itself is a permanent element of human nature.

Marxism-Leninism provides its followers with an exact answer to the question of war. It holds that "with private ownership of the means of production, society was divided into antagonistic classes and exploitative states were created."[1] How can war be eliminated? Marxists-Leninists believe that "the inevitability of the transition of all countries and nations to communism is the historical prerequisite for elimination of war from the life of society and establishing eternal peace on earth."[2] But this communist Utopia has not yet arrived. Nor have relations between "fraternal" communist countries over the years augured well for a peaceful future.

One of the greatest military philosophers of modern times, Karl von Clausewitz, wrote a monumental work entitled, simply, *On War*. This book had an important influence on Vladimir I. Lenin, who copied a number of sections from the text and made extensive marginal notes. Lenin seized on Clausewitz's definition of war as a continuation of politics and elaborated on it thus in his article "War and Revolution":

> We all know the dictum of Clausewitz, one of the most famous writers on the philosophy and history of war, which says: "War is a continuation of politics by other means." This dictum comes from a writer who reviewed the history of wars and drew philosophic lessons from it shortly after the period of the Napoleonic wars. This writer, whose basic views are now undoubtedly familiar to every thinking person, nearly eighty years ago challenged the ignorant man-in-the-street conception of war as being a thing apart from the policies of the government and classes concerned, as being a simple attack that disturbs the peace, and is then followed by restoration of the peace thus disturbed, as much as to say: "They had a fight, then they made up!" This is a grossly ignorant view, one that was repudiated scores of years ago and

3

is repudiated by any more or less careful analysis of any historical epoch of war.

War is a continuation of policy by other means. All wars are inseparable from the political systems that engender them. The policy which a given state, a given class within that state, pursued for a long time before that war is inevitably continued in that same class during the war, the form of action alone being changed.[3]

At the time Lenin was absorbing Clausewitz's concept of war, the Russian Army, like many others, did not have a precise concept of "military doctrine." That term was not even listed in the old *Russian Military Encyclopedia*.[4] The Czar and the leaders of his army did have a definite array of ideas on war, however, which were reflected in regulations and other military documents.

After the Russo-Japanese War of 1904–1905 the Czar's military theoreticians conducted, for a time, an active discussion of military doctrine. However, little information about the discussion was made available to the West, other than what was said about foreign military forces. Later, in an article entitled "The Fall of Port Arthur," Lenin sought to establish the relationship of the proletariat and its state to war and the military organization of socialism. This relationship was reflected in materials of the 7th to 12th and later Party Congresses and Central Committee Plenums. Today Soviet spokesmen assert that these materials have guided the Soviet Armed Forces from its very beginning.[5]

Lenin and his followers seized power in 1917. Immediately, the new government of Soviet Russia was in trouble. The Marxist idea that capitalism was fated to be replaced by socialism put the new socialist state at odds with the world. Soviet ideologists portrayed a class struggle between workers supported by peasants on the one side and the exploiting bourgeoisie on the other. Hopes of having the workers of other countries rise up against their governments remained an empty Soviet dream. The Bolshevik-led government stood alone. The Civil War erupted in 1918 and officially lasted until 1920, though resistance continued in many areas for much longer. Posters at the time depicted the nation surrounded by a ring of fire. The threat of capitalist encirclement was to dominate the thinking of the country's leaders for decades.

Lenin had spent his years in internal and external exile reading and writing about war and the kind of army that would be needed to bring about the revolution. The basis of what is known as the political side of military doctrine is described in Lenin's voluminous writings. This foundation forms part of the present Marxist-Leninist teachings, which include both the ideological and methodological basis of Soviet military doctrine and Soviet military science. After the 1917 October Revolution, when the new socialist state began its attempt to hammer out the "military-political" side of a military doctrine, there was opposition from all quarters. Equal opposition met the attempt to formulate the "military-technical" side.

Military Doctrine, First Stage (1917–1928)

The Beginning of Soviet Military Doctrine

In 1969, *Voyennaya Mysl'* (Military Thought), the restricted journal of the Soviet General Staff, carried an article by General of the Army Semyon P. Ivanov, then commandant of the Academy of the General Staff.[6] Entitled "Soviet Military Doctrine and Strategy," the article was addressed to generals, admirals, and officers of the Soviet Armed Forces. In it Ivanov discussed "the origin and development of Soviet military doctrine and strategy, the principles of modern military doctrine, views on the character of a possible war and requirements for preparing the country and the Armed Forces for such a war."[7]

Ivanov gave the following periodization for military doctrine:

First period, 1917–1928: Civil War to industrialization
Second period, 1929–1941: industrialization to the Great Patriotic War
Third period, 1941–1945: Great Patriotic War
Postwar period, 1946–1953: end of war to death of Stalin
Recent period, 1954–1960: revolution in military affairs
Present, 1960–   : new military doctrine

Ivanov credited Lenin with having laid the foundations of Soviet military doctrine and military science. Following the Civil War, Soviet military doctrine was further developed by Mikhail V. Frunze. In particular, it was Frunze who stipulated that military doctrine had two parts: political and technical. Ivanov did not mention the contribution to Soviet military thought made by Leon Trotskiy, the brilliant leader of the Red Army during the Civil War. Other authors writing in the open press confirmed Ivanov's statements.

The idea of "military doctrine" surfaced on the pages of the journal *Voyennoye Delo* (Military Affairs) in August 1918[8] in an article by then chief of the All-Russian Main Staff Aleksandr A. Svechin (1878–1938), one of the military specialists from the Czarist army who worked for the new regime. Svechin, later a professor at the Academy of the General Staff, is best known for his book *Strategiya*.[9] He thought that doctrine should be limited to a "tactical outlook." Many opinions about military doctrine were expressed over the next few years, but it was not until 1920 that the debate heated up in earnest.

M. V. Frunze, a Civil War hero, was a prime mover in the debates.[10] He had joined the Communist Party in 1904 when he was nineteen years old and soon became a professional revolutionary. For his part in various uprisings he was arrested, exiled, and twice sentenced to death. During the Civil War he organized and fought successful campaigns on the Eastern and Southern fronts. In March 1924, soon after Lenin's death, Frunze was made deputy chairman of the Revvoyensovyet USSR and deputy commissar for Military and Naval Affairs. A month later, he was named chief of staff of the Red Army and head of the military academy that now bears his name. In January 1925, Frunze succeeded Trotskiy as commissar for Military and Naval Affairs and chairman of the Revvoyensovyet USSR. In February, he became a member of the Council of Labor and Defense (STO), the forerunner to the present Council of Defense. His military reforms of 1924–1925 are considered by Soviet historians as critical to the development of the Soviet Armed Forces. Although he died at age forty, following a botched operation in the Kremlin hospital, he is now enshrined in Soviet folklore.[11]

During the debates on doctrine, Frunze explained that prior to the twentieth century wars might have involved but a small segment of the population and only part of the total resources of the state. But under the conditions of the 1920s, when Frunze was writing, he pointed out that a future war would demand multimillion-man armies. The entire resources of a nation might be engaged in carrying out the struggle. Under these conditions, there must be an overall plan for the conduct of war and strict coordination when the war was in progress. He expressed a concept that was repeated in later years by Soviet military leaders as military doctrine: "The state must define the nature of overall and, in particular, military policy beforehand, designate the possible objects of its military intentions in accordance with this policy, and develop and institute a definitive plan of action for the state as a whole, one that would take account of future confrontations and ensure their success by making prudent use of the nation's energy before they take place."[12]

Based on this overall concept, according to Frunze, the armed forces must be organized in a manner that will meet the general tasks of the state. Members of the armed forces must be united from the top down by common views on the nature of the missions themselves and on the means for carrying them out. This objective requires unity of thought and will, which in itself is a complex and difficult achievement. Such unity can be reached only when the leaders of the armed forces follow a plan that rests on clearly formulated premises sanctioned by the opinion of the country's ruling class.

Frunze then tried to sum up the significance that a "unified military doctrine" would have for the nation and, in particular, for the further development of its armed forces. The primary question doctrine must answer, according to Frunze, "is the nature of the military confrontations awaiting us." Once this has been determined, the next question for doctrine is to determine what action the nation must take in building up its armed forces. Should the nation concentrate on passive defense, or should it develop a force capable of offensive actions? This question is basic to any military policy, and how it is answered will determine how the armed forces will be organized, how the force will be equipped, and how military personnel will be trained. The answer to this question also determines how the nation will be "educated" with respect to military affairs. All teaching must follow a unified plan and must express the unified will of the social class in power.

Frunze then discussed the two sides of military doctrine: the technical and the political. The technical side would be concerned with the training and education of military personnel, the organization of the armed forces,

and the methods of solving combat problems. The political side would deal
with the relationship of the armed forces "with the development of the
overall structure of state life, which defines the social environment in which
military work must be conducted and the nature of military missions which
may be assigned." Frunze gave this definition of a unified military doctrine:
"a teaching adopted by the army of a particular state establishing the nature
of armed forces development, the methods of troop combat training, and
the methods of troop management, based on the state's prevailing views
on the nature of the military missions lying before it and the means for
executing them, which are dependent on the class nature of the state and
are defined by the level to which the country's productive forces have
developed."[13]

To determine what should be the basis of the military doctrine "of our
Workers' and Peasants' Red Army," Frunze first attempted to explain the
nature of the new Soviet state. He described it as "the only state in the
world in which power belongs to labor" and a "workers' and peasants'
state in which the working class has the leading role." The basic task of
the dictatorship of the proletariat is to destroy capitalist production relations
and replace them with a structure based on public ownership of the means
of production and planned distribution of goods. The ideas of the new state
"are in irreconcilable conflict with the foundations for the existence of all
other countries in the world, in which capital still reigns throughout."[14]

Equipping the Soviet Armed Forces with modern equipment was one of
the main questions of military doctrine. A number of Soviet theorists
contended that technical backwardness and general economic weakness
would preclude the Soviet Union from becoming a major military power.
Frunze maintained that the material and technical basis of the new nation's
military forces should and could be achieved by "shock" actions, to which
all other needs should be subordinated. Because Frunze's work serves today
as a basic text for Soviet officers, those in the West concerned with arms
control agreements, improved relations with the Soviet Union, and other
matters relating to the avoidance of war should find his writings of particular
interest. Western writers might consider whether some of his conclusions
and recommendations, such as the following, are still valid:

> Between our proletarian state and all the rest of the bourgeois world there
> can be only a state of long, stubborn desperate war to the death; war requiring
> colossal endurance, discipline, firmness, inflexibility, and a united will. The
> external form of this interaction can change, depending on changing conditions
> and the course of the struggle; a state of overt war might give way to some
> form of treaty relations permitting a certain degree of peaceful coexistence of
> the conflicting sides.[15]

The "peaceful coexistence" was not intended to be permanent. Frunze
concluded that each Soviet citizen must be infused with the thought that:

our country is in the situation of a besieged stronghold and will remain there as long as capital reigns in the world; that, as previously, the country's energy and will must be directed toward the creation and fortification of our military might; that state propaganda on the inevitability of an active conflict with our class enemy must prepare that sole psychological environment of national attention, concern, and care for the needs of the army in the atmosphere of which the business of developing our armed forces could go on successfully.[16]

Such was the heritage left in the writings of M. V. Frunze.

Military Doctrine of the Future

In 1923, another Soviet theoretician joined in the discussion on military doctrine. Ioakim I. Vatsetis (1873–1938),[17] a professor at the Red Army Academy who had been commander in chief of all Red Army forces (1918–1919), published an article entitled "On Military Doctrine of the Future." He began his article with a number of truisms in order to emphasize his point about the need for doctrine.

Among his statements of basic truths were the following:

1. It is one thing to win engagements and battles, but winning a campaign is another story. One can win all the engagements and battles, but lose the campaign (Napoleon, the Sino-Japanese War of 1900, Germany in 1914–1918).
2. The one who is stronger at the end of the war than at the start wins the campaign.
3. Strength can be increased by drastic annihilation of the enemy, by concluding an appropriate alliance, and so on. Increasing one's combat might solely by exhausting one's own country loses the campaign (Napoleon in 1814; Germany in 1914–1918).[18]

Vatsetis defined military doctrine as a teaching on a state's readiness for war. Military doctrine is an attribute of state power; as such it is a function of the state "having absolutely nothing to do with day-to-day problems." The main goal of a unified military school, Vatsetis wrote, is to achieve, at all costs, *a common interpretation of military affairs*. He felt that the view of those who argued that a unified military school was the result of a common interpretation of military affairs was too simplistic. Vatsetis argued that, first, it had to be determined what factors would influence the establishment of a common interpretation of military affairs. Such an interpretation is brought about through the influence of military education. Military education would lead to a common interpretation of military affairs only when it took a particular direction, unswervingly and uniformly. Finally, a unified military school "is a categorical, self-defined universal entity within the army of a given state."[19]

According to Vatsetis, military education should not be limited to one particular category of personnel, such as officers of the General Staff, as "had been the case until quite recently." Such a practice would "result in a priesthood," which "is totally inadmissible." Instead, every field commander must possess knowledge on a par with that of staff executives in order to achieve common understanding. Lacking that commonality, the General Staff and the field commanders would not be able to understand each other. Therefore, the key to achieving a common interpretation of military affairs is providing higher military education to the army on a broad scale.

Vatsetis went on to explain that an armed force is a tool for the government to use in resolving international issues. The state has the authority to create unified regulations that are binding on the entire army. Consequently *"regulations are the means for creating a unified military school within the army."* Achieving a common interpretation of military affairs within the army's ranks must be done both prior to and during a battle by means of higher education. Vatsetis asked: "What is necessary in order for everyone to function identically? The will must be nurtured identically within everyone."[20]

The Opposing View

Glasnost has not yet been extended to publishing all the writings on doctrine by Soviet theorists of the early 1920s. Opposing views on military questions and the nature of the Soviet state that were then prevalent remain blank spaces in Soviet history. In particular, the debates between M. V. Frunze and Leon Trotskiy do not appear even in the "complete" works of Frunze that are republished every few years. The myths now surrounding Frunze might be questioned if it were revealed that Lenin sided with Trotskiy.

Trotskiy became a revolutionary in 1898. Arrested and exiled to Siberia, he escaped abroad where he first met Lenin in London. When the 1905 revolution failed, Trotskiy was again exiled to Siberia and again escaped. He settled in Vienna where he became editor of *Pravda*. During World War I he lived in New York. On his return to Russia following the overthrow of the Czar, Trotskiy joined the Bolsheviks and became chairman of the Military Revolutionary Committee, which seized power in October. Between 1918 and 1925 he was the commissar of Military and Naval Affairs. In the West, Trotskiy is generally thought to have displayed exceptional talents as a tactician and strategist during the Civil War, when his popularity was second only to that of Lenin.

Trotskiy, well known for his theory of "permanent revolution," was a Politburo member from 1919 until 1926. After Lenin's death in 1924, he opposed the ruling triumvirate of L. B. Kamenev, G. Ye. Zinov'yev and Joseph V. Stalin, who advocated a policy of "building socialism in one country." Stalin regarded Trotskiy as a major rival and took steps to eliminate his influence. It was a bitter pill for Trotskiy in January 1925 when he was replaced as commissar of Military and Naval Affairs by his earlier antagonist and chief of staff, Frunze. In 1927 he was expelled from the Party and forced into internal and later external exile. His anti-Stalinist books and articles made him a target for Stalin's OGPU, forerunner of the KGB. After several unsuccessful attempts, Soviet agents finally penetrated his residence in Mexico City in August 1940. The agent who swung the ax on Trotskiy's head later returned to Moscow and received an award.

The final winner in the Frunze-Trotskiy controversy obviously was Frunze. It is ironic that the name of Trotskiy, the single individual most responsible for the success of the Red Army, has been given to Trotskiyism, a heresy defined in Soviet works as "an ideological-political petitbourgeois tendency hostile to Marxism-Leninism and the international communist movement, which hides its opportunistic essence with radical phrases of the left."[21]

When Trotskiy's writings on military matters are examined, the reason for their being banned in the Soviet Union today becomes obvious. He scorned the views of Frunze and Vatsetis, in particular those that later were stressed in Soviet doctrinal writings.

In a 1921 article entitled "Military Doctrine or Pseudo-Military Doctrinairism," Trotskiy expressed views that are, in part, still true, but which the Soviet leadership could never acknowledge. The Red Army, he claimed, "is the military expression of the proletarian dictatorship." It might be possible, he added, "to say that the Red Army is the military embodiment of the 'doctrine' of the proletarian dictatorship." He then explained the significance of military power. "First, the proletarian dictatorship is rendered secure by the Red Army; second, the dictatorship of the proletariat would be impossible without the Red Army."[22]

The situation described by Trotskiy continues. However, the Soviet leadership now asserts that its Armed Forces are not necessary for "internal purposes" and that the military will disappear altogether when capitalism ceases to exist. In actual fact, as Trotskiy explained, the Communist Party gained its control by the military might of the Red Army, and the Party maintains its control by the same method.

But doctrine, in Trotskiy's view, should be put into its proper perspective. He explained: "Certain perspicacious innovators have suddenly discovered that *we are living, or rather not living at all but simply vegetating without military doctrine*, just like the king in Andersen's fairy tale who used to go naked without knowing it."[23] (Emphasis in original.) His sarcasm continued: "From the way things are put, it turns out that we were able to create the Red Army and, furthermore, a victorious Red Army, but, you see, we failed to supply it with a military doctrine. And this Red Army continues to thrive unregenerate. To the point-blank question of what the doctrine of the Red Army should be, we get the following answer: It must comprise the sum total of the elementary principles of building, educating and applying our armed forces."[24]

In particular, Trotskiy scorned the military theories of Frunze, who claimed that the Soviet military system "derives wholly from the specific class nature of the proletarian state," that a unified military doctrine is deduced from this class nature, and that all the necessary practical conclusions flow from this doctrine. But such a method, Trotskiy asserted, "is scholastic and hopeless. Naturally, the class nature of the proletarian state determines the social composition of the Red Army, its political world-outlook and aims and methods." Although this class nature may have a certain indirect influence on strategy and tactics, "strategy and tactics are derived not from a proletarian world-outlook but from the conditions of technology, in particular military technology, from the available facilities of providing supplies, from the geographical milieu, the character of the enemy, etc."[25]

Trotskiy continued his attack: "Those comrades who spoke here in the name of a new military doctrine have completely failed to convince me. I see in it a dangerous thing." Some "comrades," according to Trotskiy, said that

> our doctrine consists not in commanding but in persuading, convincing and impressing through authoritativeness. A wonderful idea! . . . Authoritativeness is an excellent thing, but not very tangible. If one were to impress solely through authoritativeness then what need have we for the Cheka [secret police] and the Special Department [counterintelligence]? Finally, if we can impress a Tambov *muzhik* [peasant] solely through our authoritativeness, then why shouldn't we do the same with regard to the German and French peasants?[26]

He went on to warn that a military doctrine is of no use unless it is based on reality. It is necessary to continue to learn from the past and not to throw away all the old statutes. "It will do incalculable harm if we were to inculcate the military youth with the idea that the old doctrine is utterly worthless and that we have entered a new epoch when everything can be viewed superciliously and with the equipment of an ignoramus."[27]

In a further attack on Frunze's thesis, Trotskiy maintained that "the heralds of the new unified military doctrine are at fault not only in giving improper formulations of the general goals of tactics and strategy." Instead, Trotskiy insisted, those who developed the new doctrine diverted attention from more important, practical tasks "which make the real culture of the Red Army."[28] He then advocated placing more emphasis on military fundamentals, presenting them in a manner that would embarrass Soviet military leaders today: "Let us not tear ourselves away from elementary needs, rations, and boots. I think that a good ration is superior to a poor doctrine; and as touches boots, I maintain that our military doctrine begins with this, that we must tell the Red Army soldier: Learn to grease your boots, and oil your rifle. If in addition to our will to victory and our readiness to self-sacrifice we also learn to grease boots, then we shall have the best possible military doctrine."[29]

Frunze's emphasis on maneuver, especially his assertion that this concept was a result of a new "scientific view," drew more sarcastic criticism from Trotskiy. "You see—strategy must be offensive, because, in the first place, it flows from the class nature of the proletariat and, in the second place, *because this coincides with the French Field Service Regulations of 1921.*"[30] Soviet leaders today do not admit that in the early 1920s the new Soviet military leadership took military manuals, textbooks, and regulations from Britain, France, Germany, the United States, and other nations, translated them, and used them as their own. What was needed, Trotskiy continued, was not a grand theory or doctrine, but "rather a program for the development and military qualifications of squad leaders. It is the squad leader that is the basic unit of tactics and strategy."[31]

In the debate at the 11th Party Congress, Trotskiy appeared to have won. He told Frunze that "it is too early to make generalizations on military doctrine—that should wait fifteen or twenty years." This view was even supported by Lenin, who said much the same thing: "It is too early to come forth with a theory of proletarian art. . . . It seems to me that our military communists are still insufficiently mature to pretend to the leadership of all military affairs."

Trotskiy, with his massive ego, did not consider Frunze a serious rival. At the time of the debate on doctrine, Trotskiy was at the very top of the Soviet leadership, standing close to Lenin. Frunze was only a popular war hero, and he was not yet a serious competitor in power or prestige. In the end, neither Frunze nor Vatsetis fared better than Trotskiy at the hands of Stalin. Frunze died an untimely death in October 1925 after having served as military commissar for less than a year. The military reforms that he advocated were not completed. Nevertheless, a Soviet military doctrine was eventually formulated based on the concepts that Frunze and Vatsetis had outlined. Their ideas on doctrine were carried out by others, in particular by M. N. Tukhachevskiy, who had replaced Frunze as chief of staff of the Red Army.

The doctrinal concepts of Frunze and Vatsetis were further developed during the late 1920s and up to the mid-1930s. Expanding on these writings, Soviet military theoreticians calculated that a future war between the Soviet Union and a coalition of capitalist countries, if unleashed by the capitalists, would be primarily a revolutionary-class war, a war between two sociopolitical systems. In this war the imperialist states would strive to defeat the USSR and liquidate its socialist structure. From the perspective of the USSR, it would be a just, liberating war. The irreconcilable class character of future war and the decisiveness of its military-political goals would exclude any sort of compromise. "It will be a fight not to life but to death," wrote M. V. Frunze. "It will be a struggle to the end, to the victory of one side or the other."[32] As will be seen later in this book, Soviet military leaders have continued over the decades to emphasize these same basic premises.

Soviet military theorists of the 1920s also stressed that future war would be long and drawn out and would test the economic and political foundations of the countries involved. In certain cases, they did not exclude a strategy of lightning strikes. This view was supported both by Frunze and Svechin. However, Svechin's strategy of attrition was opposed by M. N. Tukhachevskiy, who "energetically defended a strategy of destruction."[33]

Military Doctrine, Second Stage (1929–1941)

The Concept of Deep Operations

The second stage in Soviet military doctrine began with the First Five-Year Plan in 1929. An industrial base was being built in order to supply the Red Army. But before weapons could be produced, Soviet leaders had to come to some agreement on military doctrine and strategy. They had to determine the possible character of a future war, the methods and forms of its conduct, and "scientifically resolve questions of the organizational structure of the army and navy and determine the direction for the preparation of the country for waging war against a coalition of imperialist states."[34]

Soviet military analysts made a careful study of World War I; in particular, they examined the reasons for the "positional warfare" that dominated the conflict. Hundreds of thousands of men had died in their efforts to advance a front only a few kilometers. The introduction of the machine gun had made trench warfare the primary method of fighting, and defense had the upper hand. Soviet theorists concluded that the major military objective in a future conflict would be to avoid positional warfare and restore maneuver to the battlefield. This objective became a cornerstone of the military-technical side of Soviet military doctrine.

Two new weapons had appeared during World War I that showed much promise—tanks and aircraft. Improved artillery could provide supporting firepower. Military strategists theorized that a mobile combined arms force based on these three weapons systems could crush enemy machine gun pillboxes, cross trenches, punch through defensive positions, and, behind the enemy lines, wage a war of maneuver. These actions would prevent the kind of positional war that had been so disastrous in World War I. As a result of the possibilities they perceived in the combined arms utilization of tanks, artillery, and aircraft, Soviet theorists began to develop a new theory of battle in the late 1920s. This theory, which came to be known as the theory of the deep operation, became imbedded in military doctrine. A further doctrinal decision was then made—that the Soviet Union should attempt to achieve superiority in the three decisive weapons needed—tanks, aircraft, and artillery.

The best minds of the Soviet military leadership supported the deep operations concept and worked out many of the details necessary for its implementation. Among them were M. N. Tukhachevskiy, A. I. Yegorov, and especially V. K. Triandafillov, chief of operations of the Red Army staff, whose career ended in an air accident in 1931. They were joined by such well-known military commanders as I. P. Uborevich, I. E. Yakir, R. P. Eideman, Ya. I. Alksnis, and others who field-tested the plan.[35]

In the Soviet Union, action follows doctrine. In the early 1930s, tanks and artillery began to roll off production lines and the Soviets started to form mechanized corps. By 1934 the Red Army had corps of this type, which later were reorganized into tank corps. The idea of deep battle was reflected in the *Provisional Field Regulations of the RKKA for 1936 (PU-36)*, in which the offensive nature of Soviet military doctrine was clearly expressed. According to these regulations, "any attack on the socialist state of workers and peasants will be beaten off with all the might of the Armed Forces of the Soviet Union, with the transfer of military actions onto the territory of the attacking enemy. . . . Only a decisive offensive in the main direction followed by relentless pursuit will lead to complete destruction of the enemy's men and equipment."[36]

The military elements of the Soviet five-year economic plans were designed to provide the means necessary to make the new doctrine effective. First priority was given to producing the weapons demanded by that doctrine—tanks, artillery, and aircraft. Neither the collectivization of agriculture, which brought starvation to hundreds of thousands of people, nor the deaths of millions of innocent men and women in forced labor camps, caused any change in the Kremlin's decision. In 1931–1932 Soviet defense industries produced 1,911 pieces of artillery; in 1938, they produced 12,687. Aircraft production was 860 in 1932 and 5,469 in 1938. During the same years tank production rose from 740 to 2,271.[37] Although Soviet expectations were not realized in the early months of Hitler's attack, the expansion of their defense industries during that period may have been a critical factor in the USSR's survival.

Along with the production of material for war, military leaders had to be trained how to implement the concept prescribed by doctrine. A unified command in the field and in the military headquarters to plan and direct the fighting had to be developed. Earlier, Vatsetis had argued that a common interpretation of military affairs, or unified military school, could only be brought about through military education. Frunze, shortly after being named chief of staff, had spoken about the role of the Red Army staff in his address to the 1924 graduating class of the military academy: "This operational staff must become not only the brain of the Red Army; it must become the military brain for all of our Soviet state."[38]

B. M. Shaposhnikov chose Frunze's words as the title of his fundamental work on staffs, *The Brain of the Army*, which was published in three volumes between 1927 and 1929. Shaposhnikov, a former Czarist officer, was chief of operations for the Field Staff during the Civil War. From February 1921 until October 20, 1925, he was first assistant to the chief of staff of the Red Army. Thus, he was Frunze's assistant during the time military reforms were being implemented. From 1928 to 1931, Shaposhnikov was chief of staff of the Red Army; he later served as chief of the General Staff, from 1937 to August 1940 and again from July 1941 to May 1942. In these varied assignments Shaposhnikov played a major role in establishing the Soviet General Staff.

As a result of Shaposhnikov's work and the urging of others, in particular those who had attended German staff schools, Soviet leaders recognized that a General Staff was needed. This need was even more obvious after the Red Army went from a territorial system for manning the Armed Forces to a cadre system. In 1935 the Staff of the Red Army was renamed the General Staff, and there were great hopes for its continued development. In 1936 an Academy of the General Staff was established to give higher military education to Soviet commanders. The unified school of thought that Vatsetis had advocated became a reality.

However, the plans of those military leaders who were primarily responsible for bringing the Bolsheviks to power were not realized. Stalin, whose agricultural collectivization program had caused widespread starvation and the deaths of millions, was ready to take personal control of the Red Army. In 1935, a military history faculty had been organized at the Frunze Military Academy. One of its first efforts was to prepare a thirty-two-hour course on the theory of strategy. But Stalin's control brought about a change in plans. After looking at the program for the course, Ye. A. Shchadenko, deputy commandant of the Academy, told the head of the faculty: "What is this course on strategy? Strategy is Comrade Stalin's personal affair and not ours." Shaposhnikov, who at this time was commandant of the Academy, did not agree. He told the faculty head that "the question of reading a lecture on strategy was approved by the Political Administration of the RKKA; the lecture course will be read in the faculty and it is your job to prepare it." The lecture was prepared but never read. The faculty was transferred to the newly created Academy of the General Staff.[39]

The planned lecture on strategy fared no better at the new Academy. G. S. Isserson, head of the department of operational art, recalled that the least hint of the need to conduct a course on strategy as the base for operational art was met by objections from "on high." When the question was raised at one of the meetings before the Academy opened, chief of the General Staff Marshal A. I. Yegorov, with some irritation, asked the Academy representative directly: "What will you be doing with strategy? Planning a war? Strategic deployment? Or waging war? Nobody is going to let you do that because it's the business of the General Staff."[40]

The Concept Abandoned and the Cadres Decimated

During the Spanish Civil War the Kremlin sent both ground and air units to Spain. Soviet military tacticians thus had the opportunity to experiment with tanks in actual combat conditions and to determine whether their new concepts were valid. But in the mountainous Spanish terrain, with the opponent in command of the air, tank units ran into serious difficulties. In a war in which there were not always clearly defined lines, the Soviet concept of deep operations had little meaning. To compound matters, most of the senior Soviet officers who were sent to Spain as "volunteers" under various aliases were shot soon after their return to their homeland.

In the 1970s, Soviet accounts portrayed the country's participation in the Spanish Civil War as a successful demonstration of the "internationalist responsibilities" of all Soviet people. In actual fact, the Soviet experience in Spain accomplished little, and the military lessons thought to have been learned turned out to be incorrect. Based on the limited combat experience with tank units during a war in which Soviet forces were on the losing side, the tank corps were abolished and cavalry were specified as the exploitation echelon in operations.

At about the same time the Kremlin was sending forces to Spain, Stalin's purges of the Soviet officer corps were under way. From May 1937 through September 1938, nearly half the regimental commanders, almost all commanders of brigades and divisions, all commanders of corps, military district commanders and their political officers, and many instructors at military schools and academies underwent repression. Among the commanders and political workers killed were outstanding military leaders like (Marshals) M. N. Tukhachevskiy, V. K. Blyukher, and A. I. Yegorov, (Generals) I. E. Yakir, I. P. Uborevich, Ye. I. Kovtyukh, I. F. Fed'ko, I. S. Unshlikht, P. Ye. Dybenko, R. P. Eideman, Ya. B. Gamarnik (who committed suicide), and others.[41] Theoreticians like Svechin who had helped to develop the deep operations concept perished. The head of Frunze Military Academy, A. I. Kork, was shot.

Stalin's direct leadership in matters of military strategy, combined with the loss of top Soviet officers in the purges, had an adverse effect on the capabilities of the Red Army. It was some time, however, before this problem became noticeable. In 1938, Soviet troops repelled Japanese units at Lake Khasan in the Far East. In the spring and summer of 1939, Soviet troops went to the support of Mongolia in defending its border, which had been violated by the Japanese at Khalkhin-Gol. In 1939, following the Hitler-Stalin Accord, which provided for the seizure of Polish territories, Soviet troops moved into Poland to digest their booty. Polish resistance was light, and the opposition was no test of Stalin's military forces. Thousands of Polish officers who were taken into custody were murdered by their Soviet captors.

The situation was different in 1939 when the Kremlin launched an attack against its neighbor, tiny Finland. Soviet planning for its aggression was clearly faulty. Wave after wave of poorly trained and badly led Soviet troops were sent to fight against thinly held Finnish positions. Finnish officers and men demonstrated what well-trained troops could do against the Red Army. Soviet casualties ran into the hundreds of thousands. But in the end Finland, overwhelmed by sheer numbers, sued for peace. The Baltic nations—Estonia, Latvia, and Lithuania—were also unable to resist as Soviet troops moved in and took control during the summer of 1940.

But the effects of Stalin's purges were to be serious indeed. In 1941, at the time of Hitler's invasion, barely 7 percent of Soviet officers had higher military education, and 37 percent did not even have the full course of instruction at a military school. Few of the officers had any knowledge of German tactics and strategy. Those officers who had attended German staff schools in the 1920s and early 1930s, which had given them good insights into German military leadership and weaponry, had almost all been "purged."

Military Doctrine, Third Stage (1941–1945)

The Beginning of the Great Patriotic War

Hitler must have watched with amazement the 1937–1938 Soviet military purges that decimated the Soviet officer corps. The extremely poor showing of Soviet troops against Finland may have caused him to think the Red Army would fall apart in a German offensive. On June 22, 1941, Hitler launched his attack.

Once war started, military doctrine was superseded by military strategy to direct the war in progress. As early Soviet theorists indicated, military doctrine is reflected in regulations. Stalin did not like the word "doctrine," but his regulations served the same purpose as doctrine. According to later Soviet writers, the *Draft Field Regulations of 1939* "gave the essence of Soviet offensive doctrine." The regulations specified:

- Any enemy attack against the Union of Soviet Socialist Republics shall be met by a crushing blow of the entire might of our Armed Forces. . . .
- If the enemy forces us into war, the Workers' and Peasants' Red Army will be the most aggressive of all the aggressive armies that ever existed.
- We will conduct an offensive war, carrying it into enemy territory.[42]

This question is sometimes asked today: "In the event of a war with NATO, would Soviet military actions be in accordance with Soviet military doctrine?" Actions taken by the Soviet leadership, especially by Stalin immediately following Hitler's invasion, may be instructive.

In World War II the Armed Forces and the people of the Soviet Union paid a heavy price for Stalin's 1937–1938 purges of the officer corps. During Khrushchev's brief de-Stalinization period in the late 1950s and early 1960s, a number of Soviet military leaders wrote that many of the 20 million lives were lost because of Stalin's leadership. Paralyzed by fear immediately following the German attack, Stalin for a time was totally ineffective and was unable to meet with his staff. Two years were to pass before Soviet commanders gained enough experience to match the capabilities of their German counterparts.

In the first weeks of Hitler's invasion, Soviet troops, in accordance with regulations, were ordered to counterattack and carry the war into enemy territory. Many Soviet generals who tried to fight rear-guard actions and make orderly withdrawals were shot for failing to launch hopeless counterattacks. Many other troops, forbidden to withdraw, were surrounded by Germans and either killed or taken prisoner. They were given no option but to follow regulations—and Stalin's directives.

Soviet troops, in general, did as Hitler anticipated. His forces took only a few months to reach the gates of Moscow. But there, with lines of communication over-extended and facing the worst Russian winter in forty years, the German forces were stopped. The next year, at Stalingrad, the German forces were unable to overcome the Soviet defense.

Stalin's "Permanently Operating Factors"

Once Stalin took full control of military matters, his was the only voice that could be heard. Concepts that had been previously worked out were rejected. Military thought was smothered by Stalin's monopoly on the "right" to develop military science. Instead of creativity in military science, which is the foundation of military doctrine, military theorists were permitted only to comment on Stalin's pronouncements on military questions, "which mostly bore a personal, incidental character." This situation enabled "the spirit of dogmatism, pedanticism and 'quilting' [the printing of sayings of Stalin pieced together to form a book] to take root in military science." Stalin's thesis of "permanently operating factors" became dogma; the limited experience of wars conducted under special circumstances (Spain and Finland) was transferred to the structuring and use of the Soviet Armed Forces. Stalin's influence during this time has been called the "cult of personality."[43]

Stalin first announced his permanently operating factors in a speech on Soviet Armed Forces Day, February 23, 1942.[44] The purpose of these factors, in part, was to help offset the impact of German victories in the first months of the war and to cover up the mistakes made by Stalin and the Soviet High Command as a group. Even though Stalin had been informed by many sources that the Germans were planning to attack, he had disregarded these warnings, and Soviet troops were caught by surprise. Stalin asserted that "the inequality, which has been created by the surprise of the fascist German attack, has been liquidated."[45] He went on to assure the Armed Forces and the nation at large that "now the fate of war will be determined not by such transitory aspects as that of surprise, but by permanently operating factors." These were listed as follows:

- stability of the rear;
- morale of the troops;
- quantity and quality of divisions;
- armaments of the army;
- organizational ability of command personnel of the army.

For the remainder of the war and up to the time of Stalin's death, these factors were accepted as the final and unquestioned authority. Any discussion of war by Soviet military strategists had to be within the framework of these five factors.

It was not until later in the war that the Soviet High Command reintroduced tank corps and put the early concept of deep operations into effect. Germany, facing a multifront war, had to withdraw much of its air power from its Eastern Front to defend the German homeland. Under conditions of general air superiority, massive Soviet forces were able to breach German defenses and execute the maneuver-type warfare that Soviet theorists, almost a decade previously, had advocated.

After Soviet forces had stopped the German advances and were ready to launch an offensive, the lack of detailed maps covering the western portions of their own country became a major problem. Maps were available in quantity for territory outside of Soviet borders. But since the regulations had specified that an offensive would be conducted on the enemy's territory, there had been no need to plan for fighting on Soviet soil. Hence, such maps were considered unnecessary and few had been produced.

Literally thousands of books have been published in the Soviet Union since 1945 describing the victory of the Red Army over both Germany and

Japan. Seldom mentioned are the battles of other nations that participated in that war. Instead, Soviet writers in both books and journals attribute the defeat "of fascist Germany and imperialist Japan . . . to the complete superiority of the Soviet state and its military doctrine over those countries and their military doctrines."[46]

Postwar Period (1946–1953)

Throughout the war and in the immediate postwar years, Soviet military-theoretical writings as a whole exaggerated the role and significance of Stalin's leadership and his pronouncements in the sphere of military affairs. Colonel P. A. Chuvikov in his 1949 book *Marxism-Leninism on War and Army*, for example, wrote:

> Our historic victory over the enemy, which led to the unconditional surrender of Hitler's Germany and imperialist Japan, was the triumph of Stalin's military science.
> One of the greatest contributions of comrade Stalin to the people is that in the period of the Great Patriotic War he further developed Soviet military science. Comrade Stalin developed and in the course of the war put into action the thesis of permanently operating factors which determine the fate of war.[47]

Of all the permanently operating factors the most important during the war and until 1960 was the "quantity and quality of divisions." Soviet histories of World War II demonstrate how the Soviets "kept score" based on how many German divisions were destroyed.[48] Percentages of personnel in each branch of the Red Army from 1941 to 1945 were as follows:[49]

Ground Forces	80.7–87.2%
Air Forces	6.2–8.7%
Navy	4.5–7.3%
National Air Defense	3.3–4.8%

In other words, the Ground Forces, measured in divisions, were the decisive element in winning the war. Once they became decisive, all services of the Armed Forces were obligated to support their leading role.

At times, the glory given to Stalin—as well as to Nikita S. Khrushchev and Leonid I. Brezhnev later—reached comical proportions. Those aspects of Soviet military science that appeared to be effective were touted as the result of Stalin's "creative genius." Soviet authors of works on military theory were limited to singing Stalin's praises.[50] During Khrushchev's brief "de-Stalinization" period, however, an official Soviet military history described how, as a result of Stalin's cult of personality, the real problems of military science were studied very little or ignored altogether.

In his 1969 article on Soviet military doctrine and strategy, General Ivanov did not mention either Stalin's purges or the effects of Stalin's personality cult. He did not indicate why he considered the postwar period to end in 1953, which happened to be the year of Stalin's death. Ivanov only stated that until nuclear weapons were available, Soviet military doctrine and strategy developed on the basis of the experience of the war.[51]

The concept of military doctrine was not to be revived until years after Stalin's death. As will be shown in detail later, change was slow to take place. The immediate post-Stalin period was called "the thaw." Souls and minds long frozen slowly came to life. Stalin's policies were questioned in the restricted military press, as will be discussed in Chapter 5. But only after Khrushchev's secret speech about Stalin's crimes at the 20th Party Congress in 1956 was it permissible to examine the lessons of the Great Patriotic War and the development of military theory. But even then, criticism was muted.

Post-Stalin Era (1953–1960)

One of the main questions that any military doctrine must answer is this: What is the degree of probability of war, and with what enemy will one have to deal? Although the question appears simple, the answer is quite complex. Determining the probability of war depends on what kind of war one is talking about. A philosophy that advocates world revolution almost automatically makes the probability of war quite high. It also raises the question of how a nation's leaders can champion peace and fight war at the same time.

Marxism-Leninism had posited that as long as "imperialism" exists, war is inevitable.[52] That position had dominated the political side of Soviet military doctrine since 1917. But nuclear weapons made such a position very dangerous. Some Communists felt the Soviet Union should "get it over with," since war with "imperialism" was considered to be foreordained. Others believed that under some circumstances, "inevitable" could, and should, be qualified. The latter position was not openly considered until the mid-1950s. In 1953 when Stalin died, the Korean War was in its third year. As the dictator was being placed in the mausoleum in Red Square alongside Lenin, his heirs were battling for succession. They did not want the distraction of a war fought thousands of miles away that presented little immediate danger to the Soviet Union. Moscow directed its satellite, North Korea, to reach agreement in the truce talks, and the war slowly wound down.

Other problems closer at hand were more difficult to solve. Riots broke out in East Germany and Poland. The Soviet Union faced a challenge for leadership of the world communist movement when Mao Tse-tung made a strong bid to become the successor to Marx, Engels, Lenin, and Stalin. In 1955, Soviet troops were prudently withdrawn from Austria, Port Arthur in China, and Porkkala-Udd in Finland. Faced with a severe decline of Soviet prestige abroad, Khrushchev launched a political offensive from the podium of the 20th Party Congress. He declared:

But war is not fatalistically inevitable. Now there are powerful social and political forces which have formidable means at their disposal to prevent the imperialists from unleashing war, and if they do try to start one, to give a crushing rebuff to the aggressors and frustrate their adventuristic plans. To do this, it is necessary that all forces opposing war be vigilant and mobilized so that they can act with a united front and not weaken their struggle to preserve and consolidate peace.[53]

The thesis that war was inevitable as long as imperialism existed, he explained, was worked out at a time when imperialism was an all-encompassing world system. Previously, sociopolitical forces of socialism had been too weak to compel the imperialists to reject war as a means of resolving differences. The thesis was right and proper for that period, according to Marxist-Leninist theorists. But after World War II, the explanation continued, the world socialist system emerged and grew in power. The international workers' movement in capitalist countries became a powerful force. The peace movement became a strong factor. Former colonies, now newly independent countries, opposed war. Under these conditions, Khrushchev continued, "Lenin's thesis that as long as imperialism exists, *the economic base* for predatory wars is preserved, remains in force. As long as capitalism exists, reactionary forces representing the interests of capitalist monopoly will seek military adventures and aggression; they will try to unleash war. Therefore constant vigilance is needed."[54]

Later, the Congress was reminded of Lenin's principles of peaceful coexistence of states with different social systems. Peaceful coexistence is defined as "a special form of class warfare between socialism and capitalism in the international arena, but a specific form."[55] Coupled with the declaration that war was no longer fatalistically inevitable, the assertion that peaceful coexistence was possible brought cries of "revisionism" from Communist Parties still loyal to Stalinism, chiefly Maoists. When Khrushchev closed the doors and made his secret speech denouncing Stalin and his crimes, he set in motion major shock waves that were to shake the foundations of international communism.

In discussing the military needs of the Soviet Union in an era of peaceful coexistence, the term "military doctrine" was not used. However, the Minister of Defense, Marshal Georgiy K. Zhukov, came close to it in his address to the Congress. He stated:

In structuring the Soviet Armed Forces, we proceed from the fact that the methods and forms of future war will be different from all past wars in many ways. Future war, if it is unleashed, will be characterized by the mass use of air forces, various rocket weapons and various means of mass destruction such as atomic, thermonuclear, chemical and bacteriological weapons. However, we proceed from the fact that the latest weapons, including weapons of mass destruction, do not reduce the decisive role of the ground armies, navies and aviation. Without strong ground forces, without strategic, long-range and frontal aviation and a modern naval fleet, without well-organized cooperation between them, modern war cannot be waged.[56]

At that time, nuclear missiles were seen as augmenting the traditional role of artillery. Traditional services were still decisive. But the Soviet High Command was getting ready to bite the bullet.

The Revolution in Military Affairs

According to Soviet writings after the event, a revolution in military affairs took place in the Soviet Armed Forces between 1953 and 1960. Today it continues as the scientific-technical revolution. It had been centuries since a revolution in military affairs of such importance had occurred. Soviet writers pointed out that this revolution affected all facets of the military, and that it was not to be compared with a "tank" revolution or an "airplane" revolution. The current change was more comparable to the discovery of gunpowder. Before gunpowder, wars were fought with cold steel weapons or with objects thrown by mechanical contrivances. The introduction of gunpowder fundamentally altered the nature of war itself. At first, only a few guns were available. The immediate effects were small and gradual. But inexorably, the changes wrought by the gunpowder revolution accumulated until the whole fabric of feudal society crumbled.

The term "revolution in military affairs" was used by Karl Marx's collaborator Friedrich Engels to describe the introduction of gunpowder. As explained in 1962 in *Military Strategy*, "the invention of gunpowder and the subsequent development of firearms caused a complete revolution in military affairs and ushered in a new era in the development of military art and in the organization of the armed forces."[57] In the same way nuclear weapons and rockets ushered in the missile age, in which the old relationships and old rules simply do not apply. The man with the gun—be it rifle, machine gun, or cannon—is no longer decisive in war. The nuclear-armed missile, with its vast destructive power, is now the decisive factor. The quantity and quality of divisions no longer matter.

According to the 1986 *Military Encyclopedic Dictionary*, the revolution in military affairs is defined as:

> the fundamental changes which are taking place under the influence of scientific-technical progress in the development of means of armed combat, in the organization and preparation of the armed forces, and of methods of conducting war and military actions. The present-day revolution in military affairs began after World War II in connection with the equipping of the armed forces with nuclear weapons, radioelectronic equipment, automatic control systems and other new means. It simultaneously encompassed all areas of military affairs. The results of the revolution in military affairs are used in capitalist countries for preparing for war, in socialist countries—for averting war and defending the socialist fatherland.[58]

The prime mover in bringing the Soviet Armed Forces into the nuclear age was Marshal of the Soviet Union Vasiliy D. Sokolovskiy. As chief of the General Staff from June 1952, before Stalin's death, until May 1960, he was the individual most responsible for bringing about the revolution in military affairs in the Soviet Union. He also was primarily responsible for setting the stage for the next formulation of military doctrine.

After World War II, military thinking among Soviet officers may have been at a standstill but military technology was not. Years ahead of Western estimates, the Soviet Union developed its own atomic bomb in 1949 and by mid-1953 had developed the hydrogen bomb. Before the war was over German scientists from the rocket installations at Penemunde were captured and spirited into the Soviet Union along with their laboratories and factories. There they developed the Soviet missile industry. In August 1957, the Soviets tested their first intercontinental ballistic missile. On October 4, 1957, a sphere the size of a basketball was put into orbit by the USSR. The Western world was shocked after listening to the beep-beep-beeps coming from the world's first artificial satellite, dubbed Sputnik. Had the Soviets stolen the edge on technology from the United States?

The marriage of nuclear warheads to missiles as the primary carrier made an enormous difference in the conduct of war. A long-range bomber needed five to eight hours to reach its target and could be recalled. A missile took only thirty minutes to arrive on target and was unstoppable once it left its launch pad.

The Party leadership had provided the impetus both to go into space and to develop missiles to deliver nuclear warheads. In the 1950s, Leonid I. Brezhnev, Politburo member and a Party secretary, and Dmitriy F. Ustinov, wartime armaments czar and head of the Soviet defense industry, were directed by the Politburo to go to Kazakhstan to ensure that the space and missile programs were successful. Building on the work begun by Stalin and continued by Khrushchev, Brezhnev and Ustinov put the Soviet Union on the road to becoming a military superpower.

Khrushchev's speech at the Extraordinary 21st Party Congress in January 1959 was bellicose. "Series production of intercontinental ballistic missiles is being organized in the Soviet Union," he asserted. "It is obvious that if the Soviet Union can send rockets hundreds of thousands of kilometers in space, then they can send powerful rockets to any place on earth." He repeated some of the themes of the 20th Party Congress:

> The conclusion drawn by the 20th Congress of the Party that war is not fatally inevitable has been fully justified. Today we have all the more reason to insist that that conclusion was correct. There are now tremendous forces capable of rebuffing the imperialist aggressors and defeating them if they should start a war. . . .
> Indeed, when the USSR becomes the foremost industrial power in the world, and when the Chinese People's Republic becomes a mighty industrial power and the industrial output of all socialist countries combined is more than half the world industrial output, the international situation will change radically. . . . The idea that war is impermissible will take still firmer root in the minds of men. . . . Backed by the might of the socialist camp, the peaceful nations will then be able to make bellicose imperialist groups abandon their plans for a new world war. . . . As long as capitalism exists it may always be possible to find people who, contrary to common sense, will want to rush headlong

into a hopeless venture. . . . Any attempt at aggression will be curbed and the adventurers put where they belong.[59]

At the same Extraordinary 21st Party Congress, the new Minister of Defense, Marshal of the Soviet Union Rodion Ya. Malinovskiy, addressed the assembled delegates. He claimed that the imperialist nations were continuing their course of preparing an aggressive war with the use of nuclear weapons, whipping up the arms race, and strengthening their aggressive military groupings and military alliances. The imperialists, Malinovskiy claimed, "threaten us with the might of their aviation and navy." However, weapons such as these were now obsolete; they had been replaced by intercontinental ballistic missiles. "You cannot in fact stop them with any means of air defense and they can inevitably deliver hydrogen charges of colossal power to any point on the globe (actually to any point—they are very accurate)."[60]

The outside world did not know what to make of these boasts by the Soviet leadership. U.S. ships had been in the vicinity where the warhead from the first test of a Soviet intercontinental missile splashed down in 1957. Powerful long-range radars were able to detect the number of missile test flights, but nothing was known of the numbers deployed. Overflights of the Soviet Union by U-2 aircraft could cover but a small part of Soviet territory. The only prudent course for the NATO nations was to attempt to narrow the military lead that Khrushchev boasted the Soviet Union then possessed.

The Development of New Military Concepts

Behind Khrushchev's public boasting and missile-rattling, the top Soviet military theorists in the General Staff, the military academies, and the military districts were pondering how to make the most effective use of this new weapon system. In the restricted Soviet military press it became apparent that "software" was being developed to go with the new hardware. Soviet writings at the time stressed that military science, which investigates the laws and regularities of war, was elaborating questions of military art. Military art, which is the basic component part of military science, includes strategy, operational art, and tactics.

This new objective was the result of a directive from the Minister of Defense as well as of a military-science conference held in May 1957. Discussions of the role of nuclear weapons were conducted widely, both in military schools and in the field. A great number of papers were produced by prominent generals, admirals, and officers on conducting nuclear war, especially on the beginning period of such a war. Some of the main problems being examined were how to stall (*sryv*) a surprise nuclear attack by an aggressor, how to train troops, and how to conduct modern battles and operations.

As a result of all the deliberations, a new military doctrine was formed. The Soviet Armed Forces were reorganized to create a new, fifth service of the Armed Forces—the Strategic Rocket Forces—in December 1959. This reorganization took place almost three years before Soviet attempts to place missiles in Cuba touched off an international incident. Owing to the Soviet obsession for secrecy, Western students of Soviet military affairs did not at once recognize the implications of the new service. Once organized, it became the prime service. The new doctrine soon found its way into field manuals and regulations. Its basic outline was publicly revealed for the first time by Khrushchev in January 1960.

Notes

1. D. A. Volkogonov and S. A. Tyushkevich, "Voyna" [War], in *Sovetskaya Voyennaya Entsiklopediya* [Soviet Military Encyclopedia] (Moscow: Voyenizdat, 1976–1980), vol. 2, p. 305.

2. Ibid., p. 308.

3. V. I. Lenin, "War and Revolution," from *The Soviet Art of War*, by W. F. and H. F. Scott, editors (Boulder, Colorado: Westview Press, 1982), p. 25.

4. M. A. Gareyev, *M. V. Frunze—Voyennyy Teoretik* [M. V. Frunze—Military Theoretician] (Moscow: Voyenizdat, 1985), p. 105.

5. Ibid., p. 107.

6. S. P. Ivanov is the author of and contributor to many books: *Leninist Basis of Soviet Military Science* (1970); *Beginning Period of War* (1974); *On the Scientific Bases of Troop Control* (1975).

7. S. P. Ivanov, "Soviet Military Doctrine and Strategy," *Voyennaya Mysl'* [Military Thought] May 1969. From Joseph D. Douglass, Jr., and Amoretta M. Hoeber, *Selected Readings from Military Thought, 1963–1973* (English translation) (Washington, D.C.: US GPO, 1982), vol. 5, Part 2, pp. 18–32.

8. Gareyev, *M. V. Frunze*, p. 108. A. A. Svechin, a general officer of the General Staff of czarist Russia, was named chief of the Red Army's All-Russian Main Staff from August to November 1918, then combined scientific research with instruction at the Frunze Military Academy and, after 1936, when it was formed, the Academy of the General Staff. Svechin was one of those shot on Stalin's orders on July 29, 1938, at the same time as I. P. Belov, Ya. I. Alksnis, Ya. K. Berzin, I. N. Dubovoy, P. Ye. Dybenko, I. S. Unshlikht, to name just a few. There were many waves of such killings, both of Party officials and the military, from 1936 to 1939. Soviet historian Roy Medvedev estimated that 400,000 to 500,000 were summarily shot. See: Roy A. Medvedev, *Let History Judge* (New York: Alfred A. Knopf, 1972), p. 239.

9. A. A. Svechin, *Strategiya* [Strategy]. The first edition was published by Voyenizdat in 1923, the second in 1927. Marshal V. D. Sokolovskiy wrote in his introduction to his classic *Military Strategy* in 1962 that "since the publication of *Strategy* by A. Svechin in 1926 . . . there have been no other publications in the Soviet Union devoted to the problems of military strategy as a whole." (V. D. Sokolovskiy, *Soviet Military Strategy*, 3rd ed., edited by H. F. Scott, revised edition [New York: Crane, Russak & Company, Inc., 1984], p. 387.)

10. In 1965, as the Soviet leadership was in the midst of its nuclear missile buildup, a book appeared in Soviet bookstores that was out of keeping with other military publications. *Voprosy Strategii i Operativnogo Iskusstva v Sovetskikh Voyennykh Trudakh, 1917–1940* [Problems of Strategy and Operational Art in Soviet Military Works, 1917–1940] (Moscow: Voyenizdat, 1965) consisted of excerpts of writings by pre–World War II Soviet strategists, approximately one half of whom had been killed

in Stalin's military purges of 1937–1938. The introduction to the book was by Marshal of the Soviet Union Matvey V. Zakharov, chief of the General Staff, who stated that the origins of Soviet military thought were laid down in the selections. The first selection in the book was Mikhail V. Frunze's "A Unified Military Doctrine for the Red Army."

11. See Soviet historian Roy A. Medvedev's *Let History Judge*, pp. 47–50, for a full account of Frunze's unnecessary operation for ulcers. Rumors persist that Lenin had wanted Frunze to replace Stalin as General Secretary.

12. M. V. Frunze, "A Unified Military Doctrine for the Red Army," from Scott & Scott, *The Soviet Art of War*, p. 28.

13. Ibid., p. 29.

14. Ibid., pp. 30–31.

15. Ibid., p. 31.

16. Ibid., p. 31.

17. I. I. Vatsetis was one of a group of military leaders shot on Stalin's orders on July 28, 1938, one day before the shooting of the group that Svechin was in. Exact dates have been published in the military biographies found in the *Sovetskaya Voyennaya Entsiklopediya*.

18. I. I. Vatsetis, "On Military Doctrine of the Future," *Voprosy Strategii*, p. 184.

19. Ibid., p. 186.

20. Ibid., p. 188.

21. A. G. Titov, "Trotskizm" [Trotskyism], in *Bol'shaya Sovetskaya Entsiklopediya* [Great Soviet Encyclopedia], 3rd ed. (Moscow: Soviet Encyclopedia Publishers, 1977), vol. 26, p. 251.

22. L. Trotskiy, "Military Doctrine or Pseudo-Military Doctrinairism," as published in the valuable work *Marxism and the Science of War* (U.K.: Oxford University Press, 1981), edited and with an introduction by Professor Bernard Semmel, pp. 189–90.

23. Ibid., p. 189.

24. Ibid.

25. Leon Trotskiy, "Our Current Basic Military Tasks" (1922), in Bernard Semmel, *Marxism*, p. 61.

26. Ibid., p. 187.

27. Ibid., p. 188.

28. Walter Darnell Jacobs, *Frunze: The Soviet Clausewitz, 1885–1925* (The Hague: Martinus Nijhoff, 1969), p. 67.

29. Semmel, *Marxism*, p. 188.

30. Jacobs, *Frunze*, p. 72.

31. Ibid., p. 72.

32. P. A. Zhilin, editor, *Zarozhdeniye i Razvitiye Sovetskiy Voyennoy Istoriografii, 1917–1941* [Origin and Development of Soviet Military Historiography, 1917–1941] (Moscow: Nauka, 1985), p. 66.

33. Ibid., p. 67.

34. Ivanov, "Soviet Military Doctrine," p. 41.

35. N. V. Ogarkov, "Glubokaya Operatsiya" [Deep Operation], in *Sovetskaya Voyennaya Entsiklopediya*, vol. 2., pp. 574–578.

36. As quoted in N. A. Lomov and S. Alferov, "On the Question of Soviet Military Doctrine," *Voyenno-Istoricheskiy Zhurnal* [Military History Journal] 7 (July 1978), p. 25.

37. H. F. Scott and W. F. Scott, *The Armed Forces of the USSR*, 3rd ed. (Boulder, Colorado: Westview Press, 1984), p. 306.

38. M. V. Frunze, *Izbrannyye Proizvedeniya* [Selected Works] (Moscow: Voyenizdat, 1965), p. 155.

39. N. Pavlenko, "Some Questions of the Development of the Theory of Strategy in the 20s," *Voyenno-Istoricheskiy Zhurnal* 5 (May 1966), p. 12.

40. Ibid., p. 12.

41. P. N. Pospelov, editor, *Istoriya Velikoy Otechestvennoy Voyny Sovetskogo Soyuza, 1941–1945* [History of the Great Patriotic War of the Soviet Union, 1941–1945] (Moscow: Voyenizdat, 1961–1965), vol. 6, p. 124.

42. Scott, *Soviet Military Strategy*, p. 133.

43. Pospelov, *Istoriya Velikoy*, vol. 6, p. 404.

44. J. V. Stalin, "Order of the People's Commissar of Defense, 23 February 1942, No. 55," Scott and Scott, *Soviet Art of War*, pp. 79–82.

45. Ibid., p. 80.

46. Ivanov, "Soviet Military Doctrine," p. 43.

47. P. A. Chuvikov, *Kratkiy Ocherk Marksistsko-Leninskoy Teorii o Voyne i Armii* [A Short Essay on Marxist-Leninist Theory on War and Army], 1st ed. (Moscow: Voyenizdat, 1949), p. 158.

48. M. V. Zakharov, ed., *50 Let Vooruzhennykh Sil SSSR* [50 Years of the Armed Forces USSR] (Moscow: Voyenizdat, 1968), p. 454. Soviets give a figure of 607 divisions of the "fascist coalition" destroyed on the Eastern Front.

49. Ibid., p. 464.

50. Pospelov, *Istoriya Velikoy*, p. 404.

51. Ivanov, "Soviet Military Doctrine," p. 43.

52. P. A. Chuvikov, *Marksizm-Leninizm o Voyne i Armii* [Marxism-Leninism on War and Army], 2nd ed. (Moscow: Voyenizdat, 1956), p. 158.

53. N. S. Khrushchev, "Report of the Central Committee CPSU to the Twentieth Party Congress" (February 14, 1956), in *On Peaceful Coexistence* (Moscow: Foreign Languages Publishing House, 1961), p. 11.

54. Chuvikov, *Marksizm-Leninizm*, p. 158.

55. A. E. Bovin, "Mirnoye Sosushchestvovaniye" [Peaceful Coexistence], in *Bolshaya Soviet Encyclopedia*, vol. 16, pp. 314–316.

56. Scott and Scott, *The Soviet Art of War*, p. 135.

57. V. D. Sokolovskiy, editor, *Voyennaya Strategiya* [Military Strategy], 1st ed. (Moscow: Voyenizdat, 1962), p. 226.

58. "Revolyutsiya v Voyennom Dele" [Revolution in Military Affairs], in *Voyennyy Entsiklopedicheskiy Slovar'* [Military Encyclopedic Dictionary], 2nd ed. (Moscow: Voyenizdat, 1986), p. 628.

59. From the "Report on the 'Control Figures for the Economic Development of the USSR for 1959–1965,'" *Vneocherednoy XXI S"yezd Kommunisticheskoy Partii Sovetskogo Soyuza* [Extraordinary 21st Congress of the Communist Party of the Soviet Union], stenographic notes (Moscow: Gospolitizdat, 1959), pp. 72–74.

60. Speech by R. Ya. Malinovskiy, *Vneocherednoy XXI S"yezd*, stenographic notes, pp. 121–22.

2
Soviet Military Doctrine, 1960–1970

Constant Features of Soviet Military Doctrine

Soviet military theoreticians and strategists do not set forth their own ideas on military doctrine; rather, they elaborate on doctrinal decisions already made at higher levels. Readers of Soviet writings on doctrine will find constant themes repeated by many authors. Once these themes are recognized it is generally possible to pinpoint shifts in doctrine when they appear in the Soviet press.

In analyzing Soviet doctrinal writings, there is a danger of being led astray by the Soviet use of the dialectic. In the United States, writers on defense issues pay little attention to formal philosophy. In the Soviet Union, some of the most significant writings on military doctrine and strategy have had titles such as "According to the Laws of Dialectics" or "The Dialectics of Development and Change in Forms and Methods of Armed Conflict." In the Western world, philosophy has been primarily speculative; in the Soviet Union, philosophy is a guide to action.

In brief, the dialectic is discussion and reasoning by dialogue used by Socrates as a method of intellectual investigation. To Hegel, it was the process in which an entity passes over into and is preserved and fulfilled by its opposite. To Karl Marx and Friedrich Engels, it was development through stages of thesis, antithesis, and synthesis in accordance with the laws of dialectical materialism. In military terms, this finds expression as follows:

> The appearance of new means of struggle always brings into being corresponding countermeans, which in the end also lead to changes of military operations. The "struggle" of tanks and antitank means, submarines and antisubmarine means, aircraft and antiaircraft defense . . . this is the axis around which revolves the development of military affairs, including the development of methods and forms of armed conflict.[1]

Therefore, in Soviet writings on military doctrine, the "opposite" will appear somewhere, or at least an acknowledgment of the opposite will be made. For example, future war may be nuclear or conventional, short or long.

Since 1960, there have been hundreds of statements of Soviet military doctrine. Although no two versions are exactly alike, it seems that the same master list of points is used each time. These points of similarity together give a fairly accurate picture of what Soviet doctrine is. Among the constant features or themes found in Soviet military doctrine are the following:

1. Doctrine has two sides: political and military-technical. From the political side, Soviet military doctrine is against aggressive, unjust, predatory wars. It supports liberating, just, revolutionary wars. At the same time, military doctrine considers that war is no longer a fatal necessity. From the military-technical side, doctrine is determined by: (1) radical changes in armaments and equipment, and (2) combat training and moral-combat qualities of troops.

2. The major positions of doctrine as described in the following account appear in italics. Doctrine is for *world* war; if not prevented, a new world war will be *unleashed by the imperialists*. If unleashed, a new world war would be a *decisive armed clash* of two opposed social systems—*capitalism and socialism*. War might begin by *surprise* with massive use of nuclear-armed long-range rockets. It is not excluded that world war could *escalate* from a local conflict. A surprise nuclear attack is most likely. Therefore the primary task is to be constantly ready to *reliably repulse a surprise attack of the enemy and to frustrate his criminal plans*.

3. The war may be *short and swift-moving* or it may be *protracted*. Nuclear rocket weapons will play the decisive role, but *final victory* over the aggressor can be achieved only as a result of *joint actions of all services* of the armed forces and service arms. Future war will demand *massive multimillion-man armies*. Troops must be ready to fight both *with use of nuclear weapons and without them*.

With these points as a guide, the first outlines of the new doctrine and its subsequent exposition will be discussed.

Basic Positions of the New Military Doctrine

The world was only two weeks into the 1960s when Nikita Khrushchev delivered a major policy speech before the 4th Session of the Supreme Soviet of the USSR. The speech was later published in pamphlet form as "Disarmament—the Way to a Sure Peace and Friendship Between Peoples." Despite this Orwellian title, in his presentation Khrushchev outlined the fundamental positions of the new Soviet military doctrine, which was based on the decisiveness of nuclear weapons.

Khrushchev emphasized that, as stated at the 20th and 21st Congresses of the CPSU, there was no longer any fatal inevitability of war. Should there be a war, it would not begin by invasion of the frontiers, as in the past. Instead, war would begin deep in the interior. He said that "not a single capital, no large industrial or administrative center, and no strategic area will remain unattacked in the very first minutes, let alone days, of the war. A surprise strike is possible but could not by itself win a war. Rockets will be duplicated in such a way that those surviving the initial strike would be able to rebuff the aggressor effectively."

The USSR, he said, had atomic and hydrogen weapons as well as rockets to deliver them. If attacked, the USSR would "wipe the country or countries attacking us off the face of the earth." The USSR would suffer a great deal and sustain great losses, but would survive. The West would suffer more. If the West started a new war, it would not only be their last, but also the end of capitalism. Rocket units had been newly formed, and the Soviet Union, having better, more perfect rockets than the United States, would do everything possible to keep its lead until agreement on disarmament was reached. However, the only point made in his speech that received significant attention in the West was that the standing army of the Soviet Union was to be reduced because a country's defense potential depended on firepower, not on the number of men under arms.[2]

The importance of this speech was highlighted almost two years later at the 22nd Party Congress in 1961, when Malinovskiy declared that Khrushchev's speech at the 4th Session of the Supreme Soviet in January 1960 had made a thorough analysis of modern war and that this analysis now formed the basis of Soviet military doctrine. Subsequent authors, even after Khrushchev's ouster, wrote of this January 1960 speech as the crucial point in the development of military doctrine.

The import of Khrushchev's statements was not immediately apparent abroad. The foreign press was more impressed with his announcement of a projected reduction in troops of 1.2 million. Some of his remarks, such as references to the creation of new "rocket units," were not clear at the time. Although the Strategic Rocket Forces had been organized in December 1959, it was several years before the word "strategic" was used in the open press when referring to these troops.[3]

Immediately after Khrushchev delivered this 1960 speech, he called on his Minister of Defense, Malinovskiy, to address the deputies and fill in the details. Malinovskiy justified the troop reduction by pointing out that in a modern war, "provided it is unleashed by the imperialists," paramount significance would belong "to massive nuclear strikes both on objectives in the deep interior and on groupings of armed forces in theaters of military actions (TVDs)."[4]

Malinovskiy stressed that the new Rocket Forces had become the main service of the Armed Forces, displacing the Ground Forces. However, the combined efforts of all services would be needed to wage war successfully. He reaffirmed the traditional position that final victory requires reliance on combined arms, not on one particular service, no matter how powerful. But once primacy was given to the nuclear weapon, all military services had to be reoriented toward being prepared for nuclear warfare. Malinovskiy specifically rejected the notion of "limited nuclear war," "tactical use of nuclear weapons," "dosed strategy," and so forth. He concluded by noting: "It must be expected that the most probable method of unleashing war by the imperialists against the Soviet Union, if they risk going to it, will be a surprise attack with the wide use of nuclear weapons. Under these conditions the main task of [Soviet] Armed Forces will be to repulse the attack of the enemy and instantly deliver a retaliatory crushing strike on him."[5]

Nuclear rocket weapons were not confined to just one service. Tactical nuclear weapons, for example, were introduced into the Ground Forces. The Soviet Air Forces' strategic bombers were referred to as "long-range rocket-carrying aviation." The Soviet Navy was charged with the delivery of nuclear weapons from submarines. The measure of military effectiveness had changed: It was no longer determined by the number of enemy divisions destroyed. Destruction of the enemy's nuclear weapons and delivery means became the number one task.

Khrushchev's Warning

In 1960, Dwight D. Eisenhower's second term was drawing to a close and in November of that year, John F. Kennedy was elected as the new U.S. president. Shortly before Kennedy's inauguration, Khrushchev defined the types of war that might be fought: world war, local war, and wars of national liberation. The first two types of war would be imperialist wars and therefore "unjust" to the Soviets. The latter—wars of national liberation—were categorized as "just wars." Although his categories were later criticized for mixing size with political content, at the time his pronouncements prevailed.

According to Khrushchev, "the imperialists are preparing war chiefly against the socialist countries, and above all against the Soviet Union, the most powerful of the socialist countries." With reference to local war, "there is much talk in the imperialist camp today about local wars, and the imperialists are even making small-caliber atomic weapons for use in such wars." The imperialists even "have concocted a special theory" about such wars. However, "a small-scale imperialist war, no matter which of the imperialists starts it, may develop into a world thermonuclear war." The Soviet Union, therefore, "must fight against world wars and against local wars."

Wars of national liberation received specific attention. "Recent examples of wars of this kind are the armed struggle waged by the people of Vietnam and the war of the Algerian people. . . . These are liberation wars, wars of independence waged by the people." Such wars are "sacred wars. We have helped and shall continue to help peoples fighting for their freedom. . . . Communists support just wars of this kind wholeheartedly and without reservation." He then summed up the basic Soviet position:

> A world war in present conditions would be waged with missiles and nuclear weapons, that is, it would be the most destructive war in history. . . . The victory of socialism on a world scale, inevitable by virtue of the [Marxist] laws of history, is now near. Wars between countries are not needed for this victory. . . . The Central Committee of the CPSU and the Soviet government will

continue to do everything to increase the military might of our country, since the imperialists are continuing the arms drive.[6]

The Soviet Union opened the manned space era in April 1961 with the flight of Yuriy Gagarin. The very rockets that launched Gagarin into space could carry devastating destruction to any point on the globe. Each Soviet space flight was a test for the soldiers of the Strategic Rocket Forces who launched them.

The 22nd Congress of the CPSU

The 22nd Congress met on October 17, 1961, only a few months after the building of the Berlin Wall began. There were five thousand delegates, which the newly completed Kremlin Palace of Congresses had been constructed to hold. Seated with the delegation from Stavropol' was First Secretary of the Stavropol' Komsomol Mikhail Gorbachev. He was only thirty years old. Khrushchev introduced the foreign delegations: Chou En-lai from China; Wladislaw Gomulka from Poland; Anton Novotny from Czechoslovakia; Walter Ulbricht from East Germany; Georgy Georgy-Dezh from Rumania; Todor Zhivkov from Bulgaria; Janos Kadar from Hungary. Xo Chi Minh came from North Vietnam; and Kim Il-sung from North Korea. Maurice Thorez headed the French delegation; Palmiro Tolatti the Italian; Elizabeth Gurley Flynn, Henry Winston and James Jackson the American.[7] Chou En-lai did not applaud Khrushchev's attack on Albania; rather he condemned it in his own speech and walked out of the meeting. His return to China before the Congress ended created a mild sensation. The Sino-Soviet split was out in the open.

Yuriy Gagarin, the first man in space, was in the hall as was the second space hero, German Titov. New gold star "Hero of Socialist Labor" medals gleamed on the chests of Premier Khrushchev; "President" Brezhnev; deputy chairman of the Council of Ministers, D. F. Ustinov; Party secretary, Frol Kozlov; president of the Academy of Sciences, Mstislav Keldysh; chairman of the State Committee on Radioelectronics, Valeriy Kalmykov; and chairman of the State Committee on Science and Technology, Konstantin Rudnev. These decorations were for "outstanding service in the development of rocket technology and assuring the successful flight of a Soviet man in space in the spaceship Vostok (East)."

Khrushchev began the report of the Central Committee to the Congress: "While conducting an unswerving policy of peace, we have not forgotten the threat of war on the part of the imperialists. Everything necessary has been done to ensure the superiority of our country in defense. The achievements of socialist production and Soviet science and technology have enabled us to carry out a genuine revolution in military affairs."[8] This was the first public use in the Soviet Union of the expression "revolution in military affairs." It was to become a major catchword in subsequent years.

Khrushchev also declared that increasing international tensions had forced the USSR to suspend the reductions in the Armed Forces planned for 1961.

He claimed the Soviet Union was forced to raise its defense budget, postpone the annual release into the reserves of soldiers and sailors who had completed their compulsory military service, and renew nuclear testing in the atmosphere.

The New Party Program of 1961

The Party Program is intended as a guide to action. The Program is to the Communist Party what military doctrine is to the Soviet Armed Forces. Every Party member is expected to study and to quote its contents and to attempt to carry out its directives. The Third Party Program, designed as the Party's basic directive from 1960 to 1980, was adopted at the 22nd Party Congress. It remained in force, for the most part, until a new, revised edition was approved at the 27th Party Congress in 1986. Although the original grandiose plans for overtaking the United States in production by 1970 failed, the general directions specified in the Program have not been altered.

The titles of the two sections of the Third Party Program speak for themselves. Part One was "The Transition from Capitalism to Communism Is the Road of Human Progress," and Part Two, "The Tasks of the Communist Party of the Soviet Union in Building a Communist Society."[9] The last section of Part One dealt with "Peaceful Coexistence and the Struggle for World Peace." In this section, it is noted that "the CPSU considers that the chief aim of its foreign policy is . . . to deliver mankind from a world war of extermination." Imperialism is the only source of the danger of war. "The imperialist camp is making preparations for the most terrible crime against mankind—a world thermonuclear war that can bring unprecedented destruction to entire countries and wipe out entire nations." The "people" must concentrate their efforts "on curbing the imperialists in good time and preventing them from making use of lethal weapons." The main objective, the Program emphasized, *"is to ward off a thermonuclear war, to prevent it from breaking out."* (Emphasis in original.) This objective, it said, could be accomplished "by the present generation."

Expressing confidence as a result of Soviet achievements in space, the Program stated that "socialism, outstripping capitalism in a number of important branches of science and technology, has supplied the peace-loving peoples with powerful means of curbing imperialist aggression."[10] One year after this Program was adopted, the USSR attempted to place nuclear missiles in Cuba.

According to the Program, *"it is possible to avert a world war . . .* to banish world war even before the complete victory of socialism on earth, with capitalism surviving in a part of the world." Before this goal can be achieved, "general and complete disarmament under strict international control is a radical way of guaranteeing peace. . . . By active and determined effort, *the peoples can and must force the imperialists into disarmament."* (Emphasis added.) The choice was either "peaceful coexistence or disastrous war," and there was no other alternative. "Should the imperialist aggressors nevertheless venture to start a new world war, the peoples will no longer tolerate a system which drags them into devastating wars. They will sweep imperialism away and bury it."[11]

After these appeals on the need for peaceful coexistence and the opportunity to avert war, the section ended with one major exception. The Party and "the Soviet people as a whole" would continue to oppose all wars of conquest, including wars between capitalist countries and local wars aimed "at strangling people's emancipation movements." The Soviet people, it said, consider it their duty *"to support the sacred struggle of the oppressed peoples and their just anti-imperialist wars of liberation."*[12] (Emphasis added.)

The Third Party Program, as noted, remained a basic Soviet directive until 1986, when Gorbachev presented a revised edition to the 27th Party Congress for approval. Despite the worldwide peace movements supported and encouraged by the Soviet Union, a basic element of Soviet military policy is the *duty* of the Soviet Union to support "just anti-imperialist wars of national liberation."

Marxist-Leninist philosophy has always asserted that there are two kinds of wars: just and unjust.[13] Soviet textbooks list four types of just wars: (1) wars in defense of the socialist Fatherland and of the countries of the socialist community; (2) revolutionary wars of the working class; (3) wars of national liberation; and (4) wars directed at the defense of state sovereignty of capitalist states from imperialist aggression. Conversely, unjust wars are identified as: (1) wars of imperialist states against socialist countries; (2) wars of exploiting classes against the working class; (3) colonial and neo-colonial wars; (4) aggressive imperialist wars inside the capitalist system.[14]

Much has been written in the West about the selective Soviet definitions of just and unjust wars. The open avowal, for instance, that support of so-called wars of national liberation is a "sacred duty" leads to the conclusion that the probability of future wars would be quite large. The question of whether the use of nuclear weapons can be just has been answered quite simply by the Kremlin: The use of nuclear weapons in response to their use by aggressors does not deprive war of its just nature from the side of the state opposing the aggressor.[15]

The New Military Doctrine

Addressing the 22nd Party Congress on the evening of October 23, 1961, Minister of Defense Malinovskiy used a term that for many years had scarcely been mentioned in the USSR—Soviet military doctrine. The theme of the Congress had been de-Stalinization. Military doctrine, a term Stalin had not liked, was revived, not surprisingly, as the dictator was being publicly denounced. Malinovskiy outlined its significance:

> One of the most important positions of this doctrine is that a world war, if it nevertheless is unleashed by the imperialist aggressors, will inevitably take the form of nuclear rocket war, that is, such a war in which the main

means of striking will be the nuclear weapon and the basic means of delivery to the target will be the rocket. In connection with this, war will also begin differently than before and will be conducted in a different way.

The use of atomic and thermonuclear weapons, with unlimited possibilities for their delivery to any target in calculated minutes with the aid of rockets, permits the achievement of decisive military results in the shortest period of time at any distance and over enormous territory. Along with groups of enemy armed forces, industrial and vital centers, communications junctions, everything that feeds war will be the targets of crushing nuclear strikes.[16]

Although Malinovskiy was reporting to the Congress that the Soviet Union was in the midst of a massive buildup of nuclear weaponry, at the same time he warned of the consequences of a nuclear war. He said that such a war would "take on an extraordinarily destructive character. It will lead to the deaths of hundreds of millions of people, and whole countries will be turned into lifeless deserts covered with ashes." This same warning had been given in the 1950s by both Khrushchev and Malenkov. Malinovskiy then admitted that this danger also was known in the West, and that therefore "they are trying to achieve their particular aggressive goals by waging local 'little' wars with the use of conventional and tactical atomic weapons."

Even though Khrushchev had announced troop cuts and deemphasized the need for air and naval forces in his speech of January 1960, Malinovskiy stated that "final victory over the aggressor" would require all services of the Armed Forces. He said that attention was being given to "the development of all kinds of weapons." A future world war would be waged, "in spite of enormous losses, by massive, multimillion-man armed forces."

Malinovskiy stressed the importance of the beginning period of a future war, stating this was of major concern both to "the Presidium [Politburo] of the Party's Central Committee and the Soviet government." The first massive nuclear strikes could, "to an enormous degree, predetermine the whole subsequent course of the war, and lead to such losses in the interior and in the troops that the people and the country might be placed in an exceptionally serious position." He then announced a basic Soviet doctrinal tenet that was to be repeated for decades to come: "The imperialists are preparing a surprise nuclear attack against the USSR and other socialist countries. Therefore, Soviet military doctrine considers the most important, the main and primary task of the Armed Forces to be constant readiness for the reliable repulse of a surprise enemy attack and to frustrate his criminal plans."[17]

Moreover, Malinovskiy asserted, "Any armed conflict inevitably will escalate into general nuclear rocket war if the nuclear powers are drawn into it." Consequently, "we must prepare our Armed Forces, the country and all the people for struggle with the aggressor first of all and mainly in conditions of nuclear war." Although a nuclear war would cause suffering and damage, "our country is big and wide. It is less vulnerable than capitalist countries." If war does occur, the socialist camp will win "and capitalism will be destroyed forever."[18]

Many Western analysts believe that the Soviet emphasis on nuclear weapons was the result of U.S. actions during the Cuban Missile Crisis in October 1962. But Khrushchev's speech in 1960 and Malinovskiy's address to the Party Congress in 1961 testify that the Soviet Union had made the doctrinal decision to concentrate on nuclear-missile forces years before the crisis. After years of research and development, production lines for missiles were started in the 1950s.

The full impact of the new military doctrine upon warfare was explained in the book *Military Strategy*, which went on sale in the Soviet Union in the summer of 1962, just a few months before the Cuban confrontation. This work, now a military classic, showed the new direction of the Soviet Armed Forces outlined by Khrushchev and explained by Malinovskiy. It was written by a group of Soviet military authors under the general direction of V. D. Sokolovskiy, who until April 1960 had been chief of the General Staff.[19]

Military Strategy was the most significant military writing of the 1960s, and perhaps of the twentieth century. It is a book about nuclear war: the type of military actions that would likely take place, the forces required, the command and control needed, and the necessity of preparing the Armed Forces, industry, and the entire population for this eventuality.

Sokolovskiy pointed out in the first edition that not since Svechin's *Strategiya* in 1926 had a book on military strategy been published in the open Soviet press. Information made available since then provides some indications why *Military Strategy* was published and why Sokolovskiy was designated as editor. A course on strategy was introduced for the first time at the Academy of the General Staff in 1958. A lecture given by Sokolovskiy in August 1959 greatly influenced the development of the course.[20] A classified textbook on strategy (592 pages) was published by the Academy in early 1960. This text was written under the direction of the Academy head General of the Army G. K. Malandin, and his deputy for military science work, General Colonel A. I. Gastilovich.[21] This book probably provided the basis for the open publication of *Military Strategy* in 1962, in which Gastilovich was one of the authors. In 1975, an updated textbook on strategy, written by a group of professors under the leadership of commandant General of the Army I. Ye. Shavrov, was published in the closed Academy press. As of early 1988, no open press version had appeared.[22]

Only 20,000 copies of the first edition of *Military Strategy* were printed. By mid-September 1962, the book was scarce in Moscow bookstores. A second edition published in 1963 included minor revisions attributed to suggestions from readers. A third edition issued in 1968 had even more changes but was still remarkably similar to the first edition, despite the fact that by this time Brezhnev had been General Secretary for four years. Military strategy does not deal with doctrine itself, Sokolovskiy explained, but with its implementation: "Military strategy occupies a subordinate position with regard to military doctrine. Military doctrine determines overall policy in principle, while military strategy, starting from this overall policy, develops and investigates concrete problems touching upon the nature of future war, the preparation of a country for war, the organization of the armed forces and the methods for conducting the war."[23]

There is not always a clear-cut distinction between writings on military strategy and military doctrine. For certain audiences, military doctrine is even called military science. What stands out is repetition of the same phrases and ideas. In the chapter entitled "The Nature of Modern War," the authors of *Military Strategy* summed up features generally found in military doctrine. They repeated Khrushchev's modification to communist ideology: There is no fatal inevitability of war. However, despite "the unrelenting struggle for peace by the Soviet Union and the entire socialist camp," the occurrence of wars is not excluded. This was due to "the unresolved economic and political contradictions of imperialism," the class struggle throughout the world; "the aggressive course of the politics of world reaction, above all, U.S. monopolists," and finally, "the intensified preparation for war by imperialist countries."

> Should the imperialist bloc unleash war against the USSR or any other socialist state, such a war inevitably will assume the nature of a world war with the participation of the majority of countries of the world. . . . A *new world war in its political and social essence will be a decisive armed clash of two opposed world social systems. This war will naturally end with the victory of the progressive communist sociopolitical formation over the reactionary capitalist sociopolitical formation, doomed to destruction by history.* The guarantee of such an outcome of the war is the real balance of political, economic and military forces of the two systems which has developed in favor of the socialist camp. However, victory in future war will not come by itself. It must be thoroughly prepared for and supported.[24] (Emphasis in original.)

The authors of *Military Strategy* then went on to say that a new world war would be a coalition war with capitalist states on one side and socialist states on the other. Because of its "acute class nature, the most decisive political and military goals will be set by both sides." Armed combat would be waged by mass armed forces, tens of millions of the people's masses would be involved in meeting the needs of war and of work in the national economy. A graphic description was given of how the war would be fought. This account still warrants careful reading:

> From the point of view of the means of armed struggle a third world war will be primarily *a nuclear rocket war*. The massive use of nuclear, especially thermonuclear, weapons will give the war an unprecedented destructive, annihilating character. Whole countries will be wiped off the face of the earth. The main means of attaining the goals of the war and for solving the main strategic and operational problems will be rockets with nuclear charges. Consequently, the leading service of the Armed Forces will be the Strategic Rocket Forces, and the role and purpose of the other services will be essentially

changed. At the same time, final victory will be attained only as a result of the mutual efforts of all services of the Armed Forces.

The basic method of waging war will be massed nuclear rocket attacks inflicted for the purpose of destroying the aggressor's means of nuclear attack and for the simultaneous mass destruction and devastation of the vitally important objectives comprising the enemy's military, political and economic might and also for crushing his will to resist and for achieving victory within the shortest time possible.

The center of gravity of the entire armed combat in these conditions will be transferred from the zone of combat contact of the sides, as in past wars, into the depth of the enemy's disposition, including the most remote regions. As a result, the war will acquire an unprecedented spatial scope.

Since modern means of combat make it possible to achieve exceptionally great strategic results in the briefest time, *the initial period of the war will be of decisive importance for the outcome of the entire war,* and also methods of frustrating the aggressive designs of the enemy by the timely infliction of a shattering attack on him. Consequently, the main task of Soviet military strategy is the development of methods of reliable *repulse of a surprise nuclear attack of the aggressor.* The successful solution of this problem is determined primarily by the constant high level of combat readiness of the Soviet Armed Forces, especially the Strategic Rocket Forces.[25] (Emphasis in original.)

Sokolovskiy and his contributors stated that achieving readiness based on the decisions of the 22nd Congress of the CPSU was the main task. "It must always be the center of attention of commanders and staffs of all ranks and of the political and Party machinery." In theory, the authors stated, the power of nuclear rocket weapons may bring about an end to the war in a relatively short time. If this can be done, it would result in the least losses. But while this is the goal, "simultaneously it is necessary to prepare seriously for a long war."

Although nuclear war would be different from any war of the past, the authors said, the Soviet people could be assured of victory not only because of "military-technical superiority, which is assured, on the whole, by the advantages of the socio-economic and political system, but also by the skill to organize the defeat of the enemy and to use effectively the available means of combat." For this purpose, "a thoroughly scientifically substantiated preparation of the country for war with an aggressor and a high level of military art of commanders and troops are required."[26]

Sokolovskiy's 1962 book was not translated and published in the United States until 1963, after the Cuban missile crisis was over. Its nuclear emphasis shocked many Western readers.

In late 1962, within a few months of the publication of *Military Strategy,* the third edition of *Marxism-Leninism on War and Army* went on sale. It was written by members of the Department of Dialectical and Historical Materialism of the Lenin Military-Political Academy. The authors of this work represented the Main Political Administration of the Soviet Army and Navy, whereas the authors of *Military Strategy* represented the General Staff. Yet this book reflected the same nuclear emphasis, as if the authors had followed the same set of guidelines used by Sokolovskiy and his contributors. *Marxism-Leninism on War and Army* described the nature of the new doctrine using statements almost identical to those made by Malinovskiy in his address to the 22nd Party Congress in 1961. The authors wrote that with respect to its "social and political character," a future war, "if the imperialists succeed in unleashing it, will be a bitter armed clash of two diametrically opposed social systems, a struggle between two coalitions—socialist and imperialist—in which each side will pursue the most decisive goals."

Such a war "inevitably will be nuclear rocket and therefore unprecedentedly destructive and annihilating." The main role in the war would be played by the Strategic Rocket Forces and "the troops of antiair and antimissile defense." Although a decisive role will be played by nuclear rocket weapons, "final victory over the aggressor can be achieved only as a result of the combined actions of all services of the Armed Forces, which must in full measure use the results of the nuclear rocket strikes on the enemy and fulfill their missions."

A nuclear war, the authors wrote, would be intercontinental. "This is determined both by its sociopolitical content and by the presence, on both sides, of rockets of any radius of action, atomic missile-carrying submarines, and also strategic bombers. War will actually engulf the whole of our planet." It would be waged quite differently from any past war. Formerly, the primary goal of military operations was to defeat the enemy's armed forces, "without which it was impossible to reach the enemy's most important strategic centers." Now, the situation had changed. The employment of atomic and thermonuclear weapons "with unlimited possibilities for their delivery to any target in a few minutes with the help of rockets makes it possible to achieve decisive military results at any distance and over enormous territory in the shortest period of time." They said that "crushing" nuclear strikes would be delivered in industrial and political centers, communications centers, and including enemy groups of armed forces.

On the ground, combat actions would "be characterized by high maneuverability and dynamism, and swift movement over many hundreds of kilometers." It would be impossible to maintain a solid stabilized front and the traditional division between the front and the rear would be erased.

The beginning period of war would be critical. Initial nuclear strikes could independently perform not only operational-tactical but also strategic tasks. Such strikes could "in large measure predetermine all the subsequent course of the war." Nuclear strikes could bring about such substantial losses in the rear and in the troops, "that the people and the country might be placed in exceptionally difficult circumstances." Soviet military doctrine, according to the authors of this work, would have to consider the fact that the imperialists were preparing a surprise nuclear attack against the USSR and other socialist countries. Therefore, the main and immediate task of the Armed Forces was to be constantly ready "to repulse a surprise attack by the enemy and to foil his criminal plans."[27]

In early October 1962 the United States learned that the Soviets were putting offensive missiles into Cuba, only 90 miles away from the U.S.

border. Meanwhile, in Moscow, Malinovskiy's booklet *Vigilantly Stand Guard over the Peace* was ready for the press. Actual printing may have started before the last of the missiles and bombers left Cuba, but not before Malinovskiy made some final additions to the text about how the crisis was settled.

Malinovskiy's booklet was essentially about the new military doctrine, and expanded on the theme stated the previous year at the Party Congress. Recognizing that the doctrine was quite new to the military, Malinovskiy began with a very basic presentation. Military doctrine has two sides: political and military-technical. The decisions of the 20th, 21st and 22nd Party Congresses provided fundamental inputs for renovating and developing the political side of military doctrine. Basically, he pointed out that although war was no longer considered to be inevitable and there was a real possibility that world war might be eradicated even before the complete victory of socialism, the prospect of the imperialists unleashing some form of aggression remained. The other component of doctrine, the military-technical side, was determined by two factors, according to Malinovskiy: first, the radical changes in armaments and equipment; second, the combat training of the troops and their moral-fighting qualities. Malinovskiy repeated essentially the same points he had made in his address to the 22nd Party Congress, which had been highlighted in Sokolovskiy's *Military Strategy*. The essence of military doctrine, Malinovskiy restated, is as follows:

> A future war, if the imperialists succeed in unleashing it, will be a decisive armed clash of two opposed social systems, in character of the means used, it inevitably will be thermonuclear, such a war in which the main means of destruction will be the nuclear weapon and the basic means of its delivery to the target, the rocket. . . . Now war might arise without the traditional clearly threatening period, by surprise, as a result of the mass use of long-range rockets armed with powerful nuclear warheads.[28]

Despite the likelihood of a surprise attack, Malinovskiy warned, world war could grow out of a local conflict. He asserted that the imperialists talk of "preventive war." He wrote, "This is why Soviet military doctrine considers as most important, the most central and primary task of the Armed Forces: to be constantly ready for the reliable repulse of a surprise attack of the enemy and for foiling [*sryvu*] his criminal plans."[29]

To escape the lethal consequences of world war, the West, including the United States, was attempting "to achieve its aggressive goals by way of waging local 'little' wars with the use of conventional, and, as the American generals say, tactical nuclear weapons." Soviet military doctrine considered such wars unjust and aggressive. "No matter where tactical atomic weapons are used against us," threatened Malinovskiy, "it will evoke a crushing retaliatory strike."[30]

As for the duration of a possible future war, Malinovskiy stated that no one could reject the possibility of a swift war because the first surprise nuclear rocket strike might bring unprecedented destruction. At the same time, he added, it might not be limited only to just strikes with the nuclear weapons. It might become protracted. Final victory would require the combined actions of all services of the Armed Forces and "all kinds of weapons." Mass multimillion-man armies would be involved. He repeated that "Since any military conflict, when the major powers are drawn into it, threatens inevitably to escalate into all-inclusive nuclear war," the Soviet Armed Forces, the country and all the people must be prepared "first of all and primarily to struggle with the aggressors in conditions of nuclear war."[31] This delineation of doctrine was quite complete. The statements made by Malinovskiy have been quoted many times by Soviet writers.

The second edition of *Military Strategy* was published in 1963. Key modifications or changes related to doctrine as compared with the first edition are as follows: "In the event of the unleashing of war against the USSR or any other socialist state by the imperialist bloc, such a war inevitably will assume the nature of a world war with the participation of the majority of countries of the world." In the second edition, the words "inevitably will" were changed to "might."

Here can be seen the one glaring change that took place in military doctrine following the publication of the first edition. After the Cuban confrontation, the Soviets no longer insisted that war against the USSR or any other socialist state "inevitably" would become a world war. Nevertheless, this passage was followed by a description of world war. This paragraph was added in the 1963 edition:

> One of the basic questions is the problem of maintaining qualitative and quantitative military-technical superiority over the probable aggressor, which demands the possession of a corresponding military economic base and the widest attraction of scientific and technical forces for the solution of this problem.

The next several paragraphs were without change, then came the following passage. (Changes in the second edition are shown in brackets.)

> The enormous possibilities of nuclear rocket weapons and other means of combat enable the goals of war to be attained within a relatively short time. Therefore, in order to ensure the interests of our country and [added—all the socialist camp], it is necessary to develop and perfect the ways and means of armed combat, expecting the attainment of victory over the aggressor first of all within the shortest possible time, [deleted—with the least possible losses, but simultaneously it is also necessary to prepare seriously for a protracted war.] [added—in the course of a rapidly moving war. However, the war may become protracted, which will demand long and extreme effort from the army and the people. Therefore we must also be ready for prolonged war, to prepare manpower and materials for this.][32]

The final paragraph was unchanged.

Khrushchev's Last Stand

In 1964, shortly before Khrushchev's ouster, the second edition of another book about nuclear war, *On Soviet Military Science*, was issued by the Soviet military press. It was written by a quartet of authors: Colonel Svatoslav N. Kozlov, General Major Mikhail V. Smirnov, Colonel Ivan S. Baz' and Colonel Petr A. Sidorov. A first edition of this work had appeared in 1960.[33] Because Khrushchev was ousted soon after the second edition was published, Western analysts relegated the strong statements on nuclear weapons found in the book to the dust heap of history, along with Khrushchev. Moreover, the authors, unlike Sokolovskiy who had edited *Military Strategy*, were virtually unknown. Thus, the book was considered not worth reading and was not taken seriously.

Over the years, Kozlov had been identified with many books, but Smirnov, Baz' and Sidorov had rarely been mentioned. It appears that Western analysts overlooked the fact that all of these authors, at one time or another, were on the editorial board of *Military Thought*, the theoretical, limited circulation journal of the Soviet General Staff. Kozlov, in fact, became the editor of *Military Thought* in 1963, after several years as deputy editor, and continued in the position until 1969. Sidorov served as secretary of the magazine from 1963 until 1972. Baz' was on the editorial board briefly, leaving in 1963, as did Smirnov.

This information, which became available when certain data was declassified by the U.S. Government, suggests that *On Soviet Military Science* should have been analyzed more carefully in the mid-1960s. *Military Thought* is put out by the Military Science Administration of the General Staff, the section of the General Staff most concerned with military doctrine and strategy.

The authors of *On Soviet Military Science* repeated, in a slightly different way, earlier statements on doctrine: "Soviet military doctrine, based on the data of military science, considers that a nuclear rocket war, if it is unleashed by the imperialists, will be a short and swift-moving war. The nuclear rocket weapon, having great power, can put out of action individual countries in only a few days or even hours." Having defined a nuclear rocket war as short and swift moving, Soviet military doctrine at the same time directed that the Armed Forces and the country as a whole must be ready to wage a more or less lengthy armed struggle.

The beginning period of war, again, was considered to be critical. In the first place, "Soviet military doctrine considers that a nuclear rocket war might be launched by surprise, without any kind of warning, without a declaration of war." At the same time, the authors warned that "war also might begin by way of escalation [*pererastaniye*] of a limited conflict into a world one, more or less gradually." But once war begins, the first strikes of the nuclear rocket weapon might be decisive. Therefore, Soviet military doctrine pays particular attention to the beginning period of war. "Events of the beginning period might have a decisive influence on the further course of the war and on its final result."

In the 1980s Soviet leaders would assert that Soviet military doctrine had always had only a defensive character. However, in the 1960s these authors stated that *"Soviet military doctrine bears an offensive character."* But this should be of no concern: "The offensiveness of Soviet military doctrine has nothing in common with aggressiveness and the predatory tendencies of the military doctrine of the United States and its allies." The Soviet Union was not planning to attack anyone, "but if attacked, then they will attempt to conduct a war, which was forced on them by their enemies, in the most offensive manner, in order to achieve the crushing of the enemy in the shortest period of time."

While giving "decisive significance" to the nuclear rocket weapons, these authors pointed out that military doctrine stipulates that along with nuclear rocket strikes on both strategic and operational-tactical targets, conventional weapons also would be used. Their purpose would be "to conduct broad offensive operations on land, at sea and in the air for the purpose of the final defeat of the enemy, for his complete capitulation."

Another basic doctrinal statement was that success in war would be achieved only by the combined efforts of all services and service branches, "with the leading role of the Strategic Rocket Forces." Soviet military doctrine also considers "that the organization of the services of the Armed Forces and service branches must be sufficiently flexible and varied to answer to the different conditions of waging armed struggle." The authors also brought up the matter of civil defense, calling it "a new important phenomenon in modern war." It is difficult to determine whether they were considering civil defense only in terms of nuclear war, or if World War II and the air raid experiences of the British and Germans were taken into account.

They wrote, "Doctrine is not dogma but a guide to action. The principles set forth in Soviet military doctrine have the force of law, and our military cadres are guided by them in all military actions." Doctrine assures unity of views and efforts directed "at raising the military might of the Soviet government and at achieving victory in war, if the imperialist aggressors unleash it. This is why all of our military cadres are required to make a deep study of military doctrine."[34]

These views on doctrine, as did previous ones, emphasized the nuclear war that might be unleashed by "imperialists." It could be short or protracted, and might begin with a surprise attack or escalate from a local conflict. Soviet military doctrine was offensive in character. Although nuclear rocket weapons were decisive, all services, using conventional weapons as well as nuclear ones, would be needed in order to completely defeat the enemy. Civil defense had increased in importance. Finally, the principles of Soviet military doctrine had the force of law and would guide the military actions of all military personnel. If "imperialist aggressors" unleashed war, victory would be the goal of the Soviet Armed Forces.

The People's Republic of China announced the successful detonation of an atomic bomb on October 15, 1964. The nation with the world's largest population had joined the nuclear club, and Soviet deliberations on strategy would soon take on a new dimension.

Beginning of the Brezhnev Era

In a 1965 article, Kozlov, then editor of *Military Thought,* stated that doctrine constantly undergoes evolutionary changes. The complete replacement of a doctrine, however, represents a rare action by a state. Kozlov wrote, "Changes in Soviet military doctrine, which during the existence of our state have taken place three times, serve as confirmation of this."[35] He did not elaborate further. As has been shown, the military doctrine introduced by Khrushchev was completely new. Would it be changed again after Brezhnev took charge?

Soviet military leadership remained the same after Brezhnev took the reins of power in the Kremlin, with one exception brought about by an unusual accident. A week after Khrushchev was ousted, the chief of the General Staff, Marshal Sergey S. Biryuzov, was killed in a plane crash while on an official visit to Yugoslavia. Questions still remain about the cause of that accident. He was replaced by the former chief, Marshal Matvey V. Zakharov. This was the only immediate change in the High Command other than the fact that Brezhnev, as Party first secretary, replaced Khrushchev as the chairman of the Council of Defense. Owing to the Soviet obsession with secrecy, it was not known in the West for more than a decade that this organization existed.

Soviet military doctrine also remained unchanged. A collection of sixteen articles by prominent marshals and generals that had been written earlier in the 1960s was published almost immediately. Entitled *Problems of the Revolution in Military Affairs,* this volume quickly set the record straight: Khrushchev or no Khrushchev, the Party's policies remained intact. The fourth article in the collection was "On Soviet Military Doctrine" by General Colonel Nikolay A. Lomov, head of the chair on Strategy at the Academy of the General Staff from 1958 to 1969. Professor Lomov had been one of the leading officers of the Operations Directorate of the General Staff during the war. The article originally had been published in the May 1962 issue of *Communist of the Armed Forces,* the journal of the Party's Main Political Administration of the Soviet Army and Navy. All reference to Khrushchev that had appeared in the original article had been removed in the new version.

Lomov advanced familiar features of a possible world nuclear rocket war. Such a war, "if the imperialists unleash it," would be a struggle between two opposed world systems—socialist and capitalist. It would require mass, multimillion-man armies, with both sides pursuing the most decisive political goals. It would inevitably assume the nature of a world nuclear war, and would be a coalitional war from both sides. Such a war would have certain inherent peculiarities. It would be the most destructive and damaging war in history, and it would be intercontinental, since both sides have intercontinental rockets, as well as nuclear submarines equipped with rockets, and strategic bombers.[36] The long range of rocket weapons, along with their speed of flight and accuracy, would permit the destruction of any target located deep in the enemy's interior. "Industrial and economic objectives and administrative and political centers with high concentrations of population might undergo nuclear rocket strikes in the very first minutes." The possibility of mass nuclear rocket strikes, together with the possibility of a surprise strike, would change the roles of the various services and would pose special demands for preparing the country and the army for war.

Lomov also stated that the next world war might be the result of either a surprise attack from the aggressive bloc or escalation of a local war. He felt that the former would be the more probable. Therefore, "Soviet military doctrine considers that the most important, the chief and primary task of the Armed Forces is to be in constant readiness to reliably repulse an enemy surprise attack and to frustrate his criminal plans." Final victory would be achieved by the joint actions of all the services of the armed forces.[37]

In late 1964 *Krasnaya Zvezda* announced that a new Officer's Library series of books would be issued, to be used for self-study by Soviet officers. One of the first books in this series was a fourth edition of *Marxism-Leninism on War and Army*, published in 1965. The authors were generally the same ones as those who had written the second and third editions. In 1966, the book was nominated for the Frunze Prize. This edition is invaluable in any analysis of the continuity of Soviet military doctrine between the regimes of Khrushchev and Brezhnev. By comparing it with the earlier edition, the evolutionary process of military doctrine that Kozlov had mentioned can be clearly seen. The following passages show which portions of the doctrine have changed and which have not. A new paragraph of general explanation was added to the 1965 edition:

> The Soviet state's military doctrine represents a scientifically based and orderly system of ideas and precepts which determines the basic tasks in the realm of strengthening the defense capability of the country and of military development. It rests on a Marxist-Leninist analysis of the modern era and the relationship of international forces and also on foreseeing the character of a future war that the imperialists might force on us. Soviet military doctrine is called on, as M. V. Frunze said, to assure the unity of thought and will of Soviet soldiers not only in the community of political ideology but also in the unity of views on the nature of the military tasks, the methods of their solution, and the methods of combat training of the troops. It is the solid foundation of preparing the country for defense; directing the troops, their training and education. Military doctrine finds its concrete expression in our military policy and also in the field regulations and manuals of the Armed Forces.

The 1965 edition dropped the assertion that modern world war will demand massive multimillion-man armies. Most of the other changes were minor except for one of the final points. The 1962 edition had said that Soviet military doctrine proceeds from the fact that the "imperialists are preparing a surprise nuclear rocket attack against the USSR and other socialist countries." Added in 1965 was this caveat: *"At the same time it takes into account the possibility of waging war with conventional weapons."* (Emphasis in original.) After this statement it concluded with the standard concept that the foremost immediate task of the Soviet Armed Forces consisted of being constantly ready "to repulse a surprise attack by the enemy and to foil his criminal plans."[38]

What caused this added possibility of waging war with conventional weapons? The United States had adopted the policy of "flexible response" in 1961, and in 1965, NATO was about to adopt this same policy. This theme was further developed in subsequent renditions of doctrine, as will be shown. Escalation to nuclear world war was no longer inevitable! Although the assertion that modern world war would demand massive multimillion-man armies was dropped, other texts retained this concept. Additional changes appeared in a later edition of *Marxism-Leninism On War and Army.*

Impact of the 23rd Party Congress

Party Congresses are considered to be milestones for Communists, providing guidance for Party strategy and tactics. Decisions, statements, and resolutions made at the Congress frequently will be quoted in books and articles as the source for some facet of doctrine. Traditionally, the most important speech at the Congress is the report of the Central Committee made by the General Secretary.[39]

The 23rd Party Congress was the first for Brezhnev as Party chief, and he was probably anxious to make his mark on Party policy. His Report to the Congress began with assurances to the collected delegates of the Party's "desire to ensure peaceful conditions for the building of communism and socialism in the countries of the world socialist community and to prevent the unleashing of a new world war."[40] He then spoke of the military cooperation and consolidation of relations with the socialist countries "in the face of growing aggressive acts on the part of the imperialist forces headed by the USA." He described the Warsaw Pact as "the reliable protector of the gains of the peoples of socialist countries" and said that its armies "are equipped with the most up-to-date weapons." The Party, he said, sees its duty "in keeping the Soviet people in a state of unceasing vigilance with regard to the intrigues of the enemies of peace and does everything to prevent the aggressors, if they try to violate peace, from ever taking us by surprise and to make certain that retaliation overtakes them inexorably and promptly." This speech was somewhat less strident than those Khrushchev had made, but it was different only in degree, not in perspective.

In 1966, shortly after the 23rd Party Congress, a major theoretical work, *Methodological Problems of Military Theory and Practice*, edited by General Major N. Ya. Sushko and Lieutenant Colonel T. R. Kondratkov, was published in Moscow. There were twenty authors, almost all of them colonels with degrees in "philosophical sciences," that is, Marxism-Leninism. Many of the authors had written chapters in the various editions of *Marxism-Leninism on War and Army*. An examination of the treatment of doctrine in this work provides another guidepost in the study of Soviet military doctrine.

One chapter of particular interest was entitled "Military Doctrine and Military Science." It was written by Kozlov, who had just been promoted from colonel to general and was also then editor of *Military Thought*. Since a section of this 1966 chapter will be compared later with a 1969 edition of *Methodological Problems of Military Theory and Practice*, only the main points made by General Kozlov will be listed here:

1. Soviet military doctrine and Soviet military science are both based on socialist methods of production, a common sociopolitical foundation and a common philosophical-methodological outlook—dialectical and historical materialism. Consequently, they are the diametrical opposite of "bourgeois" military doctrine and science.

2. Military doctrine is formed with the help of military science and based on its conclusions. Once formulated, doctrine poses important questions for military science. Doctrine is based primarily on ideas of war waged with nuclear weapons. Doctrine is wholly oriented toward the future, whereas military science studies the past as well. Military *science* can have various and even contradictory points of view, presentations, and hypotheses. In contrast, there cannot be two military doctrines within a single state. (Thus, there are no "internal doctrinal debates," as is frequently speculated in the Western press.)

3. Within doctrine, there are strategic, operational, and tactical divisions depending on the scale of operations. But there can be no independent views on conducting actions on the ground, or in the air, or at sea. All military actions would be carried out according to one common doctrine and one common strategy.

4. With the appearance of the nuclear rocket weapon, "past experience has diminished in importance and scientific prognosis of the future has increased." From this observation stems the criteria that "the main thing is to assure supremacy over the probable enemy, guaranteeing certain and full defeat for him in the event of war."

One reference appears to have been directed at Khrushchev's policies. "Military doctrine must avoid extremes and 'hare-brained' schemes." Could this statement have been an acknowledgment of placing nuclear missiles in Cuba? Whatever he might have meant by this statement, the fact remains that, on the whole, the Kremlin leadership had been carrying out the provisions of the military doctrine announced by Khrushchev in 1960.

In the West, Khrushchev's ouster in 1964 had been greeted with a sigh of relief. It was felt that Brezhnev was more sensible and reasonable. Therefore, when the third edition of *Military Strategy* appeared in 1968, very little changed from earlier editions, this was not welcomed abroad by those who were seeking an arms control agreement with Moscow. In general, it was ignored, even though the new edition was part of the Soviet Officer's Library series. A publisher for an English translation could not be found until 1975. Yet *Military Strategy* continued to be footnoted in Soviet writings throughout the 1970s and into the 1980s as a basic work.[41] One of the key changes between the earlier editions and the 1968 edition was the position that in addition to the Strategic Rocket Forces, atomic rocket-carrying submarines would play an important role in nuclear war.

Sokolovskiy died in 1968. Eulogies in the Soviet press testified to his status. His last accomplishment was to promote the establishment of a Western-type think tank within the framework of the USSR Academy of Sciences; it was initially called the Institute of the United States of America. One of its purposes was to gather information of all types—political, economic, ideological and military—about the United States to help formulate Soviet military doctrine. This institute will be discussed in some detail in a later chapter.

A fifth edition of *Marxism-Leninism on War and Army* appeared in 1968, shortly before the Brezhnev doctrine resulted in the invasion of Czechoslovakia. For followers of Soviet military doctrine, it was clear that "defense of the socialist fatherland"—in this case Czechoslovakia—was considered in Marxist-Leninist ideology as one of the *just* types of military actions.

According to its preface, *Marxism-Leninism on War and Army* was intended for study by officers, generals, and admirals. A group of fourteen authors prepared the text. They represented the *kafedras* (chairs) of Marxism-Leninism at the leading military academies: The Military Academy of the General Staff, Frunze Military Academy, the Malinovskiy Tank Academy, the Lenin Military-Political Academy, and others. These academies have a much broader scope than U.S. war colleges and command and staff schools; they also serve as the "think tanks" for the Soviet Armed Forces.

There were some significant changes in this text over the years, as will be shown below. In 1968, it was made clear that the Marxist-Leninist teaching on war and the army is closely connected to Soviet military doctrine. Whereas earlier editions had asserted that war *inevitably* would be thermonuclear, the 1968 edition said that war *"may be* nuclear." (Emphasis added.) Nevertheless, it continued,

> troops having an inflexible will to victory, enthused with the high goals of a just war, can and must wage active offensive actions with any surviving means and achieve the final utter defeat of the enemy.
>
> Soviet military doctrine proceeds from the fact that the imperialists are preparing a surprise nuclear attack against the USSR and other socialist countries. At the same time it takes into account the possibility of *conducting military operations* with conventional weapons *and the possibility of their escalation into military operations with the use of the nuclear rocket weapon.* Therefore, the main and immediate task of the Armed Forces consists of being constantly ready to repulse a surprise attack by the enemy and to foil his criminal plans no matter what means he uses.[42] (Emphasis added.)

This was another confirmation of the modification to military doctrine that first had appeared about 1965: War might begin with the use of conventional weapons, but escalation to nuclear weapons was likely. Earlier editions had not indicated this possibility. This fifth edition added that military doctrine was subject to change. With changing conditions, the state might either improve the existing doctrine or, if obsolete, replace it. For example, after the Great Patriotic War, Soviet military doctrine was improved by taking into account the experience gained in that war. But after that, a new doctrine was worked out and adopted at the beginning of the 1960s that was qualitatively different from the earlier doctrine. The authors noted that changes were being made in the present doctrine, although its essence remained the same.

In 1969, a second edition of *Methodological Problems of Military Theory and Practice* was issued. The editors of this edition were General Colonel A. S. Zheltov, Lieutenant Colonel T. R. Kondratkov and Colonel Ye. A. Khomenko. There were twenty-four contributors, almost all of whom had advanced degrees in philosophical sciences. Like the first edition, this book was prepared by the *kafedra* (chair) of Marxist-Leninist philosophy of the Lenin Military-Political Academy. In 1971 the book was nominated for the Frunze Prize.

The chapter written by General Major S. N. Kozlov, who had acquired the degree of candidate of military sciences since his contribution to the first edition in 1966, presented an exceptional essay on Soviet military doctrine and the premises on which it is based. Comparing the 1969 edition with the 1966 edition provided an opportunity to trace doctrinal shifts, especially those changes that occurred as a result of the 1967 Middle East War, the invasion of Czechoslovakia in 1968, and the continuing conflict in Southeast Asia.

Perhaps the most significant change that took place between publication of the two editions resulted from NATO's adoption of the strategy of "flexible response" in early 1967. Although President John F. Kennedy had announced this strategy almost immediately after he had taken office in January 1961, NATO's decision was necessary in order for it to have a decisive influence on Soviet military doctrine. The continuity and change between these two editions are shown below. (Changes are shown in brackets.)

The military doctrine of any state has two sides: the sociopolitical and the military-technical. Both sides are closely interconnected and influence each other, with the chief, leading one being the sociopolitical side.

The sociopolitical side of [Soviet] military doctrine determines the nature of the military tasks of the Soviet government and the main direction of the development of the Soviet Armed Forces. V. I. Lenin established its foundations. Guided by the Leninist analysis of the predatory nature of imperialism, and in the Leninist theory of protecting the socialist fatherland, our military doctrine condemns predatory, unjust, reactionary wars and supports wars that are just, liberating, and revolutionary.

Soviet military doctrine considers that a new world war, [deleted—if the imperialists unleash it,] [added—if preventing it fails,] will be an armed clash of two opposed social systems—capitalism and socialism—in its social and class character. From the side of the imperialist states, it will be an unjust, predatory and criminal war. From the side of the socialist camp, the war will be just and liberating.

This war will inevitably take on intercontinental scope and draw into its orbit the majority of countries and peoples of the world. War will have an exceptionally fierce, destructive and annihilating character.

In the composition of the opposing sides, world war will be coalitional. Such coalitions in fact already exist. To wage war against the socialist countries, the imperialists have knocked together NATO, SEATO, CENTO and other aggressive groups. In answer to this the socialist countries were forced to take measures for uniting their efforts in the event of aggression. They created [added—and are strengthening] the organization of the Warsaw Pact which is a reliable shield for the gains of socialism [added—in Europe].

The countries of the socialist camp are fighting for peace, struggling against imperialist aggression, and strengthening their armed might. In this struggle, each socialist country makes its contribution to the common goal of assuring the security of the socialist camp. The decisive role belongs to the Soviet Union. Having enormous economic and military might and the nuclear rocket weapon [added—and modern conventional weapons] the USSR is the powerful block on the path of imperialist aggression. It is well known that many times in the most critical moment, when the militaristic circles of imperialism placed the world on the brink of war, the Soviet Union used her international authority, her might, in order to stop the hand of the aggressor which had been raised over little or big countries, near or far.

While giving special significance to the preparation of the country and the Armed Forces for world war which the monopolistic circles are preparing, [added—primarily the USA,] our military doctrine takes into account the possibility of the unleashing of local, limited wars by the imperialist aggressors [added—with the use of conventional weapons].

[Deleted—Soviet] [Added—Modern] military doctrine takes into account that [deleted—modern wars are waged by the people.] [added—now wars are waged not just by armies but also by the people.]

The course and outcome of modern war depends in the final count on the relationship of the peoples' masses to its goals. Victory in such a war will be achieved by the gigantic strained efforts of the front and the rear, the Armed Forces and all of the people.

The military-technical side of our doctrine focuses its attention on the features of [deleted—nuclear rocket war] [added—modern war] and the methods of its waging. Our doctrine considers that the decisive role in [deleted—such a war] [added—nuclear war] will be played by the Strategic Rocket Forces. They will carry out nuclear strikes on the enemy's most important targets and objectives in his territory. Massive nuclear strikes can to a significant degree predetermine the whole course and outcome of war. Simultaneously with the nuclear rocket strikes or following them, all the other services of the Armed Forces and service branches will unroll their actions on land, at sea, and in the air.

Consequently our military doctrine proceeds from the fact that success in present-day war will be achieved not by any one means or any one service but by the combined efforts of all the services of the Armed Forces and service arms with the decisive role of the Strategic Rocket Forces. [Added—This position is even more true for military actions conducted without the use of the nuclear weapon.]

Taking into account that the nuclear rocket weapons have enormous power, [added—that their mass use] in just a few days and even hours might [deleted—wipe countries from the face of the earth,] [added—lead to strategic results,] our doctrine views nuclear war as short and swift-moving (*skorotechniy*). At the same time it recognizes that in certain circumstances war might take on a protracted character.

As concerns the imperialists' methods of unleashing war, Soviet military science considers it most likely to be a surprise attack of an aggressor without any declaration of war. The imperialists are banking on just exactly that. [Added—They have resorted to similar methods in the past. The aggressors will resort to them also in contemporary circumstances, as shown, for example, in the attack of Israel on the Arab countries.] It is not excluded that war might begin by way of the gradual escalation of a limited conflict into a world one.

[Added—The imperialists may start it and for some time wage it without the use of the nuclear weapon, with only conventional weapons. In this case the wealth of experience, accumulated in the past, might be used, but, undoubtedly, taking into account those important changes which have taken place in military equipment and other determining conditions of armed conflict.]

But no matter how the war begins, [deleted—the first nuclear rocket strikes might turn out to be decisive.] [added—the aggressor will try for surprise.] From this comes the main task of the Soviet Armed Forces [added—to display maximum vigilance,] to be in constant combat readiness [added—to decisively repulse the aggressor no matter from where and no matter how he carries out his attack.]

Our military doctrine teaches that in nuclear war, the methods of combat actions will be different from past wars. The nuclear rocket weapon has changed the relationship of tactical, operational and strategic acts of armed struggle. While in the past, strategic results [added—were achieved by a series of consecutive, more often efforts of long duration, and] were built up from the sum of tactical and operational successes and strategy could realize its plans only with the help of operational art and tactics, now strategy can directly achieve its goals [added—using powerful nuclear strikes. In these conditions,] the role of operational art and tactics has changed. In the course of operations (battles) troops will basically accomplish the final defeat of the enemy, which will be achieved by strikes of nuclear rocket means [deleted—of strategic designation.] [added—If military actions will be conducted without the use of nuclear weapons, then the former importance and the relationship of all parts of military art basically remain in force.]

Soviet military doctrine has always considered the offensive as the basic method of the full defeat of the enemy and the achieving of victory, and defense was viewed as a forced form of struggle used when the offensive was impossible or inconvenient. In the conditions of war the role of active offensive actions is growing even more.

[Deleted—The sphere of the use of defense has narrowed. Obviously it will be resorted to only in exceptional circumstances, and then only on a tactical or limited operational scale.]

In nuclear war, the division between the front and the rear is being erased more and more. The combat actions might unroll simultaneously on the front and in the deep interior. Nuclear rocket strikes might be carried out on objectives in the interior. Airborne troops [deleted—might be landed in the rear.] [added: probably will be landed in the rear.] All this poses special demands [added: for organizing defense of the rear, in particular] for civil defense which is called upon to protect the population from enemy nuclear rocket strikes, liquidate the results of nuclear attack, and promote the uninterrupted work of businesses, administrative organs and supply.

While giving enormous significance to nuclear rocket weapons and new combat equipment, Soviet military doctrine does not allow them to be absolutized. It views man and equipment in dialectical interdependence and gives first place in achieving victory to [deleted—man.] [added—people with high moral-political consciousness joined in a smoothly running collective, excellently mastering the mighty equipment.]

Soviet military doctrine [deleted—is the doctrine] [added—expresses the military policy] of a socialist state. . . .

Soviet military doctrine soberly and objectively evaluates the probable enemy and examines the factors of armed struggle and their interdependencies.

While admitting the decisive role in war of the nuclear rocket weapon, at the same time it affirms that victory will be achieved by the combined efforts of all forces and means, by various methods and various forms of armed conflict.[43]

Although Soviet military doctrine throughout the 1960s was primarily concerned with nuclear war, wars of lower intensity also demanded attention throughout that period. Problems with the People's Republic of China, which had been festering since the mid-1950s and were exacerbated by Soviet political and logistical support of North Vietnam, burst open in May 1969. At that time a border dispute near Damanskiy Island on the far eastern border between China and the Soviet Union resulted in considerable loss of life. Other border incidents in Kazakhstan led to the formation of a new military district, the Central Asian Military District, that same year. These developments may account for the addition on the need to be ready "to decisively repulse the aggressor no matter from where and no matter how he carries out his attack." Some modifications in military doctrine were inevitable.

Tasks of Military Doctrine

Throughout the 1960s dozens of books and hundreds of articles described the major Soviet concerns about military doctrine. However, many aspects of doctrine were not highlighted, and were not normally identified as doctrinal issues. In Sokolovskiy's *Military Strategy*, the following definition of military doctrine appeared:

Military doctrine is the expression of the accepted views of a state regarding the problems of:
• political evaluation of future war;
• the state attitude toward war;
• a determination of the nature of future war;
• preparation of the country for war in the economic and moral sense;
• organization and preparation of the armed forces;
• methods of waging war.

Later, beginning in 1974, the "problems" identified in Sokolovskiy's work were posed as "questions," with some rewording. From that point on there was little general discussion of the content of military doctrine in the same sense that it had been explained throughout the 1960s. It then became necessary to analyze Soviet writings very closely in order to determine how the questions that doctrine asked were being answered.

For purposes of showing the continuity of doctrine, the "questions" used later by Grechko and Ogarkov will be summarized in this section to make comparison easier for the reader. Each question will be answered by pertinent excerpts from the most significant writings of the 1960s that have already been described.

Question 1: What Is the Probability of a Future War and Who Will Be the Enemy?

Khrushchev, in his address to the 4th Session of the Supreme Soviet in 1960, restated the position given at the 20th and 21st Party Congresses: "There is no longer any fatal inevitability of war."[44] Following his speech, Minister of Defense Malinovskiy outlined the course that modern war might take, adding "provided it is unleashed by the imperialists."[45]

In 1961 the adoption of the Third Party Program was a milestone for the Communist Party of the Soviet Union (CPSU). Confident of Soviet economic and military power, the framers of this Program stated that "should the *imperialist aggressors* nevertheless venture to start a new world war, the peoples will no longer tolerate a system which drags them into devastating wars."[46] (Emphasis added.)

At the 22nd Party Congress Malinovskiy also talked in general terms about "a world war, if it nevertheless is unleashed by imperialist aggressors."[47] With this pattern established both by the Third Party Program and by the Minister of Defense at a Party Congress, later spokesmen could be expected to follow the general guidelines, while giving a few more details. For example, a 1961 textbook designated the enemy in these general terms: "If the *imperialist aggressors* succeed in unleashing World War Three, then it will be an armed clash of two opposed social systems and will assume a class nature."[48] (Emphasis added.)

The operative expression was "a future war, if the imperialist aggressors succeed in unleashing it"[49] or "if it is unleashed by the imperialists."[50] The first edition of Sokolovskiy's *Military Strategy* put it this way: "If a war against the USSR or any other socialist country is unleashed by the imperialist bloc."[51]

At the 23rd Party Congress in 1966 General Secretary Brezhnev said that Soviet foreign policy has the objective of "firmly repelling the aggressive forces of imperialism and delivering mankind from the threat of a new world war."[52] That same year Colonel A. A. Strokov in a military textbook again used the expression: "a future war, if the imperialists unleash it against the socialist countries."[53] Another work used almost the same words: "a new world war, if the imperialists unleash it."[54] Kozlov stated that "Soviet military doctrine soberly and objectively evaluates the probable enemy."[55] The enemy remained defined in general terms as "the imperialists." The pattern set at the very beginning of the 1960s remained, and the words used to express this idea changed only in very minor ways: "A future war, if the imperialists unleash it," "a new world war, if the imperialists succeed in unleashing it," or "a new world war, if unleashed by the imperialists."[56]

In 1969, as arms control negotiations were under way with the United States, Soviet military doctrine gave special attention "to the preparation of the country and the Armed Forces for world war which the monopolistic circles are preparing, primarily the USA. . . . Soviet military doctrine soberly and objectively evaluates the probable enemy and examines the factors of armed struggle and their interdependencies."[57] At this time General N. V. Ogarkov, later to become chief of the General Staff, was the most visible Soviet military negotiator at the arms control talks.

The following year preparations were being made for the 24th Party Congress, and arms control negotiations continued. Professor D. M. Grinishin of Kiev University agreed that world war was not inevitable, and that it could be averted by the "common efforts of the world socialist community" through three world movements: (1) the international working class, (2) the national-liberation movement, and (3) the peace-loving forces of all countries. However, he warned, "the aggressiveness of imperialism at the present time has become stronger."[58] These three movements, basic to Marxist-Leninist strategy and tactics, remained as the foundation of Soviet policies throughout the coming decades.

In summary, at the beginning of the 1960s Soviet strategists considered that war would be unleashed by the imperialists. Although the United States on occasion was singled out as the aggressor, Soviet writings more often simply described the enemy as the "imperialists." And finally, the position Khrushchev took in 1956 that war between capitalism and socialism was no longer inevitable remained: War could be prevented by a militarily strong Soviet Union, assisted by peace-loving forces throughout the world.

Question 2: What Will Be the Character of the War in Which a State and Its Armed Forces Will Have to Take Part, and What Goals and Missions Might Face Them in This War?

A consistent theme concerning the nature of a future war began to emerge in the late 1950s and continued throughout the 1960s. If "World War Three" is unleashed by the imperialists, "it will be an armed clash of two opposed social systems and will assume a class nature."[59] On occasion it was stated that war would "inevitably" be a world war;[60] at other times "might" was substituted.[61] In a 1967 work that won the Frunze Prize the following year, this question was asked: "What are the basic positions of the nature of future war if the imperialists unleash it?" The answer left little room for doubt: "War will inevitably become a world nuclear rocket war."[62]

There was little question of the destruction that a future war could cause. In his speech on January 14, 1960, Khrushchev claimed that the Soviet Union had such quantities of nuclear rocket weapons that "if some madman were to provoke an attack on our country or any other socialist countries, we could literally wipe the country or countries attacking us off the face of the earth." Although the Soviet Union would sustain great losses, it would survive; but for the aggressors, it would "not only be their last war, but also the end of capitalism."[63]

This statement was followed by other equally dramatic ones. One spokesman described the consequences of a future war as follows: "The use of nuclear missiles and also of chemical and bacteriological weapons will lead to countless victims both in the civilian population and in the troops. The losses of dead and wounded in two past world war numbered in the tens of millions, but in a future war they will reach hundreds of millions. It will be a severe, tense and exceptionally bitter war—a struggle not for life, but to the death."[64]

Malinovskiy, as already noted, also claimed that a future world war, "if not prevented," would lead to the deaths of hundreds of millions of people, and "whole countries will be turned to lifeless deserts covered with ashes. This is well understood in the West, and for this reason, they are trying to achieve their partial goals by waging local 'little' wars with the use of conventional and tactical atomic weapons."[65]

In the first edition of *Military Strategy*, published in 1962, the authors claimed that any war launched by the imperialists against the Soviet Union or any other socialist country would be a decisive armed clash between two opposed world social systems. It would be "first of all a nuclear rocket war. . . . The main means of attaining the goals of the war for solving the main strategic and operational problems will be rockets with nuclear charges."[66] Malinovskiy used almost these exact words in his 1962 booklet. A future war, he said, will be "a decisive armed clash of two opposed social systems, . . . it inevitably will be thermonuclear, the basic means of delivery [of the nuclear weapon] to the target, the rocket."[67]

The words used by Malinovskiy in his address to the Party Congress in 1961, in Sokolovskiy's *Military Strategy* and in Malinovskiy's 1962 pamphlet set the pattern for the remainder of the 1960s. The major writings of the period all repeated those basic ideas, including: *Marxism-Leninism on War and Army*, fourth edition, 1965; *History of Military Art*, 1966; *Methodological Problems of Military Theory and Practice*, first edition, 1966; and *50 Years of the Armed Forces of the USSR*, 1968.

Surprise remained a primary focus of Soviet military doctrine. When outlining his "permanently operating factors" during the Great Patriotic War, Stalin played down the significance of surprise, stating that it was only a transitory factor. Following Stalin's death, the possible consequences of a surprise nuclear strike were a major motivating factor for developing a new military doctrine. A surprise first strike, so the Soviet military and populace were assured in open publications, would never be attempted by the Soviet leadership. On the other hand, "it must be expected that the most probable method of unleashing war by the imperialists against the Soviet Union, if they risk going to it, will be a surprise attack with the wide use of nuclear weapons." A surprise nuclear strike by the imperialists became a matter of doctrine.

Malinovskiy laid out the official line in 1961: "It must be taken into account that the imperialists are preparing a surprise nuclear attack against the USSR and other socialist countries. Therefore, Soviet military doctrine considers the most important, the main and paramount task of the Armed Forces to be in constant readiness for the reliable repulse of a surprise attack of the enemy and to frustrate his criminal plans."[68] In 1962 Malinovskiy modified this statement, noting that war might arise as the result of a surprise nuclear strike, without the traditional threatening period. This is possible because of long-range nuclear missiles. At the same time, "this does not exclude a world conflict arising out of a local one. But the main danger is a surprise attack."

Other military writers quickly followed the line established with this doctrinal pronouncement. For example, the authors of *Marxism-Leninism on War and Army* (3rd edition) used almost identical wording: "Soviet military doctrine proceeds from the fact that the imperialists are preparing a surprise nuclear rocket attack against the USSR and the other socialist countries." Therefore, the main and paramount task of the Armed Forces was "to be constantly ready to repulse a surprise enemy attack and to frustrate his criminal plans."[69]

In his address to the 23rd Party Congress in 1966, Brezhnev said that the duty of the Communist Party was to keep the Soviet people in a state of unceasing vigilance. If the aggressors try to violate peace and make a surprise attack on the Soviet Union, retaliation would overtake them inexorably and promptly.[70] The Congress did not alter this aspect of military doctrine. A spokesman later that year affirmed that "as concerns the methods of unleashing war by the imperialists, Soviet military science considers it most likely to be a surprise attack of an aggressor without any declaration of war."[71]

With respect to the length of a war, Malinovskiy in 1962 postulated that the war might be "swift-moving" and end quickly as a result of the destruction brought about by the initial strike. On the other hand, "it might be protracted," and "assume a more or less lengthy nature."[72] The same assertion was found in *Military Strategy*: "Efforts should be made to attain victory over the aggressor within the shortest possible time. . . . But simultaneously it is also necessary seriously to prepare for a protracted war." In 1963, in the second edition of this work, the authors added: "We also must be ready for a prolonged war and prepare human and material resources for this contingency."[73]

Since this also was a matter of doctrine, other major writings and articles had to make the same point. For example, "War might be protracted, and demand long and extreme tension of all the forces of the army and the country as a whole."[74] Another stated: "Our doctrine views nuclear war as short and swift-moving. At the same time it recognizes that in definite circumstances war might take on a protracted character."[75]

Would the war be nuclear or nonnuclear? In the early part of the 1960s, writers on Soviet doctrine specified that the war would begin with a nuclear strike. Within a few years, nuclear weapons became smaller and more numerous, and they were included in the armaments of all of the Soviet services, in particular the Ground Forces. By 1965 Soviet spokesmen began to state that Soviet military doctrine took into account "the possibility of waging war with conventional weapons."[76] A 1967 work went further: "The Soviet Armed Forces must be ready to utterly defeat the enemy not only in conditions of using the nuclear weapon, but also with the use of just conventional means of fighting."[77]

The conventional option was carefully explained in articles providing instruction to political officers in conducting their classes. For example:

> In our times conditions may arise when in individual instances combat operations may be carried out using conventional weapons. Under these conditions, the role of conventional means and the traditional services of the Armed Forces are greatly increased. . . . This circumstance is sometimes interpreted as a negation of the contemporary revolution in military affairs, as its conclusion.
>
> One cannot agree with this opinion. The point is that the new possibilities of waging armed struggle have arisen not in spite of, but because of the nuclear missile weapons. They do not diminish their combat effectiveness, and the main thing, they do not preclude the possible use of such weapons.[78]

Soviet spokesmen, from the Minister of Defense to faculty members of the military academies continued to make this point. In an article in *Kommunist*, the Party's leading journal, Marshal A. A. Grechko stated that "much attention is being devoted to the reasonable combination of nuclear weapons with perfected conventional classic armaments, to the capability of units and subunits to conduct combat actions under nuclear as well as nonnuclear conditions."[79] That this view became a matter of doctrine could be seen clearly in two later texts in *Communist of the Armed Forces*, one by Grechko and the other by Colonel I. A. Seleznev which contained the same sentence: "The main and decisive means of conducting battle will be the nuclear rocket weapon. In it, 'classical' kinds of weapons will find application. In certain circumstances, the possibility is admitted of conducting combat actions by units and subunits with conventional weapons."[80] Word-for-word repetition of statements generally indicates a doctrinal pronouncement.

Soviet theorists gave careful attention to the matter of escalation. Herman Kahn's book *On Escalation* was read in Moscow. Although Soviet military strategists denied the validity of the concept and described his various stages of escalation as nonsense, they nevertheless gave the book careful attention. In 1961, at the Party Congress, Malinovskiy stated that "in contemporary circumstances any armed conflict inevitably will escalate into general nuclear war if the nuclear powers are involved in it."[81]

In December 1962, following the Cuban Missile Crisis, Malinovskiy again brought up the matter of escalation: "Now war might arise without the traditional clear threatening period, by surprise, as a result of the massive use of long-range rockets armed with powerful nuclear warheads. . . . At the same time, this does not exclude a world conflict growing out of a local one." This view of escalation from a local war into general nuclear war continued for the remainder of the decade.[82]

The Soviet view of "just war" was simple and straightforward. "Our military doctrine condemns predatory, unjust, reactionary wars and supports wars that are just, liberating and revolutionary. [A new world war] from the side of the imperialist states will be unjust, predatory and a criminal war. From the side of the socialist camp, war will be just and liberating."[83] These statements reflect basic Marxist-Leninist ideology, where there are no shades of gray. Soviet writers have continued to assert this view into the late 1980s.

Can either side achieve victory in a nuclear war? As the new Soviet military doctrine was being explained to the Soviet military in the early 1960s, Soviet authors did not deny that great destruction and suffering should be expected. However, they did not question that victory could be achieved. The "decisive" role would be played by nuclear rocket weapons, but final victory could be achieved as a result of joint actions of all services of the Armed Forces.[84] Another writer stated: "The ability to hold out in the face of atomic death, not losing heart or courage and the will to fight— that is the mighty weapon which will decide the outcome of future war. Not rockets with megaton nuclear warheads but the moral strength of man in the final count will achieve victory."[85]

All three editions (1962, 1963, 1968) of Sokolovskiy's *Military Strategy* gave the following prerequisite for victory: "Victory in war is determined not only by military and technical superiority, which is assured, on the whole, by the advantages of the socio-economic and political systems, but also by the ability to organize the defeat of the enemy and to use effectively the available means of combat."[86]

There was one discordant note. In 1965, within months of the ouster of Khrushchev as First Party Secretary, the "censors" may not have been as careful as they usually were. *International Affairs*, a journal published in Russian, French and English, carried an article by General Major N. A. Talenskiy, who had once been editor of *Military Thought* in Stalin's day. In the 1960s, Talenskiy was a regular participant at Pugwash (an international discussion group) meetings. The following paragraph in his article attracted world-wide attention: "In our day there is no more dangerous illusion than the idea that thermonuclear war can still serve as an instrument of politics, that it is possible to achieve political aims by using nuclear weapons and at the same time survive, that it is possible to find acceptable forms of nuclear war."[87] As it turned out, Talenskiy's article was aimed at countering Communist Chinese proposals that the Soviet Union "give a push" to world revolution by using its nuclear might. Instead, it was read in the West as a sign that there were "hawks and doves" in the new regime in the Kremlin.

The Main Political Administration of the Soviet Armed Forces responded to Talenskiy in an article carried in the "Lectures and Tutorials" section of *Communist of the Armed Forces*. It was recommended for study of the theme "nuclear war and politics." Readers were told that while "no one has a right to close his eyes to all the serious results of nuclear war," victory was nevertheless possible. A quick victory would limit the amount of destruction. Moreover, there was "a possibility of developing and producing new means of waging war which would be able to safely counter the nuclear blows of the enemy."[88]

In the final analysis, the requirement for victory, as stated in 1970, was straightforward: "Correct, scientifically substantiated doctrine makes it possible to successfully conduct preparations for a potential war, and to gain victory when a war becomes fact. An erroneous and adventuristic military doctrine can propel a state into an abyss and lead to destruction."[89]

The nature of a future war, explained at the very beginning of the 1960s by both Khrushchev and his Minister of Defense, remained much the same throughout that decade. A shift in doctrine took into account the possibility of nonnuclear fighting: If a war began with mass nuclear strikes, it probably would be short; however, it might also be protracted. Regardless of how the war might start, or for whatever reason, it would be a just war on the part of the Soviet Union, which would emerge as the victor.

Question 3: What Armed Forces Are Necessary to Accomplish the Tasks That Might Be Assigned, and What Direction Must the Development of Armed Forces Take?

As a result of the doctrinal decisions made in the late 1950s, basic organizational changes took place in the Soviet Armed Forces. In January 1960 Malinovskiy sought to reassure his military men that these changes did not invalidate the traditional services: "The rocket troops of our Armed Forces unquestionably are the main service of the Armed Forces, but we realize that one kind of troops cannot resolve all the tasks of war."[90] Later, he added: "We nevertheless come to the conclusion that final victory over the aggressor can be achieved only as a result of the joint actions of all the services of the Armed Forces."[91] An identical statement can be found in Sokolovskiy's *Military Strategy*.[92]

Another statement was made in the mid-1960s, which even today has not lost its significance: "The main role in the war will be played by the Strategic Rocket Forces and also by troops of PVO [antiair defense] and PRO [antimissile defense]."[93] As the means of attack have increased, "the development of aerospace defense proceeds with incredible speed. . . . [Soviet] Scientists and engineers are seeking development of antiaircraft and antirocket defense which will outstrip the means of attack of the enemy and also tirelessly working directly on equipment for antispace defense (PKO)."[94]

Throughout most of the 1960s the Soviet people were told that they had an effective ballistic missile defense, and the Galosh, designated as an antiballistic missile, was featured in the 1964 November Parade. However, in the latter part of the decade the United States tested MIRV warheads and made plans for a ballistic missile defense system of its own. The Soviets may have worried about the effectiveness of their own antiballistic missile system against MIRVs, as well as about the possibility of a U.S. missile defense system capable of countering their own missiles. By about 1969 all claims in the Soviet press about the efficiency of their own ballistic missile defense ceased, and new interest was given to arms control negotiations.

The Soviet leadership has always expressed confidence that the nation could produce whatever weapons might be necessary. As stated by General Secretary Brezhnev in his address to the 23rd Party Congress in 1966: "The achievements in economic development have enabled us to equip the Army and Navy with the most highly perfected nuclear rocket weapons and other armaments of the latest design. The armaments of the Soviet troops are on a level with modern requirements and their striking power and firepower are quite sufficient to crush any aggressor."[95]

In January 1960 First Secretary Khrushchev had stated that a future war would be determined by nuclear strikes and implied that the number of men under arms was no longer a major factor. This statement may have been made to impress the Chinese. Chairman Mao at one time was reported to have been willing to sacrifice well over a 100 million Chinese to world revolution, knowing perfectly well that the Kremlin did not have such excess manpower. Malinovskiy nevertheless spoke of the need for multimillion-man armed forces,[96] and this statement has been repeated ever since by scores of Soviet spokesmen.

In retrospect, it is clear that the Kremlin's first military requirement in the early 1960s was to negate the strategic nuclear forces of the United States. By the late 1960s, numbers of deployed ICBMs began to exceed those of the United States. In addition, a massive program was under way to build nuclear submarines armed with ballistic missiles to supplement those of the Strategic Rocket Forces. At about the same time the shortage of males ages nineteen to twenty-one, resulting from the low birth rate of 1941–1946, became less severe. The Ground Forces and other services were steadily built up. A major attempt was made to develop and deploy an antiballistic missile system.

Question 4: How Are Preparations to Be Carried Out for the Possibility of a Future War?

As in other matters of military doctrine, the Minister of Defense laid out the general requirement: "We must prepare our Armed Forces, the country, and all the people to struggle with an aggressor first of all and chiefly in conditions of nuclear war." Details were provided in all three editions of Sokolovskiy's *Military Strategy* in the chapter "Preparing a Country for the Repulsion of Aggression." The author of this chapter, General Colonel A. I. Gastilovich, explained the requirements in three areas: (1) the Armed Forces, (2) the national economy, and (3) the population. The latter area included civil defense.

Preparing the Armed Forces included mobilization, training in the conduct of actual combat, material and technical support, and outfitting the territory of the entire nation as a theater of military operations. In addition, there is a need for strategic intelligence, which must be obtained in times of both peace and war. Preparation of the national economy encompasses industry, transport, agriculture, and communications. The entire population must have moral-political preparations, must know the basics of military combat, and must understand and be trained in measures for defense from weapons of mass destruction. Civil defense was considered a "matter of strategic importance."[97]

The author of a later work emphasized organizing defense of the rear, in particular for civil defense, which is called upon to protect the population from enemy nuclear rocket strikes, to deal with the results of nuclear attack and to promote the uninterrupted work of businesses, administrative organs, transport, and supply.[98] Another writer described how a "scientifically substantiated military doctrine is necessary" to provide effective leadership in military development, to ensure continued improvement in weapons, combat equipment, and methods of their employment, to train and indoctrinate military personnel, and to train command personnel.[99]

Several authors stressed that the offensive was the basic method of achieving victory and the complete defeat of the enemy. Defense was a temporary phase only. At the end of the 1960s, it was noted that during military exercises, many troops simply were waiting for nuclear rocket strikes to accomplish the destruction of the enemy while they did nothing. This was one of the reasons that Minister of Defense Grechko emphasized that soldiers had to learn to fight "both in conditions with the use and without the use of nuclear weapons." The soldier must be trained so that he "will always be ready to operate successfully on the battlefield in circumstances that take shape in different ways."[100]

Question 5: By What Methods Is the War to Be Conducted?

The main task of the Soviet Armed Forces, as explained by Malinovskiy, is "to repulse the attack of the enemy and instantly deliver a retaliatory crushing strike on him. And this first of all is for what we are preparing our Soviet Army and Navy."[101] When addressing the Party Congress in 1961, he added that "the Presidium [now the Politburo] of the Central Committee of the Party and the Soviet government have demanded and are demanding from us that special attention be given to the beginning period of a possible war."[102]

Sokolovskiy was more specific: "The basic method of waging war will be massed nuclear rocket attacks inflicted for the purpose of destroying the aggressor's means of nuclear attack and for the simultaneous mass destruction and devastation of the vitally important objectives comprising the enemy's military, political and economic might, for crushing his will to resist, and for achieving victory within the shortest period of time."[103]

The ouster of Khrushchev as Party secretary did not result in any changes to this view. A future war, if unleashed by the imperialists, "will be waged by absolutely different methods. . . . The beginning period of the war will play a special role, the time in which the nuclear strikes will be carried out, having not only operational-tactical but also strategic significance."[104]

The introduction of nuclear weapons and missiles brought about major changes in the three components of military art: strategy, operational art, and tactics. In past wars, "strategic results were achieved by a series of consecutive efforts, more often of long duration, and were built up from the sum total of tactical and operational successes, and strategy could accomplish its goals only with the help of operational art and tactics." Now, "strategy, using powerful nuclear strikes, can directly achieve its goals."[105] Strategic nuclear weapons might achieve decisive results before operational and tactical weapons could be employed.

Writing in 1969, the editor of *Military Thought*, General Major Vasiliy Zemskov, pointed out that in the event of a nonnuclear war, the offensive would be waged against enemy groupings wherever deployed. First, there would be attempts to gain air and naval superiority. Commanders would have to be aware of the constant threat of the use of nuclear weapons, and all nuclear weapons would have to be maintained in readiness for immediate use.[106]

In 1960, Khrushchev announced that the Soviet Union would give primary attention to "rocket troops." The following year his Minister of Defense outlined a new military doctrine in which the Strategic Rocket Forces would play the dominant role. These doctrinal pronouncements provided guidelines for the massive, unprecedented Soviet military buildup that continued throughout that decade.

Anyone who questions the importance of the role played by doctrine need only examine the Soviet order of battle in 1960, read the works on military doctrine written in the early 1960s, and observe how closely the buildup coincided with the dictates of the stated doctrine. Such a review should also clear up a major misconception held by many in the West— those who believe that the Soviet nuclear buildup was somehow the result of the 1962 Cuban Missile Crisis. This was not the case. As Soviet writings at the time show, the decision that nuclear missiles would be the decisive factor in any future war had already been made in the 1950s. The Strategic Rocket Forces were formed in December 1959. The Cuban Missile Crisis did not change the focus of either military doctrine or the military buildup that was already under way.

Notes

1. N. Ya. Sushko and S. A. Tyushkevich, *Marksizm-Leninizm o Voyne i Armii* [Marxism-Leninism on War and Army], 4th ed. (Moscow: Voyenizdat, 1965), p. 128.

2. N. S. Khrushchev, *Disarmament—The Way to a Sure Peace and Friendship Between Peoples* (Moscow: Gospolitizdat, 1960), p. 46. Also in *Pravda*, January 15, 1960, p. 1. For a discussion of Khrushchev's speech, see H. F. Scott and W. F. Scott, *The Soviet Art of War* (Boulder, Colorado: Westview Press, 1982), pp. 162–164.

3. When Deputy Minister of Defense Chief Marshal of Artillery Mitrofan I. Nedelin was killed by an explosion of a faulty rocket on the launchpad in October

1960, his obituary simply called him "Commander in Chief (*Glavnokomanduyushchiy*) of Rocket Troops." In mid-1962, his successors were also called by that title in the official *Yezhegodnik Bol'shaya Sovetskaya Entsiklopediya, 1962* [Annual of the Great Soviet Encyclopedia, 1962]. Another Marshal of Artillery S. S. Varentsov had been commander (*komanduyushchiy*) of artillery (a branch of the Ground Forces) since 1955, and it was not clear in 1960 that a reorganization had taken place.

4. R. Ya. Malinovskiy, "Address to the Fourth Session of the Supreme Soviet USSR," *Pravda*, January 15, 1960, p. 3.

5. Ibid.

6. N. S. Khrushchev, "For New Victories of the World Communist Movement," in *Communism—Peace and Happiness for the Peoples* (Moscow: Foreign Languages Publishers, 1963), vol. 1, pp. 39–44, 47, excerpts.

7. *XXII S"yezd Kommunisticheskoy Partii Sovetskogo Soyuza* [22nd Congress of the Communist Party of the Soviet Union], stenographic notes (Moscow: Politizdat, 1962), vol. 1, pp. 4–5.

8. Ibid., p. 17.

9. *Programma Kommunisticheskoy Partii Sovetskogo Soyuza* [Programme of the Communist Party of the Soviet Union] (Moscow: *Pravda* Publishers, 1961), p. 143.

10. Ibid., pp. 56–57.

11. Ibid., p. 59. This last statement landed Khrushchev in trouble when it was simplified to read "We will bury you!"

12. Ibid., p. 61.

13. This statement can be found in I. N. Lebanov, B. A. Belyy, and A. P. Novoselov, *Marksizm-Leninizm o Voyne i Armii* [Marxism-Leninism on War and Army], 1st ed. (Moscow: Voyenizdat, 1957), p. 76, and in D. A. Volkogonov, ed., *Marksistko-Leninskoye Ucheniye o Voyne i Armii* [Marxist-Leninist Teachings on War and Army] (Moscow: Voyenizdat, 1984), p. 38. Both books were published in the Officer's Library series.

14. Volkogonov, *Marksistsko-Leninskoye Ucheniye*, p. 49.

15. Ibid., pp. 50–51.

16. R. Ya. Malinovskiy, speech, *XXII S"yezd*, vol. 2, pp. 111–112. The October Revolution of 1917 found Malinovskiy fighting in France. He also fought under an alias in the Spanish Civil War in 1937. He was commander in chief of Troops of the Far East from 1947 to 1953, before and during the Korean War. As Minister of Defense (1957–1967) Malinovskiy frequently lashed out at the "imperialists." However, at a reception at the Main Officers' Club in Moscow, when a clumsy waiter spilled a tray of ice cream on the wife of an American attache, he sprang to his feet, whipped out his own handkerchief, and attempted to repair the damage, all the while expressing his profound apologies.

17. Ibid., p. 112.

18. Ibid., p. 113.

19. Rumors abounded on the reasons for Sokolovskiy's resignation: a heart attack; disagreement over Khrushchev's troops reductions; objections to the new military doctrine. Sokolovskiy lived a vigorous life until he died eight years later at age seventy; Sokolovskiy, of all people, must have been aware of the demographic impact that the extremely low birthrate during the war was about to have on the number of nineteen-year-olds available for compulsory military training, making cuts inevitable; and, as indicated, the new doctrine was the result of Sokolovskiy's own initiative. In all probability, Khrushchev dismissed him, along with Warsaw Pact Commander in Chief Marshal Ivan S. Konev, because they both had been close to Stalin. He wanted his own marshals in those positions. It is important to note that both Konev

and Sokolovskiy remained in the Party's powerful Central Committee until their deaths.

20. *Akademiya General'nogo Shtaba* [Academy of the General Staff] (Moscow: Voyenizdat, 1976), p. 152.

21. Ibid., p. 158.

22. Ibid., p. 205.

23. V. D. Sokolovskiy, editor, *Voyennaya Strategiya* [Military Strategy], 1st ed. (Moscow: Voyenizdat, 1962), p. 49.

24. Ibid., p. 237.

25. Ibid., pp. 238–239.

26. V. D. Sokolovskiy, editor, *Voyennaya Strategiya* [Military Strategy], 1st ed. (Moscow: Voyenizdat, 1962), pp. 237–239; 2nd ed. (1963), pp. 258–261; 3rd ed. (1968), pp. 252–256. For a comparison of all three editions, see H. F. Scott, editor, *Soviet Military Strategy*, by V. D. Sokolovskiy, 3rd ed. (New York: Crane, Russak & Company, Inc., 1984), revised U.S. edition.

27. G. A. Fedorov, N. Ya. Sushko, B. A. Belyy, editors, *Marksizm-Leninizm o Voyne i Armii* [Marxism-Leninism on War and Army], 3rd ed. (Moscow: Voyenizdat, 1962), pp. 357–358.

28. R. Ya. Malinovskiy, *Bditel'no Stoyat' na Strazhe Mira* [Vigilantly Stand Guard Over the Peace] (Moscow: Voyenizdat, 1962), p. 24.

29. Ibid., p. 25.

30. Ibid., p. 27.

31. Ibid., p. 26–27.

32. V. D. Sokolovskiy, editor, *Voyennaya Strategiya* [Military Strategy], 1st ed. (Moscow: Voyenizdat, 1962), pp. 237–239; 2nd ed. (1963), pp. 258–261; 3rd ed. (1968), pp. 252–256.

33. A collection of articles with the same title, *O Sovetskoy Voyennoy Nauke* [On Soviet Military Science], had been published in 1954. Both General Major M. V. Smirnov and Colonel P. A. Sidorov had articles in it. In addition, Sidorov edited the book for publication.

34. S. N. Kozlov, M. V. Smirnov, I. S. Baz', P. A. Sidorov, *O Sovetskoy Voyennoy Nauke* [On Soviet Military Science], 2nd ed. (Moscow: Voyenizdat, 1964), pp. 388–391.

35. S. N. Kozlov, "Military Doctrine and Military Science," in P. M. Derevyanko, *Problemy Revolutsii v Voyennom Dele* [Problems of the Revolution in Military Affairs] (Moscow: Voyenizdat, 1965), p. 64.

36. N. A. Lomov, "On Soviet Military Doctrine," in Derevyanko, *Problemy Revolutsii*, pp. 49–51.

37. Ibid., p. 54.

38. G. A. Fedorov, N. Ya. Sushko, and B. A. Belyy, *Marksizm-Leninizm o Voyne i Armii* [Marxism-Leninism on War and Army], 2nd ed. (Moscow: Voyenizdat, 1962), pp. 357–358; Sushko and Tyushkevich, *Marksizm-Leninizm* (1965), pp. 337–338.

39. The title of "First Secretary" was changed back to "General Secretary" at the 23rd Party Congress in 1966, and the Central Committee's "Presidium" was renamed "Politburo."

40. L. I. Brezhnev, *XXIII S"yezd Kommunisticheskoy Partii Sovetskogo Soyuza* [23rd Congress of the Communist Party of the Soviet Union], stenographic notes (Moscow: Politizdat, 1966), p. 19.

41. M. A. Gareyev, in *M. V. Frunze—Voyennyy Teoretik* [M. V. Frunze—Military Theoretician], in 1985 wrote this about *Military Strategy*: "A deep and, on the whole, true analysis of the long-term development of the theory of military strategy, taking

into account the appearance of the nuclear weapon, was given in the book *Military Strategy* published under the editorship of Marshal of the Soviet Union V. D. Sokolovksiy. However, in the intervening more than twenty years, not all the theses of *Military Strategy* have been confirmed" (p. 29). He then brought up several principles of military strategy, some of which were erroneously considered obsolete or altered, and others which had been correctly stated.

42. S. A. Tyushkevich, N. Ya. Sushko, and Ya. S. Dzyuba, *Marksizm-Leninizm o Voyne i Armii* [Marxism-Leninism on War and Army], 5th ed. (Moscow: Voyenizdat, 1968), pp. 350–351.

43. A. S. Zheltov, *Metodologicheskiye Problemy Voyennoy Teorii i Praktiki* [Methodological Problems of Military Theory and Practice], 2nd ed. [Moscow: Voyenizdat, 1969), pp. 284–290.

44. N. S. Khrushchev, *On Peaceful Coexistence* (Moscow: Foreign Languages Publishing House, 1961), p. 140.

45. Malinovskiy, *Pravda*, January 15, 1960, p. 3.

46. *Programma*, p. 57.

47. Malinovskiy, *XXII S"yezd*, pp. 111–113.

48. Fedorov et al., *Marksizm-Leninizm* (1961), p. 331.

49. Fedorov et al., *Marksizm-Leninizm* (1962), p. 357; Malinovskiy, *Bditel'no*, p. 24; Sushko and Tyushkevich, *Marksizm-Leninizm* (1965), p. 337.

50. Kozlov et al., *O Sovetskoy Voyennoy Nauke* (1964), p. 388.

51. Sokolovskiy, *Voyennaya Strategiya* (1962), p. 237.

52. L. I. Brezhnev, *23rd Congress of the CPSU* (Moscow: Novosti, 1966), p. 15.

53. A. A. Strokov in *Istoriya Voyennogo Iskusstva* (1966), p. 608.

54. N. M. Kiryayev, *KPSS i Stroitel'stvo Sovetskikh Vooruzhennykh Sil* [CPSU and the Structuring of the Soviet Armed Forces] (Moscow: Voyenizdat, 1967), pp. 412–418; S. A. Tyushkevich et al., *Marksizm-Leninizm o Voyne i Armii* [Marxism-Leninism on War and Army] (Moscow: Voyenizdat, 1968), p. 350.

55. N. Ya. Sushko and T. R. Kondratkov, *Metodologicheskiye Problemy Voyennoy Teorii i Praktiki* [Methodological Problems of Military Theory and Practice], 1st ed. (Moscow: Voyenizdat, 1966), pp. 85ff.

56. Sokolovskiy, *Voyennaya Strategiya* (1968), pp. 252–256.

57. Zheltov, *Metodologicheskiye Problemy* (1969), pp. 284ff.

58. D. M. Grinishin, *O Voyennoy Deyatel'nosti V. I. Lenina* [On the Military Activities of V. I. Lenin] (Kiev: Kiev University Publishers, 1970), pp. 242–246.

59. Fedorov et al., *Marksizm-Leninizm* (1961), p. 331.

60. Sokolovskiy, *Voyennaya Strategiya* (1962), p. 237.

61. Sokolovskiy, *Voyennaya Strategiya* (1963), p. 258.

62. A. S. Zheltov, *V. I. Lenin i Sovetskiye Vooruzhennyye Sily* [V. I. Lenin and the Soviet Armed Forces], 1st ed. (Moscow: Voyenizdat, 1967), pp. 226–227. A think tank analyst who was asked to evaluate this book (in 1967) said it was a historical work about Lenin and "the content of the book is not directly applicable to the subject of the study of doctrine."

63. Khrushchev, *On Peaceful Coexistence*, p. 150.

64. Fedorov et al, *Marksizm-Leninizm* (1961), p. 331.

65. Malinovskiy, *XXII S"yezd*, pp. 111–112.

66. Sokolovskiy, *Voyennaya Strategiya* (1962), p. 238.

67. Malinovskiy, *Bditel'no*, p. 24.

68. Malinovskiy, *XXII S"yezd*, vol. 2, p. 112.

69. Fedorov et al., *Marksizm-Leninizm* (1962), pp. 357–358.

70. Brezhnev, *XXIII S"yezd*, p. 43; for English translation see *23rd Congress*, p. 50.

71. Sushko and Kondratkov, *Metodologicheskiye Problemy* (1966), p. 88.

72. Malinovskiy, *Bditel'no*, p. 26.

73. Sokolovskiy, *Voyennaya Strategiya* (1963), p. 261.

74. Strokov, *Istoriya Voyennogo Iskusstva*, p. 609.

75. Zheltov, *Metodologicheskiye Problemy* (1969), pp. 287–288.

76. Sushko and Tyushkevich, *Marksizm-Leninizm* (1965), p. 338.

77. Zheltov, V. I. *Lenin i Sovetskiye Vooruzhennyye Sily* (1967), p. 265.

78. V. M. Bondarenko, "The Modern Revolution in Military Affairs and Combat Readiness of the Armed Forces," *Kommunist Vooruzhennykh Sil* 24 (December 1968), p. 29.

79. A. A. Grechko, "On Guard Over Peace and Socialism," *Kommunist* 3 (February 1970).

80. A. A. Grechko, "Loyalty to Lenin's Behests on the Defense of the Motherland," *Kommunist Vooruzhennykh Sil* [Communist of the Armed Forces] 7 (April 1970); I. A. Seleznev, "V. I. Lenin—The Founder of Soviet Military Science," *Kommunist Vooruzhennykh Sil* 6 (March 1970).

81. Malinovskiy, *XXII S"yezd*, p. 112.

82. Malinovskiy, *Bditel'no*, pp. 24, 26; Sushko and Kondratkov, *Metodologicheskiye Problemy* (1966), p. 87; Zheltov, *Metodologicheskiye Problemy* (1969), p. 288.

83. Sushko and Kondratkov, *Metodologicheskiye Problemy* (1966), p. 87; *Metodologicheskiye Problemy* (1969), p. 286.

84. Malinovskiy, *XXII S"yezd*, p. 112; Fedorov et al., *Marksizm-Leninizm* (1962), p. 357; Malinovskiy, *Bditel'no*, p. 26; Sushko and Tyushkevich, *Marksizm-Leninizm* (1965), p. 338; Strokov, *Istoriya Voyennogo Iskusstva*, p. 613.

85. Fedorov et al., *Marksizm-Leninizm* (1961), p. 331.

86. Sokolovskiy, *Voyennaya Strategiya*, 1st ed., p. 239; 2nd ed., p. 261; 3rd ed., p. 256; Scott, *Soviet Military Strategy*, p. 212.

87. W. R. Kintner and H. F. Scott, *Nuclear Revolution in Soviet Military Affairs*, (Norman, Oklahoma: University of Oklahoma Press, 1968), p. 113.

88. Ye. I. Rybkin, "On the Nature of World Nuclear Rocket War," *Kommunist Vooruzhennykh Sil* 17 (September 1965), p. 50. See discussion and translation in Kintner and Scott, *Nuclear Revolution*, p. 100.

89. M. P. Skirdo, *Narod, Armiya, Polkovodets* [The People, the Army, the Commander] (Moscow: Voyenizdat, 1970), p. 123.

90. Malinovskiy, *Pravda*, January 15, 1960.

91. Malinovskiy, *XXII S"yezd*, pp. 112–113.

92. Sokolovskiy, *Voyennaya Strategiya* (1962), p. 238.

93. Sushko and Tyushkevich, *Marksizm-Leninizm* (1965), p. 338.

94. Kintner and Scott, *Nuclear Revolution*, p. 215.

95. Brezhnev, *XXIII S"yezd*, p. 93; *23rd Congress*, in English, p. 132.

96. Malinovskiy, *XXII S"yezd*, p. 112; Fedorov et al., *Marksizm-Leninizm* (1962), p. 357; Malinovskiy, *Bditel'no*, p. 26; Strokov, *Istoriya Voyennogo Iskusstva*, p. 608.

97. Sokolovskiy, *Voyennaya Strategiya* (all editions), Chapter 7; Scott, *Soviet Military Strategy*, pp. 306–333.

98. Zheltov, *Metodologicheskiye Problemy* (1969), p. 289.

99. Skirdo, *Narod, Armiya, Polkovodets*, p. 123.

100. Grechko, "Loyalty to Lenin's Behests," *Kommunist Vooruzhennykh Sil* 7 (April 1970).

101. Malinovskiy, *Pravda*, January 15, 1988.

102. Malinovskiy, *XXII S"yezd*, p. 112.

103. Sokolovskiy, *Voyennaya Strategiya* (1962), pp. 238–239.

104. Fedorov et al., *Marksizm-Leninizm* (1962), p. 358; Sushko and Tyushkevich *Marksizm-Leninizm* (1965), p. 338.

105. N. V. Ogarkov, "Strategiya, Voyennaya," *Sovetskaya Voyennaya Entsiklopediya*, vol. 7, p. 564.

106. V. I. Zemskov, "Characteristic Features of Modern Wars and Possible Methods of Conducting Them," in Douglass and Hoeber, *Selected Readings*, vol. 5, Part 2, p. 53.

3
Soviet Military Doctrine in the Arms Control Era

To reach the industrial output of the United States by 1970: This was the goal established in the Third Program of the Communist Party of the USSR, approved in 1961. Euphoric Soviet leaders, flushed with their success in space and missile developments, thought that such achievements could be transferred to other areas. But this did not happen.

Westerners in Moscow in the early 1970s who had known the economy and living conditions of the populace at the beginning of the 1960s saw few changes. There were more dismal blocks of new prefab highrise apartment buildings. People did dress somewhat better, and there was more color and style in clothing, especially in the large cities. However, a check on the origin of this finery generally disclosed that practically all of it had been brought in from one of the Eastern European satellites.

During train or auto trips through the countryside it was apparent that the economic goals promised in the Party Program had not been met. A Soviet couple might wait for years to obtain an apartment. Very few new roads had been built. Supplies of food were scarcely better than a decade previously. A train trip from Moscow to Khabarovsk differed little from what one would have experienced in Czarist days. At most of the seventy-six stations where the train stopped, local people rushed to the train's dining car hoping to buy candy, eggs, or perhaps a bottle of sweet wine not available in local stores.

There was one observable change. In the early 1960s tourists in the Soviet Union were rare. Accommodations were poor in the few Soviet hotels where foreigners were permitted to stay, with standards far below those of Western Europe. In the 1970s the Kremlin needed hard currency. For this reason, an effort was made to attract tourists from hard currency countries in Western Europe, and the United States and Canada. Since there were few manufactured goods that could be sold abroad, Party leaders hoped that tourism would act as a substitute. Special hotels were built in those cities to which foreigners are permitted to travel. Visitors then, as in the 1980s, saw a Soviet Union that bore little relationship to reality. They were given a Potemkin village tour, as carefully staged as a scene at the Bolshoi Theater. As one perceptive observer of the Soviet scene wrote:

> The tourist's image is the image of the display put on for his especial benefit in certain selected places; half a dozen great cities, half a dozen collective farms, half a dozen villages, and one or two resorts.
> And if it is objected, as it so often is, that it is impossible to turn a whole city—Moscow, Leningrad, Tashkent, Alma Ata, Tiflis—into a shop window, a display cabinet, the answer is that you don't know the Russians. Because this is precisely what the Soviet Government can do and does.[1]

The guidelines set out in Soviet military doctrine, outlined by Malinovskiy at the 22nd Party Congress in 1961, did succeed in one area. Major defense goals as stated in the Third Party Program were realized. But the announced goal to improve the living standards of the people and to bring about a huge increase in manufactured goods and ample food supplies, as well as other objectives set out in the Party Program, had failed. The growth in Soviet military strength had exceeded the highest estimates made in the mid-1960s by U.S. Government agencies.

In early April 1971 a confident Leonid Brezhnev addressed the 24th Party Congress of the CPSU. He warned that "unremitting vigilance" was necessary "in the struggle to safeguard Soviet society against the actions of hostile elements and against the intrigues of imperialist intelligence services." He repeated the standard formula: "Everything created by the people must be reliably protected." This protection was the task of the Soviet Armed Forces, and the demands placed on it were being met. "When carrying out the people's will, the Communist Party works tirelessly to strengthen the country's defense. . . . Our glorious Armed Forces are prepared to repel an enemy attack at any time of the day or night from any quarter."[2]

The Armed Forces also had another role, which went beyond purely military matters. "In our country military service is not only a school of combat skill. It is also a good school of ideological and physical hardening, of discipline and organization."[3] Males in the Soviet Union had begun to be inducted into the Armed Forces at a younger age (eighteen) for their two to three years of compulsory active military service. They became a captive audience for Party-political indoctrination of "hatred for the enemy" and the glories of the Party.

In 1972, only ten years after the first edition of Sokolovskiy's *Military Strategy* was published, U.S. President Richard Nixon went to Moscow to sign the Strategic Arms Limitation Treaty (SALT I). This treaty signaled to the world that the Soviet Union's military power now equalled that of the United States. The impression was further confirmed in 1974, when U.S. President Gerald Ford landed at an airfield near Vladivostok, a city closed to foreigners, to sign another "Accord" related to arms control.

In the United States great hopes were expressed that the signing of SALT I had changed the views of the Soviet leadership on the vital question of nuclear war. Many analysts thought that Soviet thinking on military matters had undergone a complete reversal. As presented in a popularized account of SALT: "Defending people is the most troublesome of all strategic options, for stability demands that each of the two societies stand wholly exposed to the destructive power of the other. Acceptance of this severe and novel doctrine illustrates the growing sophistication of Soviet thinking."[4]

The expected change in Soviet military thinking did not materialize. Soviet military writings at this time expressed the same viewpoint as before SALT I was signed. In 1973 the final book in the Officer's Library series was published, entitled *Military-Technical Progress and the Revolution in Military Affairs*, and edited by General Colonel N. A. Lomov, who had written previously on military doctrine. He wrote: "As long as capitalism exists, the danger of war from imperialist aggressors remains. In the event that such a war is unleashed against the Soviet Union and the countries of the socialist community, the Soviet Armed Forces are always ready to deliver crushing strikes on the aggressors and foil their criminal plans."[5]

Regardless of who might start a war, he said, strategic nuclear weapons are efficient. They are capable of bringing about "the simultaneous destruction of frontline and rear objectives [which] create real prerequisites for achieving the goals of a war in a short period of time." By using strategic nuclear forces, it was now possible "to achieve strategic results at the beginning of the war." In the past it had first been necessary to develop tactical successes into success at the operational level, and from a series of such actions strategic results could be achieved. Now these stages could be bypassed.

Although the possibility of nuclear war remained a reality, the Soviet leadership did not accept the concept of mutual assured destruction. As stated by a retired Soviet general, "mutual assured destruction is not a military concept and should not be accepted as such by either side. It might be a political concept, or a philosophical concept, but it is not valid militarily. Whenever a new weapon system is developed, a defense must be provided against it."[6] Another Soviet spokesman wrote that "now victory or defeat in war will depend on how well the state will be able to reliably protect important objectives on their own territory from destruction by strikes from the air and out of space."[7]

Despite the continued buildup of the Soviet Armed Forces following SALT I and the stated military doctrine, a period of "détente" between the Warsaw Pact and NATO powers existed, in one form or another, throughout the 1970s. But the United States construed the meaning of the word in one way and the Soviets in another. As Soviet leaders described the period, détente was in accordance with the Leninist principle of peaceful coexistence and provided an atmosphere for the building of communism and for the success of national liberation movements. In contrast, the prevalent view in the United States was that "détente" meant improved relations with the Soviet Union in all areas, an actual reduction of tensions, and "peaceful coexistence" in the general Western meaning of the expression.

In 1973, at a Party Plenum, the leaders of two powerful groups were made full members of the Politburo. The first was Yu. V. Andropov, head of the KGB. This was the first time that the head of the KGB had been given Politburo status since 1953, when the infamous Lavrenty Beria was shot. The second was Marshal A. A. Grechko, Minister of Defense. Marshal G. K. Zhukov, the famed World War II hero, had been a Politburo member for less than a year when he was suddenly removed as defense minister in 1957. His successor, Marshal R. Ya. Malinovskiy, who headed the ministry from 1957 to 1967, was never given Politburo status. Grechko, who succeeded Malinovskiy, served as defense minister for six years before being admitted into the Party's inner sanctum.

In 1974, Grechko noted a significant addition to Soviet military doctrine. In an article published in the Party's leading theoretical journal, *Problems of History of the CPSU*, he wrote of the ability of the Soviet Union to project military power over great distances: "At the present stage the historic function of the Soviet Armed Forces is not restricted to their function in defending the Motherland and the other socialist countries. In its foreign policy activity the Soviet state purposefully opposes the export of counterrevolution and the policy of oppression, supports the national liberation struggle, and resolutely resists imperialists' aggression in *whatever distant region of our planet* it may appear."[8] (Emphasis added.) It had been no secret that aid from the Soviet Union and Eastern Europe had been poured into Southeast Asia during the war in Vietnam. Grechko wrote about it in his 1974 book on the Soviet Armed Forces: "The development of the external function of socialist armies is a natural process. It will be developed even further. Fulfillment of the external function by the Soviet Armed Forces and the armies of other states of the socialist community objectively answers the interests of workers of the whole world, the progress of all mankind."[9]

A year later, Grechko revised his book and this section in particular. Writing in 1975 he said:

> The external function of the Soviet Armed Forces is inseparably linked with other most important directions of the foreign policy activity of the Soviet state. The USSR actively and purposefully opposes the export of counterrevolution; it opposes the policy of oppression; it supports the national liberation struggle of peoples, and it strongly rebuffs the imperialist policy of aggression. In carrying out these tasks the Communist Party and the Soviet government are supported by the economic and defensive might of the country. . . . The combat power of the Armed Forces of the fraternal socialist states restrains the reactionary circles of imperialism from unleashing a new world war and new local military conflicts.[10]

Commander in chief of the Soviet Navy and Admiral of the Fleet of the Soviet Union Sergey Gorshkov published *Seapower of a State* in 1976. He wrote of the expanded role of the Soviet Navy in international affairs, pointing out that "demonstrative actions of the fleet in many cases makes it possible to achieve political goals without resorting to armed conflict by just indicating pressure by their potential might and the threat of beginning military actions." He added: "The neutral waters of the world ocean permit accomplishing the transfer and concentration of forces of the fleet without breaking the positions of international law, without giving the opposing side formal grounds for protests or other forms of counteractions."[11]

Grechko died in 1976. His replacement, Dmitriy Ustinov, was better known for his genius in producing armaments than for his military prowess. Writing in the Party journal *Kommunist* on Armed Forces Day in February 1977, Ustinov reiterated what others had already said about the external function.

> The character of today's international situation and the internal life of Soviet society is introducing much that is new in the structuring, training and missions of the Armed Forces of the USSR. This primarily refers to *their external function*. Together with the armies of other countries of the socialist community, they reliably guard the revolutionary gains of their own people and with their combat might restrain the aggressive aspirations of imperialist circles, hinder their attempts to turn back the wheel of history.[12] (Emphasis added.)

Two years later, in 1979, a volume of Ustinov's speeches and writings was published. The article from *Kommunist* had been critically revised to read:

> The character of today's international situation and the development of the internal life of Soviet society is introducing much that is new in the structuring, training and missions of the Armed Forces of the USSR. This primarily refers to *their function of defending the socialist homeland from imperialist aggressors.*[13] (Emphasis added.)

This change was not surprising. Foreign involvement in Egypt, Angola, and Ethiopia in the 1970s, culminating with the invasion of Afghanistan in December 1979, was, and still is, extracting a toll from Soviet society.

In February 1976 at the 25th Party Congress, General Secretary Brezhnev told of the Soviet people's pride in providing "aid to Vietnam in its struggle against the imperialist invaders."[14] The principles of peaceful coexistence, strengthened by the meetings with U.S. Presidents Nixon and Ford, had lessened somewhat the threat of nuclear war.[15] Brezhnev stated that "political détente needs to be backed up by military détente."[16] He pointed out that his Peace Program introduced at the 24th Party Congress in 1971 was aimed at reducing armed forces and armaments in Europe. During this period of détente the General Secretary sought to present the peace-loving face of the Soviet Union.

In 1977 the Soviet Union adopted a new Constitution, which furnished a number of new insights into the Soviet defense structure. The Constitution provided for the continuance of universal military service and stated that the duty of the Armed Forces is to "be in constant combat readiness, guaranteeing that any aggressor is instantly repulsed."[17] The state "supplies the Armed Forces of the USSR with everything necessary" for "ensuring the security and defense capability of the country."[18] The Constitution further provided that the Presidium of the Supreme Soviet of the USSR shall "form the Council of Defense of the USSR and confirm its composition, appoint and dismiss the high command of the Armed Forces of the USSR."[19]

In 1978, U.S. President Jimmy Carter and General Secretary Brezhnev met in Vienna, Austria, and initialed the SALT II Treaty. However, skepticism among U.S. Senate members concerning the ability of the United States to verify its provisions delayed acceptance of the treaty. In December 1979, Soviet troops invaded Afghanistan. President Carter, disillusioned with the Soviet Union, did not press further for the Senate's approval of SALT II.

Evolution of the Concept and Purpose of Military Doctrine

The actions of the Kremlin leadership throughout the 1970s followed the dictates of Soviet military doctrine. In 1971, shortly before the 24th Party Congress, an Officer's Library book, *The Officer's Handbook*, edited by General S. N. Kozlov, appeared in Moscow bookstores. It restated the basic concept of military doctrine, differing little from what had been published in the early 1960s. For example: "Military doctrine determines the main trend in military development and establishes a common understanding of the nature of possible war and of the tasks involved in defending the state and preparing it to repel imperialist aggression."[20] The work went on to explain that military doctrine is the political policy of the Party and the Soviet government in the military field. Doctrine "determines the practical side of military development." Doctrine is *not* concerned with investigating past experience of armed combat—that task belongs to military science. The authors wrote: *"Doctrine exists primarily for the present and the immediate future."* (Emphasis added.)

They also gave an explanation of the difference between military doctrine and strategy:

> Strategy as a scientific theory elaborates the fundamental methods and forms of armed combat on a strategic scale and, at the same time, produces the guiding principles of war. . . . In wartime, military doctrine drops into the background somewhat, since, in armed combat, we are guided primarily by military-political and military-strategic considerations, conclusions and generalizations which stem from the conditions of the specific situation. Consequently, war, armed combat, is governed by strategy, not doctrine.[21]

Specific points of doctrine were made clear. The authors emphasized that "Soviet military doctrine is offensive in character." This statement would be completely reversed in the 1980s; Soviet leaders would deny that Soviet military doctrine had ever been characterized as "offensive." In modern warfare "Soviet military doctrine assigns the decisive role to nuclear missiles." However, at the same time, military doctrine "assumes that, in addition to nuclear missile strikes of a strategic and operational-tactical nature, the Armed Forces will use conventional weapons." This doctrinal modification had originated in the second half of the 1960s.

Perhaps the most important aspect of Soviet military doctrine was explained as follows: "[The doctrine's] principles have legal force; they govern all the activities of our military cadres." The frequently held idea in the United States that there are "doctrinal debates" between individual officers or different groups simply is not in accordance with the Soviet concept of military doctrine. Military doctrine, determined by the Party leadership, is not subject to open debate once it is formulated.

At the end of the section on military doctrine a list of suggested readings appeared. Four books were recommended: *Marxism-Leninism on War and Army* (1968), *Methodological Problems of Military Theory and Practice* (1969), *Military Strategy*, third edition (1968), and *History of Military Art* (1966).[22] That these books were recommended indicated that immediately prior to the 24th Party Congress, which was to meet in February–March 1971, Soviet military doctrine was unchanged from the late 1960s. In fact, the writings in three of the four books on military doctrine were virtually unchanged from previous editions of these same books that had appeared in the Khrushchev era.

But the manner in which doctrine was discussed soon changed. Following the meeting of the 24th Party Congress, Grechko's booklet, *On Guard Over the Peace and the Building of Communism*, was available in Moscow bookstores. Its purpose was to help put the "decisions of the 24th Congress into life," as they applied to the Soviet Armed Forces. He did not outline the content of Soviet military doctrine, as Malinovskiy had done in the past or even as it had appeared in the 1971 *Officer's Handbook*. Instead Grechko defined military doctrine and then stated its purpose. The definition included the following:

> Military doctrine is elaborated by the political leadership of the state with the participation of the higher military agencies on the basis of an evaluation of the international situation and the balance of forces in the world, taking into account the material, spiritual and military possibilities of [the Soviet Union] and of the probable enemies, the development of means of armed conflict and an evaluation of geographical and other factors.[23]

The purpose of military doctrine, Grechko further explained, is to determine (1) the character of future war, (2) the tasks of the state in a possible military clash and the methods of their resolution, and (3) the direction of preparing the country and the Armed Forces for war. Military doctrine not only deals with the role of the Armed Forces in war, but also the role of all of the people. Military doctrine directly involves all significant spheres of state activity.

In 1974 Grechko published another work, *The Armed Forces of the Soviet State*. He wrote that "military doctrine is understood to be an officially accepted system of views in a given state and in its armed forces on the nature of war and methods of conducting it and on preparation of the country and army for war."[24] This was almost word for word the same definition that had been given throughout the 1960s. He then listed five "basic questions" that military doctrine is to answer:

1. What enemy will the country have to deal with in a possible war?
2. What is the character of the war in which a state and its armed forces will have to take part, and what goals and missions might face them in this war?
3. What armed forces will be necessary to fulfill the given missions and what direction to conduct military development?
4. How are preparations for war to be carried out?
5. What are to be the methods of conducting the war?[25]

Grechko went on to explain that "these questions comprise the basis of the content of military doctrine." Whether the country and the Armed Forces would be prepared properly for possible war and have the necessary degree of combat readiness would depend "upon their correct solution."

In the early 1960s, Malinovskiy and other Soviet spokesmen had delineated the content of Soviet military doctrine in considerable detail. But after the meeting of the 24th Party Congress in 1971, the direction of military doctrine could be discerned only through a close analysis of how the five questions posed by Grechko were being answered.

This is not to imply that a major change in Soviet military doctrine took place at this time. Instead, Soviet military spokesmen were perhaps only being more cautious. In 1962, military doctrine had been explained in Sokolovskiy's *Military Strategy* as follows: Military doctrine is the expression of the accepted views of a state regarding the problems of (1) the political evaluation of future war, (2) the state attitude toward war, (3) a determination of the nature of future war, (4) preparation of the country for war in the economic and moral sense, (5) organization and preparation of the armed forces, and (6) methods of waging war.[26] If these problems are reworded as questions, it can be seen that Grechko's questions were very similar to the tasks of military doctrine given both in Sokolovskiy's *Military Strategy* and in Grechko's 1971 pamphlet, *On Guard Over the Peace and the Building of Communism*.

Grechko's questions were complex, with most having a number of elements. These were as follows:

Question 1. This question includes the identity of the enemy and the possibility of war.

Question 2. The character, or nature of a future war includes (1) the element of surprise at the start, (2) the anticipated length of a war, (3) whether it will be nuclear or conventional, (4) whether the war will escalate, and (5) the "justness" of the war. This question also includes another important factor, the question of the goals and missions the armed forces must accomplish.

Question 3. What armed forces will be necessary and the direction of their development, including (1) the kind of armed forces, (2) the size of the armed forces to be maintained, and (3) the question of superiority.

Question 4. How to carry out preparations for war includes the question of whether Soviet military doctrine is offensive or defensive.

Question 5. By what methods to conduct the war? The following factors must be determined: (1) whether the war will be fought with or without nuclear weapons, and (2) the declaration of no first use of nuclear weapons.[27]

In order to show the continuity of Soviet military doctrine, or lack of it, from the eve of the 24th Party Congress until the end of 1980, immediately prior to the 26th Party Congress, each of these questions will be examined in turn.

Naming the Enemy

What is the probability of a future war, and with what enemy will one have to deal? This was the first question asked of Soviet military doctrine as expained by Grechko in 1974. The first part of the question has never been specifically answered. In 1956 Khrushchev announced a fundamental change in Communist ideology when he announced that war between communism and capitalism was no longer inevitable. This reversal of the Soviet position was possible only because the Soviet Union possessed nuclear weapons. As long as the Soviet Armed Forces were strong and in a high state of combat readiness, the "imperialists" might not attack.

The answer to the second part of the question, with what enemy will the nation have to deal, is much more specific. In 1971, as the final details were being placed on an arms control agreement with Washington, Soviet officers were told that: "Soviet military doctrine determines the means, ways and methods of the reliable protection of the Soviet socialist state from imperialist aggression. . . . Of all the wars possible in the modern epoch, the main danger is presented by a world nuclear rocket war which the imperialist aggressors, first of all the USA, are preparing against the socialist community, primarily against the Soviet Union."[28]

Another book published the same year noted that "in the modern epoch, along with world wars, imperialism might use limited (in aims and means) local wars." This situation requires that the Soviet Armed Forces be prepared to counter "imperialism" at all levels, from local wars to an all-out nuclear exchange. However, the primary threat remained a direct attack against the Soviet Union.[29]

In 1971, when explaining the decisions of the 24th Party Congress, Grechko warned, "it is quite evident that, if it were not for the military might of the Soviet state, the imperialists would have already forced World War III on mankind." Therefore, "Soviet military doctrine . . . is directed not at unleashing war but preparing . . . to repel aggression, if war cannot be prevented—the war that the imperialists might force on the Soviet Union."[30]

Statements made in the Soviet press in the year immediately preceding the signing of SALT I concerning the probable enemy and the possibility of war generally were identical with those written in 1961 prior to the

Cuban nuclear confrontation. The authors of a Soviet textbook on military history declared that if the imperialists unleashed a war against the socialist nations, it would be a world war of two opposing coalitions.[31] Another book issued by Nauka, the publishing house of the Academy of Sciences, asserted that "Soviet military doctrine proceeds from the fact that in the event of an attack of imperialist aggressors on the Soviet Union . . . future war inevitably will become world war."[32]

Always it was the "imperialists" who were preparing to "unleash" war on the Soviet Union.[33] In Western books, journals, and newspapers, as well as in various seminars and conferences on security issues, one or more individuals will generally attempt to show how the West may be at fault in arms control matters or in dealing with the Soviet Union. But in the Soviet press there was only one view. The following expression was standard: "Soviet military doctrine proceeds from the fact that in the international arena there is a fierce struggle of two social systems—socialism and imperialism. . . . The Soviet Union must take this into consideration and take necessary measures in the event of the imperialists unleashing war against the countries of the socialist community."[34]

As the most powerful nation of the "imperialist bloc," the United States is singled out by Kremlin spokesmen as the primary enemy. There is no way of knowing what actual perceptions of the United States the Soviet leadership holds. Many of the statements in the Soviet media about the United States may be designed to provide justification for what they themselves are doing. For example, a *Red Star* article in 1974 claimed that "the American militarists are counting on cloaking their cherished plans for insuring U.S. strategic supremacy through the qualitative improvement of arms and development in using them, with the aim of bringing pressure to bear on the Soviet Union. . . ." The author then got to the bottom line. "These actions are forcing the Soviet Union and its Warsaw Pact allies to adopt appropriate measures to strengthen their defense capability."[35]

Soviet assertions of the types of war that the United States was planning may reflect what the Soviets themselves were considering. Grechko claimed the following types of war were under study in the Pentagon: (1) a strategic nuclear war, (2) a nuclear war in a theater of war, (3) a conventional war in a theater of war, (4) a conventional war in a theater of military operations, and (5) a conventional war in a limited region of a theater of military operations.[36] These types of war were essentially the same as those being studied by the Soviets, according to officers attending Soviet military academies.

In 1974 there was talk in the United States about a new strategy of "selective targeting," based on the possibility of a limited nuclear exchange involving perhaps less than 100 missiles. Grechko claimed that this strategy was simply a variant of all-out nuclear war, in which strikes would be made against Soviet nuclear missile launching sites, nuclear weapons stockpiles, airfields, troop concentrations, and other military targets. The purpose of such strikes would be "to prevent the Soviet Union from making a retaliatory nuclear strike."[37] Such a counterforce strike, as described by Grechko, was similar to the targeting that had been advocated for their own Strategic Rocket Forces.

In the latter part of the 1970s, "gray area" weapons became a major topic in Soviet writings. Such weapons are those that could be used in a variety of roles: tactical, operational, or strategic. Cruise missiles were a case in point, since they could strike nearby tactical targets, as well as those deep in enemy territory. One Soviet commentator admitted that while the Soviet Armed Forces did have such missiles, the U.S. plans for their use would open a new channel in the arms race. Other spokesmen repeated this argument almost word for word. One claimed that such weapons "would lead to a revolution in NATO's arsenal and strategy. . . . With fuel increase the missile becomes strategic, and conventional warheads can be replaced by a nuclear warhead."[38] It was further claimed that the U.S. adoption of cruise missiles "could destabilize the strategic situation. They can be launched from practically any platform." Instead of increasing strategic stability, the deployment of strategic cruise missiles "could alter the balance of strategic forces between the U.S. and the USSR."[39]

In the late 1970s, attention shifted to the proposed deployment of the Pershing II missile. The Soviets claimed that such "Eurostrategic weapons" had nothing to do with NATO defenses. The Pershing II, with a 1,800-kilometer range, "is not a technical replacement for the Pershing I. . . . It represents a qualitative change, and could strike Soviet territory from the FRG."[40] Nothing, however, was admitted about the capabilities of the Soviet SS-20.

The main focus of Soviet propaganda was that the USSR was surrounded by military bases and military coalitions controlled primarily by the United States. SALT, they said, limited nuclear delivery systems that could strike the United States, but U.S. forward-based systems, together with the mini-strategic forces of Britain, France, and China, could still strike the USSR. In contrast, the Soviet Backfire bomber was not strategic, and was in the same category as the American FB-111. The SS-20 did not represent a threat to NATO or to any other nation, Soviet spokesmen assured.

A major propaganda effort was undertaken to prevent the United States from deploying the neutron bomb. The Soviets said that such weapons "erect new obstacles" to a solution of the problem of strategic arms limitations. Since the neutron bomb was designed primarily as an antipersonnel weapon with minimum danger to physical structures, Soviet propagandists argued that the introduction of such weapons in Europe would lower the nuclear threshold and represent a greater threat than existing nuclear weapons.[41] The Soviet effort to prevent its deployment was successful, and Washington's plans for the neutron bomb were dropped.

U.S. programs to upgrade its weapons systems came under similar attacks. Yuriy Zhukov, a leading *Pravda* columnist, wrote that a new, modified version of the FB-111 strategic bomber could deliver nuclear weapons at a distance of 9,599 kilometers, and that such aircraft threatened the strategic balance. Another commentator said that the cruise missile and the neutron bomb were being followed by such innovations as the strategic FB-111 bomber, which in many respects was "comparable to the not unknown B-1."[42]

U.S. forward-based facilities continued to be a favorite theme for Soviet writers such as Lev Semeyko. Such bases, "located far from the United States, could strike the Soviet Union at the beginning of a conflict." These facilities were referred to as "ministrategic forces" and were grouped with facilities in the intermediate "grey" zone, which "formally were regarded as tactical forces."[43]

In arms control discussions then under way, Soviet propagandists wrote that it already had been agreed that air-to-surface cruise missiles would be limited to a range of 600 kilometers. They insisted that both ground- and sea-based missiles also be limited to the same range. The Backfire bomber is not strategic, cannot reach U.S. territory, and therefore should not be included in the talks, they said. However, cruise missiles on submarines, vessels, bombers, or on territory of U.S. allies could reach the USSR, and therefore should be included.[44]

In 1977 U.S. Secretary of State Cyrus Vance made certain proposals to the Soviets on further strategic arms limitations. But these proposals were rejected out of hand in Moscow. According to Soviet spokesmen, "imagine the end result" for the Soviet Union if both sides eliminated all ICBMs, submarine-launched ballistic missiles, and heavy bombers: "The USSR would be deprived of means of delivery to U.S. territory." However, "in the immediate proximity of the Soviet Union would remain about 800 aircraft and cruise missiles capable of nuclear delivery, plus more than 500 aircraft operating off carriers. In addition, some allies of the U.S. also have their own strategic weapons."[45] Soviet capabilities in nuclear weapons were never revealed.

But whatever the "imperialists" did to provide for their own security was a threat and a danger to civilization, as explained in *Voprosy Filosofii*, a leading theoretical journal of the Communist Party: "In imperialism's hands, nuclear missile weapons are terrible weapons of war. In the hands of the socialist states, nuclear weapons are a shield for peace. They have been created to curb an aggressor and avert war."[46]

Occasionally, Soviet writers mentioned exceptions to the rule that "imperialists," primarily the United States, were the only enemy. In his 1974 book, *The Armed Forces of the Soviet State*, Grechko first mentioned the war "which might be imposed by the imperialists on the Soviet Union or other socialist countries." He then talked about "high vigilance and strengthening the combat readiness of the Soviet Army and Navy." Following this, he added: "The Armed Forces are always ready to come to the defense of the Motherland, to repel any aggression no matter *from where* or *from whom* it comes." (Emphasis added.)

The expression "from where" had been used before. But combining these words with "from whom" was somewhat different. Could it be that Grechko was warning about someone other than the "imperialists," perhaps the Chinese? The meaning of Grechko's statement was not clear at the time. According to the discussion of military doctrine in the *Soviet Military Encyclopedia*, it was only the "imperialist aggressors" who presented a threat to the Soviet Union.[47]

However, in 1979 the prestigious Party journal *Problems of History of the CPSU* carried an article by Marshal D. F. Ustinov, then Minister of Defense. In it, Ustinov identified what Grechko had meant. An analysis had been made of "military-political conditions"; it was necessary to take timely and effective measures against aggression "no matter from where it comes."[48] Ustinov then became specific:

> In the same harness with the most reactionary forces of imperialism is the present Chinese leadership. Pursuing their expansionist and hegemonistic goals, the Peking leaders openly declare their opposition to détente, disarmament and stability in the world, in every way are trying to stir up enmity between peoples, are using unruly anti-Soviet propaganda, are talking about the inevitability of a third world war and intensively carrying out the militarization of the country, and equipping the armed forces with new modern weapons, including nuclear ones.[49]

The following year, in the first book of a new 1980s Officer's Library series, Soviet officers were informed of two enemies: the "imperialists" and the "Maoists." Although in recent years international tensions had relaxed somewhat, the military threat from imperialism continued to exist.[50] The aggressive nature of imperialism had not changed, and the threat of new world war still existed.[51]

After giving the usual warning about the "imperialists," the authors then went into a discussion of the danger that China posed to all "peace-loving" people: "[Peking's] position is incompatible with the Leninist idea of the necessity of close economic and military cooperation of people in the struggle for socialism." This position was especially dangerous at a time "when the revolution in military affairs has produced nuclear rocket weapons." In order "to curb the aggressor, thwart his plans and not let the imperialists and their accomplices start a new world war," it was necessary that the armed forces of socialist states be combined.[52]

However, the Maoist policy and ideology, which had been "unmasked" by General Secretary Brezhnev, showed "the feverish attempts of Peking to disrupt détente, not to permit disarmament, to sow distrust and enmity between states, their aspiration to provoke a world war and warm their hands in it, represent a great danger for all peace-loving people." Peking's aim deeply contradicted the interests of all people. "We will rebuff this incendiary policy, defend the interests of the Soviet state and the socialist community, and of the world communist movement."[53] Another major Soviet work the same year stated that the position of the leaders of China differed little from the aggressive policy of imperialism.[54]

China posed a difficult ideological problem for the Soviet leadership. If capitalism was the source of all wars, how could China be a threat? The primary enemy was the "imperialists, headed by the USA." Designating another primary enemy, especially one not in NATO, could confuse the Soviet people. Nevertheless, the traditional friction between these two powerful nations, stemming from cultural differences and the expansionist tendencies the Soviet empire had inherited from the Russian Empire, continued to exist.

The Nature of Future War

The second question propounded by military doctrine—how to specify the nature or character of a future war—involved a number of related questions. These included (1) the element of surprise at the start, (2) the anticipated length of a war, (3) whether it would be nuclear or conventional, (4) whether the war would escalate, and (5) the "justness" of the war. This question also included the important factor of the goals and missions of the Armed Forces.

In the early 1970s, following the 24th Party Congress, Soviet perceptions about the nature of war and how it might begin changed little. A standard assertion was that "Soviet military doctrine proceeds from the fact that a new world war, if the imperialists unleash it, might begin with a surprise nuclear attack by the imperialist powers on socialist countries or it may escalate from a local conflict." Such a world war would "be a decisive clash between two social systems. It will be a coalition war with a sharply defined class character and decisive political and military goals."[55] Statements such as this were standard, and were repeated with little variation in numerous publications.

In 1974, perhaps with the various agreements stemming from SALT I in mind, Grechko wrote about the problem of "characterizing" wars. Although an agreement had been concluded between the United States and the Soviet Union on the prevention of nuclear war, other nations possessing nuclear weapons had not joined the agreement. Furthermore, there had not been a complete prohibition and elimination of nuclear weapons. The threat of nuclear war still existed.[56]

Despite the fact that throughout the 1970s a spirit of détente was supposed to exist between the NATO nations and the USSR, the actual teachings of Soviet military doctrine showed little change. In his entry in the *Soviet Military Encyclopedia*, published in 1979, Marshal N. V. Ogarkov postulated a possible "future world war" in almost exactly the same terms that Malinovskiy had used in 1961:

[Future world war] will be a global opposition unprecedented in size and bitterness of multimillion coalition armed forces and will be waged without compromise, with the most decisive political and strategic goals. During it, all the military, economic and spiritual powers of the belligerent coalitions and social systems will be fully tested.

Soviet military strategy proceeds from the fact that if nuclear war is forced on the Soviet Union, then the Soviet people and its Armed Forces must be ready for the most severe and long testing.[57]

A surprise strike appeared to remain uppermost in the minds of the Soviet leadership. Despite all the warnings from Great Britain and the United States, as well as from some elements of Stalin's own intelligence agencies, the German attack in June 1941 had caught Stalin by surprise. In that case, the Soviet Union finally recovered at the cost of millions of lives. Hence, the possibility of a similar surprise strike remained a paramount concern.

Recognizing what a surprise nuclear strike might do to their own country, Soviet planners may well have prepared plans to do to their opponents what they accused their probable opponents of planning to do to them. In the aftermath of the 24th Party Congress, and only a few months before the signing of SALT I, Grechko had this to say:

> The armies of the United States and its allies in the aggressive blocs are being prepared with a consideration of using the element of surprise in unleashing war. For this the strategic nuclear forces, the combined units of tactical aviation, the assault carrier combined units, the airborne, tank and motorized combined units deployed close to the frontier of the USSR and other socialist countries are kept in a high state of readiness. In the armed forces of the United States and its allies, all sorts of methods for the surprise use of both nuclear as well as conventional types of weapons have been developed, they claimed.[58]

Grechko stated that no variation of a surprise attack had been overlooked, and he stressed the implications. "It is quite obvious that at the present time surprise strikes, especially with nuclear weapons, are fraught with incomparably greater consequences than was the case in the past."[59] This viewpoint was a matter of Soviet military doctrine, which "proceeds from the fact that a new world war, if the imperialists unleash it, might begin with a surprise nuclear attack by the imperialist powers on socialist countries or it may escalate from a local conflict."[60] Another work warned that "various methods of unleashing the war are possible, including the surprise use of nuclear weapons or just conventional means of destruction."[61]

But the enemy, another author said, should not expect a surprise strike to be successful: "At the present stage the Armed Forces must be able under any circumstances to foil a surprise attack of an aggressor, assuring favorable conditions for the further conduct and victorious conclusion of the war."[62] In 1979 Ogarkov assured the Soviets that although the possibility of a surprise attack remained, it could be prevented by maintaining the combat readiness of the Armed Forces.[63] This point was made even more specifically in 1980: "The Party sees the main task as the whole sum of sociopolitical, organizational-technical and educational measures to assure such a level of military might of the Soviet state and the combat readiness of its Armed Forces which would exclude any possibility of taking us by surprise and would allow the carrying out of a retaliatory crushing strike on an aggressor no matter where he is located."[64]

The duration of a possible future war remained a primary consideration. All three editions of Sokolovskiy's *Military Strategy* had emphasized the importance of the entire nation being prepared for the possibility of a protracted war, even though an all-out nuclear war might be quickly concluded. This concept was repeated throughout the 1970s. It was agreed that nuclear war might last a comparatively short time, since its main political and strategic goals might be achieved primarily through the mass use of strategic nuclear weapons. At the same time, there would be active operations of all services of the Armed Forces in the theaters of military actions (TVDs). It was necessary also to prepare the nation for conditions that might result in a "comparatively long, drawn-out war."[65] This view continued to be stressed. In 1979 Ogarkov repeated the same thesis: "With the contemporary means of destruction, world nuclear war will be relatively short. However, taking into account the enormous military and economic potential possibilities of the coalitions of belligerent states, it is not excluded that it also might be protracted."[66]

Was it possible that a future war might be either just nuclear or just conventional? Soviet writings are very vague on this issue. Grechko assured his readers that the Soviet Union also had all the types of weapons that were available to the enemy. Therefore, the Soviet Armed Forces were prepared to respond with whatever weapons the enemy might employ. They "can wage active combat actions at high tempos, to great depths, in various combinations of circumstances, with the use and without the use of nuclear weapons and thus can successfully resolve operational-tactical and strategic tasks on any scale."[67] He reminded his readers that strategic nuclear weapons could not perform all of the tasks of war. Great efforts, he said, "as before, are being attached to the creation of new types and development of existing kinds of conventional armaments."[68] However, nuclear weapons retained their importance, and it was thought that they would be used in conjunction with conventional weapons. This concept was explained as follows:

> Military theoretical thought has been enriched with new conclusions and views on the forms and methods of armed conflict with due regard for the possible utilization of the nuclear weapon.
> The question of strategic objectives and scales of wars has become different. The relationship of strategy, operational art and tactics has changed. The nuclear weapon permits the simultaneous solving both of strategic and operational-tactical tasks. In examining these new phenomena, it must be stressed that the conduct of military operations with the use of the nuclear weapon and the conduct of combat operations by units and subunits with conventional kinds of weapons are not isolated from each other, but are closely correlated and develop as a single whole.[69]

Soviet military leadership spoke with one voice repeating the doctrinal change that had occurred in the late 1960s. Nuclear missiles would still be the decisive means of armed combat in the event of a future war, but "along with this, conventional weapons will also find use, and under certain conditions, the units and subunits can conduct combat actions solely with conventional means." One spokesman added that various methods of unleashing the war were possible, including the surprise use of nuclear weapons as well as purely conventional means of destruction.[70] In 1975 Grechko again stated that great efforts were being made to develop new kinds of conventional weapons.[71]

In 1977 the perceived need to have both nuclear and conventional weapons was explained further. An analysis had been made of the "peculiarities" of modern war and the "tendencies" of fundamental changes in military affairs, and questions on the forms and methods of military actions and on the relationship of various means of armed combat were studied. Although it was still acknowledged that nuclear rocket weapons would be the major determining factor in a future war, the role of conventional weapons was also put forward. Officers were cautioned not to allow "extremes in evaluation" both of new weapons and those already deployed. The Armed Forces must be ready to perform given missions with conventional and also with nuclear means.[72]

Another work described the need to train soldiers to be able to conduct warfare "acting in conditions of use of the nuclear weapon or only with conventional means of destruction." Because of the rapid pace of scientific-technical progress in bringing about changes in military affairs, the "harmonious development and improvement of all services" were considered essential. This rate of progress required a "single military-technical policy" which was a key problem for the Party leadership of the Armed Forces.[73] Although nuclear rocket weapons had enormous power, Soviet military science "does not absolutize them."[74]

The possibility of escalation remained another dominant issue in Soviet military doctrine. Soviet theorists focused their greatest attention on the possibility of war beginning with only the use of conventional weapons, then widening to include the tactical use of nuclear weapons, and final escalation to general nuclear war.[75] This problem also entailed the possibility of war escalating from a local conflict to world war.[76] But here the Soviets wanted to have it both ways. The Soviet leadership insisted on its right to support national liberation wars, while at the same time "decisively opposing the unleashing of local wars by imperialists, taking into account not only their reactionary nature, but also the great danger, connected with the possibility of their escalation to world war."[77]

The Soviet idea of "just wars" remained. The Party-military leadership continued to affirm that the very nature of the Soviet state precluded it from waging any war that was "unjust." Wars of "national liberation" were in the "just war" category, which the Kremlin supported. On the other hand, the "imperialists" waged only "unjust" wars.[78] This reasoning determined the political character of the war, as expressed in Marxist-Leninist terms.

The nature of a future war was summed up in lectures given to foreign students at the Soviet military academies. It is not certain that these lectures represented actual views of the Kremlin leadership, although they are the same as those given in Soviet writings. As presented to foreign students, in a future war between the forces of communism and capitalism, both sides would have decisive political aims and these aims could lead to the unlimited use of all available weapons. A war might begin by a surprise attack without a prior period of tension. On the other hand, it could follow after a period of tension, or it might escalate from a military action of limited scope.

Nuclear weapons might be used in the initial stages of a war, or they might only be used later. If a war opened with a nuclear exchange, the opposing sides would try to bring about a quick end to the war by inflicting heavy losses on each other in the shortest possible time. Some small countries whose industries are concentrated in urban areas may quickly be eliminated from such a war.

Finally, students were told of the political utility of nuclear weapons. The imperialists must consider the possibility that the Soviet Union would respond with a massive nuclear strike in retaliation for even the introduction of a single tactical nuclear weapon on the battlefield. Therefore, victory could be achieved by the use of conventional weapons alone.

The Armed Forces Needed

The third question Soviet military doctrine must answer—what armed forces would be needed in a future war—requires an examination of (1) the kind of armed forces, (2) their numbers and equipment and (3) the question of superiority. In the 1960s the Kremlin leaders had described what armed forces they considered necessary. Their views on this matter remained essentially the same in the 1970s. First were nuclear forces capable of actions at many different levels—strategic, operational-strategic, operational-tactical, and tactical. At the same time, forces had to be prepared for either nuclear or conventional war or a combination of the two.[79]

There was no letup in the emphasis placed on the need for nuclear missiles. In 1971, the year before SALT I, Soviet theorists repeated the thesis that any future world war would be a coalition war fought for decisive political and military goals. In this case, the nuclear-armed ballistic missiles would be the decisive means of waging war.[80] This message was exactly the same as had been given in the 1960s.

In 1973 Minister of Defense Grechko stated that the guarantor of defense for socialist countries was first of all "the nuclear rocket shield of the Soviet Union."[81] Other writers repeated the same thesis four years later; the defense of all socialist countries was guaranteed by "the nuclear rocket shield of the Soviet Union—the most powerful state in the fraternal family of countries of the socialist community."[82]

Although all services of the Armed Forces were considered necessary and were being "perfected," Soviet military doctrine did not exclude, under certain conditions, the more rapid development "of one or another service of the Armed Forces. At the present time, for example, we are paying more attention to developing the Strategic Rocket Forces—the basis of the nuclear rocket might of our country, the main means of restraining the aggressive aims of imperialism."[83]

Grechko sounded a warning note. No matter how significant might be the role of strategic nuclear weapons, he said, they cannot perform all the tasks of war. Therefore, great efforts must continue in the science and technology necessary for creating new weapons and further developing "available" conventional kinds of armaments.[84]

Even though war might be conducted primarily with nuclear weapons, conventional weapons would also be employed, "and under certain conditions the combat actions by units and subunits might be conducted only with conventional weapons."[85] Although the nuclear weapon was significant, there must not be extremes in evaluation either of new or existing armaments. A given mission might be performed with either, or both.[86] As further specified by Ogarkov, conventional weapons might be used exclusively at the beginning of war. However, the war could later escalate to general nuclear war, where primarily strategic nuclear weapons might be employed.[87]

It was anticipated that war might extend to several continents and would be fought under varied conditions in different theaters of military action (TVDs). The complexity and variety of strategic tasks would require all services, using various means of fighting, including conventional weapons. The major nations of the world inevitably would take part in such a war, and the armed struggle would be intercontinental.[88]

Although they continued to emphasize the offense as the basic strategic action, Soviet military strategists specified the importance of defense in war. The Armed Forces, they said, must be capable of organizing its forces and conducting defensive actions on a strategic scale for the purpose of frustrating or repelling an enemy attack and holding or defending certain territory. They must be capable of winning time in order to concentrate the necessary forces to hold back the enemy in one direction and achieve superiority over the enemy in another.[89]

The United States and other NATO nations have declared that they need armed forces adequate to assure an outcome favorable to them. The Soviet leadership has a different view. In Lenin's words, "When fighting it is necessary not just to bring down the enemy but to destroy him. This thesis became the basis of Soviet military strategy." As expressed in Soviet military doctrine, "high combat activity and decisiveness of action is demanded for the purpose of utterly defeating the aggressor no matter from where he appears."[90]

In the early 1960s Soviet military theorists admitted that work was being conducted on both ballistic missile and space systems. By the late 1960s such admissions largely had ceased, and by the 1970s Soviet writings denied any interest in a military role in space. It was seldom revealed that an active ballistic missile defense actually existed around Moscow. Nevertheless, in the 1970s Sokolovskiy's book *Military Strategy* was frequently cited by Soviet authors. This work described the need for both ballistic missile and space defenses. Also in the 1970s, students at Soviet military academies were told of requirements for the military use of space as well as the need for defense against space strikes.

Formulating a single military-technical policy was necessary to produce the required weapons systems. The policy of the Party leadership of the Armed Forces involved "creating conditions for the development and improvement of those systems of weapons on which the security of the USSR depends to the greatest degree." It was added that this goal was being achieved while, at the same time, international treaty obligations were being observed.[91] Following the signing of SALT I there was no mention of the need to achieve military superiority. Now the armed forces of the Soviet Union and the United States were portrayed as being in a position of "approximate parity," but the United States was accused continually of seeking to upset that parity.

Preparing the Army and Country for War

The fourth question addressed the problem of how to carry out preparations for war and included whether Soviet military doctrine was offensive or defensive. Following the 24th Party Congress in 1971, Minister of Defense Grechko restated the general guidelines, which differed little from those given in 1966. All services and service branches were being developed further and were being improved and equipped with the most modern means of combat. This development was in accord with the requirements of the coordinated use of such forces in modern battle, operations and war as a whole.

With respect to armaments, the authors of the *Officer's Handbook* wrote that ballistic missiles had "substantial advantages over other types of weapons." They are "easy to disperse and camouflage at the site and they do not require large launch sites." Perhaps thinking of the research and development that was under way in the Soviet Union at the time, they wrote "they can also be mounted on mobile launchers. Such missiles are capable of striking objects . . . in practically any region of the globe."[92]

In structuring forces, the time factor had to be considered carefully. The enormous speed of missiles and aircraft had made new demands on time. The Armed Forces would have to be brought to a state of full combat readiness in literally a few minutes. Because the enemy might launch a surprise strike, the Strategic Rocket Forces and other nuclear forces, Troops of Air Defense, and the Air Forces must be prepared for conditions "where time is counted in seconds." As long as probable opponents have nuclear rocket weapons, "a principle of structuring and using the armed forces of a socialist state, such as maintaining constant combat readiness of the army to repel aggression, becomes especially important."[93]

Officers attending Soviet military academies were told that no longer would there be time to build up and train forces after a war started. Both must be done in time of peace. Advance plans were needed for strategic deployment, which in a period of tension should be accomplished in secret. This was exactly what had been taught in the 1960s.

The total Soviet military structure underwent significant reorganization in the 1970s. All three editions of Sokolovskiy's book *Military Strategy* had stressed how the entire nation must be prepared as a theater of military action. In the late 1970s a TVD headquarters was established in the Far East, with headquarters probably at Chita, east of Lake Baikal. It was called the High Command of the Far East. It is likely that at the same time plans were made for other TVDs. The remaining areas of the world were probably also divided into continental or oceanic TVDs, as appropriate.

Continued preparation of the nation as a theater of war was based on an overall unified plan carried out by government, Party, and military agencies. Careful advance planning for TVDs was essential to ensure successful military actions in event of war. Certain military forces within each area were maintained in a constant state of combat readiness for either nuclear or conventional war. Within each TVD a unified and developed system of communications was deemed essential. This plan required preparation of a state command and control system with all necessary communication networks. In addition, the hospital system needed to be extended. Because a nuclear strike can cause serious problems with contaminated water, provisions had to be made for emergency water supplies.

Transportation in the Soviet Union was critical in World War II and remained so in the 1970s. Planners establishing the TVDs appeared to be well aware of this factor. There would be no time to expand or improve the transportation systems once a war began. Road capacity needed improving, and major rail lines needed straightening and leveling. Since major cities might be attacked, causing transportation bottlenecks, bypass roads were needed around cities. Additional pipelines—another matter given specific attention in Sokolovskiy's *Military Strategy*—were constructed. Civilian airfields needed expansion for high-performance military aircraft, and special facilities had to be provided at such airfields so they could immediately be used for military purposes.

In preparing the nation for the possibility of war, civil defense was considered "one of the strategic factors." The head of civil defense was elevated to the position of deputy minister of defense. Additional civil defense facilities were constructed in urban areas, although evacuation for most of the population still was considered necessary. The Soviet people were told that public ownership of the means of production and the "planned system of economic management" gave the Soviet Union an advantage over the "imperialists" in providing protection against weapons of mass destruction.[94]

Particular attention was paid to preparing the Armed Forces for the conditions of nuclear war. Military textbooks emphasized preparation of the Armed Forces for fighting in conditions where nuclear, chemical, and biological weapons might be employed. Measures to limit the effectiveness of the opponent's weapons included dispersion of military facilities and personnel, utilization of the terrain for maximum concealment, and the construction of shelters. In addition, misleading the enemy and camouflage were discussed widely.

During the 1970s Soviet weapon systems and changes in the military structure coincided with the published military views. New models of MIRVed ICBMs were developed and deployed, which approximately tripled the number of warheads. There were significant quantitative and qualitative increases in submarine-launched ballistic missile forces. Missile accuracy was improved. The antiballistic missile system surrounding Moscow was updated with better radars, two new ABM systems, and improved missile guidance as a result of installing more modern computers. Combined arms forces were equipped to fight both with nuclear and conventional weapons. In light of all this, it is clear that the signing of the SALT I arms control agreement had no discernible effect on Soviet military expenditures.[95]

Soviet military developments in the 1970s bore out the stated premise that "Soviet military doctrine is offensive in character."[96] An identical statement was made about Soviet military strategy, with the explanation that "Marxists have always noted that the primacy of the offensive type of military operations over the defensive is due to the objective requirements of waging war." In the 1980s, the "offensive character" of military doctrine would be vigorously denied by the most senior Soviet Party-military leaders.

Conducting the War

The final question pertinent to doctrine related to what methods would be used to fight a war. Throughout the 1970s, as in the 1960s, nuclear war remained the primary focus of Soviet military doctrine. At the same time, increased attention was given to fighting both major conventional wars and local wars.

Foreign officers attending military academies in the Soviet Union during and immediately following the signing of SALT I have provided excellent accounts of Soviet perceptions of methods for the conduct of a future war as viewed in the early 1970s. Most of these foreign officers attended the Frunze Military Academy or the Voroshilov Military Academy of the General Staff, the most senior of all Soviet military, professional, educational institutions. Students were from such nations as Poland, Finland, Egypt, and Afghanistan. A number of them later either wrote about the instruction received, or have been available for interviews. Although they did not attend classes with Soviet officers, they were in a unique position to obtain some insights into the then-current Soviet view of how a future war between the Warsaw Pact and NATO would most likely be fought.

Their Soviet instructors estimated that the average time between the beginning of a period of "high tension" and the initial combat clash would be approximately two weeks. During this period an escalation of troop readiness and possibly the beginning of mobilization would be likely to occur. This time would be utilized to bring troops to full combat readiness and to move nuclear weapons to deployment areas. Concealment of preparations and deception would be of extreme importance during this early phase.

The war would be primarily a nuclear-missile war, with forces at the tactical, operational, and strategic level participating. The primary forces, as Soviet military doctrine has specified since the 1960s, would be the Strategic Rocket Forces. Because of the destruction that a nuclear war would cause, it is possible that a future conflict would be conducted with the use of conventional weapons only. This possibility, however, seemed unlikely. NATO's military exercises, they were told, begin with a conventional phase, but introduce operational-tactical nuclear weapons in the later stages. Such exercises, Soviet theorists asserted, provided evidence that the war probably would become nuclear.

When nuclear weapons are used either at the outset or in a later stage, said the Soviet instructors, the first strike could achieve decisive strategic goals. NATO military leaders might insist on the use of such weapons, since to achieve the same results with conventional weapons would take a number of successive operations. If nuclear weapons were used, the war could be either short or protracted. Much would depend on the capability of one side to deliver a surprise first strike and not be seriously crippled by the opponent's retaliatory strike.

The "imperialists," who no longer had superior strategic nuclear forces, would suffer untold destruction in event of a nuclear exchange. Therefore, it should be expected that they first would attempt to defeat the socialist forces with conventional weapons or with the limited use of nuclear weapons. If the war was being conducted with conventional weapons, the enemy could be expected to introduce nuclear weapons at any time that he faces defeat on the battlefield or the actual loss of his territory.

The following forms of strategic action were considered:

- attacks by strategic nuclear forces using ground-based strategic missiles, submarine-launched ballistic missiles, and long-range aircraft;
- strategic operations in a continental theater of military action;
- strategic operations in an oceanic theater of military action;
- strategic air operations against the enemy's air force in a war in which nuclear weapons are not used;
- strategic defensive actions against an enemy's aerospace strikes.

Lectures by faculty members of Soviet military academies as well as articles and books in the military and Party press gave identical views on how a future war would be fought. An aggressor must be defeated by conducting decisive actions. Strategic operations would be conducted within a theater of military action (TVD). In coastal areas there would be operations of fleets, air, antiair, airborne and naval landing, combined landing, and other actions, and nuclear rocket and air strikes also would be made. Additional kinds of strategic operations might also be conducted.[97]

If nuclear weapons were used at the beginning of war, "active operations in TVDS of all services of the Armed Forces might begin simultaneously with nuclear strikes." At this time, at the very beginning of the war, the destruction caused by the initial nuclear strikes would "determine the character and content of subsequent actions of the Armed Forces."[98]

A war might be fought with conventional forces or with the limited use of nuclear weapons. In such a war, the military goals would be to destroy operational units of air and naval forces and to obtain air superiority and the reduction or destruction of the enemy's nuclear potential. Any action conducted with only conventional weapons would be fought under the constant threat of the opponent's use of nuclear weapons.

Whether conventional or nuclear weapons were used, strategic actions would continue during the entire course of the war. The political and strategic goals for which the war was initiated would be gained only after winning victory over the enemy. If the war is nuclear, the immediate military goal would be reached through the destruction and incapacitation of the enemy by simultaneous nuclear strikes against his economic base and the main grouping of his armed forces. Victory would be achieved by the side that manages to inflict greater damage on the enemy while retaining more of its economic bases and armed forces.

If the war is fought with only conventional weapons, destruction of the enemy's nuclear means would still take first priority. Next in priority would be the battle to gain air superiority. Control of the air would provide conditions for the seizure and occupation of vital operational and strategic areas in enemy territory, which generally is carried out by conventional forces. Commanders must be prepared to use nuclear weapons at any time should their use be authorized by a higher command.

It was believed unlikely that war with only the limited use of nuclear weapons could be conducted for any significant period; all-out war soon would follow. When that happened, seizing the strategic initiative in the first minutes would have a decisive impact on future military actions. The objective would be to destroy the enemy's nuclear capability and disrupt his command and control.

Soviet sources do not provide an estimate of losses that the USSR might expect in the event of a nuclear exchange with the United States. Soviet writers quote U.S. sources that state that Washington expects 80 million casualties as well as the elimination of 40 percent to 60 percent of its industry. In a nuclear exchange, Soviets say, certain factors favor the Soviet Union. For example, 40 percent of the U.S. population is concentrated in large cities, while in the Soviet Union only 25 percent is so concentrated.

While Soviet textbooks and faculties of the military academies were describing the most likely manner in which they believed a future war would be fought, Soviet Party leaders sought to reassure the world that should nuclear war take place, it would be entirely the fault of the imperialists, primarily the United States. An attempt was made to give this view additional credence on January 18, 1977. In a speech at Tula, a city south of Moscow, General Secretary Brezhnev repeated a recent Warsaw Pact call for participants in the European Security Conference to pledge not to be the first to use the nuclear weapon against one another and not to increase membership in either NATO or the Warsaw Pact. He accused the NATO nations of maintaining their first-use policy, in order to retain the ability to threaten the Soviet Union with nuclear weapons.[99] The speech was timed so that it was made two days before President Jimmy Carter was inaugurated.

But at the time Brezhnev made his Tula speech, there was considerable concern in the West about the continued buildup of Soviet military forces. Brezhnev admitted that the Soviet Union was improving its defenses, for there can be no compromise, he said, "in matters of our own security or the security of our allies." However, he denied the allegations "that the Soviet Union is going beyond what is sufficient for defense, that it is trying to attain superiority in weapons in order to deal 'a first strike.'" He called such beliefs "absurd and unfounded." Instead, Brezhnev claimed, Soviet efforts were directed toward preventing a first strike as well as a second strike. The Soviet Union sought "not superiority in weapons" but a course that will result in reducing armaments and easing the military-political confrontation.[100]

The following year, in addressing the Communist Youth Congress, the Komsomol, Brezhnev again declared that the Soviet Union was against the use of nuclear weapons. He assured the Komsomol that only extraordinary circumstances, such as "aggression against our country or its allies made by other nuclear powers," could force the Soviet Union to resort "to this extreme means of self-protection."[101]

It was Ogarkov who next addressed the subject of no-first-use. Writing in the *Soviet Military Encyclopedia* in 1979, he stated:

> However, the widening of military actions might lead to its escalation to general nuclear war, the main means for waging of which is the nuclear weapon, primarily of strategic designation. At the base of Soviet military strategy lies the thesis that the Soviet Union, proceeding from the principles of its policy, will not use this weapon first. And it in principle is against the use of weapons of mass destruction. But any possible aggressor should distinctly recognize that in the event of a nuclear rocket attack on the Soviet Union or on other countries of the socialist community, it will receive an annihilating retaliatory strike.[102]

The Brezhnev era was drawing to a close. At the end of 1979, despite all the proclamations to the contrary, Soviet troops rolled into Afghanistan where they remained for almost a decade before starting to withdraw. The 1980s would hold some new developments in military doctrine, yet they would sound all too familiar.

Notes

1. Edward Crankshaw, *The New York Times International Edition*, January 4, 1964, p. 5.

2. L. I. Brezhnev, *XXIV S"yezd Kommunisticheskoy Partii Sovetskogo Soyuza* [24th Congress of the CPSU] (Moscow: Politizdat, 1971), p. 106.

3. Ibid.

4. John Newhouse, *Cold Dawn: The Story of SALT* (New York: Holt, Rinehart and Winston, 1973), p. 3.

5. N. A. Lomov, editor, *Nauchno-Tekhnicheskiy Progress i Revolyutsiya v Voyennom Dele* [Military-Technical Progress and the Revolution in Military Affairs] (Moscow: Voyenizdat, 1973), p. 136.

6. Mikhail A. Milstein, personal conversation in 1976.

7. G. V. Zimin, *Razvitiye Protivovozdushnoy Oborony* [Development of Antiair Defense] (Moscow: Voyenizdat, 1976), p. 191.

8. A. A. Grechko, "The Leading Role of the CPSU in Building the Army of a Developed Socialist Society," *Voprosy Istorii KPSS* [Problems of History of the CPSU] (May 1974). Translated by FBIS, May 1974.

9. A. A. Grechko, *Vooruzhennyye Sily Sovetskogo Gosudarstva* [Armed Forces of the Soviet State], 1st ed. (Moscow: Voyenizdat, 1974), p. 120.

10. A. A. Grechko, *Vooruzhennyye Sily Sovetskogo Gosudarstva* [Armed Forces of the Soviet State], 2nd ed. (Moscow: Voyenizdat, 1975), p. 107. (US GPO trans., pp. 99–100.) There is also a Soviet translation into English by Progress Publishers, 1977, see pp. 106–107.

11. S. G. Gorshkov, *Morskaya Moshch Gosudarstva* [Seapower of a State] (Moscow: Voyenizdat, 1976), p. 403.

12. D. F. Ustinov, "Guard of Peaceful Labor, Bulwark of Universal Peace," *Kommunist* 3 (February 1977), p. 13.

13. D. F. Ustinov, *Izbrannyye Rechi i Stat'i* [Selected Speeches and Articles] (Moscow: Politizdat, 1979), p. 314.

14. L. I. Brezhnev, *XXV S"yezd Kommunisticheskoy Partii Sovetskogo Soyuza* [25th Congress of the CPSU] (Moscow: Politizdat, 1976), p. 29.

15. Ibid., p. 43.

16. Ibid., p. 47.

17. *Constitution (Fundamental Law) of the Union of Soviet Socialist Republics* (Moscow: Novosti Press, 1977), Art. 31.

18. Ibid., Art. 32.

19. Ibid., Art. 121, para. 14.

20. S. N. Kozlov, editor, *Spravochnik Ofitsera* [The Officer's Handbook] (Moscow: Voyenizdat, 1971), p. 63.

21. Ibid., pp. 65–66.

22. Ibid., p. 66.

23. A. A. Grechko, *Na Strazhe Mira i Stroitel'stva Kommunizm* [On Guard Over the Peace and the Building of Communism] (Moscow: Voyenizdat, 1972), p. 53.

24. Grechko, *Vooruzhennyye Sily* (1974), p. 314.

25. Ibid., p. 315.

26. V. D. Sokolovskiy, editor, *Voyennaya Strategiya* [Military Strategy], 1st ed. (Moscow: Voyenizdat, 1962), p. 49.

27. Grechko, *Vooruzhennyye Sily* (1974), p. 315. The English translation by Progress Publishers differs from the original Russian on several points. The questions used here are translated from the Russian.

28. Kozlov, *Spravochnik Ofitsera*, pp. 74–75.
29. A. S. Zheltov, editor, *Soldat i Voyna* [Soldier and War] (Moscow: Voyenizdat, 1971), p. 8.
30. Grechko, *Na Strazhe*, pp. 49, 53.
31. I. Kh. Bagramyan, editor, *Voyennaya Istoriya* [Military History] (Moscow: Voyenizdat, 1971), p. 340.
32. A. A. Strokov, *V. I. Lenin o Voyne i Voyennom Iskusstve* [V. I. Lenin on War and Military Art] (Moscow: Nauka, 1971), p. 163.
33. Lomov, *Nauchno-Tekhnicheskiy Progress*, p. 138; A. A. Yepishev, *Ideologicheskaya Bor'ba po Voyennym Voprosam* [Ideological Struggle on Military Questions] (Moscow: Voyenizdat, 1974), p. 91; and G. V. Sredin, *Na Strazhe Rodina* [On Guard Over the Motherland] (Moscow: Voyenizdat, 1974), pp. 107, 204.
34. A. S. Milovidov and V. G. Kozlov, *Filosofskoye Naslediye V. I. Lenina i Problemy Sovremennoy Voyny* [Philosophical Heritage of V. I. Lenin and Problems of Contemporary War] (Moscow: Voyenizdat, 1972), p. 135.
35. V. V. Larionov, "Reduction of Tension and the Principles of Equal Security," *Krasnaya Zvezda* [Red Star], July 18, 1974.
36. Grechko, *Vooruzhennyye Sily* (1974), p. 347.
37. Ibid., p. 344.
38. Editorial, *New Times*, May 13, 1977; Vladen Kuznetsov, *Zarya Vostoka* [Dawn of the East], May 14, 1977; Dmitriy Ardamatskiy, *Novosti* (News), June 16, 1977.
39. Lev Semeyko, "Stability or Destruction?" *New Times*, September 1, 1978.
40. V. Mikhaylov, "A Threat to Détente," *Pravda*, February 8, 1979, and "A Nuclear Palisade," *Pravda*, February 18, 1979.
41. Editorial, *Za Rubezhom* [Abroad], August 1977; N. Polyanov, *Izvestia* [News], August 12, 1977.
42. Yuriy Zhukov, *Pravda*, September 1, 1977; Oleg Skalin, *Pravda*, September 7, 1977.
43. Lev Semeyko, "A Sinister Chain," *Krasnaya Zvezda*, May 12, 1978.
44. Editorial, *Pravda*, April 17, 1977.
45. Ibid.
46. A. S. Milovidov, Ye. A. Zhdanov, *Voprosy Filosofii* [Problems of Philosophy] 10 (October 1980).
47. "Doktrina, Voyennaya" [Doctrine, Military], in *Sovetskaya Voyennaya Entsiklopediya* [Soviet Military Encyclopedia] (Moscow: Voyenizdat, 1976–1980), vol. 3, pp. 225–229.
48. D. F. Ustinov, "The Leading Role of the CPSU in Structuring the Soviet Armed Forces," *Voprosy Istorii KPSS* (February 1979), as reprinted in D. F. Ustinov, *Izbrannyye Rechi*, p. 498.
49. Ibid., p. 500.
50. A. S. Zheltov, *V. I. Lenin i Sovetskiye Vooruzhennyye Sily* [V. I. Lenin and the Soviet Armed Forces], 3rd ed. (Moscow: Voyenizdat, 1980), p. 168.
51. Ibid., p. 415.
52. Ibid., p. 517.
53. Ibid.
54. K. A. Vorob'yev, *Vooruzhennyye Sily Razvitogo Sotsialisticheskogo Obshchestva* [Armed Forces of a Mature Socialist Society] (Moscow: Voyenizdat, 1980), p. 83.
55. Milovidov and Kozlov, *Filosofskoye Naslediye*, p. 136.
56. Grechko, *Vooruzhennyye Sily* (1974), p. 322.
57. N. V. Ogarkov, "Strategiya, Voyennaya" [Strategy, Military], in *Sovetskaya Voyennaya Entsiklopediya*, vol. 7, p. 564.

58. Grechko, *Na Strazhe*, p. 62.

59. Ibid.

60. Milovidov and Kozlov, *Filosofskoye Naslediye*, p. 136.

61. Lomov, *Nauchno-Tekhnicheskiy Progress*, p. 138.

62. Ye. Ye. Mal'tsev, *KPSS—Organizator Zashchity Sotsialisticheskogo Otechestva* [CPSU, Organizer of the Defense of the Socialist Fatherland] (Moscow: Voyenizdat, 1974), 1st ed., p. 353.

63. Ogarkov, "Strategiya Voyennaya," *Sovetskaya Voyennaya Entsiklopediya*, vol. 7, p. 564.

64. Zheltov, *V. I. Lenin i Sovetskiye Vooruzhennyye Sily* (1980), p. 163.

65. Lomov, *Nauchno-Teknicheskiy Progress*, p. 139.

66. Ogarkov, "Strategiya, Voyennaya," *Sovetskaya Voyennaya Entsiklopediya*, vol. 7, p. 564.

67. Grechko, *Vooruzhennyye Sily* (1974), p. 99.

68. Grechko, *Vooruzhennyye Sily* (1975), p. 195.

69. S. V. Baranov, "Material Basis of the Might of the Armed Forces USSR," *Krasnaya Zvezda*, March 5, 1971, p. 2.

70. Grechko, *Na Strazhe*, p. 55; Milovidov and Kozlov, *Filosofskoye Naslediye*, p. 136; Lomov, *Nauchno-Tekhnicheskiy Progress*, p. 138.

71. Grechko, *Vooruzhennyye Sily* (1975), p. 195.

72. D. A. Volkogonov, A. S. Milovidov and S. A. Tyushkevich, *Voyna i Armiya* [War and Army] (Moscow: Voyenizdat, 1977), p. 33.

73. Zheltov, *V. I. Lenin i Sovetskiye Vooruzhennyye Sily* (1980), pp. 163–164, 485.

74. Vorob'yev, *Vooruzhennyye Sily*, p. 91.

75. Ogarkov, "Strategiya, Voyennaya," *Sovetskaya Voyennaya Entsiklopediya*, vol. 7, p. 564.

76. Milovidov and Kozlov, *Filosofskoye Naslediye*, p. 136.

77. Ogarkov, "Strategiya, Voyennaya," *Sovetskaya Voyennaya Entsiklopediya*, vol. 7, p. 564.

78. Ibid., vol. 7, p. 565.

79. Milovidov and Kozlov, *Filosofskoye Naslediye*, p. 136.

80. N. N. Azovtsev, *V. I. Lenin i Sovetakaya Voyennaya Nauka* [V. I. Lenin and Soviet Military Science] (Moscow: Nauka, 1971), p. 283.

81. A. A. Grechko, "On Guard Over Peace and Socialism," *Kommunist* 7 (May 1973), p. 18.

82. Volkogonov et al., *Voyna i Armiya*, p. 366.

83. Vorob'yev, *Vooruzhennyye Sily*, p. 92.

84. Grechko, *Vooruzhennyye Sily* (1975), p. 195.

85. Milovidov and Kozlov, *Filosofskoye Naslediye*, p. 136.

86. Volkogonov et al., *Voyna i Armiya*, p. 33.

87. Ogarkov, "Strategiya, Voyennaya," *Sovetskaya Voyennaya Entsiklopediya*, vol. 7, p. 564.

88. Lomov, *Nauchno-Tekhnicheskiy Progress*, p. 135.

89. Ogarkov, "Strategiya, Voyennaya," *Sovetskaya Voyennaya Entsiklopediya*, vol. 7, p. 565.

90. Zheltov, *V. I. Lenin i Sovetskiye Vooruzhennyye Sily*, pp. 256, 432.

91. Ibid., p. 164.

92. Kozlov, *Spravochnik Ofitsera*, p. 128.

93. Vorob'yev, *Vooruzhennyye Sily*, p. 92.

94. Milovidov and Kozlov, *Filosofskoye Naslediye*, pp. 320, 334.

95. W. T. Lee and R. F. Staar, *Soviet Military Policy* (Stanford, California: Hoover Institution, 1987), p. 110.

96. Kozlov, *Spravochnik Ofitsera*, p. 78.

97. Ogarkov, "Strategiya, Voyennaya," *Sovetskaya Voyennaya Entsiklopediya*, vol. 7, p. 563.

98. Lomov, *Nauchno-Tekhnicheskiy Progress*, pp. 135, 139.

99. L. I. Brezhnev, *Na Strazhe Mira i Sotsializma* [On Guard Over Peace and Socialism] (Moscow: Politizdat, 1979), p. 490.

100. Ibid., pp. 490–491.

101. Brezhnev, *Na Strazhe*, p. 616.

102. Ogarkov, "Strategiya, Voyennaya," *Sovetskaya Voyennaya Entsiklopediya*, vol. 7, p. 564.

4
Soviet Military Doctrine in the 1980s

As the 1980s were beginning, Soviet leaders sought to reassure the world, alarmed by the invasion of Afghanistan on the eve of the new decade, that their military forces were not a threat. General Secretary Brezhnev used the meeting with other East bloc leaders in mid-May, marking the twenty-fifth anniversary of the Warsaw Pact, to issue a Declaration on the subject of Soviet and Warsaw Pact military doctrine. "There is not now, never was and never will be any strategic doctrine other than a defensive one. There is not now, never was and never will be the intention of creating a potential for a first nuclear strike." Furthermore, "the Warsaw Pact nations had never and never would aim for military superiority" and "are invariably advocating maintaining the military balance at ever lower levels, for reducing and ultimately eliminating military confrontation in Europe."

The Declaration also called for "confidence-building measures, renunciation of force or threat of force, limitation of forces and arms of each state or group of states solely to suit defense needs, and mutual renunciation of attempts at gaining military supremacy."[1] In a show of goodwill, the Soviet Union announced a unilateral withdrawal of troops and arms, including tank units, from central Europe. They reiterated a call for a conference on military détente and disarmament in Europe. On the question of Afghanistan, this 1980 Declaration stated that: "Together with the full termination of all forms of outside interference against the government and people of Afghanistan, the commencement of the withdrawal of Soviet troops from Afghanistan will be started."[2]

As will be seen later, these assertions were much the same as those made by Mikhail Gorbachev in his report to the 27th Party Congress in 1986. The major difference was the impact. In 1980, NATO members were well aware of the Soviet military buildup that had continued throughout the 1970s, and were most concerned with the deployment of the Soviet SS-20 intermediate-range missiles. Seven years later, similar announcements made by a new, more dynamic leader, touted as "new thinking,"[3] made a much greater impact on the West.

Even before the decade began, possible shifts in military policies were hinted at in Soviet publications and in conversations that many Westerners had with Soviet officials. Brezhnev made many assertions about the danger of nuclear war and the hopes of the Soviet people for peace, words that had a hollow ring after the invasion of Afghanistan. Later, however, there were significant changes that could well result in modifications to the Party's military doctrine. First, Brezhnev's eighteen-year reign ended and there was a quick succession of new Party leaders. Second, some major reassignments occurred in key command and staff personnel in the Soviet Armed Forces. Third, new technologies and scientific discoveries led to the development of new weapons and corresponding alterations in the military structure. Fourth, serious economic and social problems in the Soviet Union led the Soviet leadership to seek arms control agreements with the West, a policy that would likely last until these problems were brought under control.

In many ways Western anticipation of change in the Soviet Armed Forces in the latter part of the 1980s was reminiscent of the expectations for Soviet liberalization in the early to mid-1960s when de-Stalinization was under way. Then there had been unwarranted optimism abroad that the Soviets had backed away from reliance on nuclear weapons and were settling for strategic inferiority. This dream was shattered in the early 1970s when Soviet deployment of strategic weapons not only matched U.S. deployment but passed it in numbers. Many in the West remembered this earlier period and the hopes it had generated.

Party-military decisions that have had the most impact on military doctrine during the 1980s resulted from the meetings of the 26th Party Congress in 1981 and the 27th Party Congress in 1986. The former was Brezhnev's last congress. The latter, Gorbachev's first, approved a revised edition of the Third Program of the Communist Party, the first revision since the Program was adopted in October 1961 at the 22nd Party Congress. This Program will have a strong impact on military doctrine until the end of the century.

The 26th Party Congress and Its Aftermath

At the 26th Congress of the CPSU in February and March 1981, a failing Leonid Brezhnev struggled to deliver the Report of the Central Committee to the more than 5,000 assembled delegates. In the United States Ronald Reagan had just been inaugurated as President. Iran had just released the American hostages whom they had held for more than a year. The second year of fighting in Afghanistan had already begun, and the situation in Poland would lead to a declaration of martial law by the end of 1981.

Brezhnev noted in his address that while the Soviet Union was pursuing "the line of curbing the arms race, strengthening peace and détente, and defending the sovereign rights and freedom of nations," the "other side" was following "the line of disrupting détente, escalating the arms race, of threats and interference in other countries' affairs, and of suppressing the liberation movement." He spoke of "new victories" in the revolutions in

Ethiopia, Afghanistan and Nicaragua. However, "the aggressiveness of imperialist policy, notably that of U.S. imperialism, has increased acutely." Later, he added that "the CPSU will consistently continue the policy of promoting cooperation between the USSR and the newly free countries and consolidating the alliance of world socialism and the national liberation movement."[4]

Brezhnev devoted a large part of his Report to arms control. He pointed out that "the great unifying principle . . . enhancing the prestige of the world communist movement, is the Communists' unremitting struggle for peace, against imperialism's aggressive policy, and the arms race that carries with it the danger of a nuclear disaster."[5]

The military directives of the 26th Party Congress later were explained in detail by the most senior officers in the Ministry of Defense. Although he ranked number two in the military hierarchy, Marshal N. V. Ogarkov was the primary military spokesman on doctrine and its implications. In the first half of the 1980s Ogarkov attracted unusual attention in the West as a result of his writings, interviews, and television appearances. To the outside world, he seemed to be the dominant Soviet military figure. Many Western scholars assumed that he had primary responsibility for any revisions in the Kremlin's military doctrine and strategy.

In July 1981, a few months after the 26th Congress ended, *Kommunist*, the Party's leading theoretical journal, carried an article by Ogarkov in which he explained to the Party membership that the Armed Forces were meeting the directives of the Congress. This article was expanded into a monograph, and early the next year, on February 23, 1982—Soviet Armed Forces Day—his booklet *Always Ready to Defend The Fatherland* went on sale in Moscow bookstores.

Senior Soviet military officers are expected to sum up the decisions of Party Congresses as they relate to key military issues. Four other senior Soviet officers also published booklets, with covers identical to the one used on Ogarkov's work. Each bore the caption: "Decisions of the XXVI Congress of the CPSU—into Life." None of these booklets attracted any significant attention, even though one was written by Marshal D. F. Ustinov, the Minister of Defense. This lack of attention was not surprising since Ustinov was an armaments production expert, not a line officer.

In both the journal article and the booklet, Ogarkov discussed military doctrine. His article in the July 1981 issue of *Kommunist* gave the following definition:

> Soviet military doctrine, in full correspondence with the Leninist foreign policy of peace, is a scientifically based system of views on the essence of the nature of war, which might be unleashed by imperialism, and on the preparation of the country and the Armed Forces to repel possible aggression. "Our strategic doctrine," said comrade L. I. Brezhnev, "has a purely defensive orientation." At the same time it envisages, in the event of an attack by an aggressor on the USSR or its allies, decisive actions of the Soviet Armed Forces

who in full measure are masters of the art of waging not only defensive but also contemporary offensive actions on land, in the air and at sea.

A new world war, if aggressive imperialist forces nonetheless succeed in unleashing it, would be a decisive clash between two opposing social systems. It would cover all continents of the world and would be waged by coalition groupings of armed forces with the most decisive aims, using the entire arsenal of means of armed struggle. Many hundreds of millions of people would be caught in its maelstrom. . . . The very nature of modern weapons is such that, if they were put into use, the future of all mankind would be at stake.[6]

In his booklet, Ogarkov's discussion of Soviet military doctrine and policies were essentially the same as given in his 1981 article in *Kommunist*.

On November 7, 1982, Brezhnev, although noticeably ill, was obligated to stand in the cold on Lenin's mausoleum in Moscow's Red Square to review the traditional parade. He died within a few days, on November 10. His successor, Yuriy V. Andropov, initially gave the appearance of a strong, vigorous leader. But his health, too, soon failed, and upon his death in January 1984, he was replaced by seventy-two-year-old Konstantin U. Chernenko.

In early September 1984, the highly visible Ogarkov was to have held a television interview. Foreign officials and scholars worldwide who follow Soviet defense policies were astounded to see Marshal Sergey Akhromeyev, previously a first deputy chief of the General Staff, appear on the television screen instead of Ogarkov. A two-sentence announcement in the press noted only that Ogarkov had been "transferred to other work." Although his exact assignment was never reported in the press, later Soviet accounts of Ogarkov's activities indicate that he was sent to a command position in the Western USSR, most likely the newly formed Western TVD. Although his new position may not have been equivalent to that of the chief of the General Staff, he still was far from being "in disgrace," as some overzealous Western reporters claimed.[7] In November 1984, his article "Unfading Glory of Soviet Arms," dedicated to the 49th Anniversary of the Great Patriotic War, appeared in *Communist of the Armed Forces*, the official journal of the Main Political Administration of the Soviet Army and Navy.[8]

Then, in December 1984, Ustinov, the seventy-six-year-old Minister of Defense, died. His replacement was Marshal of the Soviet Union Sergey Sokolov, who at age seventy-four seemed to be an interim selection. A power struggle among competing Kremlin factions may have prevented the designation of a more vigorous individual. Upon General Secretary Chernenko's death in March 1985, a leader from a new generation was moved in. The fifty-four-year-old Mikhail S. Gorbachev—by Soviet standards a young man—was articulate and at ease with Western reporters. He was presented in the world press as a leader capable of bringing about the reforms necessary to revitalize the moribund Soviet society and economy.

Shortly after Gorbachev's designation as General Secretary, another booklet by Ogarkov, *History Teaches Vigilance*, was reviewed favorably in the Soviet press. Although Gorbachev had been in the position of General Secretary for a matter of weeks, Ogarkov had managed to insert the following acknowledgment:

> "In a difficult international situation," noted M. S. Gorbachev, in a speech at the special CPSU Central Committee plenum in March 1985, "it is important as never before to maintain the defense capability of our homeland at a level at which potential aggressors know well that encroachment on the security of the Soviet Union and its allies, on the peaceful life of the Soviet people, will be met with a crushing retaliatory strike. Our glorious armed forces will continue in the future to possess everything necessary for this."[9]

In this 1985 work Ogarkov defined military doctrine as follows: "Soviet military doctrine is a system of guiding principles and scientifically based views of the CPSU and the Soviet Government on the essence, nature and methods of waging war which may be unleashed by the imperialists against the Soviet Union, as well as on military construction and the preparation of the Armed Forces and the country to destroy the aggressor."[10]

There had been no significant shifts in Soviet military writings on doctrinal matters during either the brief tenure of Andropov or Chernenko as General Secretary. In general, Soviet spokesmen during that time continued to emphasize the "findings of the 26th Party Congress."

The 27th Party Congress and the New Party Program

At the 27th Party Congress in 1986, Gorbachev had been General Secretary for less than a year. In the first minute of his speech he noted that the Congress was to discuss and adopt a new edition of the Third Program of the CPSU. Exactly twenty-five years earlier, at the 22nd Party Congress, the Third Party Program had been approved. The task at hand was simply to approve a revision of that edition. The major decisions, to which the assembled Congress would give its approval, had been made in the preceding months. Unless changed by unanticipated events, these decisions would provide guidelines until the next Party meeting, expected to be held in 1991.

In the opening paragraphs of his Report on the Congress, Gorbachev claimed that "we have secured military strategic parity and have thereby substantially restricted imperialism's aggressive plans and capabilities to start a nuclear war."[11] Several hours later in his report he brought up Soviet military doctrine: "Soviet military doctrine is also entirely in keeping with the letter and spirit of the initiatives we have put forward. Its orientation is unequivocally defensive. In the military sphere we intend to act in such a way as to give nobody grounds for fears, even imagined ones, about their security."[12]

The revised Third Party Program and Gorbachev's Report to the Congress were in agreement. The Program noted that although the "aggressive circles of imperialism" present a danger, "world war is not fatally inevitable,"[13] provided the Soviet Armed Forces are equipped with the necessary weapons and are maintained at a high state of combat readiness. To ensure this, "the

Communist Party of the Soviet Union regards defense of the socialist homeland, a strengthening of the country's defenses and the ensuring of state security as one of the most important functions of the Soviet state."[14] The Program reaffirmed the leadership of the Communist Party over the Armed Forces: "It is under the Party's guidance that the country's policy in the field of defense and security and the Soviet military doctrine, which is purely defensive in nature and geared to ensuring protection against an outside attack, are worked out and implemented."[15]

In his Report to the Congress, Gorbachev declared that states should lower their military potential to the limits of "reasonable sufficiency."[16] This was reiterated in the Resolution of the Congress: "Our country is for withdrawing weapons of mass destruction from circulation and limiting the military potential with the limits of *reasonable sufficiency.*"[17] (Emphasis added.) Later, on Soviet Armed Forces Day, February 23, 1987, Sokolov wrote:

> The Soviet Union formerly advocated and advocates now the decisive lowering of the level of military confrontation, the cutting of military potentials to the level necessary and sufficient for defense, and the complete elimination of nuclear and other types of weapons of mass destruction from the strategic balance. . . . A few days ago, in his speech at the Moscow international forum "For a Nuclear-Free World, for the Survival of Mankind," M. S. Gorbachev . . . once again noted that the Soviet Union is ready to renounce its status as a nuclear power and reduce all other areas to the *minimum of reasonable sufficiency.*[18]

The expression "reasonable sufficiency" was thought by a number of NATO scholars and political leaders to herald a new chapter in Soviet military policy. Hopes increased when other Soviet spokesmen stressed the defensive nature of Soviet military doctrine: "Soviet military doctrine, as a system of state views on military development and on the preparation of the country and its Armed Forces to repulse aggression, is of a strictly defensive nature. It has essentially become a doctrine of preventing war. . . . While remaining a military means, nuclear weapons are increasingly becoming an instrument which it would be irrational to use."[19]

As this campaign was under way to emphasize the defensive nature of Soviet military doctrine and the nonutility of nuclear weapons, the Soviet leadership tried another ploy. At a meeting in May 1987, Gorbachev met with his Warsaw Pact counterparts in Berlin. The members of the Political Consultative Committee (PKK) of the Warsaw Pact discussed disarmament proposals and further steps to be taken. The meeting ended with the signing of the document "On the Military Doctrine of the Warsaw Pact Member States." It should be noted that military doctrine of the Warsaw Pact is not the same as Soviet military doctrine. The document stated that "the military doctrine of Warsaw Pact member states is strictly defensive and proceeds from the fact that in today's circumstances the use of the military way of resolving any disputed question is inadmissible [*nedopustimo*]."[20] The document provided for Warsaw Pact forces to be maintained at such a level that they "will give a crushing rebuff [*sokrushitel'nyy otpor*] to the aggressor." At the same time, the Pact forces "strictly keep to the limits of sufficiency for defense, for repulsing [*otrazhenya*] possible aggression."

A new twist was then introduced. "Authoritative" representatives from NATO nations were invited to meet with Warsaw Pact representatives to discuss the military doctrines of the two alliances. Soviet spokesmen tried to convince their readers that the major tenet of Warsaw Pact doctrine is to prevent the outbreak of war, whether conventional or nuclear. As deputy chief of the General Staff General M. A. Gareyev stated: "The Military Doctrine of the Warsaw Treaty Organization is aimed at achieving an ever lower level of military confrontation of the sides, as genuine equal security today is guaranteed not by a high but [by] the lowest possible level of the strategic equilibrium."[21] Even the Foreign Ministry got into the act, as one of its spokesmen stated: "It is time to review military doctrines, from the point of view of the principle of *reasonable sufficiency*, minimal restraint and a nonnuclear prospect."[22] (Emphasis added.)

A deputy Soviet foreign minister also took up the matter of military doctrine: "The question of military doctrines as an international factor was posed at the 27th CPSU Congress. In the Central Committee Political Report the thrust of Soviet military doctrine was described as unambiguously defensive. At the Political Consultative Committee Conference in Berlin 28-29 May this year the Warsaw Pact states adopted a document formulating the principled provisions of their military doctrine."[23]

Attempts to justify the change from what had been "offensive" doctrine to "defensive" doctrine got a boost from a group of professors at the Lenin Military-Political Academy. This Academy is under the Main Political Administration of the Soviet Army and Navy, which operates with the rights of a department of the Party's Central Committee. In a book published in 1987, the professors wrote that Lenin himself declared "that socialist states wage and will wage only *defensive* wars. However these wars are defensive in their *political goals* and not in the methods of waging." The authors went on to say that "as history shows, the Soviet state has never threatened anyone, but in the event of an attack on it by the imperialists, it will wage decisive offensive war right up to the complete destruction of the enemy."[24] (Emphasis in original.)

The Soviet Minister of Defense, General Dmitriy T. Yazov, said that "Soviet military doctrine is subordinate to the task of preventing war." However, Soviet Armed Forces are maintained in a state of alertness to avoid being taken by surprise, but if an attack occurs, "they will deal the aggressor a crushing rebuff."[25] These statements were essentially the same as those which previous Soviet ministers of defense had been making since the early 1960s. But they also complemented the new image of military doctrine that the Soviet leadership was attempting to create.

In this new approach to explain military doctrine, Soviet researchers at the Institute of the USA and Canada attempted to show that U.S. analysts were confused about Soviet military doctrine. One researcher declared that "their judgment on Soviet military doctrine is based on one book written in the sixties by late Marshal Sokolovskiy and some other people which is called *Military—SOVIET Military Strategy*—by the way, not doctrine, but strategy."[26]

Lev Semeyko from the same institute described the concept of "reasonable sufficiency":

> Among the most important political directives of the new thinking, special significance attaches to the principle of *reasonable sufficiency*. . . . Where does the essence of the concept lie?
>
> The *political* aspect lies in its emphasis on the strictly defensive function of armed forces and their readiness for defense against outside attack and not for attack and aggression. . . .
>
> The concept of *reasonable sufficiency* is oriented to the future and carries a charge of ideas for long-term action. . . .[27] (Emphasis added.)

A Soviet general, V. V. Serebryannikov, Doctor of Philosophical Sciences and a professor, explained that the concept of "sufficiency" had been approved by the 27th Party Congress. He then added:

> The sufficiency of military potentials is expressed both in terms of the precise quantity and quality of armaments and the troops themselves intended for defense, and also in terms of their structure and stationing . . . [Our] military might and combat readiness must be sufficient to permit them not to be taken unawares . . . and, if a hostile attack occurs, to deal the aggressor a crushing rebuff. . . .
>
> Sufficiency does not preclude but, on the contrary, presupposes the presence of strategic parity—that decisive factor in preventing war.[28]

Did these assertions about "sufficiency" indicate a real change in Soviet military doctrine? The answer requires an examination of the tasks that military doctrine must answer during the 1980s and beyond.

Tasks of Military Doctrine

In his discussion of military doctrine in 1982, Ogarkov listed five questions "which the military doctrine of any state answers." As previously shown, similar questions had been stated by Grechko in his 1974 book and afterward were found in a number of Soviet military writings, including the *Soviet Military Encyclopedia*.

Ogarkov's wording of the questions, coming so soon after the 26th Party Congress, was probably based on phrases from some official document. The words used by Grechko in 1974 had been polished to make the meaning more exact. For example, in the first question, Grechko simply talked about "a possible war." Ogarkov put it even more definitely: "What is the degree of possibility of a future war?" In the final question Ogarkov added, "if it breaks out," making the wording even more precise than in Grechko's questions.

Because of the difficulties of translating Russian into readable English, the extent of identical wording is sometimes lost. Below is a comparison of Grechko's wording in 1974 with Ogarkov's in 1985 in which identical wording in Russian has been printed in italics. Some of the questions had more than one part; here, each part has been treated as a separate question for the sake of comparison, although each set contains only five questions.

1. Grechko: *With what enemy will one have to deal* in a possible war?
1. Ogarkov: What is the degree of probability of future war and *with what enemy will one have to deal?*

2a. Grechko: *What* [is] the *character* of *the war* in *which the* state *and its Armed Forces might have* to take part?
2. Ogarkov: *What character* might *the war* take, *which the* country *and its Armed Forces might have* to wage?

2b. Grechko: *What goals and missions might* stand before them in this war?
3a. Ogarkov: *What goals and missions might* be assigned to the armed forces in anticipation of such a war?

3a. Grechko: *What Armed Forces are necessary in order to fulfill the assigned* missions?
3b. Ogarkov: *What Armed Forces are necessary* to have, *in order to fulfill the assigned* goals?

3b. Grechko: *In what* direction must *military structuring* be carried out?
4a. Ogarkov: *In what* way, proceeding from this, should *military structuring* be accomplished?

4. Grechko: How should preparations *for war* be accomplished?
4b. Ogarkov: [In what way should] the army and the country be prepared *for war?*

5. Grechko: *By what methods to conduct the war?*[29]
5. Ogarkov: *By what methods to conduct the war,* if it breaks out?[30]

Answers to these questions, required by military doctrine, are reflected in writings both by the Party and military leadership. The answers can also be deduced by observing the actions undertaken by the Soviet Union both internally and externally in preparing for the possibility of war. These actions include policies regarding military organization and weapon systems. Each question will now be examined separately.

Question 1: What Is the Degree of Probability of a Future War and Who Will Be the Probable Enemy?

Soviet leaders never estimate the percentage of probability of a future war. Instead, they claim that the forces of "imperialism" are becoming more aggressive every year and are planning to attack the Soviet Union and other socialist states. Only by constantly increasing the power and combat readiness of the Soviet Armed Forces can such an attack be prevented.

The probable enemy is identified and discussed in detail. In both his article and booklet published following the 26th Party Congress, Ogarkov started his first chapter with: "There has been a sharp increase in the aggressiveness of imperialism—and particularly U.S. imperialism." The attack against "imperialism" was strong enough in the article, but Ogarkov added thirteen pages to the booklet reciting all the "crimes" of "imperialist" countries since the October Revolution of 1917—the year he was born.[31] He repeated the standard refrain that the peace-loving Soviet Union has never been guilty of starting the arms race. He then gave "facts," which he claimed were "incontrovertible," among which were the following:

> We know, for example, that the United States built the world's first atomic bomb in 1945 and proceeded to use it to threaten the Soviet Union, which did not develop a similar weapon until four years later. What is more, *the United States was the first to test an even more powerful hydrogen bomb in 1952, while the USSR followed suit in 1953.* The Americans were also the first to build nuclear-powered submarines armed with ballistic missiles in 1960, while the USSR followed suit in 1967. . . . This list of strategic weapons could go on and on.[32] (Emphasis added.)

This approach was altogether new; it was a complete reversal of what Soviet spokesmen had claimed previously. In the past, they had bragged that their nation was "first" in most major military developments. For example, in 1968 an official Soviet publication, *50 Years of the Armed Forces USSR*, contained the following:

> Some leaders of the USA figured that the USSR would need 15 to 20 years to create the atomic weapon. But in 1947 our government revealed that for the Soviet Union the secret of [building] the atomic bomb did not exist, and, in August 1949 in our country, an experimental explosion of an atomic device took place. The monopoly of the USA on nuclear weapons was liquidated. Soon Soviet scientists, engineers, technicians and workers of the atomic industry achieved a new major victory: In August 1953, *earlier than in the USA*, we successfully tested one kind of hydrogen bomb.[33] (Emphasis added.)

Between 1960 and 1980 dozens of statements similar to this one had appeared in the Soviet press. In 1968 Sokolovskiy had written: "The Soviet Union created the most powerful rockets in the world—the carriers of cosmic objects. The Soviet Union was the first in the world to create the hydrogen bomb and the intercontinental ballistic missile, and also a number of new kinds of rocket armaments that are new in principle."[34] He later provided another example:

> Nuclear weapons appeared in the Soviet Union at the end of the 40s and the beginning of the 50s in the form of atomic and then hydrogen aviation bombs, and somewhat later in the form of nuclear charges of rockets of different types and torpedoes. Taking into account the fact that the Soviets created hydrogen weapons before the United States, and, most important of all, that the United States does not possess superpowerful thermonuclear charges such as those possessed by the USSR, we consider our superiority over the Western bloc in nuclear weapons to be indisputable.[35]

A 1973 Soviet book repeated essentially the same claims made by Sokolovskiy:

> Even in 1947, in the Soviet Union it was announced that the secret of [building] the atomic bomb did not exist. In August 1949, the first atomic explosion occurred in the USSR. The Soviet scientists created a hydrogen bomb even sooner, and in fact earlier than the American scientists.
> In the United States a hydrogen device was detonated in 1954. This was not yet a bomb, but namely a device, and a very heavy and cumbersome one. No aircraft of those times could have carried it. In the Soviet Union, the testing of the first thermonuclear bomb occurred in 1953, and we, thus, were ahead of the Americans in developing the most powerful and advanced type of modern weapon. Incidentally, the Americans themselves were forced to recognize this.[36]

In case readers of this Soviet book had missed the claims in the first part of the work, the following ideas were repeated:

> While at the end of the 1940s, the United States was the leader of the revolution in military affairs, *later this role gradually began to shift to the Soviet Union.* In 1947, the Soviet government announced that the secret of [building] the atomic bomb did not exist. In August 1949, an atomic explosion was carried out in the USSR. In 1953, a year ahead of the United States, the USSR tested its first hydrogen bomb. After the war, work went on successfully to create missiles of different classes and purposes. *The change in the balance of power in favor of the Soviet Union and its further successes in developing nuclear missile weapons led to a serious crisis in the ideology and policy of militarism.*[37] (Emphasis added.)

In the late 1970s the claim of being "first" was still being made. In the official history, *The Soviet Armed Forces*, published in 1978 for the sixtieth anniversary of the Soviet Armed Forces, the following statements appear:

> The broad scale of research, the powerful scientific-technical base permitted the Soviet Union to make and, in August 1953, *earlier than the United States of America*, to test such a bomb. The Soviet Armed Forces got a new kind of

unusually powerful weaponry which still further strengthened the defense capability of the USSR.

At the same time the nuclear weapon was created, another very important military-technical problem was resolved in the Soviet Union—the development of delivery means for atomic ammunition to targets. Soviet military-theoretical thought concluded that the leading strategic means of delivery of nuclear ammunition to the target would have to be the long-range guided ballistic rockets.[38] (Emphasis added.)

The first book in a new Officer's Library series, *V. I. Lenin and the Soviet Armed Forces*, published in 1980, made a similar claim: "By 1947 the production of nuclear weapons did not represent a secret for us. In 1949, a nuclear bomb was created and tested in the Soviet Union, and, in 1953— *earlier than in the United States of America*—Soviet scientists created a thermonuclear bomb."[39] (Emphasis added.) Even in 1981 yet another work, *V. I. Lenin and Soviet Military Science*, again asserted: "Under the direct leadership of the Central Committee, in an exceptionally short period of time, a powerful atomic industry was created and the massive production of nuclear weapons was organized. On 29 August 1949, an aviation bomb with a nuclear charge was tested, and on 12 August 1953, *earlier than in the United States of America*, a test of a bomb with a thermonuclear charge was conducted."[40] (Emphasis added.)

Although this book carried a 1981 publication date, it was actually printed in December 1980 prior to the 26th Party Congress. Therefore, the radical revision announced by Ogarkov following the Congress must have been a deliberate switch, and thus represents new measures concerning defense issues approved by the Congress.

From this point on, the gigantic propaganda network of the Communist Party went into action. It was now disregarded that for at least twenty years the Soviet Union had boasted about being first to have a usable thermonuclear bomb, a weapon that served as one of the paramount causes of the arms race. Nothing more would be said about being "first" in any area of weapon system development. The Party leadership at the 26th Party Congress, as had Party leaders in the past, simply rewrote history. As George Orwell had explained in his book *1984*, he who controls the present also controls the past.

Ogarkov set a pattern of accusations against the United States as being solely responsible for the arms race, a line that Soviet spokesmen have followed to this day. Among the new developments threatening the existing parity were U.S. intelligence-gathering satellites, "the multipurpose 'Shuttle' space program and the AWACS long-range radar detection system." In addition to these advanced systems, the United States also had improved its "so-called conventional weapons . . . with the aim of achieving superiority over the USSR."[41]

In the 1980s, according to Ogarkov, the United States formulated a new military strategy—a strategy of "direct confrontation" with the Soviet Union on a global and regional basis. Furthermore, the United States was poised to use nuclear weapons in everything from limited nuclear strikes to an all-out nuclear war. The creation of large "Eurostrategic" nuclear forces had raised the possibility of achieving political and military goals in limited nuclear war without it escalating to global war. "Theoretically," continued Ogarkov, "such reasoning is possible. But any sane person without too much difficulty will understand that it is impossible to keep nuclear war in any kind of limited framework."[42]

The new U.S. strategy was described as "closing the circle"—a return to massive retaliation. It was a policy of American imperialism, of trying to achieve global superiority by any means, and of not wanting to assess soberly the relationship of forces which had built up in the world. Ogarkov reminded his readers that Brezhnev had shown at the 26th Party Congress that the aggressiveness of imperialism, especially U.S. imperialism, had grown sharply. Ogarkov did not play favorites. In his July 1981 article he accused U.S. President Carter of threatening world peace. When his 1982 booklet appeared, the section on the "threat" had been updated to attack what he perceived as the policies of the new Reagan administration.

When Andropov, a former head of the KGB, succeeded Brezhnev as General Secretary, the Kremlin's line remained the same. The United States continued to be singled out as the primary enemy, and preparations for war in the NATO bloc, headed by the United States, were said to "have grown to an unheard-of scale." Officials in Washington were reported to talk of the possibility of limited, sustained, and other types of nuclear war.[43]

Even when Chernenko was designated to succeed Andropov, the nature of the propaganda attacks did not change. Chernenko claimed that in recent years there had been a "drastic escalation" in the policies of American imperialism; "a policy of undisguised militarism, striving for world supremacy, resistance to progress, and violation of the rights and freedoms of the peoples. . . . All this forces us to pay the gravest attention to strengthening our country's defenses."[44]

At the 27th Party Congress in 1986, General Secretary Gorbachev asserted that "the capitalist world has not abandoned the ideology and policy of hegemonism; its rulers have not yet lost the hope of taking social revenge and continue to indulge themselves with illusions of superior strength."[45] He further claimed that "the military-industrial machine of the USA remains the locomotive of militarism."[46]

When Brezhnev named the countries of the socialist community at the 26th Party Congress, he listed Bulgaria, Hungary, Vietnam, the German Democratic Republic, Cuba, Laos, Mongolia, Poland, Rumania and Czechoslovakia. The People's Republic of China was not listed. Nor was there any mention of the new Soviet High Command of the Far East that had been formed in December 1978 along China's border with the Soviet Union. Brezhnev noted that Vietnam had been "the target of a barbarian aggression by Peking in 1979. . . . This was also the case with Kampuchea, which had been devastated by the Pol Pot clique of Peking henchmen."[47] Later, Brezhnev devoted a considerable part of his Report to China:

Special mention must be made of China. . . . At present changes are under way in China's internal policy. Time will show what they actually mean. . . . But, unfortunately, there are no grounds yet to speak of any changes for the better in Peking's foreign policy. As before, it is aimed at aggravating the international situation, and is aligned with the policy of the imperialist powers. That, of course, will not bring China back to the sound road of development. Imperialists will never be friends of socialism. . . .

If Soviet-Chinese relations are still frozen, the reason for this has nothing to do with our position. . . . Our proposals for normalizing relations with China remain open and our respect for the Chinese people has not changed.[48]

In the summer of 1982, after Andropov took over the Central Committee department directing relations with China, the polemical statements all but disappeared. Envoys from the two countries met to improve relations. By 1986 at the 27th Party Congress, Gorbachev made specific mention of Communist China. However, he called it "socialist" China. He said: "One can say with gratification that there has been a measure of improvement in the Soviet Union's relations with its great neighbor—socialist China. The distinctions in attitudes, in particular to a number of international problems, remain."[49] The Resolution of the 27th Congress CPSU also used the term "socialist" China: "The Congress points out a certain improvement in mutual relations of the USSR with its great neighbor—socialist China, and the possibility, in spite of different approaches to a number of international problems, to develop cooperation on the basis of equality."[50]

Peace was a major theme of the 27th Party Congress. The Soviet Union sought ways to convince the world of a major change in its foreign policies, brought about by "new political thinking." Polemics against the United States decreased somewhat after the Congress, and Moscow began to seek NATO agreement on arms control measures.

Question 2: What Character Might the War Take Which the Country and Its Armed Forces Might Have to Wage?

The military-technical side of doctrine has the task of "analyzing the development of military-technical means of the opposing sides and the basic features and peculiarities of strategic operations, national and combined." Those making the analysis also must consider the total armed forces of the coalitions of states engaged.[51]

Beginning in the late 1950s, as already shown, the Kremlin leadership anticipated that a war between the Warsaw Pact and NATO would start with a massive nuclear exchange. This view was modified in the latter part of the 1960s, when Soviet spokesmen began to emphasize that "units and subunits" must be prepared to fight "either with or without the use of nuclear weapons." By the late 1960s, some attention was given to the possibility of a war fought with conventional weapons only. However, should the major powers be involved, it would be difficult to prevent the use of nuclear weapons as well as conventional ones.

This viewpoint changed little in the 1980s. In his July 1981 *Kommunist* article, Ogarkov stated: "A new world war, if aggressive imperialist forces were nonetheless to succeed in unleashing it, would be a decisive clash between the two opposing social systems. It would cover all continents of the world and would be waged by coalition groupings of armed forces with the most resolute objectives, using the entire arsenal of means of armed struggle."[52] In his 1982 booklet, Ogarkov repeated the same basic thesis. "In present-day conditions" a war between the nations of imperialism and socialism would "become a decisive armed conflict between two diametrically opposed social systems—capitalism and socialism." Such a war would "pursue decisive political and strategic aims."[53]

The author of a chapter in a book edited by General Aleksey A. Yepishev, chief of the Main Political Administration, emphasized that "a new world war, if the imperialists manage to unleash it, in character will be an uncompromising struggle of two opposed social systems, an extreme means of resolving the question *kto-kovo* [who dominates whom] in the historical fight between capitalism and socialism."[54]

In 1985, Ogarkov, who had been commander in chief of the Western TVD since 1984, reaffirmed what had already been said, with few modifications, since the late 1950s: "Soviet military doctrine presumes that a contemporary world war, if the imperialists nevertheless unleash it, will take on an unprecedented spatial scope, enveloping all continents and oceans and inevitably will draw into its orbit the majority of countries of the world. It will assume an unprecedentedly destructive character."[55]

That same year, Gareyev repeated Ogarkov's statement almost word for word, adding that "the practically unlimited reach of means of delivery of nuclear weapons, allowing the delivery of destruction in a short time to any grouping of the enemy's armed forces, has changed the idea of the character of war."[56] This "change" in the character of war was not new. As shown in previous chapters, such a change was asserted after the first successful test of a Soviet ICBM in 1957.

General M. M. Kir'yan in a 1985 work referred to the *Soviet Military Encyclopedia* to give his position on the character of a possible future war. Should such a war occur, he said, "the presence of a great arsenal of nuclear weapons at the disposal of the opposing coalitions will give a basis to propose that under certain conditions it might be used either at the very beginning or during the course of the war."[57] Otherwise, his view of the character of a future war was the same as that of other spokesmen.

While the question of the character of a future war is a matter of doctrine, according to official Soviet statements, at times it is expressed in terms of strategy. A 1986 book confirmed what other Soviet spokesmen had stated earlier:

> In determining the possible character and course of a future war, the theory of military strategy proceeds from the fact that a future war, if the imperialists unleash it, will be a decisive clash of two opposed world socio-political systems. Most likely it will be a coalition war. The existence of a great arsenal of

nuclear weapons at the disposal of the opposing coalitions provides the basis
to assume that they might be used by the aggressor for achieving strategic
goals both at the beginning and during the course of a war.[58]

There is no set way in which a war might begin. Ogarkov wrote that
the need to keep the Soviet Armed Forces "in a high state of combat
readiness, ensuring their timely deployment to repulse a surprise enemy
attack is the most important position of the military-technical content of
Soviet military doctrine." This is the result of rapid development of nuclear
weapons "and their possible surprise use by the enemy."[59] In a 1982 book
edited by Kir'yan at the Institute of Military History, the same views were
expressed: "The presence of the nuclear weapon will allow the aggressor
to use it to achieve his strategic goals from the very beginning of the war,
in connection with which, as never before, the danger of a surprise unleashing
of war is increased."[60]

A future war also "might be unleashed both by conventional and also
by nuclear weapons." If a war starts with conventional weapons only, at a
certain stage it might escalate to nuclear war.[61] This escalation could result
simply from widening military actions.[62] Ogarkov gave another condition:
"In scale, war unleashed by imperialism might be *world*—with the participation of the majority or a significant part of the countries of the world
or *local*—limited participation of two or several states. Here it is not excluded
that a war that began as local might escalate to a world war, as was the
case in the Second World War, a war with the use of conventional weapons—
to a war with the use of nuclear weapons.[63] (Emphasis in original.)

The duration of a future war would be determined in large measure by
how well the nation's economy, Armed Forces, and population are prepared.
Should a war begin with massive nuclear strikes by both sides, it might
be "comparatively short." However, because of the tremendous resources
that the two coalitions—capitalism and communism—might possess, "it is
not excluded that it might be protracted."[64]

Since the early 1960s, as well as in the 1970s, Soviet doctrine has
maintained that preparations must be made for the possibility of a protracted
war. This tenet remained part of doctrine in the 1980s. The outcome of
war more than ever before "depends on the quantity and effectiveness of
force applied in the very beginning of war," but "it is difficult to count on
war between major coalitions, with their enormous potential possibilities,
being short. Therefore it is necessary to be prepared for a long, strenuous
and fierce armed struggle."[65] This essentially was the same view expressed
in all three editions of Sokolovskiy's *Military Strategy.*

There is always uncertainty in wartime, and the Soviet leadership plans
for all contingencies. While a surprise nuclear strike might bring a quick
end to the war, many factors could cause the war to become protracted.
That possibility was addressed thus:

> The existence of nuclear weapons and powerful groupings of armed forces,
> kept at the highest state of readiness, with surprise use of them, now as never

before would make it possible at the very beginning of a war to achieve results which might have a decisive influence on the course and even the outcome of war. From this, military science reached the conclusion that in the event of the achievement of strategic surprise by an aggressor, and the unpreparedness of the other side for timely delivery of retaliatory strikes, the war might be short. However, in resolving the given problem on a theoretical plane, there are many things which say that a future nuclear war may not be ended quickly.[66]

A quick victory would depend primarily upon a successful surprise strike that, first, would be very difficult to achieve "if an opponent has well-organized reconnaissance." And second, the other side, if its weapons are in a high state of readiness, could "carry out a launch of rockets before the enemy's rockets reach the target even in the event of a forestalling strike by an aggressor." (In U.S. terms, this would mean "launch under attack.") Taking this possibility into account, "military strategy in calculating the duration of a war proceeds from the fact that after the exchange of the first strikes of the means of nuclear attack, the war might continue."[67]

Regardless of how a war begins or how it is fought, it will be a "just" war on the part of the Soviet Union. In the 1980s, according to Marxist-Leninist teachings, as in past decades, the very nature of the Soviet state makes it impossible for Soviet leaders to act in an aggressive manner.[68] The sociopolitical character of any war waged by peoples of socialist countries is always "just." This recognition and "feeling of justness" serves as a "powerful factor mobilizing the efforts of the people of the army of socialist countries to repel the aggressor."[69]

In the mid-1980s General Colonel Gareyev attracted considerable attention in the West with his work *M. V. Frunze: Military Theoretician.* In discussing the character of contemporary warfare he wrote that in the 1960s and 1970s many Soviet writers, including Sokolovskiy, "proceeded primarily from the fact that war under all circumstances would be waged with the use of nuclear weapons, and military actions with the use of only conventional weapons was viewed as a brief episode at the beginning of war."[70]

A number of prominent Soviet military strategists in the 1980s wrote of the "disutility" of nuclear weapons.[71] Gareyev, for example, claimed that both sides have so many nuclear weapons that the mass use of such weapons could "cause catastrophic results for both sides." Therefore, "a war may be conducted with only the use of conventional weapons." At the same time, "the possibility also is not excluded of the imperialists unleashing a nuclear war."[72] Another spokesman in 1987 stated that "while remaining a military means, nuclear weapons are increasingly becoming an instrument which it would be irrational to use."[73] These statements should be viewed with caution. As earlier Soviet writings show, Soviet spokesmen ranging from the Party's General Secretaries to military theoreticians had been describing the destruction that a nuclear war would cause since the 1950s. At the same time, however, the Soviet nuclear buildup continued without end.

Nevertheless, the possibility of change should be considered. In the 1960s the slogan "revolution in military affairs" was used to impress upon the Soviet people the impact of the nuclear-rocket weapon upon warfare. In 1985 Ogarkov referred to a "revolutionary transformation in military affairs [which] continues in our time in connection with the further development and qualitative perfection of thermonuclear weapons, the rapid development of electronics and also in connection with significant qualitative development of conventional means and methods of armed combat."[74] The same thought has been expressed by other Soviet spokesmen in a somewhat different context.

These slight modifications in doctrine described by different Soviet spokesmen do not indicate any "internal debate" among the Soviet leadership on the nature of a possible future war. Indeed, all appear to be writing from the very same set of doctrinal guidelines.

Question 3: What Goals and Missions Might Be Assigned to the Armed Forces and What Armed Forces Are Necessary in Order to Fulfill the Assigned Goals?

Soviet strategists charge the Soviet Armed Forces with three missions: (1) to give a decisive repulse to any aggressor; (2) to reliably protect the socialist gains of the Soviet people; (3) and to protect the socialist gains of peoples of socialist countries.

The first and foremost mission of the Soviet Armed Forces is to have the capability of "waging an uncompromising war with imperialism, if imperialism unleashes a war, to the complete and final defeat of imperialism."[75] This mission requires "constant high combat readiness—the ability at any moment to repulse and to frustrate aggression from no matter where it comes and no matter what ways and means the enemy uses for this."[76] Such readiness is essential so that "powerful retaliatory strikes" can be delivered on the enemy. High combat readiness is required of all services and "first of all the Strategic Rocket Forces."[77]

Should the war involve nuclear weapons, the Soviet Armed Forces must be prepared and capable of accomplishing: (1) the annihilation of the aggressor's strategic nuclear forces, and (2) the destruction of the most important military-economic objectives, groupings of troops, and state and military organs of command and control. While all services of the Soviet Armed Forces would have a part in these tasks, "the Strategic Rocket Forces, nuclear submarines, and long-range aviation have the leading role." Such forces must be developed and prepared in time of peace, since "the first day of the war and even the first strategic massive nuclear strike, which can have a decisive influence on the further course of the war, is taking on special significance."[78]

The 1983 *Military Encyclopedic Dictionary* restated the mission in terms of both doctrine and strategy: "In accordance with Soviet military doctrine, which has a purely defensive character, the main task of Soviet military strategy is development of methods of repulsing an attack by an aggressor and his subsequent defeat by conducting decisive actions."[79] In 1985 Gareyev also concentrated on the importance of readiness:

> Especially great significance is being given to the problem of maintaining high combat readiness to repulse an enemy surprise attack. The development of means of attack by our probable enemies, their banking on carrying out a preemptive strike, the growing role of the time factor at the beginning of the war is making new demands for combat readiness of the Armed Forces. Therefore *one of the important tasks of military science is to seek a way to further increase the combat readiness of the Armed Forces, their ability to carry out decisive actions for defeating any aggressor in any combination of circumstances.*[80] (Emphasis in original.)

While following the new line that Soviet military doctrine has a "defensive character," Gareyev sought to clarify that it "does not exclude either high combat readiness of the Armed Forces or active *offensive actions* against the aggressor if he makes an attack on our country or on its allies."[81]

Also in 1985, Ogarkov wrote that whether the war is short or protracted, "military actions will be waged simultaneously in broad zones, distinguished by extraordinary bitterness, will bear a highly maneuverable, dynamic character and will continue to full *victory* over the enemy."[82] (Emphasis added.) He also assured his readers that the "Soviet Armed Forces, the armies of countries of the socialist community, have everything necessary to give a decisive repulse to any aggression from no matter where it comes."[83] This standard phraseology has been used since the early 1980s.

Regardless of whether the war is nuclear or conventional, "the most important component of the combat task both in the offensive and in the defensive is destruction of the enemy's means of nuclear attack." This statement, made in a 1986 Officer's Library publication, reaffirmed statements made in the 1960s. As then, there was no discussion of how the Soviets would respond if their own nuclear means were destroyed during a conventional war with NATO forces.[84]

The paramount mission, then, is to have forces capable of repulsing a surprise attack. At the same time Soviet strategists also stress the "external" mission, another name for "proletarian internationalism" or "internationalist responsibilities." As explained in a Soviet military textbook, "fraternal [Communist] parties came to the conclusion that in contemporary conditions, when imperialism is increasing efforts in the struggle against peace, the defense of the revolutionary gains of socialism has become an international obligation of Communist and workers' parties."[85] The Soviet military repression of the people of Afghanistan is described in the press as "fulfilling internationalist obligations." Soviet textbooks still refer to the "internal" role of the Soviet Armed Forces, which is "gradually dying away." This role, which the Kremlin does not like to acknowledge, is the task of keeping the Soviet people in subjection, in particular the inhabitants of Central Asia and the Baltic republics.[86]

Often the external role of the Soviet Armed Forces—a key factor in proletariat internationalism—is overlooked by scholars outside the communist bloc. In his address to the 24th Party Congress in 1971, Brezhnev described the three main revolutionary forces in today's world: socialism, the international working-class movement, and the people's national liberation movement. This notion was restated in the 1980s: "The idea of proletariat internationalism now combines the three fundamental streams of the world revolutionary process: (1) the world system of socialism (in reality, existing socialism); (2) the workers' movement in capitalist countries; and (3) the national liberation movement."

The Soviet Armed Forces are concerned with ensuring the success of the national liberation movement, as defined by the Party leadership. Stated in Marxist-Leninist terms, the mission of the Soviet Armed Forces, based on "the historical experience accumulated by the Communist Party," is the "combining of national and international tasks in defense of socialism." This experience is used by both communist and workers' parties of socialist countries, "placing this experience at the base of their own military policy." When help is needed, "socialist countries and their armies are always ready to render fraternal aid to peoples struggling for social and national liberation, against aggression from the side of imperialism. In realizing this policy, studying the military activities of the CPSU, its measures to defend the motherland and military aid to other countries take on great significance."[87] Expressed more simply, the role of the Armed Forces is "defense of the gains of socialism—this is the concern of all people building and having built socialism, this task is international in its essence."[88]

Victory in war is both the goal and mission of the Soviet Armed Forces. Defense intellectuals in the United States give considerable attention to how to get opponents to negotiate after a war has started. The purpose is "war termination." It is possible that such studies have been done in the Soviet Union. It is equally possible that they have not. In the Soviet mind, as in the earlier Russian mind, war ends with either victory or defeat. In 1812, Napoleon invaded Russia. As he advanced, Russian troops fell back, destroying everything in their wake. On reaching Moscow, Napoleon found it nearly deserted. Fires, deliberately set by the Russians, destroyed the city. Napoleon sent word to Czar Alexander to negotiate peace terms, but there was no reply. Faced with the prospect of no food and no winter quarters for his men, Napoleon began a disastrous withdrawal in which most of his army perished. Russian troops then joined allies in marching on Paris where the defeated Napoleon was forced to abdicate.

In the late 1970s Brezhnev and other Party leaders stressed that there could be no victor in a nuclear war. This concept was not new. G. M. Malenkov had said much the same thing in the 1950s. The thought was also expressed during the greater part of the 1960s, at the height of the Soviet strategic nuclear missile deployments. However, the Soviet civil defense programs that began in 1961 still continue; such preparations now include a massive deep shelter program for the Soviet leadership. Some 1,500 hardened alternate facilities exist that can house more than 175,000 key Party personnel.[89]

Therefore, victory in nuclear war is possible if adequate advance preparations are made. This position has been explained as follows:

> With the appearance of the nuclear rocket weapon and the possibility of its use by the aggressor, the unification of political, economic, and military leadership allows support of purposeful decisions of common political tasks, tying them together with strategy, the selection of the optimal scale, tempo and tenseness of operations, the number of strategic forces and weapons necessary for achieving victory, the possibility of using economic conditions and other aspects of social life in the war, etc.[90]

Victory requires a defense potential, which must be effectively mobilized before war starts. If properly done this will provide "the necessary conditions for conducting military actions and achieving victory over the enemy."[91] Another key factor is the "moral might of the country," which is based on the ability of "the state, classes and party to mobilize the moral-political strength of the masses for struggling with the enemy, to maintain them at a high level, to use them for the purposes of achieving victory.[92]

Victory cannot be achieved by military means alone. Party political work is declared to be essential, for it serves "as an active means of realizing the military policy of the Party, educating personnel in the ideas of Marxism-Leninism, mobilizing soldiers to strengthen the combat might of the troops in peace time and to achieve victory over the enemy in war."[93] Such work supports combat readiness, which is "the crown of military mastery of personnel in peace time and the key to victory in war."[94]

References to victory in war, whether conventional, nuclear, or both, are found in a wide variety of Soviet writings. The Soviets do not expect that it would be achieved easily. The nation must plan for "a long, strenuous and fierce armed struggle."[95] They anticipate military actions characterized by "extraordinary bitterness . . . and will continue to full victory over the enemy."[96] Another work stated that "in nuclear war also final victory over the aggressor can be achieved only by the joint efforts of all the services of the Armed Forces."[97]

A 1987 book for officers points out the importance of Party-political work in Soviet military doctrine. "Without the high moral potential of the state, high combat readiness of the army and navy cannot be maintained nor the achievement of victory over the aggressor."[98] Another book claimed that "victory in modern operations" is impossible without well-organized troop cooperation. Cooperation must assure the unification and coordination of all systems to achieve victory over the enemy with the least material and human loses."[99] Mission statements in the U.S. Armed Forces are given in vague terms, such as "bringing about the end of a conflict on terms favorable to the United States." The Soviets are more specific; they assert clearly that the Armed Forces must constantly "be in such a degree of combat readiness which would enable them at any moment to enter into war and conduct decisive combat actions right up to the complete defeat of the aggressor."[100]

In order to accomplish this mission the Soviet Armed Forces must have the capability to conduct warfare "with or without" the use of nuclear weapons. In the event of a general war, they must be able to bring about the complete defeat of the enemy, with no allowances for a negotiated settlement. Soviet forces also must be prepared to fight at a lower intensity, and to provide whatever support the Party leadership considers necessary for "wars of national liberation" or to fulfill its "internationalist responsibilities."

Question 4: In What Way Should Military Structuring Be Accomplished and the Army and the Country Prepared for War?

The Soviet term "military structuring" has no exact equivalent in the United States. The Soviets define it as the system of economic, sociopolitical, purely military and other measures of a state that are carried out in order to strengthen its military might. The tasks of military structuring are determined by military doctrine. Geography, alliances, and treaty obligations also influence military structuring. The most important aspect of military structuring relates to the Armed Forces; that is, determining the manner in which to organize, man, train, provision and equip them. These measures are vital for maintaining constant combat readiness. In the Soviet Armed Forces, Party and political work also play important roles.[101] Attempts to set up self-sufficient economic regions also are an aspect of military structuring.

Military structuring in the Soviet Union involves a wide range of actions undertaken at all levels. One of the purposes of the youth organization, the Pioneers, is to provide facilities where children can learn the fundamentals of civil defense and basic skills that might be useful in the event of war. The Pioneers also conduct the annual paramilitary Zarnitsa sports games, which help children master beginning military training. The Komsomol—the Communist Youth Organization for young people ages fourteen to twenty-six—promotes Party policies and prepares youth to serve their country. It sponsors the paramilitary Orlenok games for youth from ages sixteen to eighteen to prepare them for the work force or for military service. For those in service, the Komsomol serves as a rallying force to fulfill training objectives and to inspire dedication to the motherland.

Another paramilitary organization for everyone fourteen and older is DOSAAF—the Volunteer Society for Cooperation with the Army, Aviation and Fleet. It serves a variety of purposes in military structuring. DOSAAF assists with the military sports games for youth and conducts beginning military training for working youth. It cooperates in civil defense, trains people for professions with military applications (driving, flying, scuba diving, boating, shooting, ham radio operation, etc.), popularizes scientific-technical knowledge, and directs military-technical sports for the whole country. Universal military service provides active duty military training to every able-bodied male, after which they are discharged into the reserves.

In military structuring, "great significance is being given to development of ways and means of counteracting surprise." This is necessitated by the availability of the nuclear weapon, which "will allow the aggressor to use it to achieve his strategic goals from the very beginning of the war."[102] Military structuring involves planning for the "possibility of conducting combat actions both with the use of the nuclear weapon and also with the use of only conventional means of combat." Soviet spokesmen claim that a "coherent organization" has been created that allows "the solution of tasks of any scale in different conditions of circumstances."[103] These tasks include planning and preparing for the possibility of a protracted world war, either nuclear or conventional, or a combination of the two.

In the 1980s major changes were made in the organization of the Soviet forces. As Ogarkov explained, before the sixteenth century, the highest form of military action was battle, and regiments were the most important form of military organization. Subsequently, the ascendant formations went from regiment to brigade, from brigade to division, from division to army, and from army to front. In World War II the basic form of Soviet military action was the front operation, an area 200 to 300 kilometers wide and 100 to 400 kilometers deep. Before the war ended, the operation of a group of fronts developed. Now commanders of fronts might have armaments of many types—missiles, missle-carrying aircraft, and other forms of weapons whose ranges and combat capabilities much exceed the area that a front normally occupies. In addition, the maneuverability of troops has increased, and the types of missions that various formations can accomplish have changed.

Ogarkov asserted: "In connection with this, the *strategic* operation in a theater of military actions [*deystviy*] (TVD) should be considered the basic operation of contemporary war.[104] In 1985, Ogarkov had reworded his earlier declaration, omitting the word "strategic." In his second booklet, he declared: "In connection with this, as the basic operation it is now customary to consider not the front or even the operation of a group of fronts, but a more modern, perfected and larger form of it—the operation in a theater of military actions (TVD)."[105] It is not likely that the omission of the word "strategic" was accidental, but the reason for its omission is not altogether clear. The earlier version was widely publicized in the West, where it was sometimes called the "theater-strategic military operation." In 1986, in the *History of Military Art*, a book in the Officer's Library series, the authors expanded on the concept.

> Within the framework of a strategic operation in a TVD [continental theater of military actions] might be conducted: initial and subsequent operations of fronts, and in coastal areas also initial and subsequent operations of fleets, air, air defense, airborne, shipborne, combined landings and other operations and also the delivery of nuclear rocket and aviation strikes. There might also be other types of strategic operations.[106]

The *Military Encyclopedic Dictionaries,* edited by Ogarkov (1983, 1984), and the 1986 edition edited by his successor, Marshal Sergey Akhromeyev, all agree that the strategic operation in a continental or oceanic TVD is the basic form of strategic action of the nuclear age. As to what "other types of strategic operations" they might have been referring to, the definition of a strategic operation might be instructive: "To repulse enemy strikes from the air and from space, strategic operations on repulsing an aerospace attack may be conducted."[107]

The need for restructuring the major operational formation of the Soviet Armed Forces in the early 1980s resulted in the formation of newly designated TVDs. A new command, Troops of the Far East, had been established in December 1978. In a protocol listing of the topmost military leaders in 1984, the names of four senior Soviet officers, including that of Ogarkov himself, appeared immediately before the names of the commanders of military districts. One of these names was already known—the commander in chief of the Troops of the Far East: General of the Army Ivan M. Tret'yak. The other three were believed to be the commanders in chief of three new TVDs—Western, Marshal Nikolay V. Ogarkov; Southwestern, General of the Army Ivan A. Gerasimov; and Southern, General of the Army Yuriy P. Maksimov. It is speculated that a Northwestern TVD has also been formed, but no commander in chief has been identified.

Formation of the TVDs has led to other changes in military structure. In the early 1980s the total air defense capability underwent a major reorganization. The service designated as Voyska PVO Strany (literally, Troops of Air Defense of the Country) was changed to Troops of Air Defense. The troops of air defense of the Ground Forces appeared to have been transferred to the Troops of Air Defense. At the same time approximately one-half of the aircraft that had been in Voyska PVO Strany were reassigned to the Air Forces. The tactical air elements were then operationally subordinated to the military district commander, who in turn might be under the TVD commander in chief. Apparently, something went wrong in this realignment. By 1986 there were indications that the troops of air defense of the Ground Forces had been reestablished, and some of the aircraft that had been assigned to the Air Forces were returned to Troops of Air Defense. Other adjustments in the Troops of Air Defense, Ground Forces, and the Air Forces appeared to be taking place.

Along with this new structure emphasizing the TVDs, command and control of forces changed. Some Navy units may now be under the operational control of the TVD commanders. However, it does not appear that this authority includes submarines carrying ballistic missiles or certain surface craft that would operate beyond the area of the TVD commanders. Soviet military art also provides for the establishment of oceanic TVDs.

When describing the services of the Soviet Armed Forces, Soviet strategists have occasionally referred to "strategic nuclear forces" and then named only four of the five services—the Ground Forces, Troops of Air Defense, Air Forces and Navy—with no mention of the Strategic Rocket Forces. In the

1960s, Sokolovskiy and other Soviet spokesmen had referred to strategic nuclear forces consisting of the Strategic Rocket Forces, ballistic missile-carrying submarines, and long-range aircraft. This omission suggests that today, as in the past, there is a structure in the General Staff that controls the strategic nuclear forces. This control would rest with the High Command, and none of the intercontinental strategic forces would be controlled by the TVD commander. In like manner, the Troops of Air Defense, even though their elements might be based in the areas of TVD commanders in chief, would remain under central control.

This new operational organization of the Soviet Armed Forces, established in peacetime conditions, provides for a wartime structure. Stavka (Headquarters) of the Supreme High Command (VGK), under direction of the Council of Defense (the equivalent of the State Committee of Defense [GKO] in World War II), through the General Staff, would control the following:

1. Theater of war (TVs). A theater of war would consist of two or more TVDs.
2. Theaters of military action (TVDs). Commanders in chief of TVDs have operational elements consisting of Ground Forces, Air Forces, Troops of Air Defense, and some Navy units. It is possible that oceanic TVDs have already been established, or would be established in event of war.
3. Those elements of strategic nuclear forces with an intercontinental capability. These elements would include certain portions of the Strategic Rocket Forces, Air Forces, and Navy.
4. Troops of Air Defense, including antirocket and antispace defense forces but excluding those elements specifically assigned to a TVD.
5. Those fleet units operating outside a continental TVD area, and oceanic TVDs if established.

At the time of Hitler's attack on June 22, 1941, a structure suitable for conducting an all-out war was not yet established in the Soviet Union. Eight days after the attack, the State Committee of Defense (GKO) was set up to direct the total war effort and to oversee the actions of all government departments and establishments as well as the general direction of military actions. Stavka (Headquarters) of the Supreme High Command ran the purely military effort, with the General Staff as its executive agency. The equivalents of TVDs were set up in the Northwest, West, and Southwest, but were soon overrun. In the latter stages of the war, after the defeat of Germany, a TVD was established in the Far East to direct the brief Soviet participation against the Japanese. Soviet strategists have been writing about the role of TVDs since at least the early 1960s. It is possible that the current structure has been in existence since then, but that commanders in chief were not specifically designated.

Another objective of military structuring in the 1980s is to ensure that the adult population of all socialist countries master military knowledge.

The necessity for such a program had been posed by Lenin.[108] An overall guideline in military structuring, and one of the "most important positions of the *military doctrine of socialist states*, is that *military structuring be accomplished under the leadership of the Communist Party*."[109] (Emphasis in original.)

Scientific and technological advances are likely to bring about new Soviet military structuring. In the late 1950s, after it was decided that nuclear rockets would be the decisive factor in a future war, the Strategic Rocket Forces were established. It is possible that the Soviets may create a sixth service, a space force, to ensure Soviet dominance in this area.

In the early 1980s, Ogarkov, then chief of the Soviet General Staff, seemed well pleased with the military structuring in effect. "The level of development of the Soviet Union which has been achieved . . . permits the successful solution of the most technically complicated defense tasks and in a short time the creation of any kind of weapon on which the enemies of peace would like to count."[110] Even before Akhromeyev became chief of the General Staff, he also had emphasized the importance of structuring. He warned that "changes in the character of war are now taking place faster, and that means also our reaction to these changes, the demands of Soviet military art and to the structuring of the Armed Forces must be more operational."[111] He appeared confident that this goal was being achieved.

But not all was well. During the late 1980s, in the period of General Secretary Gorbachev's *glasnost*, the Soviet leadership itself began to question earlier assumptions. *Perestroika* (reorganization) became Gorbachev's slogan as he launched attempts to restructure the entire Soviet economy and many aspects of its social system. *Perestroika* also became a slogan in the Soviet Armed Forces, with emphasis on higher discipline.

Question 5: If War Breaks Out, by What Methods Should It Be Fought?

Soviet military doctrine covers all bets and deals with the uncertainties inherent in preparing for war. Soviet strategists anticipate that nuclear weapons, conventional weapons, or a combination of the two might be used in a future war. Soviet leaders have repeatedly declared that their doctrine states that they will not be the first to use nuclear weapons. However, nowhere is their concept of "frustrating" or "repulsing" an enemy surprise attack spelled out. Unless the Soviets have at present an effective antiballistic missile system, the only way of "frustrating" or "repulsing" a surprise nuclear strike would be to prevent such an attack from being launched. Prevention could be accomplished in a variety of ways, from creating an electro-magnetic pulse to disrupt communications to establishing teams of saboteurs to seize launch areas. As early as 1968, Sokolovskiy pointed out that modern surveillance satellites could detect preparations being made for launches so that the leadership would be warned of impending attack. They presumably would then take some sort of action to "frustrate" such an attack.

Soviet military strategy, following the dictates of military doctrine, is the same for all services. The Soviet General Staff has made plans for specific military actions, using either conventional or nuclear weapons. The strategy underlying the planning is that war will consist "of a complex system of interconnected strategic operations, including operations in a continental and oceanic TVD, within the framework of which front and fleet operations, air, antiair, airborne, naval landing, antilanding, and other operations might be conducted." The goal of such operations could only be met "with the combined efforts of all the services of the Armed Forces and service branches closely interacting with each other."[112]

If nuclear weapons are used, "the primary forms of strategic actions might be operations of strategic nuclear forces, strategic operations in continental and ocean TVDs and operations in repulsing an air enemy."[113] The initial period of the war "may be basic and decisive, which largely predetermines the outcome of the entire war [victory or defeat]." If the war continues, "the timely delivery of nuclear and fire strikes and the skillful use by the troops of their results will take on decisive significance." When mass strikes are being delivered, troops must be dispersed in order to prevent easy nuclear targeting by the enemy.[114] Shelters, protective clothing and other means of safeguarding personnel from nuclear, chemical, and bacteriological weapons must be provided.

Soviet military doctrine in the 1980s continued to consider that war might be waged with conventional means only. However, even in this case, commanders must be "nuclear scared," at all times prepared for the possibility of a surprise nuclear strike.[115]

At the strategic level, operations in a continental (oceanic) theater (TVD) are now considered by Soviet military spokesmen to be the basic form of strategic action. The efforts of several fronts (fleets, army groups), strategic nuclear forces, aviation formations and troops of air defense are needed for the conduct of a strategic operation. "During such an operation two or more front operations might be conducted successively by each front (fleet) with small pauses or even without them."[116] Strategic operations might be conducted for defensive purposes and for repulsing enemy strikes from the air and from space.[117]

The strategic operation, as a concept, began to take shape in World War I. It was not until World War II, however, that it was fully developed.[118] Strategic operations can be either offensive or defensive. Soviet sources list fifty-one strategic operations that took place between 1941 and 1945 in their Great Patriotic War.[119] There are several characteristics that make an operation a strategic one:

1. Performance of an important strategic mission and achievement of a major military-political goal;
2. In the majority of operations, great spatial scope of combat actions and the participation of significant numbers of troops and equipment;

3. Planning by the Stavka of the Supreme High Command and coordination of actions of fronts, fleets, and other services of the Armed Forces by their representatives.[120]

In 1985, General M. A. Gareyev described strategic operations as "increasing in size with different services of the Armed Forces participating in them." They would have "high dynamism and maneuverability of combat actions." He noted that there would be an "absence of solid fronts," and "acute and rapid changes of circumstances." There would be "a fierce struggle to seize and hold the initiative."[121] In 1986, in the *History of Military Art* edited by General P. A. Zhilin, similar themes emerged. The goal of operations would be "tied with assuring the defense of and holding of important regions of one's own territory, and, if necessary, with the destruction of actual enemy strategic groupings."[122]

No First Use

Brezhnev had made the Soviet Union's proposal to the European Security Conference on no first use of the nuclear weapon a theme of his Peace Program for the 80s unveiled at the 26th Party Congress in 1981. "We will not use nuclear weapons against non-nuclear countries that do not permit the deployment of such weapons on their territory," declared Brezhnev, repeating an old theme of the 1970s. "We would like that the participants in the European Conference should undertake not to use either nuclear or conventional arms against each other first."[123]

On June 15, 1982, Brezhnev sent a declaration to the Second Special Assembly of the United Nations on Disarmament. Andrey A. Gromyko read it to the delegates: "The Union of Soviet Socialist Republics unilaterally assumes the obligation not to be the first to use nuclear weapons."[124] When Brezhnev died in November, Andropov quickly made it clear that he agreed with Brezhnev's policy. He made this statement shortly after becoming General Secretary:

> Our position is clear: A nuclear war—whether big or small, whether limited or total—must not be allowed to break out. . . . That is why the unilateral commitment of the Soviet Union not to use nuclear weapons first was received with approval and hope all over the world.
>
> It is said that the West cannot make such a commitment because, allegedly, the Warsaw Treaty has an advantage in conventional armaments. To begin with, this is untrue, and the fact and figures bear witness to it. Furthermore, as everybody knows, we are in favor of limiting such armanents as well, and of searching for sensible, mutually acceptable solutions to this end. We are also prepared to agree that the sides should renounce first use of conventional, as well as nuclear arms.[125]

In 1985, Gareyev added a few caveats to the no-first-use theme when he wrote: "The Soviet Union is against the use of weapons of mass destruction;

it will not use them first. But any possible aggressor must clearly understand that in the event of a nuclear rocket attack on the Soviet Union or other countries of the socialist community, it will receive a crushing retaliatory strike."[126]

Ogarkov repeated earlier declarations in his 1985 booklet. He wrote that "at the base of Soviet military doctrine lies the provision that *the Soviet Union will not use nuclear weapons first.* This obligation is taken by them unilaterally and declared to the whole world."[127] (Emphasis in original.)

To many in the West, the no-first-use pledge made by Soviet leaders was not convincing. "Second use" remained with only a fine line separating a first strike and preemption. Earlier Brezhnev had admitted that such weapons would be used first in a case of extreme emergency. It had never been the intent of NATO nations to do otherwise.

In the early 1960s, when Soviet strategists began writing about military doctrine, the NATO nations paid little attention to it. A review of Western journals of that period concerned with national security issues and foreign policies reveals that Soviet military doctrine was scarcely noticed. In the mid-1970s a number of Soviet military books were translated and published in the United States. From then on, greater attention was paid to Soviet military publications. Once Soviet security agencies recognized that these writings were being read abroad, the inevitable happened. Soviet censors became more stringent, and passages were rewritten so as not to alarm foreign readers. Doctrine now took on a purely "defensive" character.

The shifts and modifications in Soviet military doctrine, anticipated throughout the greater part of the 1980s by a number of scholars both in the United States and Britain, have not yet materialized. When the answers to basic questions of Soviet military doctrine are examined in detail, it becomes clear that, in the 1980s, doctrine remains much the same as in earlier periods. As new weapons are developed, however, the military-technical side of doctrine will no doubt change. It is even possible that significant changes have already taken place, but have not yet been announced.

Notes

1. "Declaration of Warsaw-Treaty Member Countries," *Pravda,* TASS, May 16, 1980, p. 1.

2. Ibid., p. 2.

3. Anatoliy Gromyko and Vladimir Lomeyko, in their book *Novoye Myshleniye v Yadernyy Vek* [New Thinking in the Nuclear Age] (Moscow: International Relations Publishing House, 1984), attributed the idea of "new thinking" to Albert Einstein: "A new way of thinking for humanity is necessary in order for man to survive and develop further. Today the atomic bomb has changed the world to its foundations; we know this and people find themselves in a new situation to which their thinking must correspond," p. 4. This book was written a year before Gorbachev became General Secretary.

4. L. I. Brezhnev, *XXVI S"yezd Kommunisticheskoy Partii Sovetskogo Soyuza* [26th Congress of the CPSU], stenographic notes (Moscow: Politizdat, 1981), pp. 20, 33.

5. Ibid., p. 35.

6. N. V. Ogarkov, "On Guard Over Peaceful Labor," *Kommunist* 10 (July 1981), p. 85. In his book, the sentence quoted from the speech was made by Brezhnev in June 1981, leaving the reader to wonder how it got into Ogarkov's article almost before it was spoken by Brezhnev. The expression "strategic doctrine" as used by Brezhnev is out of place as it does not mean the same thing as "military doctrine."

7. When Ogarkov surfaced sometime later, Western reporters who had publicized Ogarkov's "fall" were forced to invent his "rehabilitation." One major news magazine erroneously declared he was "some sort of political commissar." See: *Time*, January 14, 1985.

8. N. V. Ogarkov, "Nemerknushchaya Slava Sovetskogo Oruzhiya" [Unfading Glory of Soviet Arms], *Kommunist Vooruzhennykh Sil* [Communist of the Armed Forces] 21 (November 1984), pp. 16–22.

9. N. V. Ogarkov, *Istoriya Uchit Bditel'nosti* ([History Teaches Vigilance] (Moscow: Voyenizdat, 1985), p. 60.

10. Ibid., p. 72.

11. M. S. Gorbachev, "Report of the Central Committee to the 27th Congress CPSU," *Pravda*, February 26, 1986, p. 6.

12. M. S. Gorbachev, *XXVII S"yezd Kommunisticheskoy Partii Sovetskogo Soyuza* [27th Congress of the CPSU] (Moscow: Politizdat, 1986), p. 89. For English translation see *Political Report of the CPSU Central Committee to the 27th Party Congress* (Moscow: Novosti, 1986), p. 85.

13. "Programma KPSS, Novaya Redaktsiya," in *XXVII S"yezd*, p. 570. For English translation, see *The Programme of the Communist Party of the Soviet Union*, a New Edition, approved March 1, 1986 (Moscow: Novosti, 1986), p. 23.

14. Ibid., p. 595.

15. Ibid., p. 53.

16. Ibid., p. 98.

17. Ibid., p. 544. Also see *Materialy XXVII S"yezd KPSS* [Materials of the 27th Congress of the CPSU] (Moscow: Politizdat, 1986), p. 111.

18. S. L. Sokolov, "On Guard Over the Peace and Security of the Motherland," *Pravda*, February 23, 1987, p. 2.

19. D. A. Volkogonov, "Imperatives of the Nuclear Age," *Krasnaya Zvezda* [Red Star], May 22, 1987, p. 2.

20. "On the Military Doctrine of the Warsaw Pact Member States," *Pravda*, May 30, 1987, p. 1.

21. M. A. Gareyev,.Moscow TASS in English, June 22, 1987; FBIS (SOV), June 23, 1987, p. AA7.

22. Gennadiy Gerasimov, "International Panorama," Moscow Television Service, May 24, 1987. FBIS (SOV), June 25, 1987.

23. TASS report, "At the USSR Foreign Ministry Press Center," *Krasnaya Zvezda*, June 24, 1987, p. 3; FBIS, June 25, 1987, p. aa-11. Statement by V. F. Petrovskiy, USSR deputy foreign minister.

24. A. S. Milovidov, editor, *Voyenno-Teoreticheskoye Naslediye V. I. Lenina i Problemy Sovremennoy Voyny* [Military-Theoretical Heritage of V. I. Lenin and Problems of Contemporary War] (Moscow: Voyenizdat, 1987), p. 251.

25. Dmitriy T. Yazov, in an address to the graduates of military academies in the Kremlin, quoted in *Krasnaya Zvezda*, July 29, 1987, pp. 1, 3.

26. R. Bogdanov, "Top Priority," Moscow Radio in English, June 26, 1987; FBIS (SOV), June 29, 1987, p. cc-2.

27. Lev Semeyko, "Instead of Mountains of Arms . . . On the Principle of Reasonable Sufficiency," *Izvestia*, August 13, 1987, p. 4.

28. V. V. Serebryannikov, "The Relationship of Political and Military Means in the Defense of Socialism," *Kommunist Vooreuzhennykh Sil* 18 (September 1987), pp. 9–16.

29. A. A. Grechko, *Vooruzhennyye Sily Sovetskogo Gosudarstva* [Armed Forces of the Soviet State] (Moscow: Voyenizdat, 1974), p. 315.

30. Ogarkov, *Istorya Uchit Bditel'nosti*, p. 57.

31. N. V. Ogarkov, *Vsegda v Gotovnosti k Zashchite Otechestva* [Always in Readiness to Defend the Fatherland] (Moscow: Voyenizdat, 1982), pp. 5–17.

32. Ibid., p. 13.

33. M. V. Zakharov, *50 Let Vooruzhennykh Sil SSSR* [50 Years of the Armed Forces USSR] (Moscow: Voyenizdat, 1968), p. 482.

34. V. D. Sokolovskiy, editor, *Voyennaya Strategiya* [Military Strategy] (Moscow: Voyenizdat, 1968), p. 230. For English translation see H. F. Scott, *Soviet Military Strategy* (New York: Crane, Russak & Company, Inc., 1984), p. 190.

35. Ibid., p. 232; Scott, *Soviet Military Strategy*, p. 192.

36. N. A. Lomov, editor, *Nauchno-Tekhnicheskiy Progress i Revolyutsiya v Voyennom Dele* [Scientific-Technical Progress and the Revolution in Military Affairs] (Moscow: Voyenizdat, 1973), p. 33.

37. Ibid., p. 264.

38. S. A. Tyushkevich, *Sovetskiye Vooruzhennyye Sily* [Soviet Armed Forces] (Moscow: Voyenizdat, 1978), p. 382.

39. A. S. Zheltov, editor, *V. I. Lenin i Sovetskiye Vooruzhennyye Sily* [V. I. Lenin and the Soviet Armed Forces] (Moscow: Voyenizdat, 1980), p. 314.

40. N. N. Azovtsev, *V. I. Lenin i Sovetskaya Voyennaya Nauka* [V. I. Lenin and Soviet Military Science] (Moscow: Nauka, 1981), p. 288.

41. Ogarkov, *Vsegda v Gotovnosti*, p. 25.

42. Ibid., p. 15.

43. Yu. V. Andropov, *Sixtieth Anniversary of the USSR*, December 21, 1982 (Moscow: Novosti, 1983), p. 26.

44. K. U. Chernenko, *Safeguard Peace and Ensure the People's Well-Being*, March 2, 1984 (Moscow: Novosti, 1984), pp. 14–15.

45. Gorbachev, *XXVII S"yezd*, p. 24.

46. Ibid., p. 82.

47. Brezhnev, *XXVI S"yezd*, p. 25.

48. Ibid., pp. 27–28.

49. Gorbachev, *XXVII S"yezd*, p. 95.

50. *Materialy XXVII*, p. 112.

51. Ogarkov, *Istoriya Uchit Bditel'nosti*, p. 77.

52. Ogarkov, "On Guard," *Kommunist* 10 (July 1981), p. 85.

53. Ogarkov, *Vsegda v Gotovnosti*, p. 46.

54. A. A. Yepishev, *KPSS i Voyennoye Stroitel'stvo* [CPSU and Military Development] (Moscow: Voyenizdat, 1982), p. 83.

55. Ogarkov, *Istoriya Uchit Bditel'nosti*, p. 77.

56. M. A. Gareyev, *M. V. Frunze—Voyennyy Teoretik* [M. V. Frunze—Military Theoretician] (Moscow: Voyenizdat, 1985), p. 237.

57. M. M. Kir'yan, *Problemy Voyennoy Teorii v Sovetskikh Nauchno-Spravochnykh Izdaniyakh* [Problems of Military Theory in Soviet Scientific Reference Publications] (Moscow: Nauka, 1985), p. 113.

58. P. A. Zhilin, editor, *Istoriya Voyennogo Iskusstva* [History of Military Art] (Moscow: Voyenizdat, 1986), p. 407.

59. Ogarkov, *Vsegda v Gotovnosti*, pp. 57–58.

60. M. M. Kir'yan, editor, *Voyenno-Tekhnicheskiy Progress i Vooruzhennyye Sily SSSR* [Military-Technical Progress and the Armed Forces USSR] (Moscow: Voyenizdat, 1982), p. 312.

61. Ibid., p. 312.

62. Gareyev, *M. V. Frunze*, p. 237.

63. Ogarkov, *Istoriya Uchit Bditel'nosti*, p. 13.

64. Kir'yan, *Voyenno-Tekhnicheskiy Progress*, p. 314.

65. Gareyev, *M. V. Frunze*, p. 241.

66. Zhilin, *Istoriya Voyennogo Iskusstva*, pp. 407–408.

67. Ibid.

68. Ogarkov, *Istoriya Uchit Bditel'nosti*, p. 82.

69. N. D. Tabunov and V. A. Bokarev, editors, *Marksistsko-Leninskaya Filosofiya i Metodologicheskiye Problemy Voyennoy Teorii i Praktiki* [Marxist-Leninist Philosophy and Methodological Problems of Military Theory and Practice] (Moscow: Voyenizdat, 1982), p. 248.

70. Gareyev, *M. V. Frunze*, p. 240.

71. See, for example, Ogarkov, *Istoriya Uchit Bditel'nosti*, p. 89.

72. Gareyev, *M. V. Frunze*, p. 240.

73. D. A. Volkogonov, "Imperatives of the Nuclear Age," *Krasnaya Zvezda*, May 22, 1987, p. 3.

74. Ogarkov, *Istoriya Uchit Bditel'nosti*, p. 41.

75. Yepishev, *KPSS i Voyennoye Stroitel'stvo*, p. 41.

76. Ibid., p. 127.

77. Kir'yan, *Voyenno-Tekhnicheskiy Progress*, pp. 313–314.

78. Ibid., p. 314.

79. N. V. Ogarkov, editor, *Voyennyy Entsiklopedicheskiy Slovar'* [Military Encyclopedic Dictionary], 1st ed. (Moscow: Voyenizdat, 1983), p. 712.

80. Gareyev, *M. V. Frunze*, pp. 242–243.

81. Ibid., p. 441.

82. Ogarkov, *Istoriya Uchit Bditel'nosti*, p. 77.

83. Ibid., p. 81.

84. Zhilin, *Istoriya Voyennogo Iskusstva*, p. 414.

85. Ibid., p. 95.

86. Yepishev, *KPSS i Voyennoye Stroitel'stvo*, p. 40.

87. Ibid., pp. 254–255.

88. Tabunov and Bokarev, *Marksistsko-Leninskaya Filosofiya*, p. 249.

89. *Soviet Military Power* (Washington, D.C.: US GPO, 1987), p. 52.

90. Yepishev, *KPSS i Voyennoye Stroitel'stvo*, p. 90.

91. Ibid., p. 49.

92. Ibid., p. 81.

93. Ibid., p. 164.

94. Tabunov and Bokarev, *Marksistko-Leninskaya Filosofiya*, p. 292, quoting D. F. Ustinov.

95. Gareyev, *M. V. Frunze*, p. 241.

96. Ogarkov, *Istoriya Uchit Bditel'nosti*, p. 77.

97. Yepishev, *KPSS i Voyennoye Stroitel'stvo*, p. 114.

98. Ye. V. Zhukov, *XXVII S"yezd KPSS o Sovetskoy Voyennoy Doktrine* [27th Congress CPSU and Soviet Military Doctrine] (Moscow: Voyenizdat, 1987), p. 14. The booklet is designated for the Marxist-Leninist training of Soviet officers.

99. Milovidov, *Voyenno-Teoreticheskoye Naslediye*, p. 255.

100. Zhilin, *Istoriya Voyennogo Iskusstva*, pp. 407–408.

101. Ogarkov, *Voyennyy Entsiklopedicheskiy Slovar'*, pp. 141, 715.

102. Kir'yan, *Voyenno-Tekhnicheskiy Progress*, p. 313.

103. Ibid., p. 326.

104. Ogarkov, *Vsegda v Gotovnosti*, p. 34.

105. Ogarkov, *Istoriya Uchit Bditel'nosti*, p. 47.

106. Zhilin, *Istoriya Voyennogo Iskusstva*, p. 408.

107. S. F. Akhromeyev, editor, *Voyennyy Entsiklopedicheskiy Slovar'* [Military Encyclopedia Dictionary], 2nd ed. (Moscow: Voyenizdat, 1986), p. 710.

108. Tabunov and Bokarev, *Marksistsko-Leninskaya Filosofiya*, p. 248.

109. Ibid., p. 249.

110. Ogarkov, *Vsegda v Gotovnosti*, p. 57.

111. S. F. Akhromeyev, "Role of the Soviet Union and Its Armed Forces in Achieving the Basic Turning Point in the Second World War and Its International Significance," *Voyenno-Istoricheskiy Zhurnal* [Military History Journal] 2 (February 1984), p. 24.

112. Ogarkov, *Voyennyy Entsiklopedicheskiy Slovar'*, p. 710.

113. Kir'yan, *Voyenno-Tekhnicheskiy Progress*, pp. 314–315.

114. Gareyev, *M. V. Frunze*, pp. 237–238.

115. Zhilin, *Istoriya Voyennogo Iskusstva*, p. 410.

116. Ogarkov, *Vsegda v Gotovnosti*, p. 34, and *Istoriya Uchit Bditel'nosti*, p. 47.

117. Ogarkov, *Voyennyy Entsiklopedicheskiy Slovar'*, p. 710.

118. M. I. Cherednichenko, "Strategicheskaya Operatsiya," *Sovetskaya Voyennaya Entsiklopediya* [Soviet Military Encyclopedia] (Moscow: Voyenizdat, 1976–1980), vol. 7, p. 551.

119. "Results of the Discussion on Strategic Operations in the Great Patriotic War, 1941–1945," *Voyenno-Istoricheskiy Zhurnal* 10 (October 1987), pp. 8–24. This discussion began in 1985 and ended with this issue. The article contains eleven pages of charts about each of the fifty-one strategic offensive and defensive operations of the war.

120. V. V. Gurkin and M. I. Golovnin, "On the Question of Strategic Operations of the Great Patriotic War, 1941–1945," *Voyenno-Istoricheskiy Zhurnal* 10 (October 1985), p. 10.

121. Gareyev, *M. V. Frunze*, p. 237.

122. Zhilin, *Istoriya Voyennogo Iskusstva*, p. 408.

123. Brezhnev, *XXVI S"yezd*, p. 45.

124. L. I. Brezhnev, *Leninskim Kursom* [By Lenin's Course] (Moscow: Politizdat, 1982), p. 538.

125. Andropov, *Sixtieth Anniversary*, pp. 26–27.

126. Gareyev, *M. V. Frunze*, p. 237.

127. Ogarkov, *Istoriya Uchit Bditel'nosti*, p. 77.

5
Laws of War and
Laws of Armed Combat

Basic Premises of the Laws of War

Since the mid-1970s, there has been a heightened attention and discussion of laws of war and laws of armed combat in the Soviet Union. What previously had been referred to as "factors" or "principles" were now, in some cases, stated as "laws." One author even suggested that there were "permanently operating factors."[1] There appeared to be a move to codify certain of these laws; that is, to take them beyond the stage of discussion among strategists and place them in a category somewhat similar to that of military doctrine.

The importance of these laws of war was explained by a leading Soviet political-military theoretician, General Major S. A. Tyushkevich, Doctor of Philosophical Sciences, in a textbook designed for Marxist-Leninist officer training:

> The known laws of war are taken into account by the military policy of the Party, they are expressed in the military doctrine of a socialist state, serve as the basis of military science, and lie at the base of the principles of waging war, the activities of the command staff and of all personnel of a socialist army. Without such a foundation, military work would be limited to empty hopes of favorable coincidences of circumstances, hoping on chance.[2]

Soviet laws of war, and the laws of armed combat and principles of military art derived from such laws, form the basis for many aspects of Soviet foreign policy and the expansion of Soviet military power. They also provide insights into how Soviet military operations would be conducted in the event of a future war. The laws of war are based on certain premises:

1. According to Soviet sources, laws of war exist, but not all of them have been uncovered or correctly interpreted. One theorist may develop laws and principles of war that differ from those of others. However, all claim that the scientific methodology revealed by Marxist-Leninist teachings on war and army makes it possible for Soviet military leaders to uncover these laws in a manner impossible for bourgeois military theorists.

2. The laws are objective, and apply equally to all armed forces of the belligerent states. In other words, laws of war have the same impact upon NATO or Chinese forces as upon those of the Warsaw Pact. By knowing and utilizing these objective laws, Soviet commanders claim, they will be able to achieve victory in a future war.

3. At least one Soviet theorist asserts that "armed conflict is subordinate to statistical laws."[3] Statistical laws can be determined by generalizing the experiences of combat actions in previous wars at various levels of engagement. Statistical data derived from such laws can be entered into computers in a form that can assist commanders in making decisions on the battlefield. This third point should be of particular importance to Western military planners, war college faculty members, and others who are concerned with war gaming. Too often in such games, Soviet military forces are portrayed simply as mirror images of NATO military forces. Identification of stated Soviet laws of war and laws of armed combat should make it possible to provide inputs for such games that would, to some extent, reflect Soviet military concepts. It might even be possible for data derived from such Soviet laws at strategic, operational, and tactical levels to be entered into computers and, theoretically, the decisions based on this data could represent the most likely decisions of a Soviet field commander.

4. The laws of war, in the Soviet sense, are intermixed with the "correlation of forces in the world arena." Soviet strategists, whether in civilian clothing or in uniform, consider the economy, political structure, military forces, geographic location, and other elements of national strength when determining the correlation of forces between nations or groups of nations and in developing the laws of war. In both cases, military power is but one component. Political, economic, and scientific-technical capabilities, as well as the moral factor or national will, may be of equal or greater importance.

Neither laws of war nor laws of armed combat stemming from the laws of war are subjects taught in U.S. war colleges. "Principles of war," similar to those taught in Soviet military educational institutions, have always been studied in the United States. There was a time in the 1960s, during Robert S. McNamara's tenure as U.S. Secretary of Defense, when even these principles of war received little attention from the Pentagon. Two of McNamara's new, best-known "defense intellectuals" wrote, "What is commonly called 'military science' is not scientific in the same sense as law or medicine or engineering. It encompasses no agreed-upon body of knowledge, no prescribed curriculum, no universally recognized principles that one must master to qualify as a military professional. The so-called 'principles of war' are really a set of platitudes that can be twisted to suit almost any situation."[4]

The attitude expressed in this statement suggests why so little attention had been paid in the United States to the concept of laws of war, laws of armed combat, and principles of military art. It also may suggest why Western forecasts of Soviet actions so often prove to be incorrect. These laws of war are based on an ideology that seems illogical to many in the West. Western leaders prefer to believe that actions of the Soviet leadership are based on a logic that differs little from our own. Over the years Soviet military writings, at all levels, show otherwise.

Marxism-Leninism: The Basis of the Laws of War

Perceptions of warfare derived from the Soviet laws of war differ sharply from military concepts found in NATO nations. The laws are based on a Marxist-Leninist interpretation of the world. One who uses this logic has a different world outlook (*mirovozzreniye*), a different vision of the future of the world and how to get there. But first, before examining the laws of war in detail, a brief explanation of their place in Marxist-Leninist teaching will be given.

Many aspects of Marxism-Leninism may appear at first to be reasonable. Much of the initial formulation of this ideology, borrowed from Hegel and other philosophers, used natural laws and realistic examples. But these laws were then dogmatically applied to social phenomena. There are those in the West who would argue that the Soviets no longer take their ideology seriously and hence that Marxism-Leninism is of little consequence. The validity of this argument can neither be proven nor disproven.

Whatever the facts may be, Soviet officers are given a steady diet of Marxist-Leninist philosophy throughout their careers. Their military doctrine, strategy, force development, organization, and combat roles are explained in Marxist-Leninist terms. Soviet law requires the establishment of a department of scientific communism, headed by a general or an admiral, in each military academy.

According to Marxist-Leninist philosophy, historical materialism is the science of general laws concerning the development of society. Marx and Engels extended dialectical materialism to the study of society and its history. In doing so they evolved a theory that they claimed was "scientific" that dealt with "general laws of social development."[5] Simply put, they claimed that mankind has passed through four social formations: primitive-communal, slave, feudal, and capitalist. Now, according to this teaching, man is living in the era of transition to the next stage, which is communism, the first phase of which is called socialism. Marxism-Leninism teaches that it is inevitable that the capitalist stage will be replaced by the socialist stage.

Although the "victory of socialism" is predetermined by these laws, it is wrong to conclude, according to Marxism-Leninism, that there is no need to fight against capitalism. Neither will the "laws of history" by themselves bring about the replacement of capitalism with socialism. Such laws, without people, do not make history.

Laws of Dialectical Materialism

Marxism-Leninism regards social laws dialectically,[6] based on the three laws of dialectical materialism, as follows:[7]

The Law of the Unity and Struggle of Opposites

Opposites are two sides of one phenomenon. They constantly contradict each other, that is, they "struggle." The "struggle of opposites" is the main source of development of matter and consciousness. Applying, or rather, misapplying this "law" to society, Marxists see all of history as a struggle between "classes."[8]

This law is of particular significance to Soviet military thought. As a previous editor of *Military Thought* stated, "The unity and struggle of opposites is inherent in all processes connected with the conduct of armed conflict, with the development of its methods and forms."[9] In Ogarkov's view: "Like the other laws and categories of dialectics, this law is universal in nature and fully applicable to military activity." The law results, for example, in constant conflict between ways and means of attack and defense. In World War I automatic weapons and improved artillery gave an advantage to the defense. The situation was different in World War II, when tanks, aircraft, aircraft carriers, submarines and other weapons systems gave offense the upper hand.[10]

Tanks caused the development of antitank weapons; aircraft forced production of antiaircraft guns and missiles; submarines spurred the invention of antisubmarine weapons, and so on. According to this law of dialectics, new means of defense will always be developed to balance or overcome the offense, which in turn will cause the development of different offensive weapons. "The appearance of new means of attack always unavoidably led to the creation of corresponding countermeasures, and in the end to the development of new methods of conducting battle, engagements, operations, and war as a whole."[11] An active change from one generation of weapons to another is taking place, making it necessary for military affairs to be examined "on the basis of thorough understanding of the basic law, the core of dialectics—the law of unity and the struggle of opposites."

The Law of the Passage of Quantitative into Qualitative Changes

To explain the law of the passage of quantitative into qualitative changes, Soviet textbooks use a simple example. If water is gradually heated, at a certain stage it takes on a new quality: It turns to steam. Conversely, water remains water until a certain reduction in temperature turns it to ice. It is still H_2O but in a new, solid form, with different properties.[12] Marxists take this sensible natural law and try to make it a law of social development as well. The replacement of capitalism by socialism entails a substantial change in various quantities: an increase in the volume of industrial and agricultural output, more rapid rates of economic and cultural development, growth of the national income, wages, and so on.[13]

There is unity of continuity and discontinuity (leap) in this development. For example, the heat may be raised under the water one degree at a time. The change may be a very slow stage of quantitative accumulation. But at 212 degrees Fahrenheit, a sudden, radical, qualitative change takes place—

a leap is taken. Similarly, prolonged, painstaking work is carried out by a Marxist party in accumulating its forces, organizing the people, and gradually preparing them for the leap into revolutionary action. Marxism-Leninism teaches: "Since a leap or revolution is decisive in the development of society, the transition from capitalism to socialism can be effected neither through slow, quantitative changes nor through reforms, but only through a qualitative transformation of the capitalist system, through a socialist revolution."[14]

The replacement of capitalism by socialism supposedly will come about through a prolonged accumulation of "forces," "substantial changes" in the volume of industrial and agricultural output, and more rapid rates of economic and cultural development. Obviously, the best ways to measure these changes involve comparing economic indicators of the Soviet Union and the United States, the "world socialist system" and the "world capitalist system." Industrial and agricultural output can be compared, for example. Culture can be measured by the numbers of books and periodicals published, the number of college graduates, scientists, persons with doctoral degrees, theaters, and the like. Life expectancy is another indicator of quality of life in a country. All these factors will influence "the course and outcome" of future war.

This law takes into account that new weapons and military equipment bring about transformations in the methods of conducting military operations. As long as new weapons are used in limited numbers, they generally are merely adapted to the existing methods of armed conflict. But at some point, if increased numbers of weapons are introduced, a sudden, qualitative change will take place. For example, in the Boer war (1899–1902) British forces possessed forty machine guns. These guns did not bring about any basic change in battle formations or in combat. However, by World War I, machine guns had been improved and were used in considerable numbers. Their presence was a major factor in bringing about a qualitative change in the conduct of war as a whole.[15]

Tanks and aircraft were used in World War I, but because of their small numbers and undeveloped form they did not cause any major change in the conduct of military operations. When improved versions were introduced in quantity by both sides in World War II, qualitative changes in the method of combat took place both in the air and on the ground.[16]

The Law of the Negation of the Negation

This third law reveals the general direction and tendency of development of the material world. The passing away of the old that has outlived its age and the rise of the new and advanced proceeds constantly in every sphere of reality. The egg ceases to be an egg when the chick is hatched, to put it simply. Marxists, borrowing from Hegel, call this replacement *negation*. The history of society consists of a chain of negations of the old social order by the new: Feudalism replaced (negated) slavery; capitalism replaced (negated) feudalism; socialism will replace (negate) capitalism, say the Marxists.[17]

The old is always being replaced (negated) by something new, which is then replaced (negated) by something even newer. Thus the negation of the negation. A single egg becomes a chicken. The chicken will then produce not just one egg but many, and, if bred right, better eggs. Although a single egg will resemble the old egg, it will be different: "And so, development occurs through the negation of the old by the new, the lower by the higher. Since the new, negating the old, retains and develops the positive features of the old, development acquires a progressive character. At the same time development proceeds along a spiral, with repetition at higher stages of certain sides and features of the lower stages.[18]

With respect to military affairs, the law of the negation of the negation is considered important "for a dialectical understanding of the process of development."[19] The extent of negation may differ. In some cases only that must be eliminated "which is obsolete, out-of-date and retarding further progress," while some of the old foundations remain useful. On the other hand, on occasion a negation can be "profound and fundamental."[20] What is existing may be completely negated if it does not possess any aspect that is worth retaining. The working of this law is seen in the following example: "In 1954 because of the development of nuclear missile weapons and their entry into an army's equipment, it became clear that the old methods and forms were inapplicable to future nuclear missile war. As a result of investigations appropriate methods and forms of armed conflict were formed."[21]

These three laws of dialectics are basic to understanding Soviet military thought, and even the Soviet Armed Forces as a whole. As stated by Ogarkov: "The theory of military art and the practice of conducting operations in wars are entirely subordinated to the laws of materialist dialectics. This is also convincingly affirmed by the changes of military doctrines of states in accordance with their politics and with the specific historical situation."[22]

Marxism-Leninism teaches that any science represents not only a system of laws but also of definite categories, that is, the most general concepts which are elaborated in the process of development of each science and form its foundation. In mechanics, for example, such concepts are mass, energy, force; in political economy, they are commodity, value, money, and so on.[23] As the science of the general laws of social development and as a method of understanding social phenomena, the materialist conception of history constitutes the theoretical basis of all scientific communism, as well as the *strategy and tactics* of the Communist Party. By showing "the inevitability" in accordance with "natural law" that capitalism will be replaced by socialism, Marxism-Leninism is supposed to inspire the workers, soldiers, and the entire Soviet population with "certainty in the ultimate victory of their great cause."[24]

Marxism branches off into the "theory of class struggle." "Class" is defined so there is no doubt of its composition: in a capitalist society there are "capitalist classes" and "working classes." No middle class is possible for the dialectical thinker. The "class struggle" of the workers proceeds in various forms: economic, political, and ideological. The highest stage of the proletariat's class struggle is revolution.[25] The historic mission of the socialist revolution is the abolition of capitalist private ownership of the means of production and its replacement by public, socialist ownership.[26]

Marxism-Leninism teaches that relationships between capitalist and socialist states must be antagonistic. Détente, by Soviet definition, is a state of relations between socialist and capitalist nations that contributes to the strengthening of communism and improved conditions for wars of national liberation. Stability of relations among nations would be contrary to the "laws" of history.

Soviet laws of war and laws of armed combat must be studied in their overall Marxist-Leninist context. Some "laws" may appear logical, while others defy reason. It might be argued that it is all theory, that the Kremlin leaders act pragmatically. When Soviet writings on laws of war covering their development since the mid-1950s are studied, readers will see a close parallel between the development of military doctrine and the buildup of the Soviet Armed Forces.

Soviet laws of armed combat follow the laws of war. Within the former there are various subcategories to cover the various levels of struggle and the type of military action being waged. Principles of military art are derived from the laws of armed combat and its subçategories.

Views on the laws of war, laws of armed combat, and principles of military art that are presented here are those taught in Soviet professional military schools, which all Soviet officers must attend. Their basis is historical and materialist dialectics, as seen through the prism of Marxist-Leninist ideology.

Initial Formulation of the Laws of War

The Soviet laws of war developed and articulated in the late 1950s, and restated and reinterpreted since that time, initially appeared as an outgrowth and a response to Stalin's "permanently operating factors."[27] The nuclear weapons used at the end of World War II obviously introduced a new element into warfare. However, as long as Stalin was alive, the Soviet press barely admitted that such weapons existed or had any significance. Soviet theorists could not acknowledge that a surprise nuclear strike might seriously cripple a nation, or even suggest that such matters might warrant discussion.

In September 1953, within only a few months of Stalin's death, General Major N. A. Talenskiy, then editor of *Military Thought*, published an article in the journal entitled "On the Question of the Character of the Laws of Military Science." Although he took care not to reject Stalin's permanently operating factors outright, he wrote that they were not a basic law of military science "deciding the fate of war." He then made a number of assertions: "Any basic law of armed conflict is primarily a law of victory. . . . The political goal of war is achieved through victory in armed conflict." From this, he concluded that the correct formulation and generalization of the guiding principles in war are expressed as follows: *"Victory in modern war is achieved by the decisive defeat of the enemy in the course of armed conflict by successive strikes increasing in force, on the base of superiority in permanently operating factors, which decide the fate of war, and on the base of the comprehensive use of the economic, moral-political and military possibilities in their unity and interaction."*[28] (Emphasis in original.)

Talenskiy went on to state that there are objective laws that govern war, just as there are laws that govern all human activity. These laws, being objective, apply equally to both sides. However, if they are to be used, they must be recognized. Only Soviet military science, based on "the genuinely scientific Marxist-Leninist theory and methodology" makes correct understanding and recognition of these laws possible. Furthermore, only if commanders recognize and understand these laws can victory in war be achieved. Even military organizations cannot be effective unless they are developed within the framework of the laws of war.

Talenskiy's article attracted considerable attention, and it started a discussion in *Military Thought* on the need to reexamine military concepts. There was no general agreement that the laws of war were objective. As one officer stated in reply to Talenskiy's article: "The conditions of socialist and capitalist society are qualitatively different and the objective laws of military science, which are the expression of these conditions, must also be different."[29] Another argued that Talenskiy was attempting to develop a law of victory, similar to the concept expressed by Giulio Douhet through the use of air power, and J.F.C. Fuller through the use of tanks.[30]

No consensus was reached on what direction to take. There was agreement on the importance of surprise in nuclear war—one of the major factors that Stalin, to justify his own mistakes, had rejected. The argument about whether or not there was a single law that applied to both capitalism and socialism was closed off by an article in *Military Thought* with this brief statement: "The editors suggest that it is not yet possible to propound any final and definite formulation of the basic law."[31] In the search for new guidelines to replace Stalin's "permanently operating factors," one Soviet theorist, Colonel Pavel A. Chuvikov, attempted to show that "the basic positions of the strategy of the Communist Party form the political base for the military strategy of the Soviet Army."[32] These "basic positions" were as follows:

1. Concentration of the main forces of the revolution at the decisive moment at the most vulnerable point of the enemy;
2. Selection of the moment for the decisive strike;
3. Unswerving conduct of the course already selected in spite of difficulties and complications on the way to the goal;
4. Maneuvering with reserves intended for proper retreat, when the enemy is strong and when retreat is inevitable.

These positions appear to represent something akin to "laws" but were not stated as such. The author admitted to the danger of a surprise attack with the use of atomic and thermonuclear weapons, a danger "which would exist not only in the beginning period of war, but throughout the war's entire course." But at the same time he was not ready to break with the past. Regardless of the dangers that surprise in war represents to "peace-loving states and their armies, . . . the decisive role in modern war in the final count was played and will be played by such *permanently operating factors* as firmness of the rear, the morale of the army, the quantity and quality of divisions, the organizational ability of the command cadres, and others." No acknowledgment was made that these were the same permanently operating factors enunciated by Stalin. On the contrary, although Chuvikov's earlier 1949 book had been full of praise for "Stalin's military science," his 1956 work referred to Stalin's cult of personality as having "belittled and lowered the role of the Party and the people's masses."

New Attention to the Laws of War

One of the first serious considerations of the laws of war was found in the 1957 edition of *Marxism-Leninism on War and Army*. This book was written by a group of professors in the Department of Dialectical and Historical Materialism at the Lenin Military-Political Academy. This Academy is directly under the authority of the Main Political Administration of the Soviet Army and Navy, which reports to the Central Committee of the Communist Party. There were five editions of this work, the last of which appeared in 1968. These editions frequently are referenced by other Soviet military writers, and they represented authoritative sources at the time they were published. A number of the contributors have remained well-known Soviet spokesmen in the 1980s.

A major theme of the first edition was the "basic factors which determine the course and outcome of war." Modern war, the authors asserted, "demands exertion of all the material and spiritual forces of a country. Withstanding such stress and achieving victory are possible for that state which *is superior to its enemy in an economic, moral and purely military relationship*." (Emphasis added.) Victory over the enemy requires "all around mobilization and skillful use of the economic possibilities of the country" and also "enormous exertion of the physical and spiritual strength of all the people." Moreover, "it is necessary to know and to take into account the sum total of economic, moral and military capabilities not only of one's own country but also of the enemy."[33]

These three factors—economic, moral, and military—at that time represented the three primary factors of the "correlation of forces in the world arena." Later the "scientific-technical" factor was included. Although other elements have been added by some authors, the economic, moral, scientific-technical, and military capabilities have remained basic themes.

With this emphasis on the different components in the relationship, it followed that "Soviet military science, *while discovering and researching the laws of waging modern war, is not limiting itself to questions of military art and purely military elements."* (Emphasis added.) In particular, questions of "the economic support of the armed struggle and the role of the moral factor in war"[34] also must be included. Judging from the lack of detailed discussion of the laws of war and laws of armed combat in this first edition, it appears that specific laws of war were being studied and identified but were not ready for open dissemination.

The second edition of *Marxism-Leninism on War and Army* was published in April, 1961. Its aim was to show "the distinctive features of combat equipment and the deep upheavals in military affairs caused by it."[35] In the four years between the publication of these two editions, considerable attention appears to have been given to the laws of war and their significance. Whereas the first edition had mentioned only that laws of war were being researched and discovered, the second edition attempted to explain them in some detail. A third edition of the work, published in October 1962, only a year later, made specific reference to "the appearance of the nuclear rocket weapon and the revolution in military affairs caused by them." But insofar as laws of war were concerned, changes between the 1961 and 1962 editions were minor.

The new editions were written by the same group of instructors in the Department of Dialectical and Historical Materialism at the Lenin Military-Political Academy. Five of seven authors of the first edition contributed to the later editions, but seven new authors had been added by 1961. The authors of the 1962 edition were identical with those of the 1961 edition.

The great jump between 1957 and 1961 with respect to the laws of war corresponded to the changes that took place in military doctrine during that same period. As previously shown, a new military doctrine was formulated in the late 1950s and first announced by Khrushchev in January 1960. This doctrine was described in greater detail by Malinovskiy in October 1961 in his address to the 22nd Party Congress. In hindsight, the new military doctrine, combined with the laws of war perceived by Soviet theorists at that time, could have provided Western analysts a general indication of the direction in which the Soviet Armed Forces were moving and of the weapons systems that were being given priority.

By 1961 the authors of *Marxism-Leninism on War and Army* had declared that "the course and outcome of war depends on a multitude of reasons and conditions, which, moreover, as a rule undergo constant change, at times rapid and spasmodic." This was given as one of the reasons why it was so difficult "to establish and research the laws that determine the course and outcome of war." Because of this difficulty, many "bourgeois" military historians, theoreticians, and practitioners "wholly reject the possibility of discovering such laws and view the course and outcome of war as depending upon chance."[36] In contrast to the failure of strategists in capitalist nations to discover the laws of war, Marxism-Leninism had given the Soviet leadership the ability to determine not only the laws of war but also the origins of war. These laws show, the Soviet theorists asserted, that victory or defeat in war follow the general course of historical development.

The course of a war follows the policies of the states involved in it. However, the course and outcome of military actions are determined by the military might of these states and also the effectiveness of its use. Military might of states is derived from (1) development of the economy and natural and technical sciences; (2) the political structure of the states; and (3) the morale of the population.[37] It also was noted at the time that, along with the concepts listed above, the scientific potentials of states must also be considered. However, in 1961 these potentials were not included as a law of war.

When discussing the nature of the laws of armed combat, these Marxist-Leninist military professors emphasized that war does *not* depend on the free will of people. War represents not chaotic chance "but a process subject to certain laws." These laws represent necessary and tangible ties between the following three "values": (1) the definite conditions in which wars start and proceed; (2) the actions of enormous human masses taking part in the war; and (3) those results to which these wars lead. Following from the above "values," there are four "regularities" (*zakonomernosti*) that determine the origin, course and outcome of wars:

1. Those expressing the dependence of the origin, goals, and political leadership of wars on economic and political conditions;
2. Those expressing the dependence of the course and outcome of wars on the correlation of forces (economic, scientific-technical, moral, and purely military) of the belligerent states and their coalitions;
3. Those expressing the dependence of the course and outcome of the armed struggle on the methods of conducting combat actions;
4. Those determining the development and changes in methods of waging military actions.[38]

Note that not only the course and outcome of war, but also the *origin* of war were expressed in the above. The following "regularities" concern only the war's *course and outcome*, which depend on:

1. The level of productive forces and the economic structure of the belligerent states;
2. The level of scientific-technical development and scientific potential of these states;
3. The sociopolitical structure, ruling ideology, and morale of the population;
4. The combat might of the armed forces.

These four regularities, showing the dependence of the course and outcome of war on the resources, forces, and weapons available, "operate not with fatal inevitability, but only as certain tendencies." The correlation in the size of the forces, the degree of their development, and the qualitative status of their troops and equipment form the prerequisites, and determine a state's "objective possibilities of achieving military goals." These, however, are only "possibilities." Although the balance of power between states and armies is a major factor in determining the course and outcome of war, and thus, victory or defeat, the methods of waging military actions and the development of leadership for these actions will be equally important.[39]

Impact of the Laws of War upon Armed Combat

By the early 1960s, Soviet Party-military strategists taught that there were laws "that command cadres must take into account if they wish to achieve success in battle with the enemy." Within the framework "of laws of the economic development of society and the political struggle of classes and states," the armed struggle is subordinate to its own specific laws. These laws are as follows:

1. To conduct military actions successfully, a balance is necessary between goals (combat tasks) and the forces and equipment used in comparison to the forces and equipment of the enemy, "while also taking into account the factors of time and space."

2. Success is achieved "when superiority of forces is created at the decisive moment in the decisive direction." (In the United States this idea is stated more simply as being in the right place at the right time with the right forces.)

3. To achieve victory it is necessary to use the available forces and equipment effectively by rational and well-coordinated cooperation of service branches. This law of armed combat was said to play a primary role, especially in contemporary conditions when armies have such varied and complicated weapons.

4. Success in armed combat is possible only when correspondence between tasks and available forces, concentration of these forces at the necessary moment, and cooperation between service branches are achieved at each stage of military actions.

5. Success of attack and the complete defeat of the enemy is possible only when the offensive is waged purposefully, constantly, and at high tempos, and when the enemy is relentlessly pursued in order to prevent him from digging in along the area between defensive borders, bringing up reserves, closing the gap that has been formed in the defenses, gathering up his forces, and launching a counterattack.[40] This law was given as one of the most important for waging armed combat; it was said to have even greater significance when weapons of mass destruction are used. Under such circumstances the offensive will be conducted at exceptionally high tempos, to a great depth, constantly, and without long pauses.

By the early 1960s part of the position argued by Talenskiy in 1953 appeared settled. The laws of armed combat were considered to be objective laws, existing and operating outside of the consciousness of people and independently of their will. Laws of military science represented a more or less complete and exact reflection of those objective laws, tendencies and relationships that really exist in armed combat. These were the laws by which commanders, "proceeding from goals placed before the troops and taking into account actual circumstances, [could] make decisions, work out plans for upcoming battles and operations, and organize troops for carrying out these plans."[41]

These were the initial views at the beginning of the 1960s on laws of war and laws of armed combat as expressed by faculty members of the Lenin Military-Political Academy. Their task appeared to be that of taking approved military concepts and placing them in a Marxist-Leninist context to be used for study and indoctrination of military personnel. They attempted to show that the laws had military utility provided they were understood, and that they were more than simply theory. Further detailed discussions were soon to follow.

Views from the General Staff

In October, 1962, the month of the Cuban Missile Crisis, a small book appeared in Moscow bookstores entitled *On the Basic Laws of the Course and Outcome of Modern War*. The author of this work, General Major P. I. Trifonenkov, was head of the Department of Marxism-Leninism of the Academy of the General Staff until 1969. The preface noted that "the book represents the personal opinion of the author and bears a polemical character." It also was stated that the work had value "in the further exploration of the question of the laws of war."[42] The Soviet leadership wanted discussion of the laws of war to continue but took care to ensure that readers understood the book did not represent the final word on the subject.

The laws of war given by Trifonenkov generally were the same as those given by the authors of *Marxism-Leninism on War and Army*, but with some significant differences. He wrote that, in his opinion, there were three basic laws. First, the course and outcome of war is dependent on the correlation of purely military possibilities of the opponents. Second, the course and outcome of war is dependent on the correlation of military-economic possibilities of the belligerent states. (This was a departure from earlier writings in which only the "economies" of the belligerent states were considered, not the "military economy.") And, third, the course and outcome of war is dependent on the moral-political possibilities of the belligerent sides (which was unchanged from earlier statements).[43]

A whole chapter in his book was devoted to each of these laws. Even at this time the legacy of Stalin's views remained. The author explained that the first of the laws, the relationship of the military possibilities of the opponents, was the "military potential." In time of war, this potential would be expressed as "the permanently operating factors of the armed struggle," defined as the following:

1. The quantity and quality of troop personnel;
2. The quantity and quality of armaments;

3. The level of military knowledge, organizational ability, and the skill of the commanders to guide the organization, training, and use of troops in a strategic, operational, and tactical relationship.[44]

Superiority was the major consideration. In any battle, in each operation, and in war as a whole, victory will naturally go to that side which achieves superiority over the enemy. Superiority can be achieved in different ways but one *cannot* defeat the enemy without excelling him in a military relation. Therefore, achieving such superiority is one of the most important questions in the practice and theory of military affairs. Superiority can be achieved in one element of the armed forces or another as well as in the armed forces as a whole. More specifically, it can be achieved in the following ways:

1. Training and combat experience of the troops;
2. Quality and quantity of new kinds of weapons;
3. Skill in the conduct of war.[45]

During the 1980s Soviet spokesmen, from Politburo members to *Pravda* reporters, accused the United States of seeking military superiority over the Soviet Union. The Soviet emphasis on superiority and their insistence that the United States must not achieve such a condition are better understood when the laws of armed conflict are considered.

Aftermath of the Cuban Missile Crisis

There has been a school of thought in the United States that the Cuban Missile Crisis brought about a change in Soviet military concepts. An analysis of Soviet military writings before and after that crisis does not indicate any shift in doctrine or strategy or in the laws of war. This continuity was clearly evidenced in another book, *Essence of the Laws of Armed Conflict*, written by Colonel M. V. Popov, which appeared in 1964.[46] Later, in 1967, Popov earned the degree of doctor of philosophical sciences from the Lenin Military-Political Academy. Like the work by Trifonenkov already noted, the preface stated that the book was for discussion and represented the personal opinion of the author. At the same time, the "editor" of the book was General Colonel N. A. Lomov, one of the foremost Soviet military strategists, who then headed the Department of Strategy at the Academy of the General Staff.

In this work, Popov criticized Stalin for having prevented the development of Soviet military science and for prohibiting creative discussion of many important military-theoretical problems, including the laws of war.[47] Popov then postulated a system of laws of war, which he divided into three groups:

1. The first group of laws of war "expresses the dependence of the course and outcome of *war* on the economies of the warring powers, their socio-political system, the political-moral state of the population and the army, the level of development of science, and the quantity and quality of

armaments." (Emphasis added.) The first four elements listed were the same as those given earlier, the fourth, "the quantity and quality of armaments," was new. Trifonenkov had referred to this fourth element as one of the "permanently operating factors."

2. The second group of laws of war "expresses the dependence of the means and forms of *armed conflict* on the political content of the war, on the properties of the weapons and combat equipment, means of communications and signals, terrain and time of the year." (Emphasis added.) In this group, more attention was given to specific military factors, such as "properties" of weapons than had been expressed by earlier theorists.

3. The third group of laws of war dealt with the "internal laws of armed conflict concerning operations on strategic, operational, and tactical scales."

It was obvious in Popov's writings that he had not made a clear distinction between laws of war and laws of armed conflict. He noted that "any law of war is more or less a law of armed conflict, and each law of armed conflict is more or less a law of war as a whole."[48] A reviewer, who on the whole made very favorable comments about Popov's book, pointed out that this statement should have been discussed further, and an explanation given as to why laws of war and laws of armed conflict are the same.[49]

In his discussion of the laws of armed conflict Popov repeated, with but one exception, what had been written by previous authors. This exception was his law that "military operations on an operational-tactical scale of necessity are subordinated to the interests of strategy, which, in turn, depend on the results of individual engagements and battles."[50]

He stressed that in contemporary conditions the state of war involves the whole population of the combatant nation. It changes the nature of industry, requires a redirection of science, has a strong effect on the political and moral condition of the population, and changes the pattern of consumption. The most important aspect of war is its political content, which is primary and decisive. The armed struggle itself is secondary and subordinate, inasmuch as it is the means of politics. The political aspect exercises a decisive influence on the general character of the armed struggle, on the methods and forms by which it is waged, and on the weapons used. The more decisive the political goals that are pursued in the war, the sharper, the more intense and bitter the armed struggle. Although these laws must be known and understood by commanders, they do not give a complete answer to the question: "What determines defeat or victory?" The outcome depends on the following:

> In any battle or operation a certain number of troops take part. Although a great number of objective and subjective circumstances affect the course and outcome of every engagement, battle, and operation, the decisive importance is the quantitative and qualitative correlation of the material and spiritual forces of the troops which participate directly in a given action of armed conflict—that is, their combat power. . . . From this stems the law of the dependence of the course and outcome of armed conflict on the combat power of the troops of the opposing sides.[51]

The purpose of battle is victory, Popov said, which depends on: (1) preventing the enemy from deploying his troops, and (2) immediate follow-up offensive combat operations. He wrote: "This relationship . . . should be regarded as one of the laws of armed conflict. It may be formulated as follows: In any engagement, battle or operation the relative advantage is gained by the opposing side which is able to deploy its troops and begin combat operations ahead of the enemy. This law constitutes the objective basis of the principle of surprise."[52] For any well-trained NATO officer, the above factors would appear to be common sense for basic military operations rather than a great revelation of Marxism-Leninism. However, when basic military concepts are stated in this manner, junior Soviet officers might feel they were important and worth studying.

Reaffirmation from the Chief of the General Staff

Throughout the 1960s Soviet theorists on the laws of war, as a rule, were colonels serving on the faculties of military academies. On occasion the "reviewer" of their work might be a general. An exception was a 1967 work by Marshal of the Soviet Union Matvey V. Zakharov, chief of the General Staff, in which he explained "the factors in war that assure victory." It is not enough, he stated, merely "to study that which is necessary for war." What must be learned is "that which assures victory in war." To do this, each officer must have a sufficient knowledge of dialectical materialism and Soviet military science "to be able to formulate laws of war, laws of armed combat, regularities and tendencies in the development of military affairs."[53]

"Knowledge of the laws of war and of the laws of armed combat is obligatory for each military leader," according to Zakharov. He emphasized that the principle of teaching that which will assure victory, in essence, means that goals, tasks, and methods of combat training must be in conformity with the laws of war and laws of armed combat. Such laws show definite ties and relations that, if properly applied, will lead to definite results. He summarized the general laws of war, restating the notion that the course and outcome of war is based on the relationship of economic, moral-political, and military possibilities of the belligerent sides. The character, form, and methods of armed conflict also depend on the relationship of the social structure, economy, and politics of the belligerent states.

The political content of war influences the character of the war, the methods and forms of its conduct, and also the use of various kinds of weapons. That is, if the political goals of war are not decisive, then conventional weapons might be used. If the war is for the survival of the Soviet Union—or of capitalism—then it would be a decisive clash between two world systems, and all types of weapons probably would be employed.

Although a great deal of effort was under way to determine the laws of war, he said, "it is necessary to note that on some questions there is still not a single opinion." In general, however, "disagreement as a rule concerns some secondary questions that have only an indirect bearing on the problem."

The matter of military theory, in particular, remained a subject still requiring further research and discussion.[54] While the chief of the General Staff did not provide new insights into the laws of war, he summarized those points which the Party-military leadership considered essential and provided a point of departure for later analyses. He asserted that different views on these laws were expected and that further investigation was needed.

A few years later, in 1971, Colonel V. Ye. Savkin, Candidate of Military Science, on the faculty of the Frunze Military Academy, presented a somewhat different view of the laws of war and laws of armed conflict. He warned that determining the laws of war was so complex that "some authors express disputatious, imprecise, and even erroneous theses."[55] Although these laws must be studied and known by Soviet officers, he said, they must not tread into areas reserved for others. "We believe it necessary to stress that *military science does not investigate the laws of war in general, but strictly the laws of armed conflict*, guided herein by Marxist-Leninist theory." (Emphasis added.) In other words, only the Party leadership, in this spokesman's view, could determine the "laws of war."[56]

At the same time, he affirmed that what the military could investigate was significant. In the 1960s Soviet theorists embraced cybernetics. In the 1970s, increased attention was given to statistical laws, which can be used "to express the nature of armed conflict as a specific social phenomenon." Such laws were of particular importance when considering the laws of armed conflict, for "predictions based on statistical laws have a probabilistic nature . . . and armed conflict is subordinate to statistical laws." Savkin explained further: "The action of statistical laws in armed conflict arises as a result of a mass employment of personnel, combat equipment, and weaponry under approximately identical conditions, as well as with the manifold repetition of events, when certain attributes common to all of them are discovered."[57]

Savkin claimed that average values for characteristics of specific types of combat actions can be determined by studying the Great Patriotic War. For example, the average daily rate of advance for combined arms tank armies was 20 to 30 kilometers; the density of fire of small arms (bullets per minute per meter of defensive front) set up in front of the forward edge of defense varied from two to twelve, but the average was five to six. Statistical laws can be determined from averages such as these. "They express the nature of unregulated, chaotic processes." Such processes are found elsewhere, as in thermal, electromagnetic and quantum movements. As statistical laws can be determined for these movements, they also can be determined for certain aspects of armed combat, which to a certain extent is a chaotic and unregulated process. "On the other hand, armed conflict is in a certain sense a process which constantly is regulated by more general laws, political guidance, activity of commanders and supervisors of all echelons."[58]

This statement has many implications. In his work, *On War*, Clausewitz had stressed the "friction" of war.[59] He had posited that much depends on unforeseen events, that is, the confusion and uncertainty that is encountered in combat. Through a systematic study of the laws of armed combat, can Soviet military theorists determine statistical laws which will predict events and eliminate the "friction" in battle that has plagued military leaders over the centuries?

Nuclear Weapons and the Laws of War

The Party-military leadership began to give serious consideration to the laws of war in the late 1950s and early 1960s, at the very time they were making a massive effort to produce and to deploy nuclear weapons. It may have been the attention given to developing concepts for the use of nuclear forces that led to the attempt to develop laws of war and laws of armed conflict.

An initial view was that if nuclear weapons were used in a war, the simultaneous use of large numbers of troops would not be required. However, with respect to a war as a whole, multimillion-man armies still would be needed to replace the tremendous personnel losses. Even more important would be the troop requirements of the victor in the postwar period, for "the winning side will have to occupy great territory. This cannot be avoided because the enemy cannot be considered fully beaten until the time when his territory is occupied and he is deprived of the possibility of continuing the conflict."[60]

The assertion that multimillion-man armies are needed in order to occupy the enemy's territory following a nuclear war is seldom found in Soviet writings. Generally, the multimillion-man armies are justified as being needed to replace the heavy casualties that would result from a nuclear exchange. Would the Soviet Union have contingency plans for the possible occupation of the United States in the event of a nuclear war? It appears that this possibility is considered in conjunction with the study of the laws of war.

Soviet military theorists in the 1960s were most concerned with the significance of the laws of war for "forecasting" the nature of armed combat in a world nuclear-rocket war. A war between the two world social systems, communism and capitalism, would involve decisive political goals.[61] In such a war, they reasoned, all means of combat, including nuclear weapons, would be used. Such weapons would produce completely new qualitative changes in the nature of armed conflict and in the methods and forces by which it is carried out. Military operations would become extraordinarily intensive, fast moving and of brief duration. The development of nuclear weapons brought about a new law of armed conflict: the course and outcome of a battle would be decided by the blows of nuclear weapons. Final victory would be achieved by the combined efforts of all services of the Armed Forces, with the Strategic Rocket Forces playing the decisive role.[62]

Still, in a nuclear-rocket war, the law of the dependence of the course and outcome of engagements, battles, and operations on the relative combat power of the opposing sides would continue to operate. Success during battle in nuclear war, as in any other type of conflict, requires superiority of forces over the enemy. Each side would attempt to surpass the other in the power of nuclear strikes. At the same time, because of the decisive power of nuclear weapons, each side battling "for the achievement of victory should first of all seek out and destroy the enemy's means of nuclear attack. . . . From this flows the new principle of military art—the principle of first priority to detection and annihilation of the enemy's nuclear capability." There is yet another characteristic of a nuclear war: Each side would attempt to prevent the other side from using nuclear weapons. Therefore, "there will be a new principle—that of forestalling the delivery of nuclear attacks on the enemy in the course of the war."[63]

Moreover, the use of nuclear-rocket weapons would increase the contradiction between the tendency to concentrate troops and the tendency to disperse them. This contradiction would lead to certain problems. Because of the law of the dependence of the course and outcome of battle on the relative combat power of troops, superiority in combat power over the enemy is essential. In certain circumstances, this superiority can be achieved primarily through the concentration of superior forces—troops and weapons. But at the same time, such concentration would present the danger of these troops being destroyed by the nuclear weapons of the enemy.

For this reason, troops in a nuclear war should be dispersed. It may be necessary in certain regions and at certain times for troops to be concentrated, but care must be taken that they are not suitable targets for destruction by nuclear weapons. Where concentration is needed, such as for a specific attack, it must be for the shortest possible period. Therefore, one of the conditions of nuclear war will be concentration of troops for waging a battle, and dispersal as quickly as possible afterward. This is one aspect of the laws of nuclear-rocket war, "connected with the operation of the law of the dependence of the course of armed conflict on the relative combat power of the troops of the opposing sides."[64]

The employment of nuclear-rocket weapons brings about even greater changes with respect to this law. Simply changing the aiming points (or trajectories) of the warheads "makes it possible in many instances to oppose the enemy with superior combat power of our forces without their preliminary regrouping."[65] This capability not only applies to any target within a theater of military operations but also applies on a global scale. "Without changing their launching sites, nuclear weapons can inflict nuclear strikes of tremendous power practically anywhere on earth." Under these conditions the concentration of superior forces, even in concentrated combat formations, would cease to be necessary and would even be dangerous. From this law comes a new principle of military art—that of the concentration of effort on primary objectives by changing missile trajectories.

However, this is not to say that all previous military principles have been made obsolete as a result of nuclear weapons. It is possible that "war can be conducted only by conventional means."[66] In 1972, Savkin listed four laws of war. The first two differed from what had been presented previously because of the nuclear emphasis. These first two laws were as follows:

The First Law of War: "The course and outcome of war waged with an unlimited employment of all means of conflict are determined primarily by the correlation of strictly military forces available to the combatants at the beginning of the war, *especially in nuclear weapons and means of their delivery.*"[67] (Emphasis added.)

This law of war did not arise until the 1950s. But once it came into effect, other laws of war became secondary. Under conditions of a nuclear missile war, the outcome of a military engagement could be predetermined by the first massive nuclear strike. Victory in a nuclear-rocket war will be achieved by the effective application of a state's maximum power at the very beginning of a conflict. In such a war, nothing can compensate for the absence of nuclear weapons.

The Second Law of War: "The course and outcome of war depends on the correlation of military potentials of the combatants."[68] Efforts should be made to develop and improve the means of armed struggle so that victory can be achieved in a short time. This could be achieved by massive nuclear missile strikes delivered for the purpose of destroying the aggressor's means of nuclear attack and a simultaneous mass destruction of vital installations comprising the enemy's military, political, and economic might, as well as for crushing the will to resist.

On a nuclear battlefield the situation might change "not in a matter of hours, or even of minutes, but by seconds, and then most abruptly." Heavy losses, resulting from nuclear and fire strikes, could quickly change the composition of troops and the correlation of forces on the battlefield. However, Savkin emphasized that the capability of nuclear weapons to bring about this rapid change did not mean that other means of destruction should be ignored.[69]

In the 1980s Soviet spokesmen were less specific in relating either laws of war or laws of armed conflict to the use of nuclear weapons. However, when explaining the importance of military potentials of the warring states, one textbook contained the following: "*Nuclear missile weapons have shattered the notions which developed on troop strike force and have become the main indicator and element in the military potential of the great powers.* The organizational development of modern armies is carried out on a basis of recent achievements of scientific and technical progress."[70] (Emphasis added.) Earlier statements about the impact of nuclear weapons on both the laws of war and laws of armed conflict still seemed to apply.

Laws of War of a Military Superpower

After SALT I certified the Soviet Union as a world military superpower, the tone of military writings changed. Although the "military possibilities of the aggressive imperialist blocs are growing," one author said, their ability to force their will on other states was inexorably decreasing as a result "of the objective change in the correlation of forces in favor of socialism."[71] The "military might of socialist states" serves "the cause of preventing world war, maintaining the general peace and defending world civilization."[72] The possibilities had been reduced "for imperialism using war as a political means of achieving their reactionary goals." These themes were popular among Soviet military theorists in the mid-1970s. It is this "dynamically changing" correlation of forces in the world that predetermines "the changed form of development of laws of war."[73]

However, the laws stated throughout the 1970s, at the height of détente, were practically the same as those given in the 1960s. This continuity was seen in the eight-volume *Soviet Military Encyclopedia*, which made its appearance in the mid-1970s. Statements of laws of war in this publication, considered the most authoritative available for the period, were as follows:

- The dependence of war on its political aims is represented as the most general law.
- The dependence of the course and outcome of war on the correlation of the economic power of the warring states (coalitions).
- The dependence of the course and outcome of war on the correlation of the scientific potentials of the warring sides.
- The dependence of the course and outcome of war on the correlation of the moral-political strength of the warring states (coalitions).
- The dependence of the course and outcome of war on the correlation of the military power (potential) of the antagonistic states.[74]

Elsewhere in the *Soviet Military Encyclopedia*, under the heading "Marxist-Leninist Teachings on War and Army," the laws of war were summarized as the correlation of the economic, scientific, moral-political, and military potentials of the two sides.[75]

In 1982, a decade after the signing of SALT I, the Brezhnev leadership claimed that major shifts in the correlation of forces "in favor of socialism, peace and democracy have occurred in the past ten to fifteen years." The basic laws of war remained the same but were explained in a different way than previously. In past wars there had been times when a weakness in one element of the laws of war could be compensated by strength in another. For example, a high moral level might have compensated for poor technical equipment or, conversely, a predominant technical superiority could compensate for shortcomings in the moral level. But for the present, victory in modern war is possible "only on a basis of a harmonious combination of all the highly developed potentials" of the laws of war—economic, scientific and technical, moral-political, and military. As shown below, the Soviets believed that they led the world in all of these potentials.[76]

Economic Potential

In a textbook published in 1982, General Lieutenant of Aviation V. V. Serebryannikov, deputy commandant of the Lenin Military-Political Academy, wrote: "Without most serious economic preparations, it is an impossible thing to conduct a modern war against advanced imperialism." Such preparations depend upon the economic level of a nation, which is a measure of its economic system. Thus, the Soviet Union's economic structure is on a higher level than that of capitalistic nations. The economic level, in turn, determines "the economic potential, the material and technical bases of armed combat, the quantity and quality of weapons, military equipment, and other material for waging war."

Economic development also determines in large measure the amount of the state reserves and a superiority in this area is one of the most important conditions for victory in modern war. In addition, a high economic potential is essential for the production of modern weapons, such as nuclear weapons, missiles, and atomic submarines. Military-economic potential is a component of economic potential and determines the ability of a state to satisfy the immediate needs of its armed forces.[77]

In modern war, stockpiles of weapons, equipment, and material are indispensable. War requires the mobilization of the entire economy. Much depends on the early preparation of the economy for a possible war. These preparations are all the more necessary because the whole territory of a nation, regardless of its location, can come under attack by nuclear missile weapons.

Soviet military theorists said that, in contrast to the economic stability found in socialist states, capitalist economic systems are subject to profound upheavals. The economic potential of capitalist states is unstable and subject to unanticipated declines, resulting in serious reductions in mobilization capabilities. Such weaknesses are not found in socialist countries, whose economic systems are more stable and thus much superior to those of capitalism. In event of war, the socialist production method makes it possible to most efficiently utilize the nation's economic potential "for ensuring victory against any aggressor."

One aspect of the "crisis-free, constantly growing economy of the Soviet Union" was the creation and development of a number of territorial-production complexes (TPK),[78] predominantly in its eastern regions (Western Siberia, Bratsk, Pavlodar-Ekibastuz, Orenburg, Nizhnekamsk and others). If the transportation system of the Soviet Union was damaged in a nuclear attack, these self-sufficient economic areas would be able to operate as independent entities.

Although Soviet difficulties with food production are generally known in the West, students at higher military schools are given the impression that Soviet agricultural production leads the world. Serebryannikov's textbook, quoting Lenin's statement that "it is essential first of all to have the dependable delivery of food for a firm and reliable army," went on to describe how "the dependable defense of the nation is greatly influenced by its agricultural production." Not only must current food demands be satisfied, but it is also necessary to create the required reserves and stores of food and raw materials in the event of extraordinary circumstances. Moreover, "the advantages of socialist economic integration" make it possible in the event of war to fully mobilize the material, financial, and human resources for "repelling the aggressions of imperialism and other reactionary forces."

Scientific-technical Potential

Science and technical potential play ever-increasing roles in modern warfare. "It can be said with certainty that the dependence of the course and outcome of modern warfare upon the balance of scientific-technical potentials of the belligerents has become incomparably greater than at any other time in history." The development of this potential is essential to "ensure the development of society and to satisfy the requirements of modern warfare." Soviet spokesmen have asserted that capitalism is attempting to use the results of scientific and technical progress primarily to achieve military superiority over socialism. It is because of this that the USSR "has been forced" to be concerned with applying the advances in scientific and technical progress to strengthening its own defense capability.

Today "military history teaches that combat might to an ever greater degree has depended and depends now" upon scientific and technical progress, in both evolutionary and revolutionary changes in military affairs. This scientific and technical revolution has had the most profound and complete impact on military affairs "in causing the broad introduction of nuclear missile weapons, in changing the organization of the Armed Forces and further developing military art and the methods of troop training and indoctrination." Further results have included the production of missiles, nuclear submarines and surface vessels, supersonic aviation, and electronic development as a whole. Once again, Lenin is evoked to justify the Party's actions: "Without science, it is impossible to build a modern army." As a consequence of the scientific and technical revolution, "the role of science is fundamentally altered in shaping a state's military might."[79]

In the Soviet Union today "many nonmilitary scientific research centers and institutions are conducting developments in the interest of the military department." Such technical progress leads to a continuous shortening of the time required for weapons and equipment to become obsolete. At the same time, such progress permits weapons in the hands of the troops "to be rapidly and frequently updated."

Military science "works out the most effective ways and means for preparing the nation and the army for a war as well as the methods and procedures for conducting combat operations." The continuous development of weapons and equipment alters the nature of military service, requiring the personnel to receive a higher level of scientific and technical training than previously. It also requires personnel to develop creative thinking, "independence in carrying out complex combat missions, organization and discipline."

The Soviet Union "stands at the forefront of the scientific-technical revolution." The nation "now has a developed network of scientific institutions and approximately 1.3 million scientific workers," who comprise virtually one-quarter of all scientific workers in the world. In many areas of scientific and technical advancement, "our nation is ahead of all the world's states." Moreover, "the economy, science and technology in our nation are presently on such a high level that we are capable within the shortest period of time of developing any type of weapon on which the enemies of peace would care to wager."

Moral-Political Potential

By Soviet definition, the moral-political potential of a state is determined by its methods of production of material goods, by its socio-economic and political system, and by the nature and goals of a war. Equally important is the nature of the ideology, the degree of its dissemination and influence among the masses, and the general state of ideological indoctrination.

In modern warfare, the law of the dependence of victory upon the balance of the moral forces of the belligerents becomes even more important than before. First, "in the event that the imperialists unleash a war against socialism, in terms of its political nature it will become the greatest in the history of mankind and an exceptionally fierce and uncompromising clash between the two opposing systems." Second, the use of modern weapons, "particularly nuclear missiles, requires unprecedented moral and psychological steadfastness from the people and the army," without which "it is impossible to act in an organized and purposeful manner and conduct a decisive struggle." Third, "the exceptional dynamics, the acuteness of the engagements, the abrupt changes in the situation, and the rapid transitions from one type of operations to another places a physical and moral strain on troop personnel that is unprecedented in previous wars."[80]

At the center of moral-political training "stands the question of explaining to the personnel the basic provisions of Marxism-Leninism, the theory and policy of the CPSU, the indoctrinating of total loyalty to the cause of communism and the motherland, *class hatred for the enemies*, proletarian internationalism, unshakable belief in *victory* over the aggressors and a readiness for a feat for the sake of the triumph of the great ideas of communism." (Emphasis added.)

Military Potential

According to Marxist-Leninist teachings on war and army, the course and outcome (victory or defeat) in combat is determined primarily by the balance of combat might between the armies of the belligerent states. Combat might is composed of numerous elements, including "size, moral-political state and training level, quantity and quality of weapons, military equipment and other materials, the organizational structure of the troops; the number and training level of command personnel; and the development level of science and military art and troop control. The material basis of combat might is the quantity and quality of weapons and equipment."[81]

In light of the economic backwardness of the Soviet Union and the attempts of its officials to obtain science and technology from the West, the explanation of the laws of war given above may appear ridiculous. The textbook quoted was written in the Brezhnev era. The recognition and admission by Soviet leaders of the actual state of the Soviet economy and its impact upon the Armed Forces may have been the underlying reason why in 1986, only three years after this book appeared, an attempt was made to undertake a major *perestroika*, or reform, of the entire Soviet structure, especially the economy, science, and technology.

Relationship of Laws of War to Principles of Military Art

Principles of military art are defined as the practical military application of the laws of armed conflict, the mechanism through which the various laws of military science are applied. A law of armed conflict establishes the existence of a definite relation, but it does not define how the law may affect the actions of a commander. "Principles, on the other hand, determine the direction to be taken by the political and military leadership, and show what actions are needed to gain victory." As one Soviet textbook explained, a law of armed combat states that victory will go to the side concentrating superior forces and means at the decisive place at the decisive time. In turn, this law translates into the principle of massing of forces at the right place at the right time.

As subsets of principles of military art, the Soviets devise principles of strategy, principles of operational art, and principles of tactics, each differing in scale of actions and aims. Principles are used only for guidance. They are "directed in typical circumstances and in definite conditions for the achievement of maximum results with minimal losses." Therefore, there cannot be "any sort of chasm" between the laws of armed combat and the principles of military art.[82]

Soviet theorists also devise principles of many types that are similar to principles of military art but at a different level. Among these are principles of troop control and principles governing scientific leadership of the Armed Forces. Certain principles in the latter category involve "principles underlying the Party's decisive role in Armed Forces leadership." Although such principles are taught, they fall into a somewhat different category and will not be considered here.

The relationship between laws of armed combat and principles of military art can be summed up as follows: *That which in theory is expressed as a law of armed combat, in practice is expressed as a principle for the conducting of military action. Laws of armed combat, therefore, simultaneously are principles of military art.* This concept has been further explained as follows: "From the relationship of the laws of war and principles of military art, frequently on the basis of one law several principles come forth or, on the contrary, on the basis of several laws—one principle. Taken as a whole, they form a system of principles of military art, determining the general form of the basic sides of activity of commanders and troops in preparing for and conducting military actions."[83]

Like the laws of war and laws of armed combat, principles of military art are described in writings on Soviet military science, and these teachings "are expressed in corresponding rules and regulations." Guided by these teachings, Soviet troops "thereby conform their actions with one law or another, determining the course and outcome of armed combat."[84]

In the 1980s the view was expressed that "Soviet military science has disclosed a new view of the role in war both of permanently operating and of temporary, transient factors, indicating the dynamic relationship in them of the objective and subjective." This appeared to be something new; the idea of permanently operating factors had gone out during Khrushchev's de-Stalinization effort. Three factors were given: the role of time, the degree of combat readiness needed (determined by the qualitative level of armaments and the development of military equipment), and surprise, which in certain cases could be decisive.[85] Although these were expressed as neither laws of armed combat nor as principles of military art, they suggested that final decisions on certain principles had been made.

Except in the case noted above, principles of military art have not been firmly established. "If the objective conditions change, principles also change." However, although certain principles appear to be basic, others may be added or deleted. The following principles have appeared in writings from the 1960s through most of the 1980s:[86]

- High combat readiness;
- Surprise;
- Activeness and the retaining of initiative;
- Coordinated employment and close interaction of forces;
- Concentration of main efforts at the crucial moment.

More than one strategist have given the following:

- Decisiveness;
- Complete use of all means and methods for achieving victory;
- The simultaneous defeat of the enemy to the entire depth of his configuration;
- Firm and continuous command;
- The creation and prompt replacement of reserves;
- Complete support for battle tasks, to include material-technical support;
- Correlation of the goals and missions in war to the forces, means, and planned methods of military actions.

The following have been stated by a single author:

- Economy of forces at the expense of secondary theaters of military action or operational directions;
- Timely consolidation of achieved success;
- Bold maneuvering and building up of forces;
- Consideration and full employment of the moral-political factor;
- Mobility and high rates of combat actions.

In contrast, the principles of war taught in the United States include the following:

Objective: Clearly defined, decisive, and attainable goal.
Offensive: Seize, retain, and exploit the initiative.
Mass: Concentrate combat power at the decisive time and place.
Economy of Force: Allocate minimum essential combat power to secondary efforts.
Maneuver: Place the enemy in a position of disadvantage through the flexible application of combat power.
Unity of Command: For every objective, insure unity of effort under one responsible commander.
Security: Never permit the enemy to acquire an unexpected advantage.
Surprise: Strike the enemy at a time and/or place and in a manner for which he is not prepared.
Simplicity: Prepare clear, uncomplicated plans and clear, concise orders.

When the Marxist-Leninist trappings are removed from Soviet writings on principles of military art, much of what remains corresponds to the principles of war taught in several U.S. military academies and war colleges. However, there are significant differences. For example, the following principles are not taught in the United States.

1. The defeat of the enemy to the entire depth of its configuration: This principle is associated with the Soviet concept of deep battle and the need to surround and destroy the enemy.

2. The creation and prompt replacement of reserves: Little thought is given to this principle in the United States. In both World War I and World War II, the United States entered both wars to support its allies. Hence, there was time to mobilize its forces, and shortage of reserves was not a problem. This might not be the case in event of future war.

3. Complete use of all means and methods for achieving victory: The United States did not achieve "victory" in the Korean War of the 1950s, although it did not suffer defeat. In Southeast Asia during the 1960s and early 1970s, the United States had the means to achieve victory but did not do so.

Restatement of Basics

Most Soviet strategists refer to the laws of war and laws of armed combat in their writings, but a single officer, General Major S. A. Tyushkevich emerged in the 1980s as the major spokesman on the subject. He contributed to authoritative books such as *Marxism-Leninism on War and Army* in the 1960s, and in the 1970s he signed the entry on "Laws of War" in the *Soviet Military Encyclopedia*. In 1984 he contributed to yet another book, *Marxist-Leninist Teachings on War and Army*, published in the authoritative Officer's Library series.

In this work he restated many of the laws of war and laws of armed combat and summarized the assertions made by other Soviet writers. For example, laws of war can be determined only by those who have a deep knowledge and understanding of Marxism-Leninism: Only socialist states and their armies can use the laws of war effectively; imperialist states and their armies cannot. Such laws determine the course and outcome of war (victory or defeat in the Soviet sense) and begin to operate at the start of a conflict.[87]

First, and most important, is the law of the dependence of the course and outcome of war on the political goals of the warring sides. Politics determines the general strategic plan of the war; its economic, political, diplomatic, and ideological support; and the order in which strategic tasks and other measures are to be solved. Following this first law, four other laws were given: The course and outcome of war are dependent upon (1) the economic, (2) the scientific-technical, (3) the moral-political, and (4) the military potentials of the warring sides.[88]

He then added another "general law: the dependence of the development and change in methods of combat on quantitative and qualitative changes in military equipment and of the moral and fighting qualities of the personnel." This law is somewhat different from those given earlier, either by Tyushkevich or other Soviet military theorists. Although it would appear more as a law of armed combat, it nevertheless was specifically identified as a general law of war.

In this 1984 work Tyushkevich added little that was new in his discussion of the laws of armed combat. Once military action begins, "military movements on land and sea are subject not to the wishes and plans of diplomats but to their own laws, which are not to be broken without putting the whole expedition in danger."[89] This statement, attributed to Engels, had been quoted by other Soviet writers when stressing the importance of the laws of war and of armed combat.

Knowledge of the laws of war and its regularities (*zakonomernosti*), Tyushkevich said, must be spread not only to state and military leaders but also to each soldier and worker. These laws dictate the logic of conduct in war conditions or when the threat of war arises. The laws of armed struggle, and the theory of military art are used by troops primarily in solving strategic, operational, and tactical problems.

In the United States considerable attention is given to how a war might end. This is not the case in the Soviet Union. War ends in only one manner—victory. Laws of war somehow play a role in preventing the "imperialist aggressors" from unleashing war. The "defenders of peace" are "forced" to strengthen their defense, develop their armies, keep them in a state of high combat ability and combat readiness. This is explained as follows:

> Taking into account the real balance of forces in the international arena and actions of the general laws of war, viewed by Marxists-Leninists through the prism of the laws of social development, the objective tendencies and "*zakonomernosti*" of the modern epoch, the military-political leadership of fraternal countries solves problems of military affairs, and determines the methods of waging war which might be forced on the socialist community by imperialism.[90]

Success cannot be achieved in war unless the laws of war are considered when making decisions, formulating battle plans, and conducting operations. Laws of war set the methods of achieving victory over the enemy, and determine the choice of form and methods of military actions. They give guidelines on preparing troops in a moral-political and material-technical context and teach them what is necessary for performing the given mission. They also direct the setting up of an effective system of command, control and communications.[91] At all times the political and military goals of the war are paramount.

Although discussions of the laws of war appear most frequently in writings by Soviet military leaders, they must be known to the top Party leadership. In 1985 a booklet issued by Nauka, the publishing house of the Soviet Academy of Sciences, provided a summary of both the laws of war and laws of armed conflict. The author criticized various views on the laws of war that had been developed by different theorists. Only one met with his approval: the entry on the laws of war in the *Soviet Military Encyclopedia*,[92] written by Tyushkevich. Although this work had appeared in 1977, the author stated that in it "all basic points of view were studied" with the following being the most important:

> The laws of war represent inner, essential necessary ties of the phenomena of war, determining its character and place in the historical process, the flow, the course and outcome. At the base of the laws of war lie general social laws determining the development of society as a whole. . . . The laws of war are objective, existing independently of people, but the conditions of their action are created by the practical military activity of people. Therefore the subjective factor acts as one of the conditions for the objective laws of war.[93]

This definition of the laws of war and their purpose are essentially the same as those given by Tyushkevich in the 1970s. It appears to have been accepted as a statement of policy with which few Soviet military theorists would dare disagree.

Future Impact

Soviet concepts of laws of war are generally overlooked or scorned by national security analysts in the West. Western textbooks on international relations are concerned with various balances of power. A number of scholars have theorized that a system of balances exists among nations that makes it possible for individual states to preserve their independence and prevent their takeover by larger aggressive states. Some Western theorists assert that the balance of power has its own laws; for instance, that stability increases as parity in the power of states increases.

In the West the comparative strengths of existing military forces are often cited as the primary consideration in determining the relative power status among nations. Much attention is paid to determining the military strength of Warsaw Pact forces relative to that of the NATO nations. The balance of military power, as presented by both political and military leaders in Washington, is determined by the relative sizes of the armed forces, along with the numbers and types of weapons systems.

Soviet Party-military leaders have a different view. They stress that the total correlation of forces—economic, scientific-technical, moral-political, and military—must be kept in their favor. Stability in international affairs is not a desired goal.

In the late 1980s General Secretary Gorbachev told the Soviet public that the economy was in serious difficulty. Factories were outmoded, and scientific and technological developments, such as computers, were not being utilized. Drastic measures, he stated, must be taken for *perestroika*—restructuring—the economy and Soviet society in general, and improvements must be made in utilizing science and technology.

There was a general view in the West that Gorbachev's restructuring plan was intended to improve the living standards of the Soviet population. The needs of the Soviet Armed Forces would be held in abeyance while the economy was strengthened and production of civilian goods increased. This step was an exact mirror-image of what NATO governments would do, and had done, whenever their economies were in trouble. It would be prudent for Western planners to consider that the real reason for "restructuring" is to ensure that the laws of war are kept in the Kremlin's favor.

Notes

1. N. N. Azovtsev, *V. I. Lenin i Sovetskaya Voyennaya Nauka* [V. I. Lenin and Soviet Military Science], 2nd ed. (Moscow: Nauka, 1981), p. 321.

2. D. A. Volkogonov, editor, *Voyna i Armiya* [War and Army] (Moscow: Voyenizdat, 1977), p. 146. The chapter discussing laws of war was written by General Major S. A. Tyushkevich.

3. V. Ye. Savkin, *Osnovnyye Printsipy Operativnogo Iskusstva i Taktiki* [Basic Principles of Operational Art and Tactics] (Moscow: Voyenizdat, 1972), p. 69.

4. Alain C. Enthoven and K. Wayne Smith, *How Much is Enough* (New York: Harper and Row, 1971). Quoted in Harry G. Summer, *On Strategy* (Novato, CA: Presido Press, 1982), p. 47.

5. O. V. Kuusinen, senior editor, *Fundamentals of Marxism-Leninism* (Moscow: Foreign Languages Publishing House, 1963), pp. 125–126.

6. Ibid., p. 135.

7. V. G. Afanasyev, *Marxist Philosophy* (Moscow: Foreign Languages Publishing House, 1962), p. 97.

8. Ibid., pp. 99–100.

9. S. N. Kozlov, M. V. Smirnov, I. S. Baz', and P. A. Sidorov, *O Sovetskoy Voyennoy Nauke* [On Soviet Military Science], 2nd ed. (Moscow: Voyenizdat, 1964), pp. 321–322.

10. N. V. Ogarkov, *Istoriya Uchit Bditel'nosti* [History Teaches Vigilance] (Moscow: Voyenizdat, 1985), p. 49.

11. Ibid.

12. Afanas'yev, *Marxist Philosophy*, p. 114.

13. Ibid., p. 116.

14. Ibid., p. 118.

15. Ogarkov, *Istoriya Uchit Bditel'nosti*, p. 50.
16. Ibid., pp. 50–51.
17. Afanas'yev, *Marxist Philosophy*, p. 124.
18. Ibid., pp. 129–130.
19. Ogarkov, *Istoriya Uchit Bditel'nosti*, p. 52.
20. Afanas'yev, *Marxist Philosophy*, p. 124.
21. Kozlov et al., *O Sovetskoy Voyennoy Nauke*, p. 323.
22. Ogarkov, *Istoriya Uchit Bditel'nosti*, p. 54.
23. Afanas'yev, *Marxist Philosophy*, p. 133.
24. Kuusinen, *Fundamentals*, p. 147.
25. Ibid., p. 169.
26. Ibid., p. 61.
27. J. V. Stalin, *O Velikoy Otechestvennoy Voyne Sovetskogo Soyuza* [On the Great Patriotic War of the Soviet Union], 5th ed. (Moscow: Voyenizdat, 1949), pp. 41–48.
28. N. A. Talenskiy, "On the Question of the Character of the Laws of Military Science," *Voyennaya Mysl'* [Military Thought] 9 (September 1953).
29. H. S. Dinerstein, *War and the Soviet Union*, revised ed. (New York: Praeger Publishers, 1962), p. 54.
30. Ibid., p. 55.
31. Ibid., p. 61.
32. P. A. Chuvikov, *Marksizm-Leninizm o Voyne i Armii* [Marxism-Leninism on War and Army], 2nd ed. (Moscow: Voyenizdat, 1956), pp. 138–159, excerpts.
33. I. N. Levanov, B. A. Belyy, A. P. Novoselov, *Marksizm-Leninizm o Voyne i Armii* [Marxism-Leninism on War and Army], 1st ed. (Moscow: Voyenizdat, 1957), p. 274.
34. Ibid.
35. G. A. Fedorov, n. Ya. Sushko, B. A. Belyy, editors, *Marksizm-Leninizm o Voyne i Armii* [Marxism-Leninism on War and Army], 2nd ed. (Moscow: Voyenizdat, 1961), p. 2.
36. Ibid., p. 266.
37. Ibid.
38. Ibid., pp. 350–351.
39. Ibid., pp. 351–352.
40. G. A. Fedorov, N. Ya. Sushko, B. A. Belyy, editors, *Marksizm-Leninizm o Voyne i Armii* [Marxism-Leninism on War and Army], 3rd ed. (Moscow: Voyenizdat, 1962), pp. 329–330.
41. Fedorov et al., *Marksizm-Leninizm* (1961), p. 356.
42. P. I. Trifonenkov, *Ob Osnovnykh Zakonakh Khoda i Iskhoda Sovremennoy Voyny* [On the Basic Laws of the Course and Outcome of Modern War] (Moscow: Voyenizdat, 1962), p. 2.
43. Ibid., p. 5.
44. Ibid., p. 9.
45. Ibid., p. 24.
46. M. V. Popov, *Sushchnost' Zakonov Vooruzhennoy Bor'by* [Essence of the Laws of Armed Conflict] (Moscow: Voyenizdat, 1964), p. 2.
47. Ibid., p. 34.
48. Ibid., pp. 44–45.
49. Savkin, *Osnovnyye Printsipy*, p. 105.
50. Popov, *Sushchnost' Zakonov*, p. 92.

51. M. V. Popov, "The Laws of Armed Conflict Are the Objective Basis of the Leadership of Combat Operations," *Voyennaya Mysl'* [Military Thought] (October 1964), JPRS translation, undated, p. 16.

52. Ibid., p. 24. Later, in 1969, Popov concluded that the "basic law of war, and also the fundamental law of armed combat," is "the law of the interconnection of politics and armed violence in war." He never found a single "law of victory" that would completely determine the outcome of any battle or operation.

53. M. V. Zakharov, *O Nauchnom Podkhode k Rukovodstvu Voyskami* [On the Scientific Approach to the Leadership of Troops] (Moscow: Voyenizdat, 1967), p. 44.

54. Ibid., p. 45.

55. Savkin, *Osnovnyye Printsipy*, p. 69.

56. Ibid., p. 73.

57. Ibid., p. 77.

58. Ibid., p. 79.

59. Karl von Clausewitz, *On War*, edited and translated by Michael Howard and Peter Paret (Princeton, New Jersey: Princeton University Press, 1976), pp. 119–122.

60. Trifonenkov, *Ob Osnovnykh Zakonakh*, p. 14.

61. Popov, *Sushchnost' Zakonov*, p. 18.

62. Ibid., pp. 20–21.

63. N. Ya. Sushko and T. R. Kondratkov, *Metodologicheskiye Problemy Voyennoy Teorii i Praktiki* [Methodological Problems of Military Theory and Practice], 1st ed. (Moscow: Voyenizdat, 1966), p. 117. The same statement also is found in the second edition, 1969, edited by A. S. Zheltov, p. 338. Colonel M. V. Popov was a contributor to both editions.

64. Popov, "The Laws of Armed Conflict," p. 23.

65. A. S. Zheltov, *Metodologicheskiye Problemy Voyennoy Teorii i Praktiki* [Methodological Problems of Military Theory and Practice], 2nd edition (Moscow: Voyenizdat, 1969), p. 323–324.

66. Ibid., p. 339.

67. Savkin, *Osnovnyye Printsipy*, p. 117.

68. Ibid., pp. 118–119.

69. Ibid., p. 121.

70. V. V. Serebryannikov, *Osnovy Marksistsko-Leninskogo Ucheniye o Voyne i Armii* [Basis of Marxist-Leninist Teachings on War and Army] (Moscow: Voyenizdat, 1982), p. 173.

71. D. A. Volkogonov, A. S. Milovidov and S. A. Tyushkevich, *Voyna i Armii* [War and Army] (Moscow: Voyenizdat, 1977), pp. 39–40.

72. Ibid., p. 170.

73. Ibid., p. 163.

74. S. A. Tyushkevich, "Zakony i Obychai Voyny" [Laws and Customs of War], in *Sovetskaya Voyennaya Entsiklopediya* [Soviet Military Encyclopedia] (Moscow: Voyenizdat, 1976–1980), vol. 3, pp. 375–378.

75. S. A. Tyushkevich, "Marksistko-Leninskoye Ucheniye o Voyne i Armii" [Marxist-Leninist Teaching on War and Army], in *Sovetskaya Voyennaya Entsiklopediya*, vol. 5, pp. 153–154.

76. Serebryannikov, *Osnovy Marksistsko-Leninskogo*, p. 149.

77. Ibid., pp. 156–157.

78. Ibid., p. 160.

79. Ibid., p. 164.

80. Ibid., p. 170.

81. Ibid., p. 179.

82. B. Belyy, *Marxism-Leninism on War and Army* (Moscow: Progress Publishers, 1972), p. 413. The section on the laws of war was written by Colonel S. A. Tyushkevich. This English-language edition is essentially the same as the Russian-language *Marksizm-Leninizm o Voyne i Armii*, 5th ed. (Moscow: Voyenizdat, 1968), p. 413.

83. D. A. Volkogonov, *Marksistsko-Leninskoye Ucheniye o Voyne i Armii* [Marxist-Leninist Teachings on War and Army] (Moscow: Voyenizdat, 1984), pp. 80–81.

84. Ibid., p. 81.

85. Azovtsev, V. I. *Lenin i Sovetskaya Voyennaya Nauka*, p. 321.

86. For listings of the principles of military art see I. G. Zavyalov, "On Soviet Military Doctrine," *Krasnaya Zvezda* [Red Star], March 30–31, 1967. For an English translation, see W. R. Kintner and H. F. Scott, *Nuclear Revolution in Soviet Military Affairs* (Norman, Oklahoma: University of Oklahoma Press, 1968), pp. 385–86. Also see Savkin, *Osnovyye Printsipy*. S. A. Tyushkevich discusses the laws of war in Volkogonov, *Marksistsko-Leninskoye*, p. 77.

87. Volkogonov, *Marksistko-Leninskoye*, p. 67. Since the mid-1960s, Tyushkevich has been the major contributor covering the laws of war in books that have won Frunze Prizes or which have been in the Officer's Library series.

88. Ibid, pp. 72–75.

89. Ibid., pp. 77–78.

90. Ibid., p. 79.

91. Ibid., pp. 79–80.

92. M. M. Kir'yan, *Problemy Voyennoy Teorii v Sovetskikh Nauchno-Spravochnykh Izdaniyakh* [Problems of Military Theory in Soviet Scientific Reference Publications] (Moscow: Nauka, 1985), p. 134. On the inside cover of the pamphlet a note identifies the association with the Institute of Military History of the Ministry of Defense USSR.

93. Ibid.

Part 2
Formulation and Dissemination of Soviet Military Doctrine

6
Role of the CPSU in Formulating Military Doctrine

Every five years, delegates to a Congress of the Communist Party of the Soviet Union assemble in Moscow. Experienced observers of the Moscow scene do not expect anything new to be decided by the delegates at Party Congresses. Resolutions announced in the name of the Congress will have been made prior to its convening. The first speech at every Congress is the Report of the Central Committee made by the General Secretary. This speech is followed by a report on Party finances. The outline of the new five-year plan is then given, and some long-range plans are reported. Finally, the delegates select a new Central Committee.

Editorials and articles appearing in the Party-controlled Soviet press immediately prior to and following the meeting of each Congress warrant close study. New ideas published at such a time can be assumed to reflect Party-approved decisions. Economic goals of the next five-year plan may or may not be met, but the fact that they are announced gives economists throughout the world an indication of intent. Military goals also may not be realized, but the statements made by the Party-military leadership on military issues will reflect current military intentions.

The deployment of Soviet intercontinental ballistic missiles, which has kept the entire world on edge since the early 1960s, was a direct outgrowth of Party-military doctrinal decisions. The new doctrine first announced by Khrushchev in his speech at the 4th Session of the Supreme Soviet in January 1960 was further elaborated by Malinovskiy, the Soviet Minister of Defense, in his address to the 22nd Party Congress in October 1961.

Speeches by the Party Secretary and senior military officers immediately prior to and following Party Congresses provide an indication of shifts of emphasis on military doctrinal issues. Following the 23rd Party Congress in 1966, for example, increased attention was given to the possibility of a conventional phase in a future war, with emphasis on the need for "units and subunits to be prepared to fight with or without the use of nuclear weapons." Doctrinal modifications could also be discerned immediately following the 27th Party Congress in 1986.

Much has been published in the United States comparing policy formulation and decision-making processes in the Soviet Union with those in the United States, Western Europe, and other noncommunist nations. Differences in the basic political structure and culture, however, generally make such comparisons meaningless. In order to forecast or to anticipate Soviet political-military moves and deployments of weapons systems, it is first necessary to examine the political structure in which Soviet doctrine is developed and approved.

Those who occupy important positions within the Soviet power structure have been called the *nomenklatura*, which means simply a "list of names." The *nomenklatura* constitutes the ruling bureaucracy in the Soviet Union. Estimates of how many people make up this group range from 750,000 to 3 million.[1] Three major groups may be said to make up this power structure in the 1980s. First are those high in the Party apparatus—individuals who work full-time on Party matters. Most of the General Secretaries belonged to this group before their appointment to the top position, including Khrushchev, Brezhnev, Andropov, Chernenko, and Gorbachev. Andropov was something of an exception; originally a Party functionary, he later headed the KGB.

Second are the KGB and MVD, the security-intelligence organizations. On occasion in the past, these two organizations, under various names, have been combined, and at other times separated. In the late 1980s three individuals from this group were full members of the Politburo. Viktor M. Chebrikov, chairman of the KGB since December 1982, served fifteen years with that organization. Geydar A. Aliyev, first deputy chairman of the Council of Ministers USSR from November 1982 until October 1987, served in the KGB from 1941 until 1969, when he became First Secretary of the Azerbaydzhan Communist Party. He retired in October 1987. Eduard A. Shevardnadze, Minister of Foreign Affairs since July 1985, had been in the Georgian MVD from 1964 until 1972, when he became First Secretary of the Georgian Communist Party.

The military forms the third group. In the 1937–1938 purges, Stalin killed or sent to labor camps all of the military leaders who he thought might be a threat to his personal power. Following Stalin's death, the military as a group gained in power and influence. Children's books glorified the heroes of the Great Patriotic War, such as Marshals G. K. Zhukov, I. S. Konev, and V. I. Chuykov. Zhukov, however, was removed from his position as Minister of Defense and member of the Politburo in 1957 and went into retirement. It was not until 1973, almost two decades later, that a Minister of Defense was made a member of the Politburo again and allowed to join the inner circle of Soviet leaders. In that year the head of the KGB also became a Politburo member, for the first time since L. P. Beria, a member from 1946 until he was arrested in 1953.

In the internal Kremlin power struggle after the death of General Secretary Chernenko, the KGB was able to increase its influence in the Politburo. In contrast, the replacement for Minister of Defense, Ustinov, remained only an alternate Politburo member. In the late 1980s the head of the KGB was a full Politburo member, while the Minister of Defense still only had alternate membership. At the same time, Shevardnadze, with an MVD background, also was a full Politburo member.

It is impossible to determine all of the reasons for and implications of this change. Several of Gorbachev's predecessors had held high military rank. Stalin was a Generalissimus of the Soviet Union, Brezhnev a Marshal of the Soviet Union, while Khrushchev was a General Lieutenant. Andropov was a General of the Army by virtue of having been chairman of the KGB, although he never appeared in uniform as did Stalin, Khrushchev and Brezhnev. The Soviet press glorified the wartime exploits of both Andropov and Chernenko, although neither had been in uniform during World War II. Chernenko, however, had served in the Border Guards of the KGB from 1930 to 1933. Gorbachev, as far as can be determined, underwent training to become a reserve officer while attending Moscow State University, but it is not known whether he achieved any subsequent advances in reserve military rank.

But one thing is certain. During the period from 1957 to 1975, when the Soviet Minister of Defense was *not* on the Politburo either as an alternate or full member, the Soviet Armed Forces nevertheless brought the Soviet Union to the position of a military superpower. This accomplishment, however, was not achieved solely through the actions of the military leadership. The KGB played the paramount role in the development of nuclear weapons, and it still controls the nuclear stockpiles. The KGB also had initial responsibilities for missile development.

In addition to the three major groups, there also are less powerful groups that are part of the *nomenklatura*, such as the various ministers, scientists, and the intelligentsia. The top leaders in all groups, whether the military, the KGB, MVD, industry, or the intelligentsia, must, with few exceptions, be Party members. Their positions and privileges as well as membership in other select bodies are dependent upon their Party credentials.

Although the Kremlin power struggle does appear to have individuals seeking personal power and influence, at the same time all have a common goal: Each is seeking to make the Soviet Union the undisputed leading world power. The history of the Soviet leadership indicates that the three major groups have the same basic interest in maintaining and augmenting the Soviet Union's economic, political, scientific, and purely military position. The Communist Party structure provides the framework within which they seek to achieve their aims; thus the power apparatus of the Soviet Union embraces these several groups under the auspices of the Party. It is these groups within the Party that answer the questions posed by military doctrine: Who the enemy will be and how the nation and the Armed Forces are to be prepared for the possibility of future war.

Western observers often profess to see the Party and the Armed Forces in constant conflict, with generals, marshals, and admirals restive under the measures imposed by the Party to control the military. Others seek to identify "institutional differences" of the type that might exist in the United States or in Western European nations. The Soviet Armed Forces are visualized as opposing the "civilian" side of the Soviet economy in seeking greater military budgets. But there is no documented evidence that such institutional pressures exist. On the contrary, there is an intermarriage of Party and military leaders at the highest levels, which may have begun at the level of republics and military districts. The relationship between commanders of military districts and senior Party officials in those areas is equally close.

By law, each of the sixteen military districts into which the Soviet Union is divided must have a military council. The local Party secretary must be a member of the military council of the military district in his area. In turn, senior military leaders in each district serve in local Party organizations. For example, General of the Army M. M. Zaytsev, commander in chief of the Southern TVD, became a member of the Bureau of the Azerbaydzhan Communist Party in 1986. General of the Army I. A. Gerasimov, commander in chief of the Southwestern TVD, is a member of the eleven-man Bureau of the Ukrainian Communist Party. The local army commander is on the Bureau of the Armenian Communist Party. The commander of the Belorussian Military District, General Colonel V. M. Shuralev, sits on the Bureau of the Belorussian Communist Party, and General Colonel K. A. Kochetov, commander of the Transcaucasus Military District, does the same in Georgia. In Kazakhstan, General Colonel V. N. Lobov was selected for a seat on the Bureau in 1986 when he headed the Central Asian Military District. General Colonel A. V. Betekhtin was commander of the Baltic Military District when he was made a Bureau member of the Latvian Communist Party. In Uzbekistan, General Colonel N. I. Popov, commander of the Turkestan Military District, sits on the Bureau of the Uzbekistan Communist Party. Hundreds of top military district officers, such as first deputies, chiefs of staff, and chiefs of political administrations, are members of the Party's central committees in the republics.

Ties are thus forged between civilian Party officials and military commanders at the local level. Each of them at times may be in a position to help the other. The military district commander may help the local economy by releasing a portion of his troops to work in the fields and assist with the harvest. Party officials may help the local military commander in finding housing for military dependents. If a regional Party secretary advances to a position in Moscow, he may want a military friend occupying a key position in the General Staff, or in another important military assignment.

Although the highest leadership of the Party and government in the Soviet Union shows great interest in military policies, basic work on military fundamentals begins at much lower levels. A number of significant groups, agencies, and institutions play a role in the formulation of the major military decisions reflected in military doctrine. Much of the information necessary for a thorough analysis of these bodies and their roles in decision making is missing; however, enough information is available to show the basic structure.

It must be kept in mind that Soviet military doctrine has two sides, the political and the military-technical. Since military doctrine was first developed in the 1920s, Soviet writings have always stressed that the political side takes precedence over the military-technical side. Before any new doctrine or shift of emphasis can be announced, the Party must indicate its approval. In certain cases, the Party leadership itself initiates the change or modification to doctrine.

The role of the Party itself in formulating military doctrine, as well as that of the Party Congresses, the Central Committee, the Politburo, and the Secretariat, will be discussed first. Then the role of the Soviet government also will be examined, as well as other bodies, such as the Academy of Sciences. It may surprise many Americans that the Academy of Sciences works closely with the Soviet Armed Forces not only in weaponry but to some extent in strategy as well. Finally, the role of the Soviet Armed Forces in the development of military doctrine will be traced.

Role of the Communist Party

Basic principles and concepts of Soviet Party-military relationships, as described in numerous Soviet military publications, reflect the role of the Party in formulating military doctrine. These can be seen in frequent repetition of certain statements by one spokesman after another; this common Soviet device indicates that an official view is being presented.

A major task of the Communist Party and the Soviet government, reiterated countless times in Soviet writings, is to "take every necessary measure for further strengthening the defense of the country and raising the fighting power of the Armed Forces." In so doing, the Soviet Union "takes into account the complicated international situation and the presence in the world of a system of inimical aggressive imperialist forces."[2] There is never the slightest acknowledgment by Soviet spokesmen that their own motives are less than laudatory, or that their own military forces may be considered by some nations as a threat to world stability.

As in all other areas, Soviet spokesmen pay homage to Lenin for having formulated the basic guiding principles of Soviet military development. Since Lenin's day, Soviet spokesmen assert, these principles have been modified in accordance with changes in weapons systems and international developments. Modifications may be found in certain documents such as the Constitution of the USSR approved in 1977, the new edition of the Third Program of the Communist Party of the Soviet Union adopted at the 27th Party Congress in 1986, and in the reports and decisions of the various Plenums of the Central Committee and Sessions of the Supreme Soviet USSR.[3]

Many Party decrees relating to the Soviet Armed Forces use the expression *"voyennoye stroitel'stvo"* (military development, buildup or construction), a term that does not have an equivalent meaning in the West. In the Soviet sense, military development includes the measures that form the basis for building up military power. As explained in the *Soviet Military Encyclopedia*: "The military development of socialist states in its broadest sense represents the aggregate of economic, political, moral and purely military measures carried out under the direction of the Communist Party aimed at assuring its armed defense."[4]

This definition supposedly follows the principles of Marxism-Leninism, which Soviet writers assert guide their military development. Under these principles the armed forces are a special organ of the state. As such, the armed forces bear the specific features inherent in that particular state and are a part of its political superstructure. Soviet theorists claim that the type of armed forces of a particular state is determined by the type of political system in that state. In turn, the political system depends on the social system and the methods of production.[5]

The Soviet public is constantly reminded that their Armed Forces represent the world's first socialist army. These forces are based upon Soviet military development, which depends upon the following:

> 1. *The socialist economy*, primarily all branches of heavy industry, transport, communications, agriculture and so forth. The economic-productive and scientific-technical possibilities of the State determine the quantity and quality of the armaments that are the material basis for waging war. . . .
>
> 2. *The socialist social system* based on public ownership of the means of production, collective labor and comradely cooperation. . . .
>
> 3. *Marxism-Leninism and its teachings on war and army.* Communist ideology, which has become the ideology of all Soviet people, communist morals, high political consciousness and boundless devotion to the idea of communism. These things compose the spiritual world of the Soviet man; they produce feelings of ardent love for the socialist motherland, bitter hatred for its enemies, and invincible steadfastness in defending the socialist mother country.[6]

The official 1986 edition of the *Third Program of the Communist Party of the Soviet Union* stressed:

> The leadership exercised by the Communist Party over the country's military development and the Armed Forces is the basis for strengthening the defenses of the socialist homeland. It is under the Party's guidance that the country's policy in the field of defense and security and the Soviet military doctrine, which is purely defensive in nature and geared to ensuring protection against outside attack, are worked out and implemented.
>
> The CPSU will make every effort to ensure that the Soviet Armed Forces remain at a level that rules out strategic superiority of the forces of imperialism, that the Soviet state's defense capacity continues to be improved in every way, and that military cooperation between the armies of the fraternal socialist countries is strengthened.[7]

Since the Program was adopted, this theme has appeared in virtually every issue of the various Soviet military journals. General Colonel Makhmut A. Gareyev paid particular attention to this theme in his 1985 book *M. V.*

Frunze—Military Theoretician, in which he devoted a whole chapter to the development of the Armed Forces. In particular, he purports to trace how Frunze took the ideas of Lenin and applied them to the Armed Forces and emphasized that these ideas still apply in the 1980s, sixty years after Frunze's death.[8]

Soviet authorities write that the principles of Soviet military development are inseparable from principles of state and Party development. Three primary principles applicable to these three bodies—Party, state, and military—are as follows:

1. *The principle of Party leadership.* In the *Program of the Communist Party,* in resolutions of Congresses of the Party, Plenums of the Central Committee, and in other Party documents, the decisive role of the Communist Party in managing, organizing and educating activities in Soviet military organization is stressed. . . . Any important question of military development, before it becomes a program of activity for the State and the people, is decided by the Party. It formulates the military and military-technical policy of the state and draws up its *military doctrine.* . . . (Emphasis added.)

2. *The principle of unity of the army and the people.* The *Report of the Central Committee CPSU to the 23rd Party Congress* stressed: "Civil Defense must be perfected, military patriotic work among the workers, especially among the youth, must be improved, the patronage of factory collectives, schools, kolkhozes and sovkhozes over military units and subunits must be strengthened, and more concern for soldiers and officers of the Soviet Armed Forces and their families must be expressed."

3. *The principle of internationalism.* In the Soviet military organization, this principle is expressed in the unbreakable friendship of the peoples of the Soviet Union. This principle now is also expressed in the fraternal socialist countries, the fighting cooperation of their armies, the joint defense of the world socialist system from imperialist aggression. Organizational embodiment of this principle is found in the Warsaw Defense Pact, and also in bilateral agreements of socialist countries on friendship, cooperation and mutual aid. A clear example of such socialist internationalism was the defense of the gains of socialism in Czechoslovakia from the intrigues of internal and external counterrevolution.[9]

Each month one or more issues of *Red Star, Communist of the Armed Forces* and other military publications include articles discussing one of these principles of military development at length. Often Western observers of Soviet military affairs report on these articles, thinking they have turned up something new in an internal Soviet Party-military "debate." Confusion in the United States about the Soviet Armed Forces is likely to continue until the actual relationship between the Party and its Armed Forces is understood in light of these principles. As noted, the three principles listed above apply to the Party, the state, and to the Armed Forces. Military development principles that apply only to the Armed Forces are:

1. *The principle of cadre organization.* In the present-day complicated inter-national conditions, the presence of a cadre army is vitally necessary for

assuring the security of our country. While imperialism exists, while it has powerful regular armed forces, and great reserves of weapons of mass destruction, our country and the fraternal socialist countries must keep and strengthen in every possible way their cadre armies.[10]

2. *The principle of constant perfection of the organizational structure of our army and the harmonious development of all services of Armed Forces and branches of service.* Victory in modern war is achieved by the efforts of all services of the Armed Forces and service branches. Our Party decides questions of the structure and changes in the organizational form and relationship of the services of the Armed Forces and service branches, taking into consideration the internal situation of the country and international conditions, and also development of ways and means of armed conflict. . . .

3. *The principle of centralization.* Centralism in the organizational structure of the Armed Forces and their system of control finds expression in that all units of the army and navy, their staffs, and other organs of control are strictly subordinated to the central organ of state power, to a single Supreme Command. Lower control organs strictly carry out orders, directives and instructions of higher ones and are accountable to them in all questions of their activities. . . .[11]

4. *The principle of unity of command.* The Program of the CPSU defines unity of command as the most important principle of Soviet military organization. Unity of command in the Soviet Armed Forces is built on a Party basis. This means the commander is the representative of the Party and government in the troops, carrying out their line of action, observing Soviet laws and military regulations; he is the sole administrator of the troops entrusted to him, bearing full responsibility for all sides of their activity, for the state of combat and political training, for their combat capability and combat readiness. . . .[12]

5. *The principle of conscious military discipline.* Subordination is also found in socialist armies, but it is different in form. It is not based on class role as in bourgeois armies, but on the common interest of commanders and subordinates to assure the security of the socialist state.[13]

6. *The principle of maintaining the constant combat readiness of the Soviet Armed Forces.* The deepening of the general crisis of capitalism, [and] the aggravation of its contradictions increased the adventurousness of imperialism, its danger for [other] nations, for the cause of peace and social progress. This is convincingly confirmed by recent events. Military imperialism might unleash world nuclear rocket war. Therefore, Soviet *military doctrine* proceeds from the necessity to support high vigilance and constant combat readiness of troops and their ability in any circumstances to repulse an attack by an aggressor and deliver a crushing defeat to him.[14] (Emphasis added.)

Like the three primary principles that apply to the Party, the state, and the Armed Forces, these six military principles are frequent topics of military writers. The principle of "unity of command" and combat readiness, in particular, are frequently discussed in Soviet journals. It is likely that in the annual programs for the military journals, which are planned in advance, one or more writers will be tasked to produce articles on each of the principles listed above.

"Principles of education and training" are a subset of the "military organization."[15] The Soviet Union has the largest and in many ways the most impressive professional military training structure in the world. Approximately 140 military and higher military schools provide four- and five-year courses for officer training, similar in many respects to the three U.S. service academies at West Point, Annapolis, and Colorado Springs. The 140 Soviet schools, while not as elaborate or as large as the three U.S. service academies, are housed in well-kept facilities and are usually in or near a large city.[16]

In addition, the Soviet Armed Forces have seventeen military academies that roughly correspond to the command and staff colleges and war colleges in the United States. A primary difference is that a professional course for officers in the United States is generally one academic year or less, while courses at Soviet military academies are generally three years. Soviet officers trained and educated in this vast professional military educational structure are responsible for ensuring that the principles of education and training are implemented. These principles are as follows:

1. *The principle of unity of training and education.* It is well known that the success of a soldier in fulfilling his military duty depends on his skill and understanding. They are closely interconnected. The trainer must educate and the educator must train. Compulsory military training is for two or three years according to the new law on military obligation. . . .

2. *The principle of teaching the troops what is needed in modern war.* This means inculcating such qualities as will assure the fulfillment by them of their obligations in the most complicated conditions of modern war. Therefore training must be conducted in conditions as close as possible to battle, in the spirit of active, offensive actions. . . .

3. *The principle of taking into consideration the features of the military collective and the individual qualities of the soldiers.* Young people enter the army with different levels of education, ideological and vital erudition. Their functions in service are far from alike. The individual and the collective must be approached individually, taking into account their specifics.

4. *The principle of communist purposefulness.* Training and education is not an end in itself but a means of producing a highly principled and skillful defender of the motherland. The soldiers of the socialist army are imbued with high ideals; consciousness of patriotic and international obligations guides all their thoughts and actions, lets them achieve military mastery without tiring, bravely overcome difficulties and dangers of military life, and lets them fight to the last drop of their blood.[17]

Western readers may note that these Soviet writings contain a great deal of jargon that normally would be considered propaganda. For this reason, such writings are frequently overlooked in the West. In the examples above, no attempt has been made to translate the statements into language less offensive to noncommunist readers, because these notions and expressions are a basic part of understanding Soviet motivations and Soviet military personnel. To a greater or lesser extent, the Soviet reader believes these statements. They are repeated over and over: on radio, television, on street billboards, in the newspapers, and in magazines and books. To separate

Soviet military policy from its ideological foundations would be to study a machine without its motor.

Role of Communist Ideology

The Kremlin leadership attempts to instill in its citizens the belief that the communist ideology of Marxism-Leninism is the driving force and source of the guiding principles underlying Soviet society. Regardless of the facts and the real significance underlying ideology in Soviet actions, the Communist Party plays a unique role in every phase of Soviet military development. The importance of the Party is carefully maintained: "The leadership of the Communist Party, the increasing role and influence of Party organizations in the army and navy, as stressed in the *Program of the CPSU*, is the fundamental basis of Soviet military organization. The undivided leadership of the Armed Forces by the Party and its Central Committee is an objective rule of the life and combat activity of the army and navy."[18] In newspapers, journals, and books, spokesmen explain how the Communist Party provides the leadership. The following explanation is typical:

First: All questions of the defense of the socialist fatherland, of military organization, of military theory and practice, both in the past and at present, are decided in strict correspondence with the ideology and policy of the Party, on the basis of directives and decrees formulated in resolutions of Congresses, Plenums of the Central Committee, and the Politburo of the Central Committee CPSU.

The military policy of the Party, being part of the general policy of the CPSU, provides for the solution of the most important problems of military organization.

Second: The leadership of the Armed Forces by the Communist Party finds expression in that its Central Committee is directly concerned with questions about the life and activity of the army and navy, determines the main direction and tasks of its organization, and is concerned about strengthening its combat might, discipline and unity. The Central Committee of the Party plans the main directions in the development of the technical equipping of the army and navy [and] supplies the troops with all kinds of modern weapons and combat equipment; it determines the reasonable proportion in the development of the services of the Armed Forces and the service branches; it works out *Soviet military doctrine*; it selects and places the leading military cadres; it works out and puts into practice the principles of training and educating personnel; and is concerned with raising the vigilance and combat readiness of the troops. [Emphasis added.]

Third: The leadership of the Armed Forces by the Communist Party is shown by the fact that a strict system of political organs, [and] Party and Komsomol organizations has been created and operates within the Soviet Army and Navy which carry out enormous educational and organizational work in the troops. The Central Committee gives constant attention to questions of Party-political work in the army and navy, improving its forms and methods, [and] raising its fighting spirit and efficiency. Party-political work rallies the troops of the army and navy around the Party and the Soviet government, mobilizes them in fulfilling tasks that stand before the Armed Forces.

Fourth: The leading role of the Communist Party in the Armed Forces is revealed in the fact that in the years of military trial, the Party, by its policy and military organizational activity, assured the unity of front and rear, turned the country into a single military camp, and assured the firm leadership of the troops.[19]

On the surface, writings such as the above may appear simply as cant, for propaganda purposes without any real meaning. But it would be dangerous to dismiss the ideas that Soviet political officers work so hard to communicate. The continued indoctrination appears to work, although perhaps not as well as the Soviet leadership would like.

An area that has not yet been reconciled is the role of Stalin and the role of the Party. As noted in the fourth point above, the author tried to give all credit for Soviet successes in the Great Patriotic War to the Communist Party. In the de-Stalinization period under Khrushchev, Soviet historians described how Stalin had tried to set aside the Party and they stated that the Party's actual influence was minimal. In the 1980s the *glasnost* program of Gorbachev has encouraged some Soviet writers to declare that the role of Stalin must be reexamined, but it is uncertain what the results will be.[20]

Not content with describing the past and present role of the Communist Party in the Armed Forces, Soviet spokesmen must show how this role is constantly growing. This increasing influence has been dictated, they say, by a number of factors. First, the "motherland" is always portrayed as being in constant danger from the aggressive imperialists, headed by the United States. Therefore, the Party is the protector and ensures "the constant readiness of the people and the army to repel the aggression of the imperialists, to defend the socialist fatherland." Without external danger, the Party would have a difficult time providing a justification for its existence.

Second, Soviet spokesmen claim that the radical changes in military affairs brought about by the scientific-technical revolution make Marxist-Leninist scientific foresight more necessary than ever. Now, "thanks to the constant concern of the Party and government, our army and navy has everything necessary for defeating any aggressor." However, changes in military affairs are occurring rapidly. Imperialist nations, according to Kremlin leaders, are making great efforts to achieve advantages in the military sphere. It is of vital importance that the CPSU select the right military policy for the nation, and that the economy develop in every way possible in order to support the Armed Forces at the very highest level of present-day military technology.

Third, Soviet theoreticians assert that the history of wars shows that the deadlier the weapon, the greater the role played by the morale of those drawn into combat. This role, they say, would be incomparably higher in a nuclear war. In such a war the significance of the moral factor would be greater than ever before. Therefore, the Soviet Armed Forces must achieve a position of "moral-political superiority." To achieve this goal, the Party must play an even larger role in the communist indoctrination of troops and in their moral-political and psychological training.

Fourth, Party leaders seek to convince the Soviet people that it is more necessary than ever before to prepare the whole country and all the people "to repel imperialist aggression." Modern weapons have erased the distinction between the front and the rear. Both the troops and the interior of the country might be subject to a surprise nuclear rocket strike. Hence, the role of the Party "in guaranteeing the vitality of our state in the event of war, in strengthening the military might of the USSR in every possible way, in moral-political and military preparations of the population and in organizing civil defense, is growing."

Fifth, the Party has widened the "international obligations of the Soviet Armed Forces," and this development increases the necessity for closer cooperation and unity among action of all fraternal armies. With the "growth of the political and economic might of the world socialist system," the conditions of the armed defense of socialist states changed fundamentally. In the past a single socialist state might face an imperialist military attack alone, but in a future war, the imperialist aggressors "will be repulsed by the powerful socialist community."[21]

Role of Congresses and Conferences of the CPSU

The 27th Congress of the Communist Party of the Soviet Union convened in Moscow in February 1986. Exactly five years had elapsed since the 26th Party Congress, which had met in February and March 1981. Of the 5,000 delegates to the 27th Congress, 303 were members of the Soviet Armed Forces. Of these, twenty represented the Moscow City organization, and an additional nineteen were from the Moscow Oblast Party organization. Other military delegates were selected by Party organizations throughout the USSR.[22] They represented the central military apparatus, the five armed services, the Main Political Administration, and other military components such as Civil Defense and the Rear Services. They also included the Border Guards of the KGB and the Internal Troops of the MVD, considered part of the Armed Forces though not under the authority of the Ministry of Defense.

"Retired" marshals, generals, and admirals who are assigned to the Group of General Inspectors of the Ministry of Defense are still prominent in Party affairs. Many from this group also were delegates, including Admiral of the Fleet of the Soviet Union Sergey G. Gorshkov, who served as naval commander in chief for nearly thirty years, and Chief Marshal of Artillery Vladimir F. Tolubko, former commander in chief of the Strategic Rocket Forces. Before the end of 1987, this group included Marshal of the Soviet Union Sergey L. Sokolov, who until May 1987 was Candidate Politburo Member and the Minister of Defense; Marshal of the Soviet Union Vasiliy I. Petrov, who had been first deputy Minister of Defense; Chief Marshal of Aviation Aleksandr I. Koldunov, former commander in chief of the Troops

TABLE 6.1
Military Delegates to Party Congresses, 1961–1986

Congress	Year	Ratio of Delegates to Party Members	Number of Military Delegates	Number of Party Members in the Armed Forces
22nd	1961	1:2000	305	610,000
23rd	1966	1:2500	352	880,000
24th	1971	1:2900	(300)[a]	(870,000)
25th	1976	1:3000	314	942,000
26th	1981	1:3350	(300)[a]	(1,005,000)
27th	1986	1:3670	(300)[a]	(1,101,000)

[a]In 1971, 1981, and 1986, the Congressional Mandate Commission did not give the number of military delegates to the Party Congress. The number given is estimated.

of Air Defense; and former Civil Defense Chief General of the Army Aleksandr T. Altunin. A somewhat unusual member of the group was General of the Army Vitaliy V. Fedorchuk, previously head of the KGB. The general inspectors group is normally made up of the most senior retired officers from only the Ministry of Defense.

The senior officers in uniform form a substantial bloc at the Congresses. When gathered in Moscow, in the Kremlin's Palace of Congresses, time is set aside for them to meet both as a group and separately, by service, to take up matters of policy. The book *Troops of Air Defense*, published in 1968, shows that thirty-three delegates represented that service at the 23rd Party Congress. *The Combat Path of the Soviet Navy* contains a photograph of a group of twenty-six admirals representing the Navy.[23] Another book, *50 Years of the Armed Forces USSR*, includes a photograph of all the military delegates meeting with Party leaders in the Kremlin during the 23rd Party Congress.[24]

The number of military delegates to each Party Congress varies. For example, at the 23rd Party Congress held in March and April 1966, nearly 5,000 delegates represented the approximately 12 million Party members. Of these, 352 were military delegates. Nearly all were of the rank of general, admiral, or marshal and had previously been "selected" at local Party conferences. Each delegate at the Congress in 1966 represented 2,500 Party members; thus, the size of the Party membership in the Armed Forces in 1966 stood at approximately 880,000. (See Table 6.1.)

At the 25th Party Congress in 1976, 314 of the 5,000 delegates were identified as being in the Armed Forces. Since each delegate at that session represented 3,000 Party members, then Party membership in the military had grown to 942,000. The 26th Congress, held in 1981, had approximately 300 military delegates. That year, however, each delegate represented 3,350 Party members, which placed Party membership in the Armed Forces at about 1 million.

The roughly 300 military delegates at the 27th Party Congress (one for every 3,670 members) indicated that the Soviet Armed Forces included about

1,101,000 Party members. If the total membership of the CPSU was 18 million, approximately one out of every sixteen Party members was in uniform. Practically all of these would have been officers, since very few enlisted personnel are Party members. However, at this Congress there were a number of sergeants and junior officers, many with records of fighting in Afghanistan.

Much of the work of the Congresses consists of approving the five-year plan, the ready-made resolutions, and a new Central Committee, all of which has been carefully prepared in advance. Party Congress approval generally is thought to be a rubber-stamp process. On the other hand, there is some evidence that the Congress can force a reexamination of development plans. In 1971, for example, it appears that there was a delay in producing a new budget, it having been sent back "to committee" at least once.

Party Conferences

Congresses of the Communist Party of the Soviet Union are carefully studied in the United States. Much less is known about Party Conferences. This lack of attention is understandable, since more than forty-seven years have passed since the 18th Party Conference was held in 1941. The 19th Conference was scheduled to be convened in June 1988. Although even Party Congresses were not convened by Stalin in the thirteen years between 1939 and 1952, since then the Congresses have been held at fairly regular five-year intervals.

The difference between a Party Congress and a Party Conference is this: A Congress is the supreme, most powerful Party forum. It selects the general Party line and determines the basic directions of politics as well as the Party's strategy and tactics. It also selects a new Central Committee. A Party Conference is a form of collective discussion of Party work in the period between Party Congresses, mainly focusing on economic questions. This focus may be one of the reasons that General Secretary Gorbachev has called for a Conference in 1988. Before 1917, some Party Conferences chose a new Central Committee or made substantial changes in the existing one. The right to hold a Party Conference was dropped from Party rules in 1952 but was restored in 1966.

Activities of Military Delegates

Although we know little about the influence of military delegates on policy making at Congresses in recent years, an examination of Party Congresses of the 1920s and 1930s shows an active military role. It is likely that, to one degree or other, military delegates play a somewhat similar role today.

At the 9th Party Congress held in March 1920, the Party leadership was faced with the problem of educating both the military and the population as a whole in Party matters. Should Party work in the military be combined with Party work among civilians? The matter was discussed by the military delegates to the Congress, but no decision was reached. In the summer of

1920, at the 9th Party Conference, there was another meeting of military delegates, who thought the idea of combining all Party work under one directorate was premature. However, the Central Committee ruled otherwise, and all Party work was combined in January 1921.

National security was a central issue for Soviet leaders in the early 1920s. Lenin asserted that the Communist Party had to display "constant concern" for increasing the defense capability of the Soviet state—much the same theme that is repeated today. A key decision concerning the development of the Soviet Armed Forces at this early stage was made by the 10th Party Congress, which met in March 1921. The role of the military delegates to this and other early Congresses is illustrative.

Questions on the reorganization of the Armed Forces were debated at three closed sessions of the 10th Congress. A large group of military delegates took part in these decisions: there were 150 voting military delegates and 52 nonvoting. Among them were K. Ye. Voroshilov, S. I. Gusev, A. I. Yegorov, I. S. Unshlikht, M. V. Frunze, I. Ye. Yakir and others. The day after the close of the 10th Congress, on March 17, 1921, the military delegates held a meeting. With 158 present, they discussed "the practical realization of the decisions of the Congress."[25] Later Soviet spokesmen asserted that military reforms in the following years were derived from the decisions of this Congress.

However, not all the decisions made by Party Congresses were workable. For example, combining the political directorate of the Red Army with the Main Political Educational Directorate (*Glavpolitprosvet*) had raised many problems. It soon became apparent that combining these bodies was not feasible. At the meeting of the military delegates of the 11th Party Congress in the beginning of April 1922, it was agreed that the *Glavpolitprosvet* and its agencies could not handle their obligations and that its local agencies were too weak to carry out political education among the troops.

Other military matters, apparently of a more substantive nature, were brought up by the 11th Party Congress and discussed by the military delegates. Decrees on strengthening the Red Army adopted by the 11th Party Congress were expanded by a meeting of military delegates to the Congress. A Plenum of the Central Committee, which took place on the eve of the opening of the Congress, called for a specially selected commission to gather military delegates to discuss these issues. The meeting was given the right, if necessary, to make proposals to the Congress. As later described: "Questions of Soviet military doctrine connected with its content and role in building the Armed Forces and with their preparation for war were discussed in Congresses of the Central Committee at the 7th–11th sessions. . . . Later, questions of doctrine were brought up in subsequent Congresses of the Party in connection with judging military questions and also at Congresses of the Soviets and at Sessions of the Supreme Soviet USSR."[26]

These activities of military delegates at early Party Congresses indicate that this group operated as a sort of bloc and was tasked by the Party Congresses to perform certain studies. Although the information is sketchy, what is available shows military delegates playing an important role in the Congresses. From this evidence, the part played by military delegates to Party Congresses in contemporary times can be conjectured.

Finally, the importance of Party Congresses should not be overemphasized. Being designated as a delegate to the Congress indicates position and status. Holding the Congresses represents an attempt to give legitimacy to Party rule, and to provide a facade of democracy. At the same time, under certain conditions the Congresses could have some influence on military affairs. The intermarriage of military and Party leaders at these gatherings may carry over into cooperation for security matters in general. The most important task of the Party Congresses is to designate the members of the Central Committee. In reality, designation to this body is probably determined by a small group of Party functionaries under the control of the Politburo. It is the Central Committee which, in theory, is the ruling body of the USSR.

Role of the Central Committee

Soviet writings constantly stress that the Central Committee of the CPSU is the organization officially charged with the responsibility for Soviet military doctrine. The following statement by Marshal of the Soviet Union R. Ya. Malinovskiy, former Minister of Defense, is typical: "The basic questions connected with the content and guidance of Soviet military doctrine have been seriously elaborated in recent years thanks to the attention given to them by the Central Committee of the Party and the Soviet government."[27]

The same view of the source of military doctrine was restated by one of the leading Soviet defense-intellectuals, General Colonel N. A. Lomov, a former department head at the Academy of the General Staff. His many articles on Soviet military doctrine can be considered as reflecting "an official view." In his words:

> The bases of military doctrine are determined by the domestic and foreign policy of the Communist Party and the Soviet government in accordance with the nature and tasks of the present era. Therefore, the essence and content of military doctrine can only be correctly understood by taking into consideration those theoretical and political conclusions which are in the materials of the 22nd Congress of the CPSU and the new Program of the Party. . . .
>
> The decisions of the Central Committee of the CPSU and the Soviet government on questions of strengthening the defense of the country, the organization and logistical support of the troops, the rules and regulations of the Armed Forces on conducting combat operations, and military-theoretical works analyzing its separate positions, are the concrete expressions of military doctrine. It relies on the most important conclusions of military science disclosing the objective laws of armed conflict.
>
> The formulation of Soviet military doctrine is accomplished under the leadership of the Central Committee of the Party, under its direct control, on the basis of the theoretical and methodological principles of Marxism-Leninism.[28]

In 1921, in the magazine *Military Science and Revolution,* Frunze wrote a long article entitled "A Single Military Doctrine and the Red Army." This was said to have been based on Lenin's works and on decisions of the Party on military questions. Frunze attempted to define the military doctrine of a proletariat state as follows:

> It is the teaching accepted in the army of a given state, establishing the character of the construction of the armed forces of the country, the methods of combat training of troops, their guidance based on the ruling views in the state on the nature of the military tasks lying before them, and the methods of their solution flowing from the class nature of the state and the determining level of development of the industrial forces of the country.[29]

Another author brought in the specific role of the Central Committee:

> Questions of Soviet military doctrine, connected with its content and role in construction of the Armed Forces and with their preparation for war, were discussed at sessions of the Central Committee at the 8th and 9th [Party] Congresses. After that, questions of doctrine one way or another were brought up at subsequent Party Congresses in connection with discussions of military questions, and also at Congresses of Soviets and in Sessions of the Supreme Soviet of the USSR.[30]

The most authoritative Soviet work in 1968 was *50 Years of the Armed Forces of the USSR,* winner of the Frunze Prize for that year and in 1985 identified as an "official" publication. Authors of this work repeated the usual refrain: "All questions of preparing the Armed Forces to protect the country from aggression and to conduct the armed struggle, all sides of the life and daily routine of the army and navy are under the continual leadership of the CPSU and its Leninist Central Committee."[31]

In 1969 Politizdat (Political Publishing House) published *Army of the Soviets.* In discussing the guiding role of the Party, the authors noted that:

> The Communist Party demands from military cadres the discovery of the laws of development of modern war in connection with the appearance of the nuclear rocket weapons, the elaboration of questions of military art, and the further raising of the combat readiness of the troops.
>
> An important role in answering these questions has been played by decisions of the Central Committee of the CPSU. The Central Committee demanded that an end be put to dogmatism in the development of military theory, that new problems of conducting combat operations in conditions of nuclear war be bravely posed and solved, and that the behest of the great Lenin be studied.[32]

In 1977, another major book, *War and Army,* written by a group of authors from different military academies, again stressed the role of the Central Committee in formulating doctrine:

Soviet military doctrine in its nature and essence is the expression of the class-political line of the Communist Party and Soviet state. It is a system of scientifically based official views on the essence, character and methods of waging a war that might be forced on the Soviet Union, and also on the demands for military construction, preparation of the Armed Forces and the country to rout an aggressor. Military doctrine is elaborated by the political leadership of the country with the participation of higher military agencies.
. . .

. . . The sum total of these positions composes the political content of Soviet military doctrine. In a more concrete plan, this political content is formulated in the Program of the CPSU, in resolutions of Party Congresses and Plenums of its Central Committee, and in other Party and state documents.[33]

A 1984 book, *Marxist-Leninist Teachings on War and Army*, part of the Officer's Library series, repeated the familiar theme:

In the resolutions of our Party on military questions, the defensive character of Soviet military doctrine is clearly expressed. . . . On the basis of deep analysis of the character of modern war and its demands, the economic, social, scientific, spiritual, and purely military possibilities of our country, and also the possibilities of the probable aggressor, the Party elaborates the military policy, which guides the state in its activities in strengthening the defense capability of the country, and determines the basic direction of constructing the military and developing military affairs.[34]

The *Military Encyclopedic Dictionary*, second edition (1986) a condensed, updated version of the eight-volume *Soviet Military Encyclopedia* (1976–1980) is illustrative of those organizations and agencies that have an interest in military affairs: Authors and reviewers came from the General Staff of the Armed Forces, the Main Political Administration of the Soviet Army and Navy, the main staffs of the services of the Armed Forces, the staff of the Rear Services, the main and central directorates of the Ministry of Defense, the Ministry of Foreign Affairs, the Academy of Social Sciences of the Central Committee CPSU, the Institute of Marxism-Leninism of the Central Committee CPSU, the editors of the *Bolshaya Soviet Encyclopedia*, the Central Archives of the Ministry of Defense, the Central State Archives of the Soviet Army, the military section of the Lenin State Library, the institutes of the Academy of Sciences USSR and other scientific research establishments, and the professors and instructors of the military academies, institutes, and schools.

In summary, the Minister of Defense, faculty members of the Academy of the General Staff and the Lenin Military-Political Academy, members of the Academy of Sciences USSR, and spokesmen from organizations directly subordinate to the Central Committee, all state essentially the same thing: The Central Committee of the CPSU formulates Soviet military doctrine. The Soviet news media—newspapers, journals and books—never even hints of any other source for the formulation of military doctrine. It should be noted, however, that the Politburo is a body of the Central Committee, as

TABLE 6.2
Military Representation on the Central Committee CPSU, 1961–1986

Con-gress	Year	Total Members of the Central Committee	Military Full Members of the Central Committee	Military Candidate Members of the Central Committee	Total Military Members (% of total)	Military Members of the Central Auditing Commission
22nd	1961	330	14	18	32 (10.3%)	(3)
23rd	1966	360	15	18	33 (9.2%)	(4)
24th	1971	396	20	13	33 (8.3%)	(3)
25th	1976	426	20	10	30 (7%)	(5)
26th	1981	470	23	13	36 (7.6%)	(4)
27th	1986	477	23	14	37 (7.7%)	(3)

is the Secretariat. Key military officers also are members of the Central Committee, and it is highly probable that they, as members of this body, play a major role in doctrinal formulation.

Military Officers on the Central Committee

If the Central Committee is charged with the formulation of military doctrine, where does it get military expertise? At the 27th Party Congress in 1986, 307 full members and 170 candidate members of the Central Committee were selected. Twenty-three full members and 14 candidate members of this body were senior officers of the Soviet Armed Forces. Another 3 officers were selected as members of the Central Auditing Commission of the Central Committee. Military members on these bodies have remained fairly constant for the past two decades, as shown in Table 6.2.

As will be seen, military personnel on the Central Committee are the most powerful officers in the Armed Forces, although there does not appear to be a set rule for membership qualification. At times, it seems that certain military positions routinely carry Central Committee membership, and at other times certain individuals in the military have Central Committee membership regardless of their position. A number of World War II heroes, such as Marshals I. Kh. Bagramyan, P. F. Batitskiy, and V. I. Chuykov, held on to their Central Committee membership until their deaths.

The names and positions of those Soviet officers serving as full members and candidate members of the Central Committee (Table 6.3) suggest national security priorities and emphasis that essentially are matters of military doctrine. The table reflects new assignments in the two years since the 1986 Congress. Earlier positions will be found in Appendix A.

Table 6.3 indicates where the Kremlin leadership places defense priorities. Most of the positions of the military leaders on the Central Committee are understandable from a Western point of view. One possible exception might

184

TABLE 6.3
Military Officers on the 1986 Central Committee CPSU (changes since 1986 printed in bold)

Full Members:

Ministry of Defense:

1. D. T. Yazov	**G/A**	**Minister of Defense**
2. S. F. Akhromeyev	MSU	1st Dep MoD, Chief G/S
3. V. G. Kulikov	MSU	1st Dep MoD, CinC Warsaw Pact
4. P. G. Lushev	**G/A**	**1st Dep MoD**
5. A. D. Lizichev	G/A	Chief Main Pol Dir
6. Yu. P. Maksimov	G/A	Dep MoD, CinC Strategic Rocket Forces
7. Ye. F. Ivanovskiy	G/A	Dep MoD, CinC Ground Forces
8. I. M. Tret'yak	**G/A**	**Dep MoD, CinC Tps Air Def**
9. A. N. Yefimov	M/Av	Dep MoD, CinC Air Forces
10. V. N. Chernavin	A/F	Dep MoD, CinC Navy
11. V. M. Arkhipov	G/A	Dep MoD, Chief Rear
12. V. M. Shabanov	G/A	Dep MoD for Armaments
13. V. L. Govorov	**G/A**	**Dep MoD, Chief of Civil Def**

Theater Commanders:

14. N. V. Ogarkov	MSU	CinC Western Forces [TVD]
15. I. A. Gerasimov	G/A	CinC Southwestern Forces [TVD]
16. M. M. Zaytsev	G/A	CinC Southern Forces [TVD]

Warsaw Pact:

17. A. I. Gribkov	G/A	1st Dep Chief G/S, C/S Warsaw Pact

General Inspectors:

18. S. L. Sokolov	**MSU**	**ex-Minister of Defense**
19. V. I. Petrov	**MSU**	**ex-1st Dep MoD [Gen Affairs]**
20. A. I. Koldunov	**CMAv**	**ex-Dep MoD, CinC Tps Air Def**
21. V. F. Tolubko	CMAr	Gen Insp
22. A. T. Altunin	**G/A**	**ex-Dep MoD, Chief of Civil Def**
23. S. K. Kurkotkin	**MSU**	**ex-Dep MoD, Chief Rear**

Candidate Members:

Military District, Air Defense District, and Fleet Commanders:

1. V. M. Shuralev	G/C	Com Gen Belorussian MD
2. V. V. Osipov	G/C	Com Gen Kiev MD
3. B. V. Snetkov	**G/A**	**CinC Soviet Forces Germany**
4. N. I. Popov	G/A	Com Gen Turkestan MD
5. I. M. Kapitanets	Adl	Com Adl Northern Fleet
6. V. V. Sidorov	**Adl**	**Dep CinC Navy for Rear Services**

Political Officers:

7. A. I. Sorokin	A/F	1st Dep Chief Main Pol Dir
8. V. S. Rodin	A/F	Mem MC, Chief Pol Strategic Rocket Forces
9. M. D. Popkov	G/C	Mem MC, Chief Pol Ground Forces

Other:

10. V. I. Varennikov	G/A	1st Dep Chief G/S
11. G. M. Yegorov	A/F	Chmn DOSAAF
12. A. U. Konstantinov	**M/Av**	**ex-Com Mar Moscow Air Def Dis**

Auditors:

1. S. I. Postnikov	**G/C**	**1st Dep CinC Ground Forces**
2. N. A. Moiseyev	G/C	Mem MC, Chief Pol GSV Germany
3. D. A. Dragunskiy	**G/C**	**ex-Head, "Vystrel" Courses**

Note: See Appendix A for key to abbreviations.

be the position of the chief of Civil Defense. The head of this organization has been a four-star general, a deputy Minister of Defense, and a full member of the Central Committee. In contrast, few Americans have heard of the person who heads U.S. civil defense, such as it is. However, the need for a strong civil defense is expressed both in Soviet military doctrine and in the Constitution of the USSR. In addition, official statements concerning the composition of the Soviet Armed Forces specifically mention Troops of Civil Defense. These facts about Soviet civil defense warrant more careful study in the West.

The selection of D. T. Yazov,[35] the former commander of the Far Eastern Military District, as Minister of Defense suggests that China was still seen as a threat in 1987, though not as acutely as in 1981. All three former commanders in chief of the Troops of the Far East were subsequently promoted to top positions in the Ministry of Defense in Moscow.

The commanders in chief of the Southern and Southwestern TVDs facing Europe and the Middle East, formed in September 1984, were raised to full Central Committee membership. The commanders in chief of the Warsaw Pact Forces and the new Western TVD, bordering on NATO countries, were already full members. P. G. Lushev, who was the commander in chief of Soviet Forces Germany until he became first deputy Minister of Defense, was a full member. His successor, V. A. Belikov, was a candidate for membership, as were the commanders of the Belorussian, Leningrad, Kiev and Turkestan Military Districts. When Belikov died in 1987, he was succeeded by the commander of the Leningrad Military District.

In 1986, the selection of the commander of the Moscow Air Defense District, Marshal of Aviation A. U. Konstantinov, as a candidate member indicated that the Troops of Air Defense Troops may be assuming a more important role than previously. At earlier Congresses the commander had been only a member of the Central Auditing Commission. However, both Chief Marshal of Aviation A. I. Koldunov, commander in chief of Troops of Air Defense, and Konstantinov lost their posts (but not their seats on the Central Committee) in the wave of firings that followed the landing in Red Square of a West German teenager who had flown his light plane from Helsinki unimpeded. Koldunov, one of the top aces of World War II and twice a Hero of the Soviet Union, was replaced by General of the Army I. M. Tret'yak, a combined arms commander. Tret'yak had been commander in chief of Far Eastern Forces at the time the unarmed South Korean airliner, KAL 747, was shot down by the Troops of Air Defense in September 1983.

The commanders of the most important fleets—Northern and Pacific—were candidate members of the Central Committee. Admiral V. V. Sidorov was subsequently promoted and assigned to naval headquarters. Admiral of the Fleet G. M. Yegorov was chairman of DOSAAF, and Admiral A. I. Sorokin was first deputy chief of the Main Political Administration. These four admirals, who were candidates, plus the Navy commander in chief, Admiral of the Fleet V. N. Chernavin and General Inspector S. G. Gorshkov, who were both full members, give the Navy six admirals on the Central Committee.

Of the twenty-four senior Soviet officers who are full members of the Central Committee, two are admirals, two are aviation marshals, and two generals of the army have political or defense industry backgrounds. The other eighteen, which includes the commanders in chief of the Strategic Rocket Forces and Troops of Air Defense, have spent most of their careers in the Ground Forces.

It should be noted that there have been a number of major changes in the Ministry of Defense since the 27th Party Congress was held in 1986: Positions that have undergone changes include the Minister of Defense, one first deputy Minister of Defense, the commander in chief of Troops of Air Defense, the Inspector General (twice), and the chief of Civil Defense. Most of these positions were filled by men who were already full members of the Central Committee. One position, the Minister of Defense, was filled by a candidate member who subsequently was elevated to full membership. The new Inspector General—General of the Army Mikhail I. Sorokin—was not on the Central Committee at all, although he had been a candidate member from 1981 to 1986.

The number of general inspectors increased from two to seven largely because of the round of dismissals following the accident at the Chernobyl nuclear plant and the incident of the German teenager who landed just off Red Square. As of January 1988, none of those dismissed had lost their seats on the Party's Central Committee.

An analysis of the backgrounds of officers who are candidate members of the Central Committee and members of the Central Auditing Commission indicates a heavy predominance of Ground Forces officers—seven of the fifteen. The Navy and Main Political Administration are tied for second with four each, counting Sorokin as both a political officer and a naval officer. Konstantinov, the lone airman, is in the general inspectors group.

In 1986, twenty-seven of the forty officers in the Central Committee and Central Auditing Commission had Ground Forces backgrounds. Six came from the Navy and five from the Main Political Administration. Only three were airmen—two from the Troops of Air Defense and one from the Soviet Air Forces. One officer had a military industrial background—deputy Minister of Defense for Armaments V. M. Shabanov.

The preponderance of Ground Forces officers on the Central Committee follows the same pattern as found on the General Staff. There, the chief and his major deputies are all from the Ground Forces, except for one deputy, who is an admiral. The Party-military hierarchy, as represented by the officers on the Central Committee and Central Auditing Commission, suggests the following:

- First priority among the Soviet services continues to be given to the Strategic Rocket Forces, although it is controlled by officers previously with the Ground Forces.
- Apart from the strategic nuclear forces, the Soviet Armed Forces are structured primarily to fight a continental war on the periphery of the Soviet land mass or in areas contiguous to the Soviet Union.

- TVD commanders in chief are the key operational link in forces facing both NATO countries and the People's Republic of China.
- Even in the late 1980s concepts of military strategy may be significantly influenced by the experiences of senior officers who served in the Great Patriotic War. By the early 1990s most senior officers will not have had World War II experience; rather, they will have been conditioned by the method of fighting in Afghanistan.
- Although the Kremlin's interest in the Far East, along the Chinese border, is significant, it does not compare with its interest in the area opposing NATO countries.
- "Combined arms battle," which Soviet military theoreticians emphasize, may really mean that air and naval forces simply provide support to ground forces.
- Political officers play a vital role throughout the Soviet Armed Forces.
- Military district commanders are key elements in administration and control of the Soviet military structure.

The senior Soviet military-Party leadership, as shown above, is dominated by officers with Ground Forces backgrounds. The Air Forces, Troops of Air Defense, Strategic Rocket Forces, and Navy have little more than token representation.

Work of the Central Committee

The Central Committee must hold at least one Plenum every six months. Plenums are one- or two-day meetings where resolutions are approved which are then obligatory for all Party organizations. They legalize the work of the Politburo, giving the appearance of collective leadership. The most important speeches between Congresses are made at Plenums. Central Committee members meet for only a few days a year. It is through their positions in the Party, government, military, the arts and sciences that they carry the Party's influence into every area of Soviet life.

Major decisions are made by the Politburo of the Central Committee, and daily work is handled by the Secretariat. Specific accomplishments of the Central Committee with respect to national security decisions are difficult to document. The effort to maintain an aura of secrecy surrounding the Party's decision-making process is most effective. Past events and statements made by Soviet military strategists suggest, however, that important matters of Soviet foreign and military policies are brought before the Central Committee. For example: "The decisive role in working out the fundamental instruction in the area of military science, military doctrine, strategy, operational art, and tactics and in determining the content, form, and methods of educating and indoctrinating the personnel of the Armed Forces belongs to the Central Committee of the CPSU."[36]

In the early stages of the Soviet state, military delegates to the Party Congresses worked together in formulating plans and programs to be considered by the entire Party Congress. It would appear that military members of the Central Committee today do the basic work on questions that are of a primarily military nature and then submit their findings to the Committee as a whole. Major decisions of a military nature are also made by the Council of Defense, but there still is room within the Party structure for military members of the Central Committee to exercise power and influence.

In the post–World War II period there have been two occasions on which military members of the Central Committee played major roles. One was in 1953, during the arrest and trial of L. P. Beria, the secret police leader, when Khrushchev and other top leaders went outside the Politburo to certain members of the Central Committee for support. Details of the events were published in early 1988 for the first time. Key figures in the Soviet Armed Forces were involved, including Marshal G. K. Zhukov and General (later marshal) K. S. Moskalenko, then commander of the Moscow Air Defense District.[37] The commander of the Moscow Military District was controlled by Beria, who was head of the MVD, and it was reported that Marshal S. K. Timoshenko brought tanks in from the Belorussian Military District to ensure that Beria's MVD troops and other supporters did not gain the upper hand.

The Central Committee, and especially its military members, also played a decisive role in Khrushchev's 1957 struggle with what he called the "anti-Party group." Expecting to lose the support of the Politburo in a major battle with his opponents, Khrushchev managed to call for a meeting of the Central Committee. Zhukov, then Minister of Defense, used military aircraft to bring Central Committee members known to favor Khrushchev to the meeting in Moscow. Khrushchev's gamble was successful, and he retained Party leadership.

There is considerable speculation among Western analysts about the role of the Soviet military in the selection of the Party's General Secretary. Facts are few: once again Soviet secrecy on matters such as this is effective. But lacking facts, it is well to remember that military personnel achieve high rank only with Party approval and that the military officers themselves on the Central Committee are also senior Party members.

The Politburo

In theory, the Central Committee is the decisive voice of the Communist Party of the Soviet Union in formulating the major policies. In fact, the ruling body is the Politburo. Its members have clawed their way to the top of the Party power structure. Politburo members largely control the composition of the Party Congresses, as well as the selection of the Central Committee. The power held by the thirteen full Politburo members and the six candidate members is unequalled by any body in any other major nation of the world.

The Politburo is the Political Bureau of the Central Committee of the Communist Party. The Politburo sits at the apex of the vast Party bureaucracy that controls the USSR. Party rules limit it to not more than fifteen full members and nine candidates. The Politburo decides the most important political, economic, and internal Party questions, many of which are prepared for discussion by the Secretariat, and creates specific commissions to work out special problems.[38] It is from the Politburo that most of the members of the Council of Defense are selected.

The role of the Politburo in formulating Soviet military doctrine has been stated as follows:

> In the Soviet state, the structuring of the Armed Forces is determined by the policy of the CPSU. . . . The basic questions of military structuring in the USSR are decided by the Party, its Central Committee, and the highest agencies of the state. Party directives lie at the base of military laws. One of the official expressions of the CPSU's political line in structuring the Armed Forces of the USSR is *Soviet military doctrine*. It expresses the system of views adopted by the government on questions of the political evaluation of the nature of future war and on other fundamental questions of military structuring. The higher military-political leadership elaborates the strategic use of the Armed Forces and directs the Armed Forces during the course of a war.[39] (Emphasis added.)

The Politburo is responsible for setting and approving all policy in the Soviet Union. It meets weekly on Thursdays. Short summaries of the proceedings now appear in all major Soviet newspapers on Fridays. But members of this body are not merely concerned with Politburo duties. All of them have other major responsibilities. The current members include the chairman of the KGB, the chairman of the Council of Ministers, the chairman of the Presidium of the Supreme Soviet, and the Minister of Foreign Affairs. Some current members are first secretaries of powerful communist bodies, such as the Ukrainian Communist Party. The names and tasks of these men are shown in Table 6.4.

Mikhail Sergeyevich Gorbachev was already a Politburo member when he became the General Secretary of the Communist Party at the Extraordinary Plenum of the Central Committee held March 11, 1985. He was the third new General Secretary in a little over two years. Eight of the thirteen members have been appointed since Gorbachev came to power, and only two—A. A. Gromyko and V. V. Shcherbitskiy—have been on the Politburo longer than Gorbachev.

On May 30, 1987, seventy-five-year-old Minister of Defense Sergey L. Sokolov, a Marshal of the Soviet Union, was abruptly retired as a direct result of the penetration of Soviet air space by a West German teenager in a light plane. It did not matter that Sokolov had been in uniform for fifty-five years or that at the time of the intrusion he had been in East Berlin with Gorbachev, ostensibly the Supreme Commander in Chief of the Armed Forces. A Minister of Defense had not been dismissed in such a fashion since Khrushchev ousted Zhukov in 1957. Sokolov was also relieved of his position as candidate member of the Politburo at the same time. He did, however, keep his seat as a member of the Central Committee of the CPSU.

TABLE 6.4
Members of the Politburo, February 1988

Name	Nationality	Age	Position
Full Members:			
Mikhail S. Gorbachev	R	56	General Secretary, CPSU
Viktor M. Chebrikov	R	64	Chairman KGB, USSR
Andrey A. Gromyko	R	78	Chairman, Presidium, Supreme Soviet USSR
Yegor K. Ligachev	R	67	Secretary, Central Committee
Viktor P. Nikonov	R	58	Secretary, Central Committee
Nikolay I. Ryzhkov	R	58	Chairman, Council of Ministers
Vladimir V. Shcherbitskiy	U	70	First Secretary, Ukrainian CP
Eduard A. Shevardnadze	G	60	Minister of Foreign Affairs
Nikolay N. Slyun'kov	B	58	Secretary, Central Committee
Mikhail S. Solomentsev	R	74	Chairman, Party Control Committee
Vitaliy I. Vorotnikov	R	61	Chairman, Council of Ministers RSFSR
Aleksandr N. Yakovlev	R	64	Secretary, Central Committee
Lev N. Zaykov	R	64	Secretary, Central Committee,[a] First Secretary Moscow City Party Committee
Candidate Members:			
Petr N. Demichev	R	69	First Deputy Chairman, Presidium Supreme Soviet
Vladimir I. Dolgikh	R	63	Secretary, Central Committee
Yuriy D. Maslyukov[b]	R	50	Chairman of GOSPLAN
Georgiy P. Razumovskiy[b]	R	51	Secretary, Central Committee
Yuriy F. Solov'yev	R	62	First Secretary, Leningrad Oblast Committee
Nikolay V. Talyzin	R	58	First Dep Chmn, Council of Ministers USSR
Dmitriy T. Yazov	R	64	Minister of Defense USSR

R = Russian, U = Ukrainian, G = Georgian, B = Belorussian

[a]May be dropped from the Secretariat after becoming first secretary of Moscow City Party Committee.
[b]Added to Politburo at the February 1988 Central Committee Plenum.

He had been one of twenty-three high ranking officers selected by the 5,000 delegates at the 27th Party Congress in 1986. The new Minister of Defense, sixty-three-year-old General of the Army Dmitriy T. Yazov, became a candidate member of the Politburo shortly after he was appointed.

In summary, the Politburo, as a body, must approve major shifts of or modifications to military policy. In all probability, it would endorse whatever was recommended by the Council of Defense. The military policy approved by the Party then becomes the military doctrine of the state.

The Secretariat

The Secretariat of the Central Committee of the Communist Party of the Soviet Union is a Party organ selected by a Plenum of the Central Committee to manage the routine work, chiefly selecting cadres and organizing verification of performance. The very nature of its work and the decisions its members make largely correspond to questions of military doctrine. The Secretariat carries out its operational activities with the assistance of the Central Committee apparatus, primarily its departments. The size of the Secretariat varies. In 1960, there were only five secretaries; in 1988, there were thirteen. The Secretariat is headed by the General Secretary of the Communist Party, who also is a member of the Politburo. There is no more important and powerful leader in the Soviet Union than the General Secretary, who has his own "cabinet" of assistants who help him perform his work.

As already noted, the Secretariat prepares the materials to be presented to the Politburo for discussion. The Secretariat also carries out the decisions made by the Politburo, by placing Party cadres throughout the government and controlling the gigantic Party bureaucracy.

Questions of national defense are always at the forefront of the work of the Secretariat. Each member of the Secretariat has one or more Central Committee departments in his or her portfolio. The departments correspond to government ministries or state committees and other societal bodies such as the trade unions, DOSAAF, the Znaniye Society (see Chapter 8), War Veterans' Committee, Peace Fund, Soviet Committee to Defend the Peace, Red Cross and Red Crescent, artists and writers unions, friendship societies and others. See Table 6.5 for a list of Secretariat members.

Secretaries who are also Politburo members are called "double-hatters" and are considered to be particularly powerful in the decision-making process. The promotion of Slyun'kov, Yakovlev, and Nikonov in June 1987 to full membership considerably raised the number of double-hatters in the Politburo/Secretariat. These men play especially important roles in formulating defense-related policies and decisions; their roles will be discussed more fully in the section on the Council of Defense.

There was a good deal of turbulence in the Secretariat in the early 1980s due to the rapid turnover in the post of General Secretary. Gorbachev has had to work carefully to eliminate potential rivals and insert secretaries loyal to him. By mid-1987, the only secretaries remaining from the prior regime were Ligachev, Demichev and Dolgikh.

Departments of the Central Committee

In 1925, there were nine departments with 767 full-time workers in the Secretariat. By 1984, the number had increased to about twenty departments, not counting the Main Political Administration of the Soviet Army and Navy, which operates with the rights of a department of the Central

TABLE 6.5
Secretariat of the Central Committee CPSU, February 1988

Name	Year of Birth	Position
Mikhail S. Gorbachev	1931	Politburo member
Yegor K. Ligachev	1920	Politburo member
Lev N. Zaykov	1923	Politburo member[a]
Viktor P. Nikonov	1929	Politburo member
Nikolay N. Slyun'kov	1929	Politburo member, Economics Dept. (Belorussian)
Aleksandr N. Yakovlev	1923	Politburo member
Vladimir I. Dolgikh	1924	Candidate Politburo member
Georgiy P. Razumovskiy	1936	Candidate Politburo member
Oleg D. Baklanov	1932	Defense Industry (Ukrainian)
Aleksandra P. Biryukova	1929	(Only woman in top leadership)
Anatoliy F. Dobrynin	1919	International Department
Vadim A. Medvedev	1929	Liaison with Socialist Countries
Anatoliy I. Luk'yanov	1930	

[a]May be dropped from Secretariat as a result of becoming 1st Secretary of the Moscow City Party Committee.

Committee. Some of the departments are identified regularly in the press, while others are rarely mentioned.

Ten of the departments (Table 6.6) are concerned with industrial production, and several of them are concerned with the production of weapons, military equipment, and preparing the nation as a whole for the possibility of a future war. Three are concerned with foreign affairs. Most of the departments deal with internal Party work. Many departments of the Secretariat play vital roles that relate to military doctrine. For example, the International Department is headed by the experienced A. F. Dobrynin, who for many years while serving as the Soviet ambassador to the United States was allowed to park his limousine in the basement of the U.S. Department of State building and take a private elevator to the office of the Secretary of State. His role in advising other Soviet leaders on arms control and defense-related issues may have a direct bearing on Soviet military doctrine. The secretaries of the Central Committee supervise one or more departments and in some cases they head departments themselves. Each secretary has his or her own field of expertise.

Main Political Administration

Although the Main Political Administration of the Soviet Army and Navy is not a Central Committee department, it operates with the rights of one. Its primary responsibility is for the ideological indoctrination of Soviet Armed Forces personnel. There is nothing in the U.S. Armed Forces to which its structure and activities can be compared. According to the Soviet laws of war, the moral-political potential of a nation is one of the factors that

TABLE 6.6
Departments of the Central Committee CPSU, January 1, 1988

Department	Head
Industrial:	
Agriculture and Food Industry	I. I. Skiba
Chemical Industry	V. G. Afonin
Construction	A. G. Mel'nikov
Defense Industry	O. S. Belyakov
Economics	N. N. Slyun'kov
Heavy Industry and Power	I. P. Yastrebov
Light Industry and Consumer Goods	L. F. Bobykin
Machine Building	A. I. Vol'skiy
Trade & Domestic Services	N. A. Stashenkov
Transport and Communications	V. S. Pasternak
Foreign Affairs:	
Cadres Abroad	S. V. Chervonenko
International	A. F. Dobrynin
Liaison with Communist and Workers' Parties of Socialist Countries	V. A. Medvedev
Training:	
Culture	Yu. P. Voronov
Science and Educational Institutions	V. A. Grigor'yev
Propaganda	Yu. A. Sklyarov
Party Affairs:	
Administration of Affairs	N. Ye. Kruchina
Administrative Organs	N. I. Savinkin
General	V. I. Boldin
Organizational Party Work	G. P. Razumovskiy

determines victory or defeat, and so it is one aspect of military doctrine. The work of the Main Political Administration and its political organs is guided by the Program and Rules of the CPSU, resolutions of Party Congresses, Party Conferences, the Central Committee of the CPSU, and by the "Position of the Political Organs and the Instructions to the Organizations of the CPSU in the Soviet Army and Navy," a formal document confirmed by the Party's Central Committee.

The Main Political Administration was "formed by decision of the Central Committee of the CPSU" to assure "collectiveness in solving the most important questions of Party-political work" and "the education of cadres of Party-political workers in the Armed Forces in the spirit of observing Leninist norms of Party life and principles of Party leadership." Decisions of the Administration are put into practice "by directives and decrees of the chief of the Main Political Administration." Directives on questions of

Party-political work in the Soviet Armed Forces are issued "over the signatures of the Minister of Defense and the chief of the Main Political Administration with the approval of the Central Committee of the CPSU." Routine directives and decrees on continuing questions of Party-political work are issued by the chief of the Main Political Administration.

> Corresponding political administrations and political departments have been created for organizing and guiding Party-political work at all levels in the Armed Forces—in each of the services, groups of forces, military districts, and fleets. Each of these organizations has a military council, headed by the commander in chief or commander. Members of the military council are the senior officers on the staff, which must also include the chiefs of the political administrations (political departments).[40]

There are also political leaders in smaller units, ships, military schools, scientific research organizations, in the central apparatus of the Ministry of Defense and in the staffs and administrations of districts, groups of forces, and fleets. Party Commissions attached to the political organs examine the decisions of Party organizations on such matters as taking in new Party members and in cases of delinquencies of members of the Party and the Young Communist League (Komsomol).

One of the most important functions of the Main Political Administration is continuing indoctrination of the troops in maintaining high vigilance and in ensuring constant combat readiness. This task involves inculcating "political consciousness and psychological stability in the troops, fostering bravery, firmness of will to victory over a strong and crafty enemy, and the readiness to fulfill the fighting order at any price, right up to self-sacrifice."[41]

The Lenin Military-Political Academy comes directly under the authority of the Main Political Administration. Faculty members of this Academy are among the most articulate and influential spokesmen on military doctrine and strategy. They write and publish work on Party-military decisions, placing them in a Marxist-Leninist context for study and indoctrination of Soviet military personnel. All of the Soviet books published by the Military Publishing House (Voyenizdat), as well as military journals and newspapers, are under control of the Main Political Administration, which in turn is responsible to the Central Committee. Nothing is published in the military press that is counter to the wishes of the Communist Party. Western analysts sometimes interpret an article in *Krasnaya Zvezda*, the official newspaper of the Ministry of Defense, as being in disagreement with an article in *Pravda*, the official newspaper of the Communist Party; but this mistake is simply a result of mirror-imaging.

Council of Defense USSR

In 1976 a review of the first volume of the *Soviet Military Encyclopedia* appeared in *Krasnaya Zvezda*. The reviewer called attention to an entry on General Secretary Brezhnev, noting that among his other duties he was chairman of the Council of Defense. This mention was the first time the existence of this body, the successor to the all-important State Committee of Defense (GKO) of World War II, was publicly acknowledged. Later biographies have shown that Brezhnev actually became the chairman of the Council of Defense in 1964 when he was designated First (General) Secretary of the Communist Party. It is also now known that when the Higher Military Council was renamed the Main Military Council in November 1957, it was said to be attached to (*"pri"*) the Council of Defense.[42]

It was not surprising that such a body exists. In *Military Strategy*, Sokolovskiy had explained the importance of GKO, adding that all leadership of the country in wartime would be by the Central Committee of the Communist Party "with the possible organization of a higher agency of leadership of the country and the Armed Forces. This higher agency . . . may be given the same powers as the State Committee of Defense (GKO) during the Great Patriotic War." Since a nation may come under attack within the first minutes of a war, an organization must be formed in time of peace to prepare the nation for the possibility of war and be capable of taking on additional duties during the war.

The Constitution of the USSR, adopted in 1977, specifically provided for the Council of Defense. However, its members, other than the General Secretaries of the CPSU, who have been its chairmen, have never been identified, nor have any details been given concerning its mandate. Its purpose and functions are best derived from a study of its precursors.

The original Council of Defense, created November 30, 1918, was the highest agency of Party-military control in the Civil War. Its activities included all matters related to strengthening the fighting capability of the Red Army. It directed the war effort and carried out the policies of the Communist Party and Soviet government, putting the country on a war footing. Russian casualties in World War I had been extremely heavy, and the Red Army was short of personnel. Among the initial tasks of the new Council of Defense was providing manpower reserves for the forces, and ensuring that military personnel were provided with arms, ammunition, food, and clothing. In endangered areas the Council of Defense could declare martial law, giving full power to revolutionary councils. The Council of Defense usually met twice a week, with decisions made by majority vote. Commissions were created to carry out its directives. When in the field, its members were given authority to act in the name of the Council. Its chairman was Lenin with, among others, Stalin and Trotskiy as members.[43]

As the Civil War wound down, there was a great demand for labor. Soldiers of the Red Army were called upon to help with the task of restoring the economy. The Council of Defense, along with its overall direction of the war effort, now had to deal with the economy as well. In April 1920, the Council of Defense was incorporated into the new Council of Labor and Defense (STO) to direct both the economic development and defense of the country. It was also responsible for coordinating and strengthening the activities of the central departments and agencies in matters of national defense and economic construction. Until the Civil War was completely over, it operated with the rights of a commission of the Central Executive Committee.

This new Council of Labor and Defense was assigned major responsibilities: developing a unified economic plan and presenting it for confirmation and also for directing the work of the national economy and controlling the fulfillment of the plan. To ensure that its policies were followed, it was given the right to issue orders and directives that were binding on all central and local departments and establishments. Even the collectivization of agriculture became one of its responsibilities. With the industrialization of the Soviet Union and the First Five-Year Plan, the role of the Council of Labor and Defense grew enormously. It developed plans for producing aircraft, ships, artillery, tanks, and other equipment necessary for the Red Army and Navy. Stalin himself and other Politburo members took an active part in its work.

As industrial production mushroomed, a Commission of Defense headed by V. M. Molotov was created to simplify decision making on military matters for the Council of Labor and Defense. Its major task was to screen proposals to be presented for the approval of the Council of Labor and Defense. Thus, by the mid-1930s, there were three basic bodies carrying out the higher military leadership: (1) the Commission of Defense; (2) the Council of Labor and Defense (STO); and, under STO, (3) the Revolutionary Military Council USSR, which acted as the *Kollegiya* of the People's Commissariat for Military and Naval Affairs and was chaired by Commissar K. Ye. Voroshilov, who was also the Commissar of Defense.[44]

The Council of Labor and Defense was abolished April 28, 1937, and its functions were reassigned to the Economic Council of the Council of People's Commissars USSR. At the same time, the Commission of Defense was reorganized to become the Committee of Defense.[45] This new Committee of Defense USSR (Komitet Oborony), an agency of the Council of People's Commissars USSR, started with seven members. On January 31, 1938, a special Commission was attached to the Committee of Defense. This Commission later became the Military-Industrial Commission, known as the VPK. Its main task was to mobilize and prepare defense and nondefense industry to support plans and orders of the Committee of Defense for armaments production and delivery to the Army and Navy.[46] In 1940, K. Ye. Voroshilov, then deputy chairman of the Council of People's Commissars, was named the chairman of the Committee of Defense.

On June 22, 1941, Hitler's invasion of the Soviet Union began. The Committee of Defense was not at a sufficiently high level to direct the nation's defense. On June 30, 1940, just a week after the invasion, the Committee of Defense was abolished and replaced by the State Committee of Defense (GKO—*Gosudarstvennyy Komitet Oborony*). In theory this decision was made by the Presidium of the Supreme Soviet, the Central Committee CPSU, and the Council of People's Commissars. In reality it was by Stalin's order. Throughout the Great Patriotic War, as the Soviets refer to that part of World War II in which they participated, he served as chairman of GKO.

GKO directed the activity of all departments and establishments engaged in the war effort—economic, political, diplomatic, and military. Its representatives were given authority to make decisions on the spot. Decrees of GKO were law and had to be carried out by all citizens without question. Strategic leadership of the war by GKO was conducted through Stavka of the Supreme High Command (VGK). The members of GKO were the chairman, Stalin, who was also the General Secretary, Politburo member, Chairman of the Council of People's Commissars, Commissar of Defense, Supreme Commander in Chief of the Armed Forces; and the deputy chairman, Molotov, who was a Politburo member, first deputy chairman of the Council of Commissars, and Commissar of Foreign Affairs. Members also included K. Ye. Voroshilov, Politburo member, G. M. Malenkov,[47] Secretary (for cadres) and candidate Politburo member, and L. P. Beria, candidate Politburo member and head of the People's Commissariat of Internal Affairs (NKVD). The following were added in 1942: A. I. Mikoyan, Politburo member; N.A. Voznesenskiy, candidate Politburo member and chairman of GOSPLAN; L. M. Kaganovich, Politburo member, and in 1944, N. A. Bulganin, deputy commissar of Defense.[48]

According to Marshal G. K. Zhukov's memoirs, meetings of GKO took place at any time of the day or night, either in the Kremlin or at Stalin's *dacha*. Both the Politburo and GKO examined all plans for military actions. Commissars in charge of arms and equipment production were invited to meetings, and sharp disagreements were a common feature. If agreement was not reached, a commission was formed from among the disputers to reach a decision to be presented at the next meeting.[49] During the war, GKO handed down approximately 10,000 major decisions and resolutions on military and economic matters. On September 4, 1945, GKO was formally abolished.[50]

There is no clear picture of what body replaced GKO after the war. Early Soviet history shows that similar Civil War bodies were carried over into peacetime and played significant roles in national security matters. It is logical to assume that GKO was replaced by a body somewhat similar to it but structured for a peacetime role.

The present Council of Defense plays an important role in guiding the defense of the country. According to the Constitution of the USSR, the Council of Defense is formed by the Presidium of the Supreme Soviet. Endowed with broad powers in determining the status and perspectives of development and strengthening the defense of the country, it is a collegial interdepartmental organ of state direction. From 1976 to 1985, it was headed by the successive chairmen of the Presidium of the Supreme Soviet, who were also General Secretaries of the CPSU.[51]

The apex of decision making in the Soviet Union is the Politburo of the Central Committee. Matters of national security are the primary responsibility of the Council of Defense. The relationship of these two bodies is unique. It might be argued that the role of the Council of Defense in the formulation of Soviet military doctrine should be considered in the context of the Soviet

FIGURE 6.1
Members of the Politburo and the Secretariat, February 1988

Politburo Members	"Double-Hatters"	Secretariat
V. M. Chebrikov A. A. Gromyko N. I. Ryzhkov V. V. Shcherbitskiy E. A. Shevardnadze M. S. Solomentsev V. I. Vorotnikov	M. S. Gorbachev Ye. K. Ligachev L. N. Zaykov N. N. Slyun'kov A. N. Yakovlev V. P. Nikonov	A. P. Biryukova A. F. Dobrynin A. I. Luk'yanov V. A. Medvedev O. D. Baklanov
Candidate Members		
P. N. Demichev Yu. D. Maslyukov D. T. Yazov Yu. F. Solov'yev N. V. Talyzin	V. I. Dolgikh G. P. Razumovskiy	

government rather than the Party. This is particularly true since, according to Soviet law, the Council of Defense is headed by "the Chairman of the Presidium of the Supreme Soviet." However, as one Western scholar suggests, "While the Defense Council is unquestionably a state body, in practice it may operate more as a subcommittee of the Politburo."[52]

Very little is known of the workings of either the Politburo or the Council of Defense. Since 1982, a summary of the weekly Politburo meetings has been published in the Soviet press. Almost nothing is released, however, about the work of the Council of Defense. The Politburo is responsible for many decisions that are attributed to "the Central Committee."

Power in the Kremlin is held by those key members of the Politburo who are the "double-hatters," meaning that they are also members of the Secretariat. No one has ever become the General Secretary without first belonging to both the Politburo and the Secretariat. It is only logical that national security would be a main concern of these "double-hatters." An examination of these individuals may provide some indication of the Council of Defense membership. (See Figure 6.1.)

As previously noted, the only member of the Council of Defense specifically identified is its chairman, General Secretary Gorbachev. As of January 1, 1988, the most probable Council of Defense members are Ye. K. Ligachev, the number two Party leader, who runs the Secretariat for Gorbachev just

as Gorbachev ran it for Chernenko;[53] N. N. Slyun'kov; and A. N. Yakovlev.
These men would form its nucleus. In addition, A. A. Gromyko, chairman
of the Presidium of the Supreme Soviet; N. I. Ryzhkov, chairman of the
Council of Ministers; KGB Chief V. M. Chebrikov; Foreign Minister E. A.
Shevardnadze; and Defense Minister D. T. Yazov appear to be likely members.
L. N. Zaykov was appointed first secretary of the Moscow City Party
Committee after Boris Yel'tsin was fired in November 1987, and Zaykov is
expected to yield up his seat on the Secretariat. The chief of the General
Staff, Marshal of the Soviet Union S. F. Akhromeyev, is thought to act as
the secretary of the Council of Defense. Leading experts can be called on
to report to the Council as necessary. Similar defense councils exist in each
Warsaw Pact country, and they are chaired by the General Secretaries of
the Communist Parties of the corresponding countries.

When it is recalled that Soviet military doctrine is the defense policy of
the Communist Party, the peacetime role of the Council of Defense comes
into focus. Its role is to prepare the nation and its Armed Forces for the
possibility of war. In effect, Council members must answer the basic questions
demanded by military doctrine: who the enemy will be, what will be the
nature of the future war, what kind of Armed Forces will be needed, how
the Armed Forces and the nation are to be structured for war, and by what
methods the war is to be fought. In time of war the Council of Defense
might retain its present designation or be renamed. In any event, it would
have much the same role as that performed by GKO in World War II.

Notes

1. Michael S. Voslensky, *Nomenklatura* (Garden City, N.Y.: Doubleday & Company,
Inc., 1984), pp. 95–96.
2. S. N. Kozlov, editor, *Spravochnik Ofitsera* [Officer's Handbook] (Moscow, Voyenizdat, 1971), p. 5.
3. Ibid., p. 6.
4. V. I. Os'kin, "Voyennoye Stroitel'stvo," ["Military Structuring"] in *Sovetskaya
Voyennaya Entsiklopediya* [Soviet Military Encyclopedia] (Moscow: Voyenizdat, 1976–
1980), vol. 2, p. 219.
5. Ibid. See also I. A. Grudinin, *Dialektika i Sovremennoye Voyennoye Delo* [Dialectics
and Contemporary Military Affairs] (Moscow: Voyenizdat, 1971), pp. 49–54.
6. Kozlov, *Spravochnik Ofitsera*, p. 8.
7. *The Programme of the Communist Party of the Soviet Union—a New Edition*
(Moscow: Novosti Press, 1986), p. 53.
8. M. A. Gareyev, *M. V. Frunze—Voyennyy Teoretik* [M. V. Frunze—Military
Theoretician] (Moscow: Voyenizdat, 1985), p. 247. In spite of its title, this book is
about the Soviet Armed Forces of today. General Gareyev, a deputy chief of the
General Staff since 1985, was for many years the head of the Military Science
Administration of the General Staff, the section most concerned with the elaboration
of Soviet military doctrine.
9. Kozlov, *Spravochnik Ofitsera*, pp. 11–12. See also Gareyev, *M. V. Frunze*, p. 250.
10. These principles are also confirmed in Gareyev, *M. V. Frunze*, p. 292. The
"cadre" army of the Soviet Union consists of the regular officers, warrant officers,

and a few extended-duty noncommissioned officers. The task of this "cadre" is to be the regular force and to train the military callups. Between 1.6 million and 1.8 million Soviet youths are taken into the Armed Forces each year, and about the same number of personnel are discharged "into the reserves."

11. See also Gareyev, *M. V. Frunze*, p. 276.

12. See also Gareyev, *M. V. Frunze*, p. 286.

13. See also Gareyev, *M. V. Frunze*, p. 284. Gareyev wrote of "iron military discipline."

14. Kozlov, *Spravochnik Ofitsera*, pp. 12–16, excerpts. See also "Voyennoye Stroitel'stvo," in *Sovetskaya Voyennaya Entsiklopediya*, vol. 2, p. 219.

15. See Gareyev, *M. V. Frunze*, p. 244.

16. For a fuller discussion and listing of the schools, see H. F. Scott and W. F. Scott, *The Armed Forces of the USSR* 3rd edition (Boulder, Colorado: Westview Press, 1984), pp. 348–395.

17. Kozlov, *Spravochnik Ofitsera*, p. 16.

18. Ibid., p. 18.

19. Ibid., pp. 20–21. The Main Political Administration of the Soviet Army and Navy is not under the Ministry of Defense but operates under the Central Committee of the Party as one of its departments.

20. See Konstantin Simonov's candid interviews with World War II hero Marshal Georgiy Zhukov in *Voyenno-Istoricheskiy Zhurnal* [Military History Journal] beginning in June 1987.

21. Kozlov, *Spravochnik Ofitsera*, pp. 27–29.

22. *XXVII S"yezd Kommunisticheskoy Partii Sovetskogo Soyuza* [27th Congress of the Communist Party of the Soviet Union], stenographic notes (Moscow: Politizdat, 1986), vol. 3, pp. 365–571.

23. P. F. Batitskiy, editor, *Voyska Protivovozdushnoy Oborony Strany* [National Air Defense Troops] (Moscow: Voyenizdat, 1968), p. 401; and N. A. Piterskiy, editor, *Boyevoy Put' Sovetskogo Voyenno-Morskogo Flota* [History of the Soviet Navy] (Moscow: Voyenizdat, 1967), p. 561.

24. M. V. Zakharov, editor, *50 Let Vooruzhennykh Sil SSSR* [50th Anniversary of the Armed Forces of the USSR] (Moscow: Voyenizdat, 1968), p. 520a. For an interesting picture of the military delegates to the 10th and 15th Party Congresses (1921 and 1927), see N. M. Kiryayev, Ye. F. Nikitin, Yu. I. Korablev, editors, *KPSS i Stroitel'stvo Sovetskikh Vooruzhennykh Sil* [CPSU and the Development of the Soviet Armed Forces] (Moscow: Voyenizdat, 1967), pp. 160a and 160b.

25. Yu. P. Petrov, *Stroitel'stvo Politorganov, Partiynykh i Komsomol'skikh Organizatsiy Armii i Flota* [Structuring of Politorgans, Party and Komsomol Organizations of the Army and Navy] (Moscow: Voyenizdat, 1968), pp. 124ff.

26. N. P. Prokop'yev, *O Voyne i Armii* [On War and Army] (Moscow: Voyenizdat, 1965), pp. 257–258.

27. R. Ya. Malinovskiy, *Bditel'no Stoyat' na Strazhe Mira* [Vigilantly Stand Guard Over the Peace] (Moscow: Voyenizdat, 1962), p. 17.

28. N. A. Lomov, in P. M. Derevyanko, *Problemy Revolyutsii v Voyennom Dele* [Problems of the Revolution in Military Affairs] (Moscow: Voyenizdat, 1965), pp. 40–41.

29. M. V. Frunze, "A Unified Military Doctrine for the Red Army," in H. F. Scott and W. F. Scott, *The Soviet Art of War* (Boulder, Colorado: Westview Press, 1982), p. 27. See also Prokop'yev, *O Voyne i Armii*, p. 257.

30. Prokop'yev, *O Voyne i Armii*, p. 258.

31. Zakharov, *50 Let*, p. 520.

32. S. S. Lototskiy, editor, *Armiya Sovetskaya* [Army of the Soviets] (Moscow: Politizdat, 1969), p. 431.

33. D. A. Volkogonov, A. S. Milovidov, S. A. Tyushkevich, *Voyna i Armiya* [War and Army] (Moscow: Voyenizdat, 1977), pp. 389–390.

34. D. A. Volkogonov, editor, *Marksistsko-Leninskoye Ucheniye o Voyne i Armii* [Marxist-Leninist Teachings on War and Army] (Moscow: Voyenizdat, 1984), p. 313.

35. Yazov was raised to full membership from candidate status at the June 1987 Plenum of the Central Committee. He also was made a candidate member of the Politburo at that Plenum.

36. A. S. Zheltov, *Metodologicheskiye Problemy Voyennoy Teorii i Praktiki* [Methodological Problems of Military Theory and Practice] (Moscow: Voyenizdat, 1969), p. 284.

37. S. Bystrov, "Task of a Special Nature," *Krasnaya Zvezda* [Red Star] 18, 19, 20 March 1988. This was the first published account by an eye-witness of Beria's arrest and trial to appear in the Soviet press.

38. "Politburo TsK KPSS" ["Politburo of the Central Committee CPSU"), *Bol'shaya Sovetskaya Entsiklopediya* [Great Soviet Encyclopedia] (Moscow: Soviet Encyclopedia, 1970–1978), vol. 20, p. 215.

39. A. Ye. Lunev, editor, *Upravleniye v Oblasti Administrativno-Politicheskoy Deyatel'nosti* [Control in the Sphere of Administrative-Political Activity] (Moscow: Legal Literature, 1979), p. 20.

40. Kozlov, *Spravochnik Ofitsera*, p. 32.

41. Ibid., p. 39.

42. V. S. Golubovich, *Marshal R. Ya. Malinovskiy* [Marshal R. Ya. Malinovskiy] (Moscow: Voyenizdat, 1984), p. 207.

43. S. S. Khromov, editor, *Grazhdanskaya Voyna i Voyennaya Interventsiya v SSSR* [The Civil War and Military Intervention in the USSR] (Moscow: Soviet Encyclopedia, 1983), p. 547.

44. Zahkarov, *50 Let*, p. 198. Functions of this body will be discussed in Chapter 7.

45. Ibid., p. 199.

46. A. A. Yepishev, *KPSS i Voyennoye Stroitel'stvo* [CPSU and Military Development] (Moscow: Voyenizdat, 1982), p. 53.

47. Georgi M. Malenkov, once Stalin's heir, died in Moscow on January 14, 1988, at the age of eighty-six.

48. "Gosudarstvennyy Komitet Oborony" ["State Committee of Defense"], in *Sovetskaya Voyennaya Entsiklopediya*, vol. 2, p. 621.

49. G. K. Zhukov, *Vospominaniye i Razmyshleniya* [Reminiscences and Reflections] (Moscow: Novosti, 1974), vol. 1, p. 345.

50. *Sovetskaya Voyennaya Entsiklopediya*, vol. 1, p. 345.

51. See *Sovetskoye Administrativnoye Pravo* [Soviet Administrative Law] (Moscow: Legal Literature, 1981), p. 375. This stipulation that the Council of Defense was to be headed by the Chairman of the Presidium of the Supreme Soviet was dropped when Andrey Gromyko became the Chairman of the Presidium of the Supreme Soviet under Gorbachev.

52. Ellen Jones, *Red Army and Society* (Boston: Allen & Unwin, 1985), p. 6.

53. This interesting bit of information comes from Andrey Gromyko, who mentioned it when nominating Mikhail Gorbachev to become General Secretary. See *Spravochnik Partiynogo Rabotnika—1986* [Party Worker's Handbook—1986] (Moscow: Politizdat, 1986), p. 10.

7
Role of the Soviet Government in Formulating Military Doctrine

The Supreme Soviet

Before examining the role of the Soviet government in formulating military doctrine, a reminder is in order. The new Constitution of the USSR, adopted in 1977, stressed the primacy of the Communist Party. Its provisions were specific:

> Article 6. The leading and guiding force of Soviet society and the nucleus of its political system, of all state organizations and public organizations, is the Communist Party of the Soviet Union. . . . The Communist Party, armed with Marxism-Leninism, determines the general perspectives of the development of society and the course of the domestic and foreign policy of the USSR, directs the great constructive work of the Soviet people, and imparts a planned systematic and theoretically substantiated character to their struggle for the victory of communism.[1]

Although the Soviet Union actually is under the complete control of the Communist Party leadership, its edicts are approved and carried out through a legislative and government structure. However, this procedure is more form than substance. All the upper echelons of the vast Soviet government bureaucracy are headed by influential Party members, and any major disputes within the government apparatus probably would be settled by Party organs.

The Supreme Soviet occupies the highest place in the state organization; it is the formal legislative body in the Soviet Union. (The Russian word *soviet* means "council.") Elections of deputies (or members) of the Supreme Soviet are held every five years. There is but a single name on the ballot and voting is compulsory. It is the only election in which all the people participate, although in actual fact the voting is meaningless.

Sessions of the Supreme Soviet are convened twice a year and may last as long as a week. Its deputies, numbering 1,500, are divided equally into two councils: the Soviet (or Council) of the Union and the Soviet (or Council) of the Nationalities. The Supreme Soviet has thirty-four permanent commissions, seventeen in each chamber. Slightly over 1,200 of the deputies serve on these commissions (1984).

Approximately 40 percent of the deputies are reelected every five years, forming the experienced nucleus. The remaining 60 percent serve only once. More than half the deputies are milkmaids, tractor drivers, and various individuals from the Soviet labor force. They are "elected" to give some appearance of democracy. When they return to their factories and state farms in the remotest parts of the Soviet Union after a week in Moscow with first-hand reports of rubbing elbows with the Party leaders, they are celebrities.

The 40 percent who serve more than one term are leading members of the Party apparatus as well as heads of key ministries, senior KGB and MVD officials, leading scientists, and the like. All of the latter group are Party members as well. Of the 30 percent of the deputies who were not Party members in 1984, one-half were Komsomol (Young Communist League) members. One-third of the deputies were women; 331 deputies were under thirty and 235 were over sixty. Most important, sixty-three "nationalities" were represented. This representation is intended to have a unifying effect on the Soviet people and gives them confidence in their leadership. This support, in turn, promotes Party and state policies, including military policy.

For the 11th Convocation of the Supreme Soviet in 1984, 30 of the 750 deputies in the Soviet of the Union and 25 of the 750 deputies in the Soviet of the Nationalities were senior military officers. Table 7.1 contains the names of those elected in March 1984 and their positions as of September 1984.

The nationalities of the military deputies identified in Table 7.1 should cause reflection. Only five are *not* Great Russian by nationality. Of those five all are Slavs, including four Ukrainians and one Belorussian. One of the four Ukrainians is a delegate simply because he is a cosmonaut. At a time when the callup of youth into military service shows a constantly increasing number from Central Asian minority groups, the lack of representation from these nationalities could lead to major problems, especially if General Secretary Gorbachev's policy of *glasnost* continues.

It is doubtful that the Supreme Soviet, as such, considers substantive matters of military doctrine. However, being a member of this body reflects a high military position and to some extent also reflects standing in the Party. The fact that Soviet military personnel are listed as members of the Supreme Soviet could be an important element in the whole Party-military-government relationship and in the formulation of doctrine.

Being a deputy of the Supreme Soviet enables members to consider themselves legitimate parliamentarians, "duly elected" as in democratic societies. In this way, high Party officials can travel abroad and meet with government and state leaders on equal terms. In turn, they can entertain visiting members of Congress, governors, or members of parliament in their capacity as deputies.

TABLE 7.1
Military Deputies of the Supreme Soviet, 11th Convocation (as of September 1984)

Position/Name	Birth/Death	Nationality	Rank
Minister of Defense:			
D. F. Ustinov	1908–1984	Russian	Marshal of the Soviet Union
First Deputy Ministers of Defense:			
S. F. Akhromeyev	1923	Russian	Marshal of the Soviet Union
V. G. Kulikov	1921	Russian	Marshal of the Soviet Union
S. L. Sokolov	1911	Russian	Marshal of the Soviet Union
Chief, Main Political Administration:			
A. A. Yepishev	1908	Russian	General of the Army
Deputy Ministers of Defense:			
V. F. Tolubko	1914	Ukrainian	Chief Marshal of Artillery
V. I. Petrov	1917	Russian	Marshal of the Soviet Union
A. I. Koldunov	1923	Russian	Chief Marshal of Aviation
P. S. Kutakhov	1914–1984	Russian	Chief Marshal of Aviation
S. G. Gorshkov	1910	Russian	Admiral of the Fleet of the Soviet Union
V. L. Govorov	1924	Russian	General of the Army
S. K. Kurkotkin	1917	Russian	Marshal of the Soviet Union
V. M. Shabanov	1923	Russian	General of the Army
N. F. Shestopalov	1919	Russian	Marshal of Engineer Troops
A. T. Altunin	1921	Russian	General of the Army
I. N. Shkadov	1931	Russian	General of the Army
Political Officers:			
A. I. Sorokin	1922	Russian	Admiral
M. D. Popkov	1924	Russian	General Colonel
P. A. Gorchakov	1917	Russian	General Colonel
TVD Commanders in Chief:			
N. V. Ogarkov	1917	Russian	Marshal of the Soviet Union
I. A. Gerasimov	1921	Russian	General of the Army
Yu. P. Maksimov	1924	Russian	General of the Army
I. M. Tret'yak	1923	Ukrainian	General of the Army
First Deputy Chiefs, CinCs:			
A. I. Gribkov	1919	Russian	General of the Army
Yu. A. Yashin	1930	Russian	General of the Army
A. M. Mayorov	1920	Russian	General of the Army
A. N. Yefimov	1923	Russian	Marshal of Aviation
N. I. Smirnov	1917	Russian	Admiral of the Fleet
V. N. Chernavin	1928	Russian	Admiral of the Fleet
V. K. Meretskov	1924	Russian	General Colonel

TABLE 7.1 *(continued)*

CinCs and Commanders of Groups Abroad:

M. M. Zaytsev	1923	Russian	General of the Army
A. D. Lizichev	1928	Russian	General Colonel
G. G. Borisov	1924	Russian	General Colonel
Yu. F. Zarudin	1923	Russian	General Colonel

Military District Commanders:

K. A. Kochetov	1932	Russian	General Colonel
A. V. Betekhtin	1931	Russian	General Colonel
Ye. F. Ivanovskiy	1918	Belorussian	General of the Army
V. A. Belikov	1925	Russian	General of the Army
D. T. Yazov	1923	Russian	General of the Army
B. V. Snetkov	1925	Russian	General Colonel
P. G. Lushev	1923	Russian	General of the Army
A. S. Yelagin	1930	Russian	General Colonel
S. I. Postnikov	1928	Russian	General of the Army
V. M. Arkhipov	1933	Russian	General Colonel
N. I. Popov	1930	Russian	General Colonel
I. A. Gashkov	1928	Russian	General Colonel
A. Ya Ryakhov	1929	Russian	General Colonel

Air Defense District Commander:

A. U. Konstantinov	1923	Russian	General Colonel of Aviation

Fleet Commanders:

I. M. Kapitanets	1928	Russian	Admiral
A. M. Kalinin	1928	Russian	Admiral
A. P. Mikhaylovskiy	1925	Russian	Admiral
V. V. Sidorov	1924	Russian	Admiral

DOSAAF Chairman:

G. M. Yegorov	1918	Russian	Admiral of the Fleet

Miscellaneous:

K. S. Moskalenko	1902	Ukrainian	Marshal of the Soviet Union
P. I. Ivashutin	1909	Russian	General of the Army
L. I. Popov	1945	Ukrainian	Cosmonaut

Note: Since the 1984 elections, there have been several deaths of military deputies (P. S. Kutakhov, D. F. Ustinov, A. A. Yepishev, and K. S. Moskalenko) and four new military appointees: (1) A. A. Demidov, General Colonel, Commander of the Southern Group of Forces (1985); (2) V. V. Osipov, General Colonel, Commander of the Kiev Military District (1985); (3) V. N. Lobov, General Colonel, Commander of the Central Asian Military District (1986) now First Deputy Chief of the General Staff (1987); and (4) A. V. Kovtunov, General Colonel, Commander of the Central Asian Military District (1987).

Source: Deputaty Verkhovnogo Soveta SSSR [Deputies of the Supreme Soviet USSR] (Moscow: Izvestia, 1984), pp. 3–4.

In addition to the Supreme Soviet of the USSR, the various republics and autonomous republics also have their own Supreme Soviets. Individuals elected to these bodies represent much the same variety of Soviet society as do those elected to the "all-union" body. Several thousand military personnel serve as deputies of Soviets at lower levels.

Presidium of the Supreme Soviet

The functioning body of the Supreme Soviet of the USSR is its Presidium.[2] In theory, this is the body that forms the Council of Defense and confirms its composition, appoints and dismisses members of the high command of the Armed Forces. The Presidium is also authorized to declare martial law and general or partial mobilization.[3] Between Sessions of the Supreme Soviet, the Presidium has the authority to proclaim a state of war in the event of an armed attack on the USSR or on a country to which it is committed by a treaty of mutual defense, and to act on matters critical to the Soviet state.

The chairman of the Presidium of the Supreme Soviet is the formal head of the Soviet state, or "President." In 1985, Andrey A. Gromyko, for decades the Minister of Foreign Affairs, was appointed to this position. In addition to the chairman, there is a first deputy chairman, fifteen deputy chairmen— one from each republic—a secretary, and twenty-one other members. Seven Presidium members are also Politburo members (as of January 1988).[4] The Presidium of the Supreme Soviet met seven times in 1985.

Role of the Council of Ministers

The primary action taken by the Supreme Soviet is to form the Council of Ministers of the USSR, which provides the actual management of the Soviet government.[5] This Council and its various agencies are second only to the Party in the formulation of military doctrine. The Council members play a leading role in planning and implementing measures for the defense of the Soviet state. The Ministry of Defense depends, in part, on actions of the Council of Ministers because the technical side of military doctrine depends on what the state is able to produce and the trained manpower available for both the economy and the Armed Forces. These matters come under the authority of the Council of Ministers.

The new Constitution of the USSR restated the role of the Council of Ministers and its responsibilities in defense matters.

Article 128. The Council of Ministers of the USSR, i.e., the government of the USSR, is the highest executive and administrative body of state authority of the USSR. . . .

Article 131. The Council of Ministers USSR shall: . . .

(5) exercise general direction of the development of the Armed Forces of the USSR, and determine the annual contingent of citizens to be called up for active military duty.[6]

TABLE 7.2
Presidium of the Council of Ministers USSR, September 1987

Position/Name	Title
Chairman of the Council of Ministers:	
Nikolay I. Ryzhkov	
First Deputy Chairmen:	
G. A. Aliyev	Chairman, Bureau of Social Development
N. V. Talyzin	Chairman, GOSPLAN—State Planning Committee
V. S. Murakhovskiy	Chairman, State Agroindustrial Committee
Vice Chairmen:	
A. K. Antonov	Permanent Representative, Council for Mutual Assistance
Yu. P. Batalin	Chairman, State Construction Committee
V. K. Gusev	First Deputy Chairman, Council of Ministers RSFSR
V. M. Kamentsev	Chairman, State Foreign Economic Commission
Yu. D. Maslyukov	Chairman, Military-Industrial Committee (VPK)
B. Ye. Shcherbina	Chairman, Bureau for Fuel and Energy Complex
I. S. Silayev	Chairman, Bureau for Machine Building
B. L. Tolstykh	Chairman, State Committee on Science and Technology
G. G. Vedernikov	—
L. A. Voronin	Chairman, GOSSNAB—State Committee for Material-Technical Supply

Source: *Yezhegodnik Bol'shoy Sovetskoy Entsiklopedii 1986* [Annual of the Great Soviet Encyclopedia] (Moscow: Soviet Encyclopedia, 1986), 12; and *Vedomosti Verkhovnogo Soveta SSSR* [Bulletin of the Supreme Soviet USSR], published weekly.

Although there is separation both in theory and in function between the Communist Party and the Soviet government, there is a clear overlap in personnel. This overlap is no accident; it is another means by which the Communist Party maintains it control. The chairman of the Council of Ministers, Nikolay Ryzhkov, is also a Politburo member. Geydar Aliyev, a Politburo member until 1987, was a first deputy chairman. Nikolay Talyzin, another first deputy chairman, is a candidate Politburo member. Members of the Presidium of the Council of Ministers are listed in Table 7.2.

In November 1986, there were thirty-seven All-Union Ministries, twenty-three Union Republic Ministries, nine All-Union State Committees and sixteen Union Republic State Committees. There were an additional four ministers at large. The number and names of ministries and state committees frequently change depending on the needs of the government. Two of the ministers, Eduard A. Shevardnadze (Minister of Foreign Affairs) and Dmitriy T. Yazov (Minister of Defense), and a state committee chairman, Viktor M. Chebrikov (head of the KGB), are also Politburo members or candidate members. A number of ministries belong to the military-industrial complex of the Soviet Union and are involved in the production of weapons and military equipment (Tables 7.3 and 7.4). These ministries form a very

TABLE 7.3
Defense Production Ministries, October 1987

Ministry	Minister	Product
Aviation Industry	A. S. Systsov	Aircraft and helicopters
Communications Equipment Industry	E. K. Pervyshin	Communications equipment
Defense Industry	P. V. Finogenov	Conventional armaments
Electronics Industry	V. G. Kolesnikov	Radars
General Machine Building	O. D. Baklanov	Rockets and space equipment
Heavy, Energetics (Power), and Transport Machine Building	V. M. Velichko	Power
Machine Building	B. M. Belousov	Munitions
Medium Machine Building	L. D. Ryabev	Military applications of atomic energy
Radio Industry	V. I. Shimko	Radios
Shipbuilding Industry	I. S. Belousov	Naval products and ships

Source: *Yezhegodnik Bol'shoy Sovetskoy Entsiklopedii 1986* [Annual of the Great Soviet Encyclopedia] (Moscow: Soviet Encyclopedia, 1986), pp. 13–14; and *Vedomosti Verkhovnogo Soveta SSSR* [Bulletin of the Supreme Soviet USSR], published weekly.

TABLE 7.4
Some Military-related Ministries

Ministry	Minister	Product
Installation and Special Construction Work	B. V. Bakin	Construction
Civil Aviation	A. N. Volkov	Assists Air Forces
Electrical Equipment Industry	O. G. Anfimov	Electrical products
Machine Tool and Tool Building Industry	N. A. Panichev	Rocket and space instrumentation
Maritime Fleet	Yu. M. Vol'mer	Assists Navy
Instrument Making, Automation Equipment, and Control Systems	M. S. Shkabardnya	Guidance systems
Petroleum Refining and Petrochemical Industry	N. V. Lemayev	Gas and oil products

important part of the Soviet defense capability and make an essential input to the military-technical side of military doctrine. Without their ability to supply the Soviet Armed Forces with the latest in armaments, the Soviet Union would not be a military superpower. Only one of this group of industrial ministries, however, is openly identified as a "defense" ministry.

There also are a number of military-related ministries and state committees that have close connections with the military. Among these are:

State Planning Committee (GOS-PLAN)	Yu. D. Maslyukov (since February 1988)
Ministry of Communications	V. A. Shamshin
Committee of State Security (KGB)	V. M. Chebrikov
Ministry of Internal Affairs (MVD)	A. V. Vlasov
State Committee on Science and Technology (GKNT)	B. L. Tolstykh
State Committee for Computer Equipment and Information Service	N. V. Gorshkov

Two of the above bodies, the KGB and the MVD, have their own military organizations. The Border Guards of the KGB number between 200,000 and 300,000. They are well-trained troops, armed with tanks and armored personnel carriers, light aircraft, helicopters, and ships. The Internal Troops of the MVD are armed with similar weapons. Both the Border Guards and the Internal Troops, although not subordinate to the Ministry of Defense, are considered part of the Soviet Armed Forces.

The Military-Industrial Commission (VPK), the major defense body under the Council of Ministers, maintains program control over the defense industries. It coordinates and controls research, design, development, testing, and production activities. It also provides its requirements for the acquisition of foreign technologies and ensures that such technologies are assimilated into new equipment. The State Planning Committee (GOSPLAN) serves as the central coordinating body for assigning production targets and allocating resources to the defense industries.

The general direction of scientific research in the Soviet Union also is established by the Council of Ministers, which examines and confirms the general plan of development of science and technology. Directives are worked out by the State Committee on Science and Technology, which is charged with determining the basic direction of science and technology in the country, organizing research on scientific and technical problems involving more than one discipline, and raising the effectiveness of scientific research. It also is responsible for introducing scientific and technical advances into the economy as quickly as possible, organizing scientific and technical information, and establishing ties with foreign countries on questions of scientific and technical cooperation.

As much as 80 percent of Soviet science and research is for defense purposes and the State Committee on Science and Technology plays a key role. One of its primary objectives is to acquire by any possible means scientific and technological information and advanced technological products from other nations. Toward this end, it works with both the KGB and the GRU (Main Intelligence Directorate of the Ministry of Defense). The State Committee on Science and Technology deals directly with other state agencies, in particular with the Academy of Sciences, USSR.

GOSPLAN, which works out the national plan for economic development, determines the total allocations for science and technology. Since the Armed

FIGURE 7.1
Hierarchy of Military Decision Making

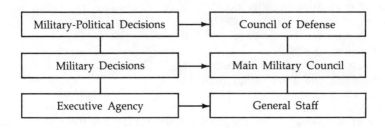

Forces are so dependent upon utilizing science and technology in new weapons systems, senior military officers often occupy high positions in GOSPLAN in order to ensure that military needs are met. GOSSTROI (State Construction Committee) is charged with carrying out a united technical policy and ensuring technical progress for the nation as a whole. This includes a single military-technical policy for the Armed Forces.

Long-range scientific and technological forecasts for the next ten to fifteen years are worked out jointly by four government agencies: the State Committee on Science and Technology, the Academy of Sciences, GOSPLAN, and GOSSTROI. Together these agencies provide direction to corresponding branches of the economy, giving priority to research and development for military purposes.

Ministry of Defense

The Ministry of Defense of the USSR is both directed by, and a contributor to, military doctrine. In its daily activities it is guided by the Main Military Council, which consists of first deputy and deputy ministers of defense, chaired by the Minister of Defense, with the participation, when appropriate, of the General Secretary. The Main Military Council comes directly under the authority of the Council of Defense. (See Figure 7.1.)

Since it is more a Party agency, the role of the Council of Defense was examined in Chapter 6. The Main Military Council and the General Staff, on the other hand, are in the Ministry of Defense and hence technically are agencies of the Soviet government. Prior to November 1957, the Main Military Council (Glavnyy Voyennyy Sovyet) had been called the Higher Military Council (Vysshiy Voyennyy Sovyet).[7] Traditional Soviet secrecy precludes any detailed knowledge of either of these two councils. We can best gain some insight into their current functions by examining the workings of their predecessors.

Histories of the Soviet Armed Forces before World War II can be most instructive. In this period the Red Army went from the poorly equipped soldiers in the Civil War of 1918–1920 to an armed force equipped in large part with state-of-the-art weaponry. At the same time, it went from a mixed territorial system to an organized cadre. These changes occurred in response to Soviet military doctrine worked out in the mid-1920s when special military agencies were established to ensure that doctrinal decisions were carried out.

Main Military Council

The Main Military Council of the 1980s traces its origins from Lenin's Higher Military Council established on March 4, 1918.[8] Created by the Council of People's Commissars, the Higher Military Council was the first of the supreme military agencies for strategic leadership of the Armed Forces of Soviet Russia. It originally consisted of three men, a military leader and two political commissars. The Council was enlarged only two weeks later, on March 19, and Commissar for Military Affairs Leon D. Trotskiy was appointed chairman, and as members, the Commissar for Naval Affairs, two military specialists and one naval specialist and two political commissars.

On September 2, 1918, the Higher Military Council was abolished and its staff turned over to the Revolutionary Military Council of the Republic[9] (Revvoyensovyet Respubliki, or RVSR). This collegial agency of supreme military authority in Soviet Russia functioned during the Civil War with a number of bodies subordinated to it. First was the All-Russian Main Staff, which organized logistical support, mobilization, and training of troops. Second was the Field Staff, which dealt directly with military actions. Third was the All-Russian Bureau of Military Commissars, as well as other central military agencies.

As the first chairman of this body, Trotskiy played a leading role in the Civil War. Other members included: E. M. Sklyanskiy, vice chairman (October 22, 1918–March 11, 1924); I. I. Vatsetis, supreme commander in chief (September 6, 1918–July 8, 1919); and S. S. Kamenev, who eventually replaced Vatsetis as supreme commander in chief (September 6, 1918–April 28, 1924).

On August 28, 1923, the Revvoyensovyet of the Republic was redesignated the Revolutionary Military Council USSR[10] (Revvoyensovyet USSR). Referred to as the collegial agency of supreme military power, this Council was charged with carrying out measures to strengthen the defense of the country, maintain combat readiness, direct local military agencies, register and call up citizens for military training and service, form and staff the army and navy, train and educate military personnel, conduct political indoctrination of the troops, and supply them with everything needed in peace or war. The Revvoyensovyet USSR was made up of a chairman (the commissar for Military and Naval Affairs); deputy chairmen (the deputy commissars for Military and Naval Affairs); the commander in chief of the Armed Forces of the USSR (until March 1924); and others.

Chairman Trotskiy was removed as commissar for Military and Naval Affairs and chairman of the Revvoyensovyet USSR on January 26, 1925, and replaced by M. V. Frunze. K. Ye. Voroshilov became Frunze's deputy. The principal members of the Revvoyensovyet USSR in 1925 were:[11]

—*M. V. Frunze,* chairman, commissar of Military and Naval Affairs (until his death in October, 1925)
—*P. I. Baranov,* chief of the Air Forces of the Red Army
—*A. S. Bubnov,* chief of the Political Directorate of the Red Army
—*S. M. Budennyy,* assistant to the commander in chief for the Cavalry
—*K. Ye. Voroshilov,* deputy chairman, then chairman from November 1925 until June 1934, commissar of Military and Naval Affairs
—*A. I. Yegorov,* chief of staff of the Red Army, 1931–1935
—*S. S. Kamenev,* member, 1924–1927, then deputy chairman as deputy commissar of Military and Naval Affairs (1927–1934)
—*G. K. Ordzhonikidze,* chairman of the Caucasus Bureau of the Central Committee
—*M. N. Tukhachevskiy,* deputy commissar for Military and Naval Affairs, deputy chairman (1931–1934), and commissar for Armaments of RKKA
—*I. S. Unshlikht,* chief of Supply of the Red Army

The Revvoyensovyet USSR carried out the military reforms of the 1920s and worked out plans to develop and employ certain types of weapon systems, aircraft in particular. The edict of the Central Committee dated July 15, 1929, for the First Five-Year Plan specified the direction for the development of the Red Army. In essence, this was the military-technical side of Soviet military doctrine, formulated by the Central Committee. Reviewing the plan of military development in 1931, the Central Committee and Soviet government asked the Revvoyensovyet USSR to achieve the following: (1) to assure that the Red Army would not be inferior in numbers to the probable enemy in the main theater of war; (2) to assure superiority in the decisive types of armaments—aircraft, artillery and tanks; and (3) to strengthen the Red Navy.[12]

These were doctrinal decisions, and the Party intended that they be implemented. The second objective, to be stronger than the enemy in aircraft, artillery, and tanks, was a consequence of adopting the concept of deep operations. As in post–World War II years, the nature of future war and the types of weapons that would be needed were determined by doctrine. The next step was to ensure that the weapons were produced.

The Revvoyensovyet was abolished in 1934 when Stalin called for the abolishment of collegiality in all commissariats at the 18th Party Congress. Since the Revvoyensovyet was the *kollegiya* of the Commissariat for Military and Naval Affairs, that move eliminated it. The Commissariat was reorganized as the Commissariat of Defense USSR, and in November 1934 a new Military Council (*Voyennyy Sovyet*) took the place of the defunct Revvoyensovyet. The Military Council, a consultative body attached to the Commissariat of

Defense, had nearly eighty members but had little power. Most of its members were later killed in Stalin's purges, and meetings simply ceased. It was officially abolished in 1940.[13]

In 1938, the second year of the military purges, two Main Military Councils were established, one for the Red Army and another for the Red Navy. Both were collegial agencies; the first was attached to the Commissariat of Defense, the second attached to the Commissariat of the Navy. Members of the Main Military Council of the Red Army[14] were:

Chairman: *K. Ye. Voroshilov*, Marshal of the Soviet Union, commissar of Defense

Members:

—*J. V. Stalin*, General Secretary

—*V. K. Blyukher*, Marshal of the Soviet Union, commander of the Far Eastern Front (shot during purges, November, 1938)

—*S. M. Budennyy*, Marshal of the Soviet Union, commander of the Moscow Military District

—*G. I. Kulik*, chief of Artillery Directorate of RKKA

—*L. Z. Mekhlis*, chief of Political Directorate of RKKA

—*I. F. Fed'ko*, 1st deputy commissar of Defense (shot in purges, Feb. 1939)

—*B. M. Shaposhnikov*, chief of the General Staff

—*Ye. A. Shchadenko*, deputy commissar of Defense, chief of the Directorate of Command and Staff Personnel

—*K. A. Meretskov*, secretary, deputy chief of the General Staff

The first meeting took place March 19, 1938. Note that Stalin was just a member of the Council, and that the deputy chief of the General Staff acted as secretary. The Main Military Council continued to function until Hitler's troops invaded on June 22, 1941. It was then necessary to create a more powerful agency to direct the war effort.

As a result, Stavka of the Supreme High Command (VGK) was formed.[15] Soviet military doctrine calls for the preparation of the military and the nation as a whole to repel aggression. The General Staff had made a proposal to the commissar of Defense for a supreme military control agency before the war started and had recommended that Stalin be designated the Commander in Chief of the Armed Forces. In his memoirs, Marshal G. K. Zhukov wrote that in the spring before Hitler invaded, he tried to convince Stalin to consider the General Staff proposal and even to test it during an exercise. Stalin finally agreed, but only if the exercise were held away from the borders. Hitler invaded before the exercise was conducted.[16]

Stavka of the High Command (*Glavnogo Komandovaniya*) was organized the day after Hitler invaded, on June 23, 1941, with S. K. Timoshenko, the commissar of Defense, as chairman. On July 10, it was reorganized into the Stavka of the Supreme Command (*Verkhovnogo Komandovaniya*), and then, on August 8, after Stalin had been named Supreme Commander in

Chief of the Armed Forces, it was again renamed the Stavka of the Supreme High Command (*Verkhovnogo Glavnokomandovaniya*—VGK).

Stavka directed strategic tasks for the Armed Forces, planned the combat actions of the army and navy, and determined the allocation of troops and equipment among the fronts. It maintained large reserves of both soldiers and equipment (reserves of the Supreme High Command) at its disposal. The "Katyusha" mortars, for example, were in this category. After July 10, 1941, the members of Stavka were:

Chairman: *J. V. Stalin*, General Secretary, Politburo member, chairman of the Council of People's Commissars, chairman of the State Committee of Defense (GKO), Supreme Commander in Chief and commissar of Defense

Deputy Chairman: *V. M. Molotov*, Politburo member, GKO member

Members:

—*S. K. Timoshenko*, had been chairman as commissar of Defense

—*K. Ye. Voroshilov*, Politburo member, GKO member

—*G. K. Zhukov*, chief of the General Staff (until July 31 1941)

—*B. M. Shaposhnikov*, chief of the General Staff (until May 1942)

—*S. M. Budennyy*, deputy commissar of Defense

—*N. G. Kuznetsov*, commissar of the Navy

On February 17, 1945, the State Committee of Defense (GKO) reorganized Stavka's membership as follows:

Chairman: *J. V. Stalin*

Members:

—*G. K. Zhukov*, deputy Supreme Commander in Chief

—*A. M. Vasilevskiy*, chief of the General Staff (until February 1945)

—*A. I. Antonov*, chief of the General Staff (until 1946)

—*N. A. Bulganin*, deputy commissar of Defense and GKO member

—*N. G. Kuznetsov*, commissar of the Navy

During the first days after the invasion, it was difficult for the Kremlin to determine exactly what was happening. All communication with the fronts had been cut. To facilitate command and control in Moscow, intermediate High Commands were established in various geographical areas: Northwestern (Marshal K. Ye. Voroshilov); Western (Marshal S. K. Timoshenko); and Southwestern (Marshal S. M. Budennyy).[17] These intermediate commands were operational for only a short time, while Stavka tried to regain control of the fronts directly from Moscow. The High Commands were not given enough authority, nor did they have any reserves to influence operations. In addition, it was not long before Hitler's troops overran the intermediate areas and were at the gates of Moscow. After the war with Germany ended, a High Command of the Far East was set up to direct military operations against Japan. Marshal Vasilevskiy, by then an experienced campaigner, had little trouble operating at a distance from Moscow.[18] These High Commands were the forerunners of the TVDs established in the 1970s and 1980s.

Stalin remained in Moscow throughout the war. Control over actions at the fronts was maintained by sending representatives of Stavka into the field where they coordinated the actions of several fronts. Most often, the former chief of the General Staff, Zhukov, or the incumbent chief, Vasilevskiy, served as Stavka representatives. They had no authority to change the plans drawn up by the General Staff and approved in Moscow; it was their job to see that the plans were carried out. Stavka did have the Reserves of the VGK[19] to call on to reinforce the fronts as needed. Stavka representatives also reported directly to Stalin, and gave him an accurate picture of what was happening at the front, something front commanders were afraid to do at times. Stavka also had a large group of specialists as "permanent advisers," who were always on call. For example, the Chief of Artillery of the Red Army General N. N. Voronov, a veteran of the fighting in Spain, was one such adviser who was called on when artillery was being discussed.

In April 1946, the year after the war ended, a Higher Military Council (Vysshiy Voyennyy Sovyet)[20] was formed as a collegial body; it was attached to the Ministry of the Armed Forces when the latter was created. Its members were also Politburo members, Central Committee members, and the foremost military leaders. This Higher Military Council was abolished in 1950. At this time the Ministry of the Armed Forces was split into the Ministry of War, and the Ministry of the Navy, and two Main Military Councils (Glavnyy Voyennyy Sovyet), were established, one for each of the ministries. This structure lasted until the two ministries were combined into the Ministry of Defense in 1953.[21] With this reorganization, there is evidence that the Higher Military Council was revived. There are several references to it in the proceedings recording the ousting of Marshal G. K. Zhukov in 1957. In November 1957, it was renamed the Main Military Council[22] and remains as a collegial agency of the Ministry of Defense. The Minister of Defense is the Council chairman.

Based on precedent, the Main Military Council of today is no doubt concerned with such matters as military discipline, combat readiness, mobilization capabilities, military and political-military training, and future military developments. In event of war, the Main Military Council likely would be redesignated as the Stavka of the Supreme High Command. In this case, its chairman would be the General Secretary, who also would be on the Politburo and chairman of the Council of Defense. Stavka would again direct the total military effort, with the General Staff acting as its executive agency.

Role of the General Staff

The Soviet General Staff is the executive agency for the Ministry of Defense and its Main Military Council[23] and it directs the work of all central and local military agencies. As already indicated, in event of war the General

Staff would probably serve as it did during the last war, as the basic agency of Stavka for strategic planning and directing the Armed Forces on the fronts. The Soviet General Staff coordinates the work of the Main Staffs of the services, the staff of the Rear Services, and the main and central directorates of the Ministry of Defense.

The General Staff, through the Main Military Council, is subordinate to the Council of Defense, which in turn is linked to the Politburo. Since military doctrine, by Soviet definition, is the military policy of the Communist Party, the General Staff participates in the formulation of this doctrine. It is a major player in ensuring that the questions stipulated by doctrine are answered and implemented.

Although Soviet military historians attempt to show that the origins of the General Staff are completely Russian, it is likely that the concept of its operation was significantly influenced first by the French General Staff and later by the Austro-Hungarian and the German general staffs. At the time the Soviet General Staff was established in 1935, a number of Soviet military leaders had attended German staff colleges. The main tasks of the Soviet General Staff at that time were (1) operational planning, (2) guiding the operational training of higher command personnel and staffs, (3) providing material support for troops, (4) planning orders for industry to develop and produce equipment and armaments, and (5) preparing for and carrying out mobilization measures.

When the Germans invaded in 1941, the Soviet General Staff had the following directorates: operations, organization and mobilization, intelligence, military communications, military cartographic service, coding, and various special sections,[24] including armaments, supply planning, fortified regions, vehicular transport and roads, and military history.[25] During the wartime years, the General Staff came into its own. Soviet military historians are lavish in praising the manner in which it operated. Although this adulation may be a bit overdone, the fact remains that both the Party and military leadership were well satisfied with the organization.[26]

While the war was in progress, sections and departments in the central apparatus and in staffs had been formed to study the lessons of the war and to communicate information on the latest combat methods to the troops. From 1946 to 1953 research increased: The Military History Section of the General Staff became a directorate and faculties were formed in the Frunze Military Academy and the Academy of the General Staff to train military historians for research and teaching.[27]

By 1953, the year of Stalin's death, the General Staff, the Main Political Administration, service staffs, and military academy presses had published a great deal of information on the war. Almost immediately this entire network was shut down. Stalin's "personality cult," as it was called, had had a stifling effect on the development of military theory. Yet it was not until after Khrushchev secretly denounced Stalin at the 20th Party Congress in 1956 that changes were made.[28]

In the postwar period the Soviets have been most secretive about the operations of the General Staff. The primary directorates are operations, organization and mobilization, military intelligence, Staff of the Warsaw Pact, external relations, foreign military assistance, military cartography, signal communications, negotiations, military science and some others. Certain individuals in the General Staff have been designated to deal with foreigners, especially on arms control matters. In the mid-1980s work was in progress on the construction of its new headquarters, located within walking distance of the Kremlin. The chief of the General Staff, Marshal of the Soviet Union Sergey F. Akhromeyev, accompanied General Secretary Gorbachev to the Reykjavik meeting in Iceland in 1986, and to the Washington, D.C., summit meeting in 1987, where he was a primary participant.

The Military Science Directorate[29] is the single most important section concerned with military doctrine within the General Staff. The military-technical side of doctrine is based primarily on the data supplied by military science. It is the Military Science Directorate that elaborates the program of research to be conducted by the Ministry of Defense in support of the development of military science. Information about this directorate is extremely limited. Among its responsibilities is the publication of the restricted circulation journal *Military Thought*. One of the elements in this directorate is the Military History Section. The Institute of Military History of the Ministry of Defense, part of the Academy of Sciences, also is associated with the Military Science Directorate.

The Directorate's interest in the relationship between military science and military doctrine was evident in a military-theoretical conference it conducted in May 1963, on "The Essence and Content of Soviet Military Doctrine." The conference was opened by General Colonel K. F. Skorobogatkin, who for many years headed the Military Science Directorate. At the conference, he noted that "military science constitutes the military-technical basis of Soviet military doctrine. It recommends the most acceptable ways and means of solving problems designated by the political leadership."[30]

The main speaker was General Major A. A. Prokhorov, one of the authors of *Military Strategy*, who spoke on "The Essence and Content of Soviet Military Doctrine." Colonel V. V. Larionov, another major contributor to *Military Strategy*, stressed the difficulty in defining military doctrine, military science, and military strategy. He noted that some feel that military doctrine is subordinate to strategy. Others deny even the existence of military doctrine, arguing that military science completely absorbs it. He went on to say that "Soviet military doctrine mainly echoes everything new found in military science and in the practice of armed conflict."

Colonel V. M. Kulish in his presentation said that not since the 1930s had a thorough scientific study of questions of military doctrine been made, "but reality is forcing the study of these important questions." He then gave what in essence was a definition of military doctrine, noting that it represents the view officially adopted by the state on the character, form and methods of waging a future war and also on structuring the armed forces and preparing the country for that war.

Another speaker, Engineer Colonel V. I. Vaneyev, stressed that military doctrine determines the buildup for war and the training of all services of the Armed Forces. In contemporary circumstances, he said, the introduction of mathematical methods and the development of cybernetics have special significance. Close attention must also be given to questions of psychological training for nuclear rocket war and in doing so, moral-political conditions have to be considered realistically.[31]

Several of those attending the conference received Frunze Prizes in 1966 for writing a work on military theory: General Colonel K. F. Skorobogatkin, General Major A. A. Prokhorov, Colonels V. V. Glazov, V. K. Denisenko, and V. V. Larionov. The title was not given in the announcement.

From 1975 to 1983, General Lieutenant M. A. Gareyev headed the Military Science Directorate. Gareyev became a deputy chief of the General Staff in 1985 and was promoted to general colonel. His 1985 book, *M.V. Frunze— Military Theoretician*, won the Frunze Prize in 1987.

More information about the Military Science Directorate was published in *Military Thought* in April 1969. It was revealed that the Military Science Directorate coordinates translations of military-technical material for the Academy of the General Staff's Department of Military-Technical Information and the Ministry of Defense's Central Institute of Military-Technical Information. From all available evidence, it is reasonably certain that the Military Science Directorate is the center of scientific research that branches out into the Academy of the General Staff, other military academies and the vast network of military schools.

Role of the Military Academies

In the United States, the nearest equivalent to military doctrine and strategy is worked out, to a large degree, in civilian "think tanks," such as RAND or Systems Planning Corporation. Within the U.S. Armed Forces there is little place for an individual or even a group to consider matters such as military strategy. As General David Jones, a previous chairman of the Joint Chiefs of Staff remarked, "If Clausewitz were alive today and serving in our armed forces, he would have retired as a colonel and would be working in a beltway think tank." In the Soviet Union the military academies perform much the same role as "think tanks" and other research institutions in the United States. These military academies have no exact counterparts in the West. They are higher professional military institutions for the education and training of officers. It is mandatory that all Soviet marshals, generals, and admirals attend the two year course at the senior academy, the Voroshilov Military Academy of the General Staff,[32] either when they are colonels (or Navy captains) expected to be promoted, or as newly promoted generals or admirals.

Traditionally, the Voroshilov Military Academy of the General Staff has fallen in the portfolio of the chief of the General Staff. In addition "the Academy of the General Staff is a center for advanced military science and conductor of the latest achievements of military theory. It carries out major scientific research work in elaborating problems of modern war and in successfully training highly qualified cadres."[33] Between 75 and 200 generals and admirals may be assigned to the faculty of the Academy, serving as instructors and doing research and studies as directed by the General Staff. They serve as a high-level military "think tank" supporting the General Staff. When one considers the questions military doctrine is to answer, such as the direction that development of the Armed Forces must take, how preparations are to be carried out for the possibility of a future war, and by what methods the war is to be conducted, the role of these academies in support of military doctrine can be more clearly seen.

Prior to attending the Voroshilov Military Academy of the General Staff, all officers also will have attended another academy appropriate to their branch or service. The most prestigious of these is the Frunze Military Academy. Before the Academy of the General Staff opened in 1936, the Frunze Military Academy was the highest military professional educational institution in the USSR. After the war, scientific research work increased at the Academy; textbooks, lectures, and other materials were rewritten; and the number of advanced degrees increased. When nuclear weapons were introduced, intense research began.[34] Other military academies that an officer might have attended before the Voroshilov Academy of the General Staff are the Gagarin Air Academy,[35] the Grechko Naval Academy, the Dzerzhinskiy Rocket Academy, the Malinovskiy Tank Academy, the Zhukov Military Command Academy of Air Defense or the Govorov Military Engineering Radiotechnical Academy of Air Defense. The length of the course of study at these academies is three years, with one exception: The course of study at the Zhukovskiy Military Air Engineering Academy is five years. These academies have faculties far in excess of what would be needed for purely instructional duties. For example, the Frunze Military Academy may have more than 35 general officers on its faculty, many of whom do research. Other academies may have an equivalent number of faculty members of high rank.

Soviet sources show that at the Gagarin Military Air Academy there are 13 doctors of science, 233 candidates of science (a degree somewhat higher than a master's degree in the United States), 10 professors, and 170 associate professors and senior researchers. Its library has more than 500,000 books. The advanced degrees of candidate of science and doctor of science can both be awarded by the Academy. As a leading "scientific center" for the Soviet Air Forces, "not a single problem, not a single complex theme connected with the combat use of aviation is decided without the active participation of this center. In most cases, it acts as the leading performer of complex research in the sphere of tactics and operational art for the Air Forces."[36] The Gagarin Military Air Academy and the Zhukovskiy Military Air Engineering Academy are closely tied to all aspects of the Soviet manned space program. At least 15 of the Soviet cosmonauts are graduates of the Gagarin Academy. Another 13 have attended the Zhukovskiy Academy.

While providing high level professional education and training for students and serving as think tanks for their respective services or branches, some faculty members of the military academies also are Academicians of the Academy of Sciences.[37] All of the academies appear to have close ties with that organization.

Role of the Academy of Sciences

The highest scientific establishment in the Soviet Union is the Academy of Sciences, USSR, which is directly subordinate to the Council of Ministers. It is responsible for general scientific guidance of research on important problems of natural and social sciences. Much of its actual research is accomplished by the Academies of Sciences of the republics and by other scientific establishments. The Academy supports Soviet military doctrine in two areas: first, in scientific research and development, and second, in the formulation of military strategy, which in turn impacts directly upon military doctrine, since the level of scientific and technological achievement in a country must be considered on the formulation of military doctrine. This accounts for the military-technical side of military doctrine. Further, as previously noted in examining the laws of war, the course and outcome of war are dependent upon the correlation between the scientific-technical potentials of the warring sides.

The Academy has four broad divisions covering seventeen branches as shown in Table 7.5. There is a Siberian Branch of the Academy of Sciences, located at Akademgorodok near Novosibirsk, and there are also two science centers and eleven filials. On January 1, 1986 there were 274 academicians, 542 corresponding members, and 98 foreign members in the Academy. At the same time the Academy had more than 280 scientific establishments, in which there were 55,583 scientific workers, including 5,740 doctors of science and 25,874 candidates of science.

In the early 1960s the Academy of Sciences was reorganized and given more authority for coordinating scientific research throughout the nation. More than 200 scientific councils were formed to work on what were considered to be the most important problems of the time. This coordinating effort was intended to ensure avoidance of duplication and to make possible speedy and broad dissemination of new scientific discoveries. The Academy operates its own translation service and it reproduces foreign scientific journals with great rapidity. It has a network of more than 170 scientific libraries with four major centers.

The Academy of Sciences works closely with the State Committee on Science and Technology. Indicative of this association was the appointment of Guriy Marchuk, chairman of the State Committee on Science and Technology, to the position of president of the Academy of Sciences in 1986. The Academy is also involved with Soviet military institutions that do basic research on scientific matters, such as the Military Academy of Chemical Defense.

TABLE 7.5
Academy of Sciences

COUNCIL OF MINISTERS
GENERAL ASSEMBLY OF THE ACADEMY OF SCIENCES
PRESIDIUM OF THE ACADEMY OF SCIENCES

SECTIONS

Division of Physico-Technical and Mathematical Sciences

Branches:
Mathematics
General Physics and Astronomy
Nuclear Physics
Physico-Technical Problems of Energetics
Computer Equipment and Automation
Mechanics and Processes of Guidance

Division of Chemico-Technological and Biological Sciences

Branches:
General Biology
General and Technical Chemistry
Physico-Chemistry and Technology of Inorganic Materials
Biochemistry, Biophysics, and Chemistry of Physiological Active Compounds
Physiology

Division of Earth Sciences

Branches:
Geology, Geophysics, and Geochemistry
Oceanology, Geography, and Physics of the Atmosphere

Division of Social Sciences

Branches:
History
Philosophy and Law
Economics
Literature and Language

Source: Yezhegodnik Bol'shoy Sovetskoy Entsiklopedii [Annual of the Great Soviet Encyclopedia] (Moscow: Soviet Encyclopedia), published annually.

Role of the Academy of Sciences in Space Activities

On the surface, the Academy of Sciences plays the directing role in Soviet space programs. Although Western intelligence agencies estimate that at least eighty percent of Soviet space efforts are for military purposes, the Kremlin does not admit that its military space activities even exist. Only a small segment of the Soviet space program is widely publicized by Soviet propaganda organs. The purpose of such propaganda is to demonstrate the scientific and technical progress of a world superpower and to give the appearance of international cooperation in space matters. What is displayed to the outside world may be to divert attention from military programs rather than to reveal the true nature of the space effort.

Glavkosmos USSR (The Main Directorate for the Development and Use of Space Technology for the National Economy and Scientific Research) was established in early October 1985, just before the Geneva summit. A. I. Dunayev, its first chief, asserted that its formation was in the interests of the national economy, science, and international cooperation. There was no mention in Soviet news releases that the new organization might have military implications.[38]

During the summit meeting in November 1985, U.S. television viewers frequently saw and heard Soviet Academician Roald Sagdeyev, director of the "Space Research Institute" under the Academy of Sciences. Soviet news releases had stated that a purpose of this institute is to provide centralized coordination of Soviet civil space programs. Academician Sagdeyev, with his command of the English language, appeared more as a propagandist than a scientist. This impression was supported when he appeared on television along with Georgiy Arbatov, head of the Institute of the USA and Canada, to denounce the United States SDI program (Strategic Defense Initiative).

Also under the USSR Academy of Sciences is the Intercosmos Council, formally referred to as the Council for International Cooperation in the Exploration and Uses of Outer Space. Chaired by Academician V. A. Kotelnikov, this council is subordinate to the Presidium of the Academy of Sciences and appears to concentrate on maintaining contact with foreign scientists under the pretext of "international space cooperation." It is reasonable to assume that its major purpose is to collect as much scientific and technical information as possible on space-related activities from foreign countries, in particular Western Europe and the United States.

These leading Soviet personalities in the Academy of Sciences, such as Sagdeyev, may actually be unaware of what is taking place in their own country. During the early SALT I negotiations it became apparent to U.S. participants that the civilian members of the Soviet team were denied access to information about their own capabilities. This tight compartmentalization is not new to the Soviet security system. The formation of certain Soviet reserve armies during World War II, for instance, was revealed only to a few key members of the Soviet General Staff. Individuals such as Sagdeyev would not be permitted to travel in foreign countries and talk freely with foreign scientists if they had sensitive security clearances.

Kremlin leaders maintain that they are against the "militarization of space." Billions of rubles are being spent worldwide on a massive propaganda campaign to kill the U.S. SDI program. Perhaps other billions are being spent to conceal both from the Soviet people and the outside world that the Kremlin rulers themselves have had the equivalent of an SDI program under way for years.[39] Finally, in 1987, Gorbachev announced that the Soviet Union had been working on such a program, but gave no details.

Military Strategy and the Social Sciences

In the United States it may seem strange that an organization such as the Soviet Academy of Sciences would play a role in the formulation of military strategy. However, in the Soviet Union the social sciences come under the Academy of Sciences and, as will be seen below, military strategy is regarded as one of its components.

Following the ouster of Khrushchev in 1964, one of the first actions of the new leadership was to examine the status of the social sciences in the USSR. Deficiencies were found, and at the 23rd Party Congress in 1966, the Central Committee was charged with making the necessary corrections. The problem with respect to the social sciences appeared to extend to the military. In April 1966, at the time the Congress met, Marshal V. D. Sokolovskiy and his frequent colloborator, General Major M. I. Cherednichenko, published an article entitled "On Contemporary Military Strategy." They noted that working out questions of military strategy had taken on paramount significance. The United States and other NATO nations, they claimed, had established "think tanks"—RAND, the Hudson Institute, and the British Institute of Strategic Studies, for example—to serve as "original factories of military thought." They explained further: "*As with the other social sciences, the theory of military strategy* is called on to expose pressing problems and tasks, to indicate the valid path of their solution, to serve as a scientific basis of Party policy in questions of protecting the country. It is fully understood that the deficiencies of social sciences being printed in our periodical press are inherent to military strategy as well." (Emphasis added.)

The authors went on to claim that Soviet military strategy is built on a scientific basis. "It takes into account the development of foreign military strategy and bases itself on the level of development achieved by other sciences." The authors concluded: "Expanding the front of strategic research makes necessary a bolder involvement in this work of scientists of different specialties, generals, admirals, and officers having corresponding preparation. The collective comparison of different points of view in order to rule out erroneous opinions has important significance in the discussion of problems of strategy."[40]

The subsequent August 1967 Plenum of the Central Committee resulted in a resolution on "Measures for the Further Development of the Social Sciences and for Raising Their Role in Communist Construction."[41] This resolution introduced far-reaching changes. V. V. Zagladin of the Central Committee's International Department wrote in 1972 that social science problems needed to be solved not just for scientific purposes, "but also for the Party's practical activity and for determining the most effective ways and means of insuring the victory of socialism over capitalism." Zagladin summed up the progress to that date:

The work of the Academy of Social Sciences has been broadened and clarified; considerable work is being done within the framework of the Academy of Sciences of the USSR by the Institute of World Economy and International Relations [IMEMO], the Institute of Economics of the World Socialist System, and also the Institutes of the Far East, Oriental Studies, Latin America, Africa, and a number of others. New institutes were created for this: the Institute of the International Workers' Movement, the Institute of Scientific Information for the Social Sciences, and the Institute of the United States of America [IUSA].[42]

It was no accident, as the Russians are fond of saying, that in November 1967 the IUSA was given an old mansion on a street within a few minutes walk of the apartment building where Sokolovskiy and other senior Soviet officers lived. Colonel V. V. Larionov, who had prepared *Military Strategy* for publication in addition to being one of its authors, became head of a section on military-political problems at the Institute. General Colonel N. A. Lomov, who in 1965 had been listed as the author of a book entitled *Soviet Military Doctrine*, was identified as a consultant. Other Soviet officers who had written previously on matters of military doctrine and strategy were assigned either full-time or consulting positions.

The older, more prestigious Institute of World Economy and International Relations (IMEMO) also apparently became more involved in strategic issues. Recognized strategists such as Colonel V. M. Kulish, Doctor of Historical Sciences, whose published works on military affairs were well known, were assigned as full-time institute members.

IMEMO had already been performing an important service since 1958 by publishing the *International Political-Economic Yearbook*. In accordance with the law of war that specifies that "the course and outcome of war depends on the correlation of economic potentials of the belligerent sides," Soviet military scientists keep a close watch on the economic balance in the world. IMEMO provides annual political and economic profiles of socialist, capitalist, and developing countries. Each annual contains a number of essays. Generals M. A. Milstein (later of the IUSA) and A. K. Slobodenko (later at IMEMO) wrote a lengthy piece on U.S. military-strategic concepts in 1958. Milstein at the time was on the faculty of the Academy of the General Staff.

Members of these institutes also play another important role in Soviet military affairs. They are the leading members of a very select group of Soviets who are permitted to meet with foreigners; in fact, this is one of their primary tasks. Prominent foreigners who visit the Soviet Union— presidential aspirants, senators, business leaders, scholars, scientists, and so on—generally are hosted by the Institute of the USA and Canada. Members of this Institute determine where the visitors may travel, with whom they may speak, and what kind of treatment they will receive. A prominent person's visit will be as carefully staged as a scene at the Bolshoi Theater and as realistic as Catherine the Great's visit to the world-famous Potemkin Village.

In return, when these Soviets travel to the United States, the courtesies they have extended to prominent Americans are returned in full, and they are able to call upon leaders in many fields. With their extensive study of the United States, these knowledgeable Soviets are able to obtain information on a variety of subjects from highly placed individuals in the United States. It is doubtful if any American researcher or reporter would have the access to U.S. leaders enjoyed by some members of the Institute of the USA and Canada.

In their discussions with Americans, the Soviet defense-intellectuals obtain information that might be called strategic intelligence—information on the political, economic, scientific-technical and military potentials of their possible opponent. Such information helps them answer questions of military doctrine such as: the degree of the probability of a war with their most likely opponents, the United States and its allies; and the character the war might take that the Soviet Armed Forces might be "forced" to wage.

Members of Soviet research institutes also provide another valuable service to the Kremlin. They seek to portray Soviet policies, such as the approach to arms control, in the most favorable light. Many defense-intellectuals in the United States, Canada, and Western Europe feel that when they meet with this group of Soviets they are having a face-to-face dialogue with individuals seeking to find mutually beneficial solutions to international security issues. They fail to realize that these Soviets are highly trained professionals, dedicated, as stated in the Party's leading journal, "to determining the most effective ways and means of ensuring the victory of socialism over capitalism."

*   *   *

The Party provides the guidelines for the formulation of military doctrine and has an overriding interest in its political side. At the highest level, the major players are the members of the Council of Defense. How they receive inputs, how often they meet, and their exact composition are not known. The military-technical side, which changes with new technologies, is worked primarily by government agencies.

Since military doctrine is concerned with many areas—from foreign policy and arms control negotiations to military-patriotic indoctrination of youth and the problem of ethnic minorities—many players take part in its formulation. These range from members of the Politburo and Secretariat to individuals working in the various ministries and in other government bodies. With few exceptions, these people and their organizations are located in Moscow. All are Party members and participate to some degree in Party activities. They must profess to be guided by Marxist-Leninist teachings, which are sufficiently flexible to cover any situation.

Notes

1. The Supreme Soviet of the USSR is legally described in the *Constitution (Fundamental Law) of the USSR* (Moscow: Novosti, 1977), English translation, Section V, Chapter 15, Articles 108–127.

2. *Constitution of the USSR*, Articles 119–125.

3. H. F. Scott and W. F. Scott, *Soviet Control Structure* (New York: Crane, Russak & Company, Inc., 1983), p. 14.

4. Politburo members A. A. Gromyko, M. S. Gorbachev, N. I. Ryzhkov, N. N. Slyun'kov, V. V. Shcherbitskiy and candidate Politburo members P. N. Demichev and Yu. F. Solov'yev are members of the Presidium of the Supreme Soviet USSR. *Yezhegodnik Bol'shoy Sovetskoy Entsiklopedii 1986* [Annual of the Great Soviet Encyclopedia 1986] (Moscow: Soviet Encyclopedia, 1986), p. 12.

5. *Constitution of the USSR*, Articles 122, 128–136.

6. Ibid., pp. 93, 96.

7. V. S. Golubovich, *Marshal R. Ya. Malinovskiy* [Marshal R. Ya. Malinovskiy] (Moscow: Voyenizdat, 1984), p. 207.

8. *Sovetskaya Voyennaya Entsiklopediya* [Soviet Military Encyclopedia] (Moscow: Voyenizdat, 1976–1980), vol. 2, p. 566. See also V. D. Danilov, "General'nyy Shtab RKKA v Predvoyennyye Gody (1936—iyun' 1941 g.)" [General Staff of the RKKA in the Prewar Years], *Voyenno-Istoricheskiy Zhurnal* [Military History Journal] 3 (March 1980), pp. 68–73, 84, and V. D. Danilov "Sovershenstvovaniye Sistemy Tsentral'nykh Organov Voyennogo Rukovodstva v 1929–1939 gg." [Perfecting Systems of Central Agencies of Military Control in 1929–39], *Voyenno-Istoricheskiy Zhurnal* 6 (June 1982), pp. 74–79.

9. V. D. Danilov, "Revolyutsionnyy Voyennyy Sovet Respubliki" [Revolutionary Military Council of the Republic], in *Sovetskaya Voyennaya Entsiklopediya*, vol. 7, p. 79.

10. *Sovetskaya Voyennaya Entsiklopediya*, vol. 7, p. 80. See also: V. D. Danilov, "Perfecting Systems of Central Agencies of Military Control in 1929–39," pp. 74–79.

11. S. A. Tyushkevich, editor, *Sovetskiye Vooruzhennyye Sily* [Soviet Armed Forces] (Moscow: Voyenizdat, 1978), p. 158.

12. Ibid., p. 185.

13. M. V. Zakharov, editor, *50 Let Vooruzhennikh Sil SSSR* [50 Years of the Armed Forces USSR] (Moscow: Voyenizdat, 1968), p. 199; A. A. Yepishev, "Voyennyy Sovet" [Military Council], in *Sovetskaya Voyennaya Entsiklopediya*, vol. 2, p. 273.

14. "Glavnyy Voyennyy Sovyet" [Main Military Council], in *Sovetskaya Voyennaya Entsiklopediya*, vol. 2, p. 566. See also *Voyenno-Istoricheskiy Zhurnal* 3 (March 1980), p. 84; 6 (June 1982), p. 75; S. F. Akhromeyev, editor, *Voyennyy Entsiklopedicheskiy Slovar'* [Military Encyclopedic Dictionary], 2nd ed. (Moscow: Voyenizdat, 1986), p. 195.

15. N. A. Sbytov, "Stavka Verkhovnogo Glavnokomandovaniya" [Stavka of the High Command], *Sovetskaya Voyennaya Entsiklopediya*, vol. 7, p. 511. See also *Voyenno-Istoricheskiy Zhurnal* 8 (August 1980), p. 80; 6 (June 1987), pp. 24ff.

16. G. K. Zhukov, *Vospominaniya i Razmyshleniya* [Reminiscences and Reflections] (Moscow: Novosti, 1975), vol. 1, p. 320.

17. "Glavnoye Komandovaniye" [High Command], in *Sovetskaya Voyennaya Entsiklopediya*, vol. 2, p. 562. See also "Glavnokomandyushchiy" [Commander in Chief], p. 564; V. D. Danilov has a good article in *Voyenno-Istoricheskyy Zhurnal* 9 (September 1987), pp. 17ff.

18. Zakharov, *50 Let*, p. 269.

19. V. I. Belyakov and N. I. Reut, "Strategicheskiye Rezervy" [Strategic Reserves], in *Sovetskaya Voyennaya Entsiklopediya*, vol. 7, p. 553.

20. A. A. Yepishev, "Voyennyy Sovet" [Military Council], in *Sovetskaya Voyennaya Entsiklopediya*, vol. 2, p. 274; Tyushkevich, *Sovetskiye Vooruzhennyye Sily*, p. 389.

21. "Glavnyy Voyennyy Sovyet" [Main Military Council], in *Voyennyy Entsiklopedicheskiy Slovar'*, p. 195.

22. Golubovich, *Marshal Malinovskiy*, p. 207.

23. M. V. Zakharov, "General'nyy Shtab" [General Staff], in *Bol'shaya Sovetskaya Entsiklopediya* [Great Soviet Encyclopedia] (Moscow: Soviet Encyclopedia, 1971), 3rd edition, vol. 6, pp. 223ff; V. G. Kulikov, "General'nyy Shtab" [General Staff], in *Sovetskaya Voyennyy Entsiklopediya*, vol. 2, pp. 510ff.

24. S. M. Shtemenko, *General'nyy Shtab v Gody Voyny* [General Staff in the War Years] (Moscow: Voyenizdat, 1983), vol. 1, especially chapter 7.

25. Danilov, "Perfecting Systems of Central Agencies of Military Control in 1929–39," *Voyenno-Istoricheskiyy Zhurnal*, June 1982, pp. 75–76.

26. For an intimate look at the workings of the General Staff before and during World War II, see the memoirs of two of its chiefs: G. K. Zhukov, *Vospominaniya i Razmyshleniya* [Reminiscences and Reflections] and A. M. Vasilevskiy, *Delo Vsey Zhizni* [Business of a Whole Life] (Moscow: Politizdat, 1975). Both have been translated into English. See also the notes of candid conversations with Marshal Zhukov by Konstantin Semonov over a thirty-year period which have finally been released for publication: *Voyenno-Istoricheskyy Zhurnal* (June, July, September, October, November, 1987).

27. Zakharov, *50 Let*, p. 494.

28. A. N. Grylev, "Sovetskaya Voyennaya Istoriografiya v Gody Velikoy Otechestvennoy Voyny i Poslevoyennyy Period" [Soviet Military Historiography in the Years of the Great Patriotic War and in the Postwar Period], *Voyenno-Istoricheskiy Zhurnal* 1 (January 1968), p. 98.

29. M. V. Filimoshin, "Iz Opyta Raboty Organizatsii Veteranov Voyny" [From the Experience of Work of War Veterans' Organizations], *Voyenno-Istoricheskyy Zhurnal* 10 (October 1987), pp. 79–81. Past heads of the Military Science Administration have been: General Colonel A. P. Pokrovskiy (1946–1956), General of the Army V. V. Kurasov (1956–1961), General Colonel K. F. Skorobogatkin (1961–1970), General Major A. N. Grylev (1970–1973), General Lieutenant G. M. Zavizion (1973–1974) and General Colonel M. A. Gareyev (1975–1983). The present head is General Lieutenant Ye. A. Kuznetsov (1983–).

30. K. F. Skorobogatkin, "Sushchnost' i Soderzhaniye Sovetskoy Voyennoy Doktriny" [Essence and Content of Soviet Military Doctrine], *Voyenno-Istoricheskiy Zhurnal* 10 (October 1963), p. 126.

31. Others at the conference were: General Lieutenants V. S. Golushkevich, V. F. Mernov and K. V. Krainyukov; Colonels G. P. Goncharov, A. N. Grylev, K. I. Ivanov, I. S. Khrebtovskiy, V. V. Mochalov, N. V. Nazarov, Ya. I. Stepnykh, P. Ye. Varezhnikov, and Captain I. I. Argunov. Since that time there have been dozens of practical science conferences conducted by the Ministry of Defense, organized by the Military Science Directorate.

32. See *Akademiya General'nogo Shtaba* [Academy of the General Staff] (Moscow: Voyenizdat, 1976] and the second edition of the same book *Voyennaya Akademiya General'nogo Shtaba* [Military Academy of the General Staff] (Moscow: Voyenizdat, 1986) for a history of the Voroshilov Academy.

33. Zakharov, *50 Let*, p. 521.

34. S. S. Lototskiy, "Akademii imeni M. V. Frunze—50 Let" [Frunze Military Academy—50th Anniversary], *Voyenno-Istoricheskiy Zhurnal* 12 (December 1968), pp. 46–55. See also *Akademiya Imeni M. V. Frunze* [Academy Named for M. V. Frunze] (Moscow: Voyenizdat, 1973) and *Voyennaya Akademiya Imeni M. V. Frunze* [Military Academy Named for M. V. Frunze] (Moscow: Voyenizdat, 1980) for more information.

35. See *Voyenno-Vozdushnaya Akademiya Imeni Yu. A. Gagarina* [Military Air Academy Named for Yu. A. Gagarin] (Moscow: Voyenizdat, 1984) for history of this Academy.

36. Ibid., p. 176.

37. H. F. Scott and W. F. Scott, *Armed Forces of the USSR* (Boulder, Colorado: Westview Press, 1984), p. 382.

38. *Izvestia*, October 13, 1985, p. 2.

39. At the Washington summit in December 1987, General Secretary Gorbachev revealed for the first time that the Soviet Union had their own strategic defense program.

40. V. D. Sokolovskiy and M. I. Cherednichenko, "O Sovremennoye Voyennoye Strategii" [On Contemporary Military Strategy], *Kommunist Vooruzhennykh Sil* [Communist of the Armed Forces] 7 (April 1966), p. 59.

41. K. U. Chernenko, editor, *Spravochnik Partiynogo Rabotnika* [Handbook of a Party Worker] (Moscow: Politizdat, 1968) p. 245.

42. V. V. Zagladin, "Revolyutsionnyy Protsess i Mezhdunarodnaya Politika KPSS" [The Revolutionary Process and the International Policy of the CPSU], *Kommunist* 13 (September 1972), pp. 14–15.

8
Dissemination of
Soviet Military Doctrine

Widespread dissemination of the basic tenets of military doctrine is an established Kremlin policy. This requirement was stressed by Frunze in the 1920s and remains just as important today. Such dissemination is necessary "to ensure a psychological situation of national awareness and concern for the needs of the army, for only in such an atmosphere can the business of building up our Armed Forces proceed successfully."[1] In order to be prepared for the possibility of a future war, the population must know what is expected of them.

Marshal R. Ya. Malinovskiy, the Soviet Minister of Defense from 1957 to 1967, sought to ensure that "the task of propagandizing the progressive views and conclusions of Soviet military doctrine" was carried out. In this effort, he called upon "military newspapers and magazines, and Voyenizdat, our military publishing house," to provide "a thorough explanation of the nature of the revolution in military affairs and the resulting demands produced in the training and education of personnel of different branches and services of the Armed Forces."[2] The hundreds of articles and dozens of books published on the new military doctrine in those years attest to the importance Soviet leaders place on its dissemination. The same pattern has continued since.

The information that is disseminated is carefully censored. Many answers to key questions of military doctrine, such as what armed forces are needed, are never openly revealed. In the Western press, especially in the United States, scholars concerned with national security issues argue unceasingly about matters such as the needs of the armed forces, the possibility of a future war, and other topics that in the Soviet Union would be considered military doctrine. The Kremlin does not permit contradictory views on security needs to be aired publicly.

There were hints in the Soviet press in 1987 that greater "openness" about military matters was being considered. However, by early 1988 nothing had changed. On the contrary, after 1985 foreign subscribers could no longer get *Herald of Air Defense*, the journal of the Troops of Air Defense, and after 1986 the *Foreign Military Observer* was also cut from foreign circulation.

Such a thing had never happened under Khrushchev, Brezhnev, Andropov, or Chernenko. In both 1986 and 1987 fewer books on military matters were published than previously.

The present Soviet leaders have inherited a legacy that will be difficult to overcome. George Orwell's book *1984* described how a totalitarian state can control information of all kinds. His model was Stalin's Soviet Union; this control did not cease after Stalin's death. Even in the 1980s published photographs were retouched to eliminate individuals who were out of favor. In cities throughout the Soviet Union there are large towers; Intourist guides tell questioning foreigners that they are for radio or television transmission, but in reality, they are very sophisticated radio jammers to prohibit Soviet listeners from hearing foreign news broadcasts that the leadership might consider objectionable.

Within the Armed Forces the Main Political Administration of the Soviet Army and Navy (MPA) is responsible for ensuring that the military press carries only Party-approved material. Because the MPA operates with the rights of a department of the Central Committee, this means that the Soviet military press is controlled by the Party, not the Ministry of Defense. Since 90 percent of Armed Forces personnel belong either to the Party or the Komsomol, the distinction is a fine one.

All Soviet publications, except the underground press, carry a censor's identification, which generally is a letter followed by a five-digit number. These can be found in books, journals, and every issue of every newspaper. If the publication is on a military theme, more than one censor will go over the material.

The vast Soviet propaganda and news organizations disseminate selected portions of military doctrine to soldiers and the citizenry, and even to different levels within various groups. Kremlin leaders recognize that modern war involves not only those in uniform but the entire population as well. In event of war the interior of the nation may come under attack. Dissemination takes many forms: The press, radio, television, and lectures are the most common. Probably no other nation on earth has placed so much emphasis on the dissemination of information, or misinformation, as the Soviet Union. The various means of that dissemination will be discussed in detail in this chapter.

Role of the Press

Material relating to military doctrine is found in Soviet publications of all types—newspapers, journals, and books—published under the auspices of many organizations and groups. The publishers include major houses such as Voyenizdat (Military Publishing House), Politizdat (Political Publishing House), newspapers at both national and local levels, theoretical Party journals, and even publications for youth. The authors include the Minister of Defense, the chief of the General Staff, and other officers on the General Staff or on the faculties of military educational institutions.

Members of Soviet research institutes, such as the Institute of the USA and Canada, also frequently write on military themes. Finally, references to military doctrine may be made by the Party's General Secretary in his report of the Central Committee.

Newspapers

Newspapers are of particular importance in the dissemination of doctrine because they are current. Each segment of Soviet officialdom has its own "organ," or publication. In each case the masthead notes that such-and-such is the "organ" of this or that. "News" is not an item high on the agenda of the editorial boards; their primary purpose is propaganda.

Pravda (Truth), the single most influential Soviet newspaper, is the organ of the Central Committee of the Communist Party of the Soviet Union. It routinely carries articles or editorials on defense issues, including military doctrine, by TASS reporters, military officers, and members of the Soviet institutes under the Academy of Sciences. On occasion an article of exceptional significance will appear as an unsigned editorial. *Pravda* is read by Party members throughout the entire nation.

Izvestia (Information), the government paper, is published by the Presidium of the Supreme Soviet USSR. Like *Pravda*, this newspaper informs its readers of the Kremlin's views on key security issues. For example, on August 13, 1987, an article by Lev S. Semeyko, Doctor of Historical Sciences, explained what is meant by Gorbachev's policy of "new political thinking" as it relates to "reasonable sufficiency" and strategic parity. These topics were of particular interest not only to Soviet readers but to governments worldwide concerned about Soviet military power.

Krasnaya Zvezda (Red Star) is the organ of the Ministry of Defense. Articles in this newspaper may stress a specific aspect of military doctrine. Some Western analysts profess to see this newspaper as presenting a "hard-line" view, differing from the more "moderate" view found in *Pravda*. This, however, may be "mirror-imaging," reflecting a prevalent U.S. view that there must be friction between the Soviet military and the Party leadership. The Main Political Administration of the Soviet Army and Navy ensures that *Krasnaya Zvezda*, and the entire Soviet military press as well, follow the dictates of the Party.

Moscow News is another newspaper that attracts considerable attention in the West. A weekly newspaper of "Soviet Societies for Friendship and Cultural Relations with Foreign Countries," it is published in a number of languages, including English, French, and Russian. This newspaper is available without charge to the tens of thousands of foreign tourists to the Soviet Union each year, few of whom can read Russian. The so-called news published in this journal is simply official propaganda, some of which would not be suitable for Soviet readers. In 1987 when General Secretary Gorbachev was attempting to convince the West of the success of *glasnost* and *perestroika*, a number of articles in this newspaper were on military matters, including military doctrine. In these cases, the purpose was to convince foreign readers of the sincerity of the Soviet position on arms control.

Readers outside the Soviet Union are sometimes surprised when a number of articles on military topics suddenly appear in Soviet newspapers. They may be unaware that on military holidays, the commander or commander in chief of whichever service or service branch is being honored will have a lengthy piece published in *Pravda*, and *Krasnaya Zvezda* will carry a long article by one of the first deputies or perhaps the chief of the political administration of that service. Other papers around the country will also carry articles by senior officers. If someone abroad reads those stirring words written for special anniversaries, it may seem that the head of the Air Force or Navy, for example, is making some special plea for his service or is somehow advocating changes in existing doctrine. The date of the article will show, however, that it was Air Force Day or Navy Day and that the chiefs were simply performing routine duties in making the nation aware of the role of their service or branch and improving the morale of their troops. (See Appendix B giving military holidays.)

The major holiday is the anniversary of the October Revolution (November 7), during which there are parades in Moscow and capitals of the various republics. These parades begin with a display of military power. Another holiday is May 9, which marks the end of the Great Patriotic War. Articles on military matters will be found throughout the Soviet press during and following these events. Of the purely military holidays, the most significant is Armed Forces Day (February 23). For example, on February 23, 1987, government and military newspapers published articles written by these senior Soviet military officers:

Minister of Defense; in *Pravda*
Chief of the General Staff; in *Sovietskaya Rossiya*
Commander in Chief of the Warsaw Pact (interview); in *Trud*
First Deputy Minister of Defense (interview); in *Krasnaya Zvezda*
First Deputy Minister of Defense; in *Izvestia*
Chief of the Main Political Administration; in *Literaturnaya Gazeta*
Commander in Chief of the Ground Forces; in *Sovietskaya Moldavia, Baku Rabochiy*
Chief of the Rear (interview); in *Sotsialist Industriya*
Inspector General; in *Ekonomicheskaya Gazeta*

Other articles by commanders and political officers were carried in military journals that same month.[3]

Rocket Troops and Artillery Day (November 19) has been a favorite day for the Soviets to start arms talks or have high-level meetings. On that day the press can be counted on to stress the power and readiness of Soviet missiles. For example, on November 19, 1985, General Secretary Mikhail Gorbachev and President Ronald Reagan held a summit meeting in Geneva. Foreign correspondents thought that the many articles in the Soviet press concerning Soviet missile forces were due to the arms control discussions under way. They failed to realize that the day for the meeting had been set deliberately by the Soviets to coincide with a military holiday.

The Party-military leadership also uses the anniversaries of major battles to expound in the press on points of military doctrine. More than 1,000 articles were published in the three months prior to May 9, 1985, to commemorate the fortieth anniversary of the victory over fascist Germany. It may be of some significance that the majority of these articles were published or planned for publication before Gorbachev became General Secretary.

Journals

Four of the Soviet services—Ground Forces, Troops of Air Defense, Air Forces, and Navy—are known to have their own journals. The Strategic Rocket Forces probably has one as well, but if so, it is classified. There are also journals for other elements of the Armed Forces, including a special journal for "officers, generals, and admirals," another for warrant officers, and still another for conscripts. Each of the military journals, depending on its orientation, presents to its readers various points of Soviet military doctrine. The following journals, as a rule, contain the most significant articles.

Voyennaya Mysl' (Military Thought), a monthly restricted-circulation theoretical journal of the Ministry of Defense, is the most interesting of the Soviet military publications. Many issues published before 1972 have been translated into English and excerpted and printed by the U.S. Government Printing Office. Subscriptions to noncommunist nations are not permitted.

Kommunist Vooruzhennykh Sil (Communist of the Armed Forces), the military-political journal of the Main Political Administration of the Soviet Army and Navy, is published twice monthly and contains articles to be used for Marxist-Leninist training of officers and detailed plans for political studies with the conscripts. Some of the best and most authoritative articles on doctrine are published in this journal.

Voyenno-Istoricheskiy Zhurnal (Military History Journal) is an organ of the Ministry of Defense and carries interesting historical material, often dealing with development of current military thought.

Voyennyy Vestnik (Military Herald) is the monthly journal of the Soviet Ground Forces. Most of its articles are intended for company grade officers.

Vestnik Protivovozdushnoy Oborony (Herald of Air Defense) is the monthly journal of the Troops of Air Defense.

Aviatsiya i Kosmonavtika (Aviation and Cosmonautics) is the monthly journal of the Soviet Air Forces and publishes articles on flying and space.

Morskoy Sbornik (Naval Collection) is an extremely well-written publication of the Soviet Navy.

Zarubezhnoye Voyennoye Obozreniye (Foreign Military Review) is the monthly journal of the Ministry of Defense and provides wide coverage of the armed forces of nations outside of the Soviet military orbit.

Soviet Military Review (in Russian, English, French, Spanish, Portuguese, Dary, and Arabic) combines information and disinformation for foreign consumption. Many articles are translations from regular Soviet military journals, often drastically condensed or edited to be more palatable to non-Soviet readers.

In addition to the journals of the Ministry of Defense and the various services, another journal, *Voyennyye Znaniye* (Military Knowledge), is of particular interest. This is a DOSAAF publication and has two major purposes. First, many of its articles are about "beginning" military training, which male youth are expected to receive before being called up for active military duty. Second, it is concerned with civil defense training for all Soviet youth. Each of these areas helps prepare the nation for the possibility of a future war, as required by military doctrine.

Kommunist (Communist), the theoretical and political journal of the Central Committee, is published every twenty days. At times a major statement or modification to doctrine will appear in a Party journal, such as *Kommunist*, before publication in a military journal. For example, Ogarkov's article "On Defense of Peaceful Labor" appeared in the July 1981 issue of *Kommunist*. His pamphlet the following year, *Always On Guard in Defense of the Fatherland*, closely followed his earlier article.

MEMO: World Economy and International Relations, the journal of the Institute of World Economy and International Relations, and *SShA: Economy, Politics, Ideology*, the journal of the Institute of the USA and Canada, often carry articles on matters of military doctrine. However, such articles are intended primarily for foreign perusal, and give a skewed view of Soviet defense issues. The articles provide both information and disinformation. Their primary purpose is to portray Soviet policies in the best possible light and to convince the foreign reader of Moscow's hopes for peace. It is important that journals such as these two not be regarded as independent publications in which the contributors express their own views. Rather, they are Party publications expressing the policies of the Party leaders.

Books and Pamphlets

Most of the significant military books are issued by Voyenizdat, the publishing house of the Ministry of Defense. Between 200 and 250 titles are announced each year. Approximately sixty will be novels, historical fiction, and fictionalized documentaries. Probably thirty more will be translations of fiction from other socialist countries. Ten or twenty will be volumes of poetry, a popular subject in the Soviet Union. There will also be a handful of dictionaries of military terms and a half dozen textbooks for the military translator (German, English, French and Arabic, in order of popularity). The Military Memoir series will include a dozen or so titles and there will be two or three dozen titles on military history. Twenty or more books and pamphlets will be on Party-political work. Another fifty books probably will be on military art, combat training, military equipment, aviation, navy, rear services, and civil defense. Finally, only three or four significant books each year will be on military theory.

Military doctrine will be specifically mentioned in only a dozen or so books published annually. Textbooks for cadets and junior officers at times may refer to doctrine as "military science." However, most of the military books relate, in one way or another, to the questions that doctrine is to answer in preparing the nation for the possibility of a future war. All will carefully follow the approved line established by the Main Political Administration of the Soviet Army and Navy; nothing in these books will contradict policies approved by Party-military leaders. In addition, the censors will ensure that nothing considered classified will be released.

Military books are not published only by Voyenizdat. DOSAAF has its own presses and publishes four basic types of books: military-patriotic, civil defense, military-technical, and books about military sports. DOSAAF publications are intended to develop feelings of military patriotism in youth and to provide information on skills that will be needed by the Armed Forces. Many books are for sportsmen, most of whom are military reservists who want to hone their skills. DOSAAF books also reflect current trends in military doctrine.

The Znaniye (Knowledge) presses are managed by Znaniye societies, both at the national level and in the various republics. This press publishes many lectures on military themes, including military doctrine. The lectures usually are written by professors at military academies who are well known in the field. Lecturers around the country then use them as the bases for military lectures at Znaniye Society meetings. A classic example of one such lecture was "Soviet Military Doctrine," by General Colonel and Professor N. A. Lomov, published in 1963.[4]

Politizdat, the Political Publishing House, has issued some of the more significant books on military themes. Since war is considered a continuation of politics by other—that is, violent—means, it is natural that the political press should take an interest in questions of peace and war. One work of particular interest was *The Soviet Army* (1969), which later was identified as being an official military publication. For some reason, the publishers did not state that the author, S. S. Lototskiy, was a general lieutenant who then headed the Department of History of Wars and Military Art at the Frunze Military Academy. The last section of this work discussed the revolution in military affairs and the basic tenets of Soviet military doctrine. Another worthwhile work for the military researcher is *The Great Patriotic War: 1941–1945*, a "dictionary-handbook." This 1985 work identified the "official" Soviet military books, which we will discuss later.

Nauka (Science), the publishing house of the Academy of Sciences, has issued a number of significant books on both military history and military theory. In the latter category are *Philosophy and Military Theory* (1975) by General Major S. A. Tyushkevich and *V. I. Lenin and Soviet Military Science* (1981) by Colonel N. N. Azovtsev. Both of these authors were affiliated with the Institute of Military History of the Ministry of Defense which is part of the Academy of Sciences USSR. The views on military doctrine and strategy presented in Nauka publications do not differ from those of Voyenizdat, the publishing house of the Ministry of Defense.

Many regional presses outside of Moscow publish a variety of books related to the military. Some concentrate on publishing books in the languages of the various republics, but the majority of military books from the regional presses are histories of the war and biographies of local war heroes. The larger cities such as Leningrad and Kiev produce better-quality books. Although all of these presses follow the guidelines established by the Party-military leadership, few delve into higher military theory. Most serve military-patriotic purposes, a vital aspect of military doctrine.

Each year these presses turn out between 400 and 600 military titles. The most significant works are reviewed in *Krasnaya Zvezda* and in various military journals. Voyenizdat annually announces the books to be published the following year. As might be expected, some of these books will live up to their advance billing while others will be disappointments.

Those abroad concerned with national security issues are most interested in which Soviet military writings are the most authoritative. There are no "private" publishing houses in the Soviet Union; all published works must bear the government censor's approval. While the most important writings on military doctrine and strategy will be those of the Minister of Defense or chief of the General Staff, the writer's rank is not necessarily a criteria. An article by a colonel at the Frunze Military Academy or the Lenin Military-Political Academy may prove to be more significant than one written by a general colonel on the General Staff.

Official Books. Seventy-five titles on Soviet military issues, primarily the historical works, were listed as being "official" in a 1985 publication. These included all eight volumes of the *Soviet Military Encyclopedia* and the second edition (1984) of the *Military Encyclopedic Dictionary*. Among the other books in this category were *The Soviet Armed Forces* (1978) and *Party and Army* (1980). At the time these books appeared there was no indication that they were in an "official" category. The acknowledgment that certain writings are considered "official" is of importance to the researcher. (See Appendix C.)

Books in the Central Museum of the Armed Forces. A display of "significant" military books can be found in the Central Museum of the Soviet Armed Forces. As exhibits in the museum are arranged chronologically, visitors start with the October Revolution, then move on to the Civil War, the engagements with the Japanese in the 1930s, and then the Great Patriotic War. After this there are a few displays of postwar equipment, now obsolete. In 1986, in the very last section was a glass case displaying fourteen publications with dates ranging from the early 1960s to 1986. Among the titles were as follows:

V. I. Lenin on Defense of the Socialist Fatherland
CPSU and the Armed Forces of the Soviet Union

Problems of the Revolution in Military Affairs (1965)
One of the volumes of the eight-volume *Soviet Military Encyclopedia*
Military Encyclopedic Dictionary (1984)
The journal *Voyennaya Mysl'* (Military Thought) 2, February 1986
Sea Power of the State (1979)
Tactics (1966 edition, from the Officer's Library series of that period)
Military Strategy (1968 edition, from the Officer's Library series of that
period)

Had these publications been studied, the reader could have gained a
comprehensive knowledge of Soviet military doctrine, strategy, operational
art and tactics covering the period from 1960 to the mid-1980s. The writings
also give the history and organization of the Soviet Armed Forces, including
regulations. Specific attention was given to Marxist-Leninist teaching on
war. The most recent work was the February 1986 issue of *Military Thought*,
the restricted journal of the Soviet General Staff, shown probably only to
indicate the journal's significance. That particular issue was to commemorate
Soviet Armed Forces Day.

Encyclopedias

Using an encyclopedia as a basic source for research on military doctrine
ordinarily would not be considered by serious scholars. In the Soviet Union,
however, encyclopedias are published by the government and represent
official policy. Many people are familiar with the story of Lavrenty Beria's
entry in the second edition of the *Bol'shaya* (or "Great") *Soviet Encyclopedia*
published in the 1950s. After the notorious chief of the secret police was
arrested and shot, encyclopedia subscribers were sent an article on the
Bering Straits and told to remove the page with Beria on it and glue in
the new page.

In 1972 a decision was made to publish a *Soviet Military Encyclopedia*
(SVE).[5] This work was most ambitious; the first of its eight volumes appeared
in 1976, the last in 1980. Minister of Defense Marshal Andrey Grechko
chaired the Main Editorial Commission for the first two volumes. After his
death he was replaced by Chief of the General Staff Ogarkov. Deputy
chairmen for the project included the chief of the Main Political Administration
of the Soviet Army and Navy, the director of the Institute of Military History
of the Ministry of Defense (a part of the Academy of Sciences), and the
deputy director of the Central Committee's Institute of Marxism-Leninism.
Thus, the encyclopedia was clearly a major Party-military effort.

In 1973, 20,000 terms were proposed for inclusion in the SVE. The
Commission spent an entire year determining what should be included.
Finally, 11,000 terms were selected for final publication.[6] "Doctrine, Military"
was one of the main entries, but the piece was not signed. The entries on
"Strategy, Military" and "Deep Operations" were signed by Ogarkov.

The staffs of military academies were assigned the task of writing many
of the theoretical articles and entries. Professors and instructors at Frunze

Military Academy wrote more than 3,000 entries, or more than one-fourth of the total.[7] More than 2,400 articles were on theoretical military themes, and more than 1,300 were on military art.[8] The relationship between war and politics was noted in more than 1,000 entries.

The first edition of *The Military Encyclopedic Dictionary* was published in 1983. It included most of the 11,000 terms in the *Soviet Military Encyclopedia* plus an additional 3,000, making 14,000 entries in all. The additions were mostly new terms that had come into use since 1974, the year in which the selection of terms for the SVE was basically completed. Although the entries were short, many of them, especially on military science, were revised versions of what had appeared in the *Soviet Military Encyclopedia* and reflected new developments.[9] A second, updated edition of the *Military Encyclopedic Dictionary* was published in 1986. These two editions enabled Western scholars to keep abreast of shifts in emphasis on military doctrinal issues.

Earlier postwar reference books of military terms had laid the foundation for the *Soviet Military Encyclopedia*. One, published in 1958, was *Kratkiy Slovar' Operativno-Takticheskikh i Obshchevoyskovykh Slov (Terminov)* (Short Dictionary of Operational-Tactical and Combined Arms Words [Terms]), written by the faculty of the Frunze Military Academy and containing 1,500 terms. The *Slovar' Osnovnykh Voyennykh Terminov* (Dictionary of Basic Military Terms), a product of the Military Academy of the General Staff, appeared in 1965. Nuclear weapons, space, and electronics were included in its 1,640 entries. This work was later criticized for errors and lack of precision in defining terms. A year later, in 1966, the *Tolkovyy Slovar' Voyennykh Terminov* (Explanatory Dictionary of Military Terms) appeared, containing 2,000 terms, many of them improvements on the 1965 *Slovar'*. Of particular interest to military analysts in the 1980s were the identification of PKO (antispace defense) and PRO (antimissile defense). These dictionaries were designed to promote a common understanding of military terms in the Soviet forces and to provide Soviet officers with authoritative reference sources on the essentials of military doctrine.

The *Spravochnik Ofitsera* (Officer's Handbook), published in 1971, presented essays on themes rather than just short definitions. Some of the topics covered were: principles of military structuring, Marxist-Leninist military theory, Soviet military science, Soviet military doctrine, military psychology, and military pedagogy. Each section ended with a list of writings for further reference. At the time this work appeared many Western readers were surprised to find that the discussion of military doctrine and strategy differed little from that found in the first edition of Sokolovskiy's *Military Strategy* (1962).

The *Bol'shaya Soviet Encyclopedia*, published by the government, states official policy. For example, general directions for the third edition of this encyclopedia were published in a decree of the Central Committee of the CPSU, and these Party guidelines were expected to be closely followed. Entries were written by the most qualified authors. The Party saw to it that every entry adhered to the Marxist-Leninist point of view and portrayed the Soviet Union and its accomplishments in the most favorable light.[10] Representing the Soviet Ministry of Defense on the editorial board and editorial councils at different times were Marshals of the Soviet Union M. V. Zakharov, V. G. Kulikov and N. V. Ogarkov, the successive chiefs of the General Staff between 1970 and 1978 when the encyclopedia's thirty-one volumes were being published.

The entry on military doctrine in the third edition was disappointing. It described what military doctrine was supposed to do in general but failed to give its content. Half of the entry was devoted to U.S. and NATO military doctrine, and the entry was not signed. However, the entry on military science was written by a group of authors under Zakharov's editorship. "Voyennaya Strategiya" (Military Strategy) was entered as "Strategiya, Voyennaya" to put it alphabetically in a later volume. It was signed by Kulikov who by that time had replaced Zakharov as chief of the General Staff.[11]

Officer's Libraries

The Soviet military press began publishing a series of books designated the Library of the Commander in the 1920s. Since the end of World War II similar series of books have been called the Officer's Library. These books provide Party-approved general guidelines for ensuring that officers have a common understanding of Soviet military doctrine and military science.

Eighteen books in the first Library of the Commander were published by 1925. Among them were *Cavalry, Military Chemical Matters, Infantry, Troop Organization and Control* and several books on tactics of small units. The print run for each book was 10,250 copies. The precedent having been set, the series was expanded in the 1930s. Forty-seven books were prepared for a new library, with the first ones released in 1936. Among these were V. K. Triandafillov's *Character of Operations of Contemporary War* (the basis of deep operations) and A. K. Mednis's *Tactics of Ground Support Aviation* (a textbook for flying schools).

This series contained many foreign books that had been translated into Russian.[12] Among these were Clausewitz's *War of 1812*, F. Mol'tke's *Military Lessons: Operational Training for Battle,* F. Mering's *Essays on the History of War and Military Art,* and W. Sikorski's *Future War.*

Three sets of Officer's Library books have been published since the end of World War II: one in the 1950s (the gray library); one in the late 1960s and the early 1970s (the blue); and the most recent started in 1980 and still in progress in 1988 (the red). These books have been unique collections of the best and most authoritative works of Soviet military writing for their eras. Many of them deal specifically with matters related to military doctrine.

The announcement for the "blue" series in 1965 promised seventeen books in three years. Soviet authors and publishers did not, however, keep to this schedule. Seven books went to the printers in 1965, three more went to press in 1966, and four in 1967 (three of them, including the third edition of *Military Strategy*, in the last week of November) making a total of fourteen books. After that, the whole series came to a grinding halt for over two-and-a-half years. The *Officer's Handbook*, typeset in February 1968, did not get approved for printing until late in 1970. The final two books were typeset in early 1972 and sent to the printers later that year.

The purpose of the Officer's Library series is "to arm the reader with knowledge of the fundamental changes that have taken place in recent years in military affairs." Authors of these books have been on the faculties of the Voroshilov Military Academy of the General Staff, the Frunze Military Academy, the Malinovskiy Tank Academy, and the Lenin Military-Political Academy, and others have served in the various departments of the Ministry of Defense. The key points of Soviet doctrine and strategy are the same regardless of where the book was written. Each academy or administration simply handles the topic that is within its competency. (See Appendix D.)

The Frunze Prize

Those in the United States and elsewhere who have followed Soviet military affairs are interested in what the Soviets themselves consider significant and worthwhile among their military writings. This problem was somewhat simplified in March 1965 when the Council of Ministers of the USSR reintroduced an annual award, the Frunze Prize for "excellent military or military historical works."[13] For a book to win this prize, or even to be mentioned for it, means that the Ministry of Defense as well as the Communist Party has placed high value on the book's content. At times the prize will go to a group of authors for making specific contributions, but the title of their publication is not mentioned. This usually indicates the book was published in the closed press.

Books nominated for the Frunze Prize represent a wide spectrum of interests. Books written by faculty members of the Voroshilov Military Academy of the General Staff, the Frunze Military Academy, the Lenin Military-Political Academy, and the Gagarin Air Force Academy have received nominations. Titles over the past twenty years have included *Military Strategy, V. I. Lenin and the Soviet Armed Forces, Party-Political Work in the Soviet Armed Forces in the Years of the Great Patriotic War,* and *Tactics.*

In March 1966, the first Frunze Prize winners for 1965 were announced, but the title of the work was not given. Three of the individuals listed had contributed to Sokolovskiy's *Military Strategy*. In 1988 one of them, Colonel V. V. Larionov, was a general major and on the faculty of the Academy of the General Staff. Two other Frunze Prize winners that year were Colonel S. A. Tyushkevich and Major D. A. Volkogonov. In 1988 these two officers, both of whom were promoted to general, remained among the most authoritative Soviet spokesmen on matters of military doctrine and strategy. The writings of another prizewinner for 1965, General Major Engineer I. I. Anureyev, were being quoted in the West for the following two decades.

The 1966 Frunze prize went to a group of authors representing the Frunze Military Academy. Again the title of the work was not given.[14] Later it was described as a work on combined arms battle[15] and even later as a specific work on *tactics* of combined arms battle.[16] One of these authors, General Major R. G. Simonyan, remains a major Soviet spokesman in the late 1980s. Another, Colonel A. A. Sidorenko, was the author of *The Offensive*, published in 1971, a work that has been carefully studied and frequently quoted in the United States.

V. I. Lenin and the Soviet Armed Forces was awarded the Frunze Prize for 1967. A second edition was published in 1969 and a third in 1980, as the first volume in the "red" Officer's Library series. The three editions of this work are a valuable source for analyzing continuity and change in Soviet military thought, in particular military doctrine. Five books were nominated for the 1968 Frunze Prize. Two of the best known were[17] *Military Strategy*, third edition, 1968, edited by Marshal V. D. Sokolovskiy and *Tactics*, 1966, edited by General Major V. G. Reznichenko. Both were part of the 1960s "blue" Officer's Library series. But the winner of the Frunze Prize for 1968 was apparently never announced. For some reason, both books nominated for the 1969 Frunze Prize were about aviation.[18] One was *Soviet Air Forces in the Great Patriotic War*, 1968, by Marshal of Aviation S. I. Rudenko; the other was *Aviation and Cosmonautics*, 1968, by Marshal of Aviation S. A. Krasovskiy. However, in March 1970 *Krasnaya Zvezda* announced that on February 17, 1970, at the meeting of the commission, the book *50 Years of the Armed Forces USSR* had been awarded the Frunze Prize for 1969.[19]

Four books were nominated for the 1970 prize. Two of them were on the Great Patriotic War and another on the history of the Kiev Military District.[20] The fourth, *Methodological Problems of Military Theory and Practice*, 1969, edited by General Colonel A. S. Zheltov, was a major work on doctrine and strategy.

After 1969, announcements of awards for prize-winning publications were greatly curtailed. Winners of the Frunze Prize for 1971 were never announced. Coincidentally, it was rumored that first deputy Chief of the General Staff General of the Army N. V. Ogarkov had been given the task of ensuring that no information on military matters that might be of use to the West would be disseminated. However, six books were nominated for the 1973 Frunze Prize.[21] Four of these discussed military doctrine at considerable length. They were:

1. *V. I. Lenin and Soviet Military Science*, Nauka, 1971, by Colonel N. N. Azovtsev.
2. *Soviet Army*, Politizdat, 1969, edited by S. S. Lototskiy. (There was no indication in the book that Lototskiy was a General Lieutenant on the faculty of the Frunze Military Academy.)
3. *Philosophical Heritage of V. I. Lenin and Problems of Contemporary War*, Voyenizdat, 1972, edited by General Major A. S. Milovidov.

4. *Questions of Strategy and Operational Art in Soviet Military Works 1917–1940* and *Questions of Tactics in Soviet Military Works 1917–1940*, Voyenizdat, 1965 and 1970, edited by Marshal M. V. Zakharov.

Even a cursory reading of these four books would indicate to the reader that significant shifts were taking place in Soviet military doctrine and strategy. It should be noted that the first work listed above was published by Nauka, the publishing house of the Soviet Academy of Sciences, and the second by Politizdat, the Political Literature Publishing House. The first three books on the list stressed the role of strategic nuclear forces but at the same time noted that "units and subunits" must be prepared to fight with or without the use of the nuclear weapon.

The Philosophical Heritage of V. I. Lenin and Problems of Contemporary War attracted renewed interest in 1987, when a follow-up work, *Military-Theoretical Heritage of V. I. Lenin and Problems of Contemporary War*, appeared, also edited by A. S. Milovidov. One of the major contributors was General Colonel D. A. Volkogonov, a most influential Soviet writer in the 1980s. The recension was by General Major S. A. Tyushkevich, on the staff of the Institute of Military History of the Ministry of Defense of the Soviet Academy of Sciences.

The fourth entry consisted of two books listed as a pair, both dealing with the period 1917–1941. Each began with a long introduction by Marshal M. V. Zakharov, then chief of the General Staff. The purpose of these writings was to show that the study of military fundamentals was still essential. Although nuclear weapons would still be the decisive factor in a future war, a nonnuclear war was also still possible. Apart from the introduction by Zakharov, the books consisted of excerpts from the writings of Soviet military commanders and strategists that had been published in the pre–World War II years. Zakharov pointed out that many younger officers would be seeing the names of these earlier officers for the first time since, in a number of cases, all but one copy of their writings had been destroyed.

The winner of the 1974 Frunze Prize was *Methodological Bases for Determining Losses*. In 1975 the award went to *Rear Services of the Armed Forces in the Great Patriotic War, 1941–1945*, and a series of five books entitled *Tactics in Combat Examples* won the prize in 1982. A three-volume work, *The Navy of the Soviet Union in the Great Patriotic War, 1941–1945* won a Frunze Prize, but the year was not given.[22]

In March 1987, the Frunze Prize was awarded to General Colonel M. A. Gareyev, Doctor of Military Sciences, for his 1985 work, *M. V. Frunze: Military Theoretician*. Another group of authors, headed by Marshal of Engineer Troops S. Kh. Aganov, was awarded for *Engineer Troops of the Soviet Army 1918–1945*. A collective headed by Rear Admiral N. S. Solomenko got honorable mention for an unnamed work.

Books nominated for the Frunze Prize, as well as the authors cited for having written unspecified works, should be of major interest to scholars interested in Soviet military and foreign policies. These writings provide

Party-approved guidelines for the Armed Forces and population to follow. In hindsight, the guidelines specified in these books can be checked against the actual Soviet force structure that followed upon their publication. (See Appendix E.)

The Soviet officer is expected to devote two hours a day to professional reading. However, in a country that praises the *kollektiv*, it is not intended that all study be done alone. In addition to reading, there must be discussions with others, and some information may be passed verbally to members of specific groups and organizations. This need is filled by the Military Science Society, the Znaniye (Knowledge) Society, DOSAAF, and Party organizations.

Military Science Societies and Related Organizations

The Military Science Society

The Red Army and Navy of 1917 was long on enthusiasm for building a new type of armed forces but short on knowledge of how to accomplish this task. Marshal Georgiy K. Zhukov wrote that the new Red commanders and the political workers frequently met to discuss the past war and the shape of the future. He confessed that he and his comrades at that time knew a great deal about military practice but little about military theory. However, he claimed, they avidly read everything they could get their hands on and endlessly discussed the various subjects.

In late 1920 a "military science circle" was formed at the Military Academy of the RKKA (Workers' and Peasants' Red Army); later it was designated the Military Science Society. The very top military leaders attended the meetings: "The Military Science Society of the Military Academy discussed the most crucial questions: The nature of future war. M. V. Frunze, K. Ye. Voroshilov, S. S. Kamenev, V. K. Triandafillov, M. N. Tukhachevskiy, R. P. Eideman, and others frequently spoke at their meetings. Collections of articles of the society were published, and later the Military Science Societies (VNO) of the Military Academy published its own magazine."[23]

At the suggestion of M. V. Frunze, the idea of military science societies quickly spread to troops in the Crimea and the Ukraine. The first conference of Military Science Organizations was held in May 1925 for the purpose of forming a central council. The resulting military science societies first became "all-army" and then turned into national societies, drawing on all the people to help in building the new Red Army.

In October 1925, Frunze died and Voroshilov succeeded him in heading the Armed Forces. The first Congress of the Military Science Society of the USSR was held in March 1926. To stress the all-encompassing nature of the society's new task, the name was changed to OSO—Society for Cooperation with the Defense of the Country. In addition, its tasks were enlarged to include beginning military training for young men before entering service. In 1927 the mission of OSO was altered; its new task was propagandizing military knowledge to the population. As a result, scientific research received less and less attention. OSO joined up with Aviakhim (the Society for Friends of Aviation and Chemical Industry) and the two were designated OSOAviakhim.

After World War II Stalin stopped all initiative in the study of military theory; writings at that time had to refer to him as the genius in military affairs and no other views were permitted. His legacy continued after his death, until he was condemned at the 20th Party Congress in 1956. Only then were VNOs again formed. Their purpose was "to cooperate in the development and dissemination of military and technical knowledge among generals, admirals, and officers."[24] VNOs were established in military units, on ships, in military schools, and also at officers' clubs.

At the present time the VNO at the Central Officers' Club in Moscow serves as a headquarters for other VNOs. It is divided into eleven sections for studying military-political, operational-tactical, historical, military-technical, and other themes. Other VNOs have similar programs, although usually on a smaller scale. Members are encouraged to participate in various activities, such as writing their memoirs, taking part in writing unit histories or ship histories, giving lectures on military themes to the public, holding military science conferences, organizing trips to historical places, and writing book reviews. Local VNOs are organized and directed by the staffs of the military districts, fleets or garrisons at whose clubs they function.[25]

DOSAAF

The paramilitary Volunteer Society for Cooperation with the Army, Aviation, and Fleet plays a major role in preparating the nation for the possibility of future war, as demanded by military doctrine. Two of its tasks are military-patriotic indoctrination and physical training for the population, especially youth. Much of their activity involves military-sports games. At the beginning of 1986, DOSAAF had 110 million members, belonging to 361,000 organizations. These "primary" organizations trained 2 million drivers, radio operators, scuba divers, electricians, motor cyclists, and other specialists for the national economy and the military services. Training youth for skills needed by the Armed Forces starts at age seventeen.[26]

The Znaniye Society

The All-Union Znaniye Society was formed in 1947. In 1986 it had 2.7 million members, which included more than 2,000 academicians and corresponding members of the Academies of Sciences both of the USSR and of union republics. It also numbers among its members 215,000 doctors and candidates of sciences. It is a prestigious organization; members of the Institute of the USA and Canada, for example, are active participants in its activities. The purpose of the Znaniye Society is to propagate political and scientific knowledge through lectures, films, and slide shows, to form a Marxist-Leninist world view in the general population, and to enlist their aid in solving tasks in building communism in the USSR.

Experts in various fields prepare lectures which are printed as brochures. These lectures are then read by a designated speaker to an audience, after which a discussion period follows. In 1985, 20 million such lectures were heard by nearly a billion people. Lectures are also given on radio and television. In 1985, 59,000 conferences and 591,000 thematic evenings were held. Znaniye also organizes "people's universities" which are attended by nearly 20 million people.

Znaniye publishes a large amount of popular science literature. For instance, 681 book and brochure titles appeared in 1985, with a total of 52.5 million copies being printed. Moreover, brochures are published in several foreign languages. A sizeable slice of the Znaniye work is directly related to military themes. Some titles in the series "To Help the Lecturer," published in the 1980s, are the following:

Actual Questions of Military-Patriotic Education of Workers
Military-Patriotic Education in Conditions of Mature Socialism
DOSAAF—Mass Patriotic Organization of the Soviet People
Military Cooperation of Socialist States
Always Be Ready to Protect the Motherland
27th Congress CPSU on Strengthening the Defense Might of the Country and Its Armed Forces
On Guard Over Peace and Socialism
On the Path of Strengthening the Defense Capability of the Country
Military-Patriotic Education of Workers: Forms and Methods
Civil Defense of Uzbekistan Today

Individuals with higher academic degrees are often called upon to deliver the lectures, for which they receive honoraria. Although military matters are not the Znaniye Society's sole interest, they do receive considerable attention. This organization provides yet another means for the political-military indoctrination of the population and disseminating information that serves the purposes of Soviet military doctrine.[27]

Marxist-Leninist Officer Training

Since the 1960s a number of Western scholars have argued that ideology is dead in the Soviet Union and that the Soviet leadership no longer takes Marxism-Leninism seriously. This claim was made particularly in the late 1980s, after General Secretary Gorbachev stressed the policy of *glasnost.* There is no way of actually proving what the beliefs of the Kremlin leadership might be or to what extent, if any, the dictates of Marxism-Leninism are followed. The fact remains that the study of Marxism-Leninism receives considerable attention throughout the Soviet Armed Forces, and in this study, military doctrine is stressed.

General Lieutenant N. I. Smorigo, deputy chief of the Propaganda and Agitation Directorate of the Main Political Administration, declared in his entry in the *Soviet Military Encyclopedia* on "Marxist-Leninist Training of the Officer Cadre," that "deep study of Marxist-Leninist theory by officers in the system of commanders training . . . is one of the most important forms of ideological tempering of military cadres."[28] A 1986 textbook for *kursants* (cadets) at higher military schools repeated the requirement: "In the postwar years, the necessary steps were taken to create a single system of Marxist-Leninist education of officers." At various times further guidance has been given in instructions and resolutions.[29]

Throughout their military careers Soviet officers, generals, and admirals are expected to improve their understanding of Marxism-Leninism by attending classes, seminars, and lectures 50 to 70 hours a year, that is, approximately one hour a week.[30] In addition, officers are expected to do independent reading of political and military theoretical literature. These will include the classics of Marxism-Leninism, the Program of the CPSU, materials and decisions of Party Congresses, resolutions of Party Plenums of the Central Committee CPSU, and important documents of the international communist movement.

According to Soviet sources, compulsory studies of Marxist-Leninist teachings began in 1923.[31] Until the end of the 1950s, most officers studied only the history of the CPSU. After that, they were required to study the fundamentals of Marxism-Leninism which consists of (1) Marxist-Leninist philosophy, which is subdivided into dialectical materialism and historical materialism, (2) political economy, and (3) beginning in 1964, scientific communism.[32]

The next cycle of studies began in the mid-1960s; its theme was philosophical problems of military theory and practice. Then came Leninist teachings on defense of the socialist Fatherland, ideological-political behests of V. I. Lenin, and actual problems of the theory and policies of the CPSU in contemporary circumstances.[33] Tests on these subjects were required.

For their Marxist-Leninist studies, officers are advised to read the newspapers *Pravda* and *Krasnaya Zvezda* (Red Star) and the journals *Kommunist* (Communist), *Politicheskoye Samoobrazovaniye* (Political Self-Education), and *Kommunist Vooruzhennykh Sil* (Communist of the Armed Forces).[34] These magazines frequently contain footnotes indicating that an article is recommended for officers studying certain themes. *Kommunist Vooruzhennykh Sil* from time to time publishes detailed outlines "to help the group leaders of Marxist-Leninist training of officers," with eight to ten articles assigned for reading listed at the end of the article. Beginning in 1979, Voyenizdat began publication of these outlines as separate brochures. Two lecture themes are in each booklet of fifty to seventy pages, which sells for five kopeks (less than a dime). These booklets indicate how the lectures can be used to disseminate the fundamentals of Soviet military doctrine to the officer corps.

Universities of Marxism-Leninism

A strict system of Party studies was introduced in 1965. The highest form of these studies is the two-year university of Marxism-Leninism formed at local officers' clubs.[35] Three basic faculties in the universities of Marxism-Leninism concentrate on: (1) Party structure and Party-political work, (2) propaganda, and (3) fundamentals of Marxism-Leninism. In addition, faculties for studying international relations and the foreign policy of the CPSU are sometimes formed, and where possible, a faculty on economics also is established. Both Party and non-Party members, including family members, may attend such universities. Appropriate textbooks are provided for each topic.[36]

When examining the Marxist-Leninist universities, it should be kept in mind that they come under the Main Political Administration of the Soviet Army and Navy (MPA), which is the arm of the Party's Central Committee in the Soviet Armed Forces. In 1977 the MPA issued new regulations for their students. While attending the universities, students do not have to attend the regular sessions of Marxist-Leninist officer training. Graduates receive a diploma indicating their completion of the equivalent of higher political education in the system of Party studies.[37]

Garrisons not having such universities are to establish two-year schools for Party activists, for which detailed regulations were issued in 1983. These are for all officers, warrant officers, extended duty servicemen, women in uniform, and civilian military workers who are Party or Komsomol members. One-year schools for Party Activists are to serve soldiers, sergeants, sailors, and petty officers. In remote regions or when located abroad, family members may also attend such schools. The one-year school can have either a 130-hour or a 60-hour program. Those attending the two-year school or the 130-hour program at the one-year school do not have to attend political training sessions.[38]

Other institutions and activities in the Soviet Armed Forces for the study of Marxism-Leninism include schools for the Komsomol and political schools, schools teaching the fundamentals of Marxism-Leninism, schools teaching scientific communism, schools for Party housekeeping activists, and theoretical and methodological seminars.[39]

Both defectors and emigrés from the Soviet Union state that people who attend Marxist-Leninist lectures and training have no enthusiasm for them, that people are inattentive, and that the students pay little attention to the subject. Although this observation may be true and certainly reflects their own experience, the fact remains that the study is required and that the leadership's outward actions must conform with what is taught, in particular, with respect to military doctrine as contained in Marxist-Leninist writings.

Conferences

Within military districts Party Conferences are held every two or three years. The most significant ones are those held shortly before the Party Congresses. For example, prior to the 27th Party Congress, which opened in late February 1987, Party Conferences were held in December 1985 and January 1986 in every military district, fleet and group abroad. The new edition of the Party Program and details of the new long-range economic plan that were to be approved by the Party Congress in Moscow were discussed at these Party Conferences by military Party members. During these conferences more than 300 military delegates were designated to attend the 27th Party Congress.

There are a number of other methods by which changes in the military policies of the Party are communicated to military personnel. Among these are military-theoretical conferences, military science conferences, and practical science conferences. These meetings are held on a national level and within military districts, in groups abroad, and in fleets. The most important gatherings are addressed by the Minister of Defense or the General Secretary.

It can be surmised that classified matters are discussed at the many military conferences. For instance, when, shortly after Gorbachev became General Secretary, he met with military leaders at Minsk, there was no report on the purpose of the meeting or what subjects might have been covered.

Indoctrination of the Rank and File

Compulsory political indoctrination is required for all conscripts. Each issue of *Kommunist Vooruzhennykh Sil*, the journal of the Main Political Administration, contains the outlines of studies to be used by the political officers. Detailed instructions, usually consisting of seven pages or more, outline how each hour of study is to be conducted. For example, six hours were to be devoted to the opening theme for the 1986 study year. Two hours of this time were to be spent in lecture, two hours on self-preparation and two in discussion. Learning objectives are clearly spelled out, and recommendations are made for films to be shown before studying the theme.

The opening study theme for 1987 was "The 27th Congress of the Communist Party of the Soviet Union on the Necessity for High Vigilance and Constant Combat Readiness of the Army and Navy." According to the summary of the lecture, it was to give the listeners deeper understanding of the basic tendencies of contemporary developments in the world, the "increased imperialist aggressiveness and, because of this, the growing military danger." More than two pages were devoted to details on this topic alone.[40]

The ideological indoctrination of the eighteen- to twenty-year-old soldiers and sailors stresses their role in preparation of the nation for war, including civil defense, and other types of moral-political training such as hatred of "imperialism."

Radio and Television

Soviet marshals, generals, and admirals regularly appear on television and radio. Their normal appearances are in conjunction with the numerous military holidays, such as Navy Day, Tank Day, Armed Forces Day, and the like. They also may appear to commemorate some battle of the Great Patriotic War. For example, General of the Army Aleksey D. Lizichev, chief of the Main Political Administration, was interviewed on radio on the 45th anniversary of the German invasion of the Soviet Union. Each presentation is designed to show the role of the Soviet Armed Forces in defending the country and to instill patriotic feelings in the viewer or listener.

On Sundays, there is a regular TV program for the Soviet Armed Forces called "I Serve the Soviet Union!" There are also programs on world events called "Novosti" (news) and "Vremya" (time). "Studio 9" and "International Panorama" are similar to talk shows. Radio shows like "International Observers Round Table" are popular for propagandizing Soviet policy as well. At times Soviet military doctrine is specifically discussed. TV commentators Valentin Zorin (host of "Studio 9"), Vadim Zagladin, and Aleksandr Bovin and radio political observers like Aleksandr Zholkver and Vladimir Posner are as well known to Soviets as Dan Rather, Tom Brokaw and Peter Jennings are to Americans. But there is a major difference: All of the Soviet commentators must carefully hew to the Party line and follow Party directives. They are paid Party employees.

Televised press conferences on certain military-related matters have become more prevalent, especially after a Soviet fighter plane shot down a South Korean commercial aircraft on September 1, 1983. Marshal Nikolay Ogarkov, chief of the Soviet General Staff, dominated the press conferences given to explain the action, although representatives from the Party's Information Department and the Ministry of Foreign Affairs were also present. Since then, televised press conferences featuring senior Soviet officers are not unusual. During the 1987 summit in Washington, Soviet officers appeared on television on a number of occasions to present the Soviet view of arms control and disarmament.

Moscow Radio Peace and Progress broadcasts to the world in many foreign languages each day. Prevalent themes are the "peace-loving" policies of the Soviet Union and the need to resist Western "imperialism." A major purpose of the broadcasts is to encourage wars of national liberation. Many programs are extremely well done, and the transmissions often can be heard more clearly than any other foreign station. Projection of Soviet military power and presence is one of the demands of Soviet military doctrine.

*   *   *

Foreign scholars beginning the study of Soviet military affairs may at first have trouble sorting out the various authors and publications. For matters of military doctrine and strategy, the books in the various Officer's Library series should be of particular help. It also is worthwhile to review the books and authors who have been awarded Frunze Prizes. The fundamentals of doctrine will be found in the Party Program, the reports of the Party Congresses, and in writings by the Minister of Defense and the chief of the General Staff. Finally, specific items will be discussed in publications by faculty members of the Soviet military academies.

It may be dangerous for the West to ignore the attention given by the Soviet Party leadership to the dissemination of military doctrine, as it is a vital aspect of the military-political indoctrination of the population and of the Armed Forces in particular. This dissemination, itself a requirement of doctrine, is accomplished by every means available and by the best propagandists the nation can produce. The results may not always bear a label, but the questions doctrine is to answer, as listed by Marshals of the Soviet Union Ogarkov and Grechko, are never far from the minds of these propagandists.

Notes

1. M. A. Gareyev, *M. V. Frunze—Voyennyy Teoretik* [M. V. Frunze—Military Theoretician] (Moscow: Voyenizdat, 1985), p. 117.

2. W. R. Kintner and H. F. Scott, *Nuclear Revolution in Soviet Military Affairs* (Norman, Oklahoma: University of Oklahoma Press, 1968), p. 21.

3. *Letopis' Gazetnykh Statey* [Chronicle of Newspaper Articles] (1987) no. 17, p. 19; no. 18, pp. 20–21.

4. N. A. Lomov, *Sovetskaya Voyennaya Doktrina* [Soviet Military Doctrine] (Moscow: Znaniye, 1963); and *Nauchno-Tekhnicheskiy Progress i Razvitiye Voyennogo Dela* [Scientific-Technical Progress and Development of Military Affairs] (Moscow: Znaniye, 1970).

5. In 1928, by decision of the Revvoyensovyet USSR, publication of an earlier edition of the *Soviet Military Encyclopedia* was approved. R. P. Eideman was the editor in chief. The editorial commission was chaired by K. Ye. Voroshilov, Commissar for Military and Naval Affairs, with Yan Gamarnik as his deputy, and members A. S. Bubnov, A. I. Yegorov, M. N. Tukhachevskiy, I. P. Uborevich, R. P. Eideman and I. Ye. Yakir. All but Voroshilov were later killed in Stalin's purges. Gamarnik, threatened with arrest, committed suicide.

6. M. M. Kir'yan, *Problemy Voyennoy Teorii v Sovetskikh Nauchno-Spravochnykh Izdaniyakh* [Problems of Military Theory in Soviet Scientific Reference Publications] (Moscow: Nauka, 1985), pp. 34ff.

7. *Voyennaya Akademiya Imeni M. V. Frunze* [Military Academy Named for M. V. Frunze], 2nd ed. (Moscow: Voyenizdat, 1980), p. 247.

8. Kir'yan, *Problemy Voyennoy Teorii*, p. 41.

9. Ibid., p. 44.

10. Ibid., pp. 31–46.

11. As with other Soviet encyclopedias a complete set is not purchased all at once; the individual volumes are purchased as they appear. For example, the fifty-one-volume second edition of the BSE was published volume by volume over a period of eight years, from 1950 to 1958. Preparations for the third edition of the BSE started immediately, although the first volume did not appear until 1970. The thirty-one-volume series was completed by 1978. Volume 32, containing a name index, finished the set in 1981.

12. P. Sharpilo, "Voyenizdat's Glorious Jubilee," *Voyenno-Istoricheskiy Zhurnal* [Military History Journal] 10 (October 1979), pp. 89–91.

13. The original Frunze Prize was introduced in July 1926, following the death of M. V. Frunze in October 1925. The first prize was awarded to A. N. Lapchinskiy for his book *Tactics of Aviation and Questions of Antiaircraft Defense* (1926).

14. *Krasnaya Zvezda* [Red Star], March 2, 1967, p. 3.

15. *Akademiya Imeni M. V. Frunze* [Academy Named for M. V. Frunze], 1st ed. (Moscow: Voyenizdat, 1973), p. 245.

16. *Voyennaya Akademiya Imeni Frunze* (1980), p. 211.

17. *Krasnaya Zvezda*, December 19, 1968, p. 3.

18. *Krasnaya Zvezda*, November 23, 1969, p. 4.

19. *Krasnaya Zvezda*, March 8, 1970, p. 2.

20. *Krasnaya Zvezda*, November 28, 1970, p. 3.

21. *Krasnaya Zvezda*, November 12, 1973, p. 3.

22. P. A. Zhilin, *Problemy Voyennoy Istorii* [Problems of Military History] (Moscow: Voyenizdat, 1975), p. 376.

23. Gareyev, M. V. *Frunze*, p. 66. The journal of the Military Science Society of the Military Academy from 1921–1922 was *Krasnaya Armiya* [Red Army]; from 1923–1924 *Voyna i Tekhnika* [War and Equipment]; and from 1925–1936 *Voyna i Revolutsiya* [War and Revolution]. See: N. A. Lomov and T. Kin, "Volunteer Military Science Societies," *Voyenno-Istoricheskiy Zhurnal* 5 (May 1975), pp. 122–126.

24. N. A. Lomov and T. Kin, "The Volunteer Military Science Society," p. 124.

25. See M. I. Skoptsov, "Voyenno-Nauchnoye Obshchestvo" [The Military Science Society], *Sovetskaya Voyennaya Entsiklopediya*, vol. 2, p. 244.

26. *Yezhegodnik Bol'shoy Sovetskoy Entsiklopedii, 1986* [Annual of the Great Soviet Encyclopedia, 1986] (Moscow: Soviet Encyclopedia Publishers, 1986), p. 25.

27. *Yezhegodnik, 1986*, p. 24.

28. N. I. Smorigo, "Marksistsko-Leninskaya Podgotovka Ofitserskogo Sostava" [Marxist-Leninist Training of Officer Personnel], *Sovetskaya Voyennaya Entsiklopediya*, vol. 5, p. 152.

29. A. A. Karalyuk, P. T. Mokryakov, A. I. Orlov et al., *Voyennyye Voprosy v Kurse Istorii SSSR* [Military Questions in the Course of History of the USSR] (Moscow: Voyenizdat, 1986), p. 186. This book is a textbook for *kursants* (cadets) of higher military-political schools.

30. M. G. Sobolev, editor, *Partiyno-Politicheskaya Rabota v Sovetskoy Armii i Flote* [Party-Political Work in the Soviet Army and Fleet] (Moscow: Voyenizdat, 1984), p. 120.

31. L. A. Bublik, M. D. Popkov, N. S. Smorigo et al, *Partiyno-Politicheskaya Rabota v Sovetskoy Armii i Voyenno-Morskom Flote* [Party-Political Work in the Soviet Army and Navy] (Moscow: Voyenizdat, 1982), p. 112. This book was part of the Officer's Library series.

32. *Voyennyye Voprosy*, p. 190.

33. Ibid., p. 190.

34. Ibid., p. 116.

35. Ibid., p. 192.

36. A. N. Agafonov, editor, *Spravochnik Politrabotnika* [Handbook of a Political Worker] (Moscow: Voyenizdat, 1985), p. 148.

37. Ibid.

38. Ibid., p. 150.

39. Ibid., p. 148.

40. I. Aristov, "27th Congress CPSU on the Necessity for High Vigilance and Constant Combat Readiness of the Army and Navy," *Kommunist Vooruzhennykh Sil* 19 (October 1986), p. 77. See also: Ellen Jones, *Red Army and Society* (Boston: Allen & Unwin, 1985), p. 156.

Conclusions:
Continuity or Change?

There are great hopes in the West that fundamental changes are taking place in the Soviet Union. At the 27th Party Congress in early 1986, Mikhail Gorbachev declared that Soviet military doctrine "is unequivocally defensive." He also assured the world that "in the military sphere we intend to act in such a way as to give nobody grounds for fears, even imagined ones, about their security."[1] Does this mean a new era in Soviet policies and a revision of military doctrine is under way?

Gorbachev's statement on military doctrine was explained as part of the Kremlin's "new political thinking." The possibility of change in the Soviet Union, especially with respect to the Kremlin's new assertions on the use of military power, has dominated Western discussions of foreign affairs in the late 1980s.

There have been similar hopes before. In the 1960s, following the Cuban Missile Crisis, leaders in Washington as well as in most European capitals thought that the Kremlin's military policies had changed. In particular, it was believed that the new team of Leonid Brezhnev and Aleksey Kosygin would reject the nuclear madness of Nikita Khrushchev. Instead, as the record shows, the military doctrine formulated in the late 1950s continued with only minor modifications. Again, in the 1970s after the signing of SALT I, Washington was euphoric about the changed nature of Soviet thinking. The United States had established such firm ties with the Soviet Union that détente was thought to be irreversible. However, the same pattern as in the 1960s was repeated. Soviet military doctrine remained the same.

In the 1980s the Kremlin has sought to convince the West that a new era has begun. Assertions of change in military doctrine have appeared in the Soviet press, were broadcast by Soviet shortwave to the West, and have been topics of conversation when NATO political leaders and scholars visit Moscow to meet with selected members of the Soviet General Staff and research institutes. In 1987, Warsaw Pact Party leaders proposed that "authoritative" representatives from the Warsaw Pact and NATO meet to

253

discuss their respective military doctrines.[2] This proposal was thought by some NATO leaders to signify a new attitude in the Kremlin toward arms control and force reductions.

The signing of the Treaty on Intermediate Range Nuclear Forces in December 1987, sparked further optimism in the West that Soviet military policies had changed for the better. A few NATO strategists, however, were concerned about the possible consequences of the Treaty. From the Soviet side, this would mean the elimination of NATO's Pershing II missiles which could strike Soviet territory within ten minutes after launch. With this capability removed, NATO's remaining short-range missiles and nuclear-capable artillery could not engage attacking Soviet forces until they were within only a few kilometers of NATO borders. Although under the Treaty provisions the Soviets would destroy their intermediate range missiles, to include the SS-20, they would retain their operational-tactical missiles and nuclear-capable artillery. When its intermediate range missiles are withdrawn, NATO will be faced with Soviet superiority in conventional forces, both ground and air.

Gorbachev's announcement in early 1988 that Soviet forces would be withdrawn from Afghanistan was welcomed throughout the noncommunist world. Should the withdrawal take place as announced, major problems in Afghanistan, caused by the Soviet invasion, will still remain. Will Moscow permit the Afghans to have a truly independent government? It would be naive to assume that the withdrawal of Soviet troops from that area signals a change in Soviet long-term aspirations toward the Indian Ocean. But whatever the outcome might be, Gorbachev's announcement caused a world-wide rise in Soviet prestige.

Before actions are based on such perceptions of Soviet behavior, it is more important than ever before that defense planners outside the Soviet orbit examine the total Soviet concept of military doctrine and its purpose— a concept quite different from Western military doctrine, which is merely a set of principles for the use of armed forces in combat. Soviet military doctrine transcends the Soviet Armed Forces. It impacts all aspects of Soviet life, whether it be the military-patriotic education of Soviet youth, the location of new industries, or scientific exchanges with the noncommunist world. Soviet military doctrine provides the overall framework for preparing the country against the possibility of a future war. It is concerned with the very essence of war, its aims and nature, the weapons that will be used as well as how they will be used.

The expansion of Soviet military power is governed by the directives of doctrine. These directives give not only the probability of a future war but also name the enemy, which, since the time of Lenin, has been the "imperialists." The United States, as the major "imperialist" power, is considered the primary threat. Communist China, which secretly may concern the Soviet leadership even more than the United States, is difficult to explain to the Soviet populace; any threat from "socialist" China, as they now call it, must be portrayed as a result of its having strayed from Marxist-Leninist teachings.

The questions of military doctrine include whether a future war will be between single nations or coalitions, what type of weapons will be used, what will be expected of the Armed Forces, and what their size and composition should be. Doctrine also gives guidelines for preparing the nation as a whole for war, including both the general population and industry. These requirements of doctrine were well explained in the early 1960s. Preparations for the possibility of future war continue today and are much more advanced.

Soviet military doctrine does not necessarily reflect existing military capabilities. It provides guidance, and its edicts have the force of law. In the early 1960s Soviet military doctrinal writings stressed nuclear war and how it would be fought. At that time the Soviet Union did not have the strategic nuclear forces needed to fight the type war their doctrine described; thus, some Western scholars thought the Soviets had two types of doctrine— a "declaratory" doctrine to mislead the West, and an "operational" doctrine that reflected the existing force posture. Western analysts did not understand socialist realism: If it is planned, it exists. It is only a matter of time before plans become realities.

Military doctrine is a military-political statement of long-term objectives, a set of national directives pertinent to planning for future war. It gives answers to questions that are vital to planning. We know only a few of these answers. Open Soviet publications barely touch the tip of the iceberg. One of the questions that doctrine is to answer concerns the forces needed for a future war. The requirements of doctrine for research and development of specific weapon systems, however, are kept in the greatest secrecy.

For those who have studied the Soviet Union in detail over a period of years, the importance of military doctrine there is not surprising. All aspects of Soviet society are planned. Factory workers have a planned goal, or "norm," to meet each month. The January issue of most Soviet military journals gives their publication plans for the coming twelve months. Economic output, even under *perestroika*, is expected to meet goals planned for the next five years. Some long-range economic goals are set for the next ten or fifteen years. Military doctrine is that aspect of Soviet planning that prepares the Armed Forces and the nation for future war.

There are dangers inherent in this type of long-range planning. If the wrong weapons systems are developed, the Armed Forces—and the nation— may be placed in a very disadvantageous position. For example, command and control procedures might be adopted that could be impractical in a nuclear environment, or, conversely, on a nonnuclear battlefield. Even the strategy that flows from doctrine might prove to be unworkable when the anticipated war takes place.

There is no indication thus far that the Soviets have made serious long-range planning mistakes in the military area. Weapons selection appears to be under continuous review, and adjustments are made as needed. Although there is centralized control in the military-industrial complex, there also can be rapid response to altered circumstances. If the judgment of the leadership is good, centralized long-range planning can be efficient and cost-effective.

Soviet military doctrine is not something promulgated primarily by senior military officers. On the contrary, doctrine is the military policy of the Party. In its formulation, however, the military does have a direct voice. As has been shown, the most senior officers are also members of the Party's Central Committee. Basic tenets of doctrine, or modifications to it, generally can be traced back to official sources, such as the Party Program, a speech made by the Party's General Secretary at the Party Congress, or an article by the Minister of Defense or chief of the General Staff. Often such an article will appear not in a military publication but in a Party journal such as *Kommunist*. There are no open "doctrinal debates," as sometimes reported in the Western press.

The two sides of doctrine, the political and military-technical, permit the leadership great flexibility. The political side, which identifies "imperialism" or "capitalism" as the enemy, has remained relatively constant since Lenin's time. Since the end of World War II, the United States has been designated as leader of the enemy camp. New weapons systems, command and control procedures, and consideration of enemy capabilities are among the concerns of the constantly changing military-technical side of doctrine. Soviet weapons are built to meet goals established by doctrine. Since existing scientific and technological capabilities permit the development of an almost infinite number of different weapons systems, research and development must be specified and channeled.

Soviet military doctrine defines the purposes of weapons. After doctrine answers the basic questions—the designation of the enemy, the nature of the future war, its aims, and what is expected of the Armed Forces—the selection of weapons systems and identification of technologies that need to be further developed becomes a rational process. This process was demonstrated by the part military doctrine played in the buildup of Soviet military power beginning in the late 1950s.

Doctrine in Action

By the 1980s the military doctrine that had taken the Soviet Union to the position of a military superpower appeared once again to be in a cycle of modification. It is impossible to determine precisely what the outcome will be. Many emerging technologies hold promise, in particular directed energy weapons. Manned military space systems also appear to be high on the Kremlin's priority list. It is likely that current military doctrine calls for primary emphasis on these weapons, just as the doctrine announced in the 1960s was based on nuclear-armed ballistic missiles that then were only under development. Probably attention also is given to chemical and bacteriological weapons, two classes of weapons that the United States tends to reject.

The doctrine formulated and approved in the 1950s, with modifications in its operational aspects as military technology evolved, served the nation well. In the aftermath of World War II, possession of the atomic bomb by the United States was one of the major political-military concerns of the Soviet Union. Working in the greatest secrecy, Soviet scientists exploded an atomic bomb years ahead of Western estimates. Similar priority was given to the development of ballistic missiles.

In the late 1950s the Party decreed that should war occur the nuclear-armed missile would be the decisive weapon. To ensure that this weapon system received priority attention, the Strategic Rocket Forces were formed in December 1959 to implement this element of doctrine. The doctrine was modified in the late 1960s to include the possibility of a nonnuclear phase; that is, that a war might begin with the use of only conventional weapons. This modification required a new emphasis on combined arms forces capable of fighting with either conventional or nuclear weapons.

The arms control agreement signed in Moscow in May 1972 signaled to the world that the Soviet Union was a military superpower. Now the Soviets believed the base of communism to be secure. The strategic nuclear forces of the United States were capped, and Soviet combined arms forces, capable of fighting with either conventional or nuclear weapons, dominated two continents.

The second major modification of doctrine was publicly announced when Minister of Defense A. A. Grechko described the new, "external" role of the Soviet Armed Forces. The modification probably had been made several years previously but was not announced until 1974. This modification involved military support for national liberation wars, declared to be the "sacred duty" of the Soviet people. This addition to doctrine had been tested during Moscow's support for North Vietnam: Success there confirmed that power could be projected to areas not adjacent to Soviet territory.

Soviet strategic nuclear forces were seen as providing the umbrella under which combined armed forces could fight, either with tactical nuclear or conventional weapons. This same nuclear umbrella made it possible for the Soviet Union to project its military power and presence without interference from other nations. It gave the Kremlin a considerable degree of escalation control and options for the use of military power. This explains why even in the 1980s Soviet leaders have reaffirmed that first priority is given to strategic nuclear forces.

Since the early 1960s Soviet military doctrine had made clear that no weapon system, in particular the nuclear-armed ballistic missile, should be "absolutized." According to the laws of dialectics often stressed by Soviet theorists, the history of past wars shows there is a continuing struggle between offense and defense. Soviet theorists have consistently warned that the development of new offensive weapons has always led to the development of offsetting countermeasures. In particular, they emphasized that this law applies to ballistic missiles.

A Defensive Military Doctrine?

General Secretary Gorbachev's assertion at the 27th Party Congress that Soviet military doctrine is "unequivocally defensive" has become a major feature in Soviet propaganda. There has been no admission in the Soviet press that the Party's military doctrine had ever been otherwise. The fact was ignored that throughout the 1960s and 1970s Soviet authorities, writing for both military and Party publications, had emphasized that "Soviet military doctrine is offensive in character." This offensive doctrine had been asserted since the 1920s.

NATO planners should not forget that the change from an "offensive" to a "defensive" doctrine was purely nominal, a change in words and nothing more. Soviet military textbooks continue to teach that the major form of strategic action is offensive operations in theaters of military operations (TVDs). This would seem to conflict with the declaration that doctrine is "purely defensive." However, military doctrine has two sides, the political and military-technical. Only the political side is "defensive." To ensure that there is no question about the military-technical side of doctrine being offensive, Lenin's words, still quoted frequently in the late 1980s, only need be read: "If we, in the face of such forces that are constantly, actively hostile to us, would have to give a pledge, as has been proposed to us, that we would never resort to certain actions which in military-strategic relations might turn out to be offensive, then we would be not only fools but criminals. . . . When fighting, one must not 'wear down' the enemy, but destroy him."[3]

How the Kremlin defines a "defensive" military doctrine is attested to in Marxist-Leninist writings on "just" and "unjust" wars. All military actions undertaken by the Soviet Union have been for "defensive" purposes, including the 1939 Soviet attack on Finland, the 1968 invasion of Czechoslovakia, and the 1979 invasion of Afghanistan. Sending nuclear-armed missiles to Cuba in 1962 was for defensive purposes, insofar as doctrine was concerned. As Soviet textbooks explain to readers, the very nature of the Soviet state makes it impossible for its leaders to ever act in an aggressive manner.

After its military doctrine became "unequivocally defensive," Moscow had to show that all along it had only been reacting to NATO's military buildup. However, from the mid-1950s to 1980, both Soviet Party and military leaders had stated that the Soviet Union was first to develop a hydrogen bomb that could be dropped from an aircraft, first to develop an intercontinental ballistic missile, and first with other new types of missiles. With the new assertions about the defensive nature of Soviet military doctrine, Soviet leaders could no longer claim "firsts" in new weapons. The United States now is portrayed as being "first." The Kremlin has even given up the claim of being first with the hydrogen bomb. What Moscow previously had termed a "device" detonated by the United States in 1952 is now considered a "powerful hydrogen bomb."

Soviet propagandists dwell on the theme of the "imperialists fanning the arms race." A review of past Soviet practices indicates that once military doctrine specifies the nature of a future war and the forces needed, the required weapons systems are then developed. What the United States or other nations do with respect to their own weapons production may have little impact on Soviet military research and development, or on weapons production and deployment. The "action-reaction phenomenon" that was "discovered" by former U.S. Secretary of Defense Robert McNamara inhibited the United States from developing some new weapons and increasing the deployment of others. The notion of action-reaction was put to rest by former Secretary of Defense Harold Brown in 1979 when he told the Congress, "When we build, they build. When we reduce our forces, they build up theirs."[4] It would be dangerous for NATO planners to assume that claims of a "defensive" military doctrine will change this pattern.

The Consequences of Nuclear War

It may seem a paradox that with Soviet nuclear throw-weight considerably greater than that of the United States, and with its superpower status derived from its nuclear forces, the Soviet leadership is most vocal about the consequences of nuclear war. General Secretary Gorbachev's declaration at the 27th Party Congress in 1986 that the Soviet Union seeks "to prevent nuclear war, in order that civilization can survive" was not new. His predecessors had made similar statements. In the 1950s and 1960 both Georgiy Malenkov and Nikita Khrushchev warned that entire continents would be devastated if a nuclear war should occur.

But the utility of nuclear weapons apparently was more important than saving continents. When in 1956 Khrushchev announced a major change in one of the basic tenets of communism—that war between capitalism and communism was no longer inevitable—he added that this change was due to the fact that the forces of communism now had "formidable means" that permitted them "to give a smashing rebuff to the aggressors and frustrate their adventurist plans."[5] The "formidable means" was the small stockpile of nuclear weapons then possessed by the Soviet Union.

Warnings about the dire consequences of nuclear war have been a standard feature of Soviet Party-military writings for four decades. The concern expressed may have been sincere; nevertheless primary emphasis since the late 1950s has been on the development, production, and deployment of ballistic nuclear weapons, principally of strategic range. The military superpower status of the Soviet Union was gained primarily through its ground-based ICBMs. Without military power, the nation would be in the underdeveloped category and Gorbachev's visit to Washington in December 1987 would scarcely have made the evening news.

Since 1981 Soviet military leaders have claimed that nuclear weapons are now so numerous that their military usefulness has been negated. Should they be introduced in a war, their destructive power would bring about an end to civilization. Many believed such statements to be a signal that the Soviets no longer seriously considered the possibility of a nuclear war and were placing increased emphasis on conventional weaponry. This hope was thought to be borne out by Brezhnev's 1982 declaration that the Soviet Union would not be the first to use nuclear weapons—a pledge also made by his successors.

A no-first-use pledge, however, is not a renunciation of nuclear weapons and should not be sufficient to change U.S. policy. At one time in the 1970s Brezhnev had caveated his no-first-use statement with the qualification that nuclear weapons would be used "only in case of extreme necessity." The leaders of NATO could in all conscience give a similar promise. Despite assertions of the consequences of nuclear war, Soviet development of nuclear weapons continues.

To prepare for an "uncompromising and crushing war," the moral-political and psychological training of all the Soviet people, an element of doctrine, remains critical. "Pacifist" attitudes among the soldiers are "impermissible." Soldiers must be ready to fight "to the last drop of blood." In order to achieve victory, it is necessary to be prepared for any condition, without reservation, "taking into account the use of any kind of weapon."[6] Members of the Strategic Rocket Forces have been told that an order to deliver a nuclear counterstrike on an opponent must be obeyed without question, regardless of the personal feelings of the individual pressing the button.

The Concept of Reasonable Sufficiency

NATO nations placed great hopes on the Resolution based on General Secretary Gorbachev's statement at the 1986 27th Party Congress, which stated that "our country stands for removing weapons of mass destruction from use, for limiting the military potential to reasonable sufficiency [*razumnoy dostatochnosti*]."[7] Following the Congress, there appeared to be a carefully orchestrated Kremlin move to portray reasonable sufficiency to overseas audiences as synonymous with plans for actual reductions in military forces. The current Soviet emphasis on reasonable sufficiency, made at a time when there were hopes in the West for a meaningful arms control agreement with Moscow, demands careful study. At first glance the idea of reasonable sufficiency may appear to be a new Kremlin concept. But the words had a familiar ring.

General Secretary Gorbachev's statement on reasonable sufficiency echoed those that had been made twenty years previously. In March 1966, General Secretary Leonid Brezhnev in his Report to the 23rd Party Congress said that "the armaments of Soviet troops are maintained at the level of contemporary requirements and their striking power and fire power are fully sufficient [*vpolnye dostatochny*] to crush any aggressor."[8] In his speech at Tula in January 1977 Brezhnev stated that the allegations that the Soviet Union is "going further than is sufficient [*dostatochno*] for defense . . . is absurd and totally unfounded."[9]

Just before his brief period as the Party's General Secretary, Yuriy Andropov made a similar statement: "The defense capabilities of the Soviet Union and the countries of the socialist community are supported at the necessary level [*dolzhnom urovnye*]."[10] There is little if any difference in the meaning of "fully sufficient," as stated by Brezhnev, and "reasonable sufficiency" as used by Gorbachev. At any rate, is it not reasonable to ask: Sufficient for what? To deter attack on the USSR or to support its long-term strategic objective?

The Need for *Perestroika*

It is assumed by many in the West that the purpose of *perestroika* (restructuring) is to improve the living standard of the Soviet people. Both Russian and Soviet history suggest otherwise. Ivan the Terrible instituted a number of changes and welcomed architects, doctors, and artisans from abroad. Peter the Great travelled widely in Europe and his reforms were even more far-reaching than those of Ivan. Both men sought to increase the prestige of the Czar and the power of Imperial Russia. Improving the living conditions of the people was incidental, if considered at all.

This pattern did not change with the Communist revolution. In 1921 Lenin's New Economic Policy (NEP) offered concessions to foreign capitalists. Soviet leaders allegedly observed that "the capitalists will sell us the rope with which we will hang them." The West helped to rebuild the economy ruined by the Civil War. When starvation threatened Soviet Russia, Herbert Hoover organized a massive famine relief program. Stalin's name is linked with the First Five-Year Plan of industrialization, and he had the help of many of the most prestigious firms in the West, which supplied funds and skills. This invigoration of the Soviet economy was for the same purpose as in the days of the Czars: to increase the power of the Soviet state and its rulers.

When Gorbachev became General Secretary in March 1985, *perestroika* became the centerpiece of the "new political thinking" in the Kremlin. Attention was focused on the floundering Soviet economy. The facts, which Gorbachev pointed out, were plain. The gross national product (GNP) of the USSR was increasing at such a slow rate that if it were not improved, either the standard of living (more new apartments) would decrease or the program of material well-being (health and education) would be reduced.[11] Nothing was said about the effect on defense spending.

Articles in the Soviet press also revealed that in a number of areas the Soviet Union was lagging in science and technology. This admission was in marked contrast to the late 1950s and early 1960s when Soviet successes in ballistic missiles and space activities convinced the Soviet people that their scientific-technical capability led the world. The admitted relative decline in scientific-technical potential represented a major problem for the Soviet military-industrial complex, as advanced weapons systems require sophisticated computers and microelectronics.

Military doctrine directs moral-political indoctrination of the population as one means of preparing the nation for future war. Admissions of social problems represent one of the greatest changes in the Soviet press. A number of Soviet writers have noted growing pacifism among the youth. Corruption is rampant and no longer is ignored by the media. By the mid-1980s drunkenness had reached such levels that severe restrictions were placed on the sale of alcohol. In the past, Soviet writings had asserted that their system, based on Marxism-Leninism, assured moral-political superiority over the "imperialists." Such writings became more circumspect.

The laws of war, as taught in higher professional Soviet institutions and explained in Party publications, provide cogent reasons why "restructuring" is given such high priority in the Soviet Union. Military doctrine, in part, is drawn from these laws. Since the laws of war state that the course and outcome of war are dependent upon the economic, scientific-technical, moral-political, as well as the military potentials of the belligerent sides, the military superpower status of the Soviet Union could be endangered. Military leaders had reason to support *perestroika*.

The danger is not immediate. In the 1980s the Soviets have a clear-cut numerical lead over NATO in conventional forces. In a number of areas the quality of weapons also is superior. Where quality might be lacking, quantity was used to compensate. In the strategic area new Soviet mobile missile systems could put the U.S. deterrent nuclear force at risk.

Should the Soviet economy and its science and technology continue to lag, within ten to twenty years the Soviet Armed Forces could fall behind those of its potential opponents. For this reason General Secretary Gorbachev may be embarking on the best course possible to ensure the Soviet Union's future as a military superpower. The economy needs Western inputs, from advanced technology to hard currency credits. Present Kremlin leaders are well aware that in the détente period of the 1970s Soviet scientists roamed the United States and Western Europe, visiting defense plants and research institutes. During the visit of General Secretary Gorbachev to Washington in December 1987 his advisors were seeking to reestablish and even to increase contacts with the U.S. scientific community.

Marxism-Leninism requires that the Kremlin seek to keep the laws of war in its favor. This is what *perestroika* hopes to accomplish. It and its fellow traveler, *glasnost'*, are more than blueprints for economic and social reform. They are elements in the economic and moral-political content of Soviet military doctrine.

Peace and Peaceful Coexistence

There is a danger that the Kremlin's propagandizing of its many "peace programs" will blind some NATO leaders, or at least some of their electorates, to the realities of Soviet military doctrine. What is meant by "peaceful coexistence" in Moscow is not the same as in Washington, London, Bonn, Paris, or Tokyo. For the Soviet people, "peaceful coexistence of states with different social systems is today a struggle against imperialism."[12] It is "a special form of the class struggle between two opposing world systems, a continuation of the struggle by peaceful means, without war."

It is difficult to understand why the leaders of NATO nations, in particular the United States, do not strive to make the general public aware of this Soviet definition. The Soviet meaning is clear. Peaceful coexistence is explained as "economic, political and ideological struggle but not a military struggle."[13] It provides for peace programs while at the same time communism must "energetically promote the revolutionary and national liberation struggle." Whenever it might occur, "détente does not in the slightest abolish, nor can it abolish or alter, the laws of class struggle."[14] But while advocating peace and security, "the socialist countries constantly strengthen their defense capacity and equip their armed forces with the latest types of weapons to enable them, in the event of attack, to repel imperialist aggressors."[15] It also goes without saying that Soviet military power scale provides powerful political leverage in pursuing Soviet goals without open conflict.

Since the very beginning of the Soviet state, Lenin and his heirs have used the emotional appeal of peace. The day after the Bolsheviks seized power in the October Revolution, Lenin issued a "Decree of Peace." One of the most comprehensive proposals for disarmament was issued in 1928, while Joseph Stalin was General Secretary. It contained thirteen articles dealing with control measures alone. After World War II the Soviets offered repeated proposals to the United Nations prohibiting atomic weapons. Only days before the Korean War began, the Soviet Union called for a declaration that would make officials of the first government to use atomic weapons guilty of war crimes.

Khrushchev was quick to make proposals on disarmament when he became Party First Secretary in 1953. The following year he submitted a grand plan for European security. Brezhnev also called for eliminating military bases in other countries, cutting military budgets, and signing a nonaggression pact between the Warsaw Pact and NATO.

A Peace and Security Program for the 1990s

Before the December 1987 Washington summit between President Reagan and General Secretary Gorbachev, Party propagandists saw to it that a book by Gorbachev was published in the West. Entitled *Perestroika: New Thinking for Our Country and the World*,[16] it purported to give the Communist Party's strategic plan for foreign and domestic policy in the immediate five-year period into the early 1990s.

During his eighteen-year tenure as General Secretary, Leonid Brezhnev had similar plans, which he called his Peace Program. Gorbachev called his a System of International Security. Carefully packaged for both domestic and foreign consumption, this plan seemingly has many implications for military doctrine. It includes renunciation of war by the nuclear powers, prevention of an arms race in space, a strictly controlled reduction of military forces to limits of "reasonable sufficiency," disbandment of military alliances, balanced and proportional reduction of military budgets,[17] and so on. Similar programs had been introduced by his predecessors—Lenin, Stalin, Khrushchev, Brezhnev, Andropov, and Chernenko.

Are these putative, basic aims of the "all-embracing System of International Security" listed by Gorbachev really "new thinking"? Do they indicate major changes in Soviet military doctrine, or perhaps a completely new doctrine? We must not forget that similar words have been used in the past. The "Stalin Constitution" of 1936 was an effort to make the Soviet system appear more democratic in order to win support from Britain and France. Gorbachev's book, *Perestroika*, was intended for much the same purpose, only for a wider audience.

While we should not ignore the possibility of actual change in the Kremlin's goals, we must be realistic about the chance of that happening. The military doctrine announced by Khrushchev in 1960 remained essentially unchanged under Brezhnev. After Mikhail Gorbachev became the Communist Party's General Secretary, new slogans appeared in support of the image he sought to project. Although some of the words have been altered, the substance remains.

Neither the Moscow summit meeting of President Ronald Reagan and General Secretary Gorbachev in May 1988 nor the 19th Party Conference held the following month produced any reversal of previously announced Soviet military policies. Both the Soviet Minister of Defense, General of the Army D. T. Yazov, and the chief of the General Staff, Marshal of the Soviet Union S. F. Akhromeyev, have discussed military doctrine with senior Pentagon officials and with prestigious civilian groups. These Soviet leaders have hinted of changes to come, but how much should we take on trust? The questions and answers are still the same.

What does the future hold for Soviet military doctrine? Even in the most normal of times forecasting events is fraught with danger. The wall of secrecy that has surrounded the Soviet Union has been breached by shortwave radio broadcasts and television programs via satellite and the VCR. Type-writers and copying machines have made the underground *samizdat* press a mass medium. Many films and books long banned in the Soviet Union are being circulated at home as they have been abroad. Some of the darkest secrets of the past are being publically aired. Once taboo subjects now appear in the pages of *Pravda*. But severe restraints on information still remain.

Gorbachev's attempt to restructure the Soviet economy and government, together with his push to reexamine the nation's history, may set in motion events that cannot be controlled. He may be forced to modify his program or be ousted. But whoever may be the Party's General Secretary, it is improbable that any change will alter the Marxist-Leninist goal of scientific communism: the overthrow of capitalism, which in the final analysis means any nation outside of the Soviet orbit. This objective will remain the basic thrust of Soviet military doctrine.

Notes

1. Mikhail S. Gorbachev, *XXVII S"yezd Kommunistickeskoy Partii Sovetskogo Soyuza* [27th Congress of the CPSU], stenographic notes (Moscow: Politizdat, 1986), p. 89.

2. V. F. Petrovskiy, "At the USSR Foreign Ministry Press Center," *Krasnaya Zvezda* [Red Star], June 24, 1987, p. 3.

3. V. I. Lenin, quoted in A. S. Milovidov, *Voyenno-Teoreticheskoye Naslediye V. I. Lenina i Problemy Sovremennoy Voyny* [Military-Theoretical Heritage of V. I. Lenin and Problems of Contemporary War] (Moscow: Voyenizdat, 1987), p. 251.

4. Harold Brown, *Washington Post*, February 19, 1979, p. 23.

5. N. S. Khrushchev, *On Peaceful Coexistence* (Moscow: Foreign Languages Publishing House, 1961), p. 10.

6. G. G. Kostev, "Our Military Doctrine in the Light of New Political Thinking," *Kommunist Vooruzhennykh Sil* [Communist of the Armed Forces] 17 (September 1987), p. 13.

7. *XXVII S"yezd*, p. 544.

8. Leonid Brezhnev, *XXIII S"yezd Kommunisticheskoy Partii Sovetskogo Soyuza* [23rd Congress of the Communist Party of the Soviet Union], stenographic notes (Moscow: Politizdat, 1966), p. 93.

9. Leonid Brezhnev, *Speech in the City of Tula*, January 18, 1977 (Moscow: Novosti, 1977), p. 22.

10. Yuriy Andropov, *Izbrannyye Rechi i Stat'i* [Selected Speeches and Articles] (Moscow: Politizdat, 1983), p. 202.

11. Mikhail S. Gorbachev, *Perestroika: New Thinking for Our Country and the World* (New York: Harper & Row, 1987), pp. 19–20.

12. V. Afanas'yev, *Fundamentals of Scientific Communism*, 2nd ed. (Moscow: Progress Publishers, 1977), p. 116.

13. V. Afanasyev, *Marxist Philosophy* (Moscow: Foreign Languages Publishing House, 1962), p. 343.

14. Afanasyev, *Fundamentals*, pp. 121–122.

15. Ibid., p. 126.

16. The idea of "new thinking" was not really new. *New Thinking in the Nuclear Age* was the title of a book published by Anatoliy Gromyko and Vladimir Lomeyko in 1984, a year before Gorbachev came to power. Mikhail Gorbachev was the protégé of Andrey Gromyko, who nominated him for the post of General Secretary and still remains one of his strongest supporters, as apparently, is his son. As pointed out earlier, Gromyko and Lomeyko attribute the original idea of the need for new thinking in the nuclear age to Einstein.

17. Gorbachev, *XXVII S"yezd*, p. 98.

Appendix A: Military Members of the Central Committee CPSU (March 1986)

Alphabetical List

	Position	Joined CPSU	23	24	25	26
Full Members:						
1. Akhromeyev, S. F.	1st Dep MoD, Ch G/S	1943				
2. Altunin, A. T.	Dep MoD, Ch of Civil Def	1943			M	M
3. Arkhipov, V. M.	Com Gen Moscow MD	1957				C/M
4. Chernavin, V. N.	Dep MoD, CinC Navy	1949				C
5. Gerasimov, I. A.	CinC SW Forces [TVD]	1942			C	C
6. Gorshkov, S. G.	Gen Insp	1942	M	M	M	M
7. Govorov, V. L.	Dep MoD, Main Insp MoD	1946			C	M
8. Gribkov, A. I.	1st Dep Ch G/S, C/S WTO	1941			C	M
9. Ivanovskiy, Ye. F.	Dep MoD, CinC Ground Forces	1941			M M	M
10. Koldunov, A. I.	Dep MoD, CinC Tps Air Def	1944		C		M
11. Kulikov, V. G.	1st Dep MoD, CinC WTO	1942		M	M	M
12. Kurkotkin, S. K.	Dep MoD, Chief Rear	1940		C	M	M
13. Lizichev, A. D.	Chief Main Pol Dir	1949				
14. Lushev, P. G.	CinC Sov Forces Germany	1951				M
15. Maksimov, Yu. P.	Dep MoD, CinC SRF	1943				C
16. Ogarkov, N. V.	CinC Western Forces [TVD]	1945	C	M	M	M
17. Petrov, V. I.	1st Dep MoD, [Gen'l Affairs]	1944			M	M
18. Shabanov, V. M.	Dep MoD for Armaments	1947				C/M
19. Sokolov, S. L.	Minister of Defense	1937	C/M	M	M	M
20. Tolubko, V. F.	Gen Insp	1939		C	M	M
21. Tret'yak, I. M.	CinC Troops of Far East	1943		C	M	M

| 22. Yefimov, A. N. | Dep MoD, CinC Air Forces | 1943 | | | | |
| 23. Zaytsev, M. M. | CinC Southern Forces [TVD] | 1943 | | | | M |

Candidate Members:

1. Belikov, V. A.	Com Gen Carpathian MD	1949				
2. Kapitanets, I. M.	Com Adl Baltic Fleet	1952				
3. Konstantinov, A. U.	Com Gen Moscow Air Def Dis	1943				A
4. Osipov, V. V.	Com Gen Kiev MD					
5. Popkov, M. D.	Mem MC, Ch Pol Ground Forces	1943				C
6. Popov, N. I.	Com Gen Turkestan MD	1953				
7. Rodin, V. S.	Mem MC, Ch Pol SRF					
8. Shuralev, V. M.	Com Gen Belorussian MD					
9. Sidorov, V. V.	Com Adl Pacific Fleet	1949				C
10. Snetkov, B. V.	Com Leningrad MD	1945				
11. Sorokin, A. I.	1st Dep Ch Main Pol Dir	1943				
12. Varennikov, V. I.	1st Dep Ch G/S	1944				
13. Yazov, D. T.	Com Gen Far Eastern MD	1944				C
14. Yegorov, G. M.	Chmn DOSAAF	1942				

Auditors:

1. Dragunskiy, D. A.	Head, "Vystrel" Courses	1931	A	A A	A
2. Moiseyev, N. A.	Mem MC Ch Pol GSV Germany				
3. Postnikov, S. I.	Com Gen Transbaykal MD	1957			A

Analysis by Year of Birth

	Year of Birth
Full Members:	
1. Gorshkov, S. G.	1910
2. Sokolov, S. L.	1911
3. Tolubko, V. F.	1914
4. Kurkotkin, S. K.	1917
5. Ogarkov, N. V.	1917
6. Petrov, V. I.	1917
7. Ivanovskiy, Ye. F.	1918
8. Gribkov, A. I.	1919
9. Altunin, A. T.	1921
10. Gerasimov, I. A.	1921
11. Kulikov, V. G.	1921
12. Akhromeyev, S. F.	1923
13. Yefimov, A. N.	1923
14. Zaytsev, M. M.	1923
15. Koldunov, A. I.	1923
16. Lushev, P. G.	1923
17. Tret'yak, I. M.	1923
18. Shabanov, V. M.	1923
19. Govorov, V. L.	1924
20. Maksimov, Yu. P.	1924
21. Lizichev, A. D.	1928
22. Chernavin, V. N.	1928
23. Arkhipov, V. M.	1933
Candidate Members:	
1. Yegorov, G. M.	1918
2. Sorokin, A. I.	1922
3. Varennikov, V. I.	1923
4. Konstantinov, A. U.	1923
5. Yazov, D. T.	1923
6. Popkov, M. D.	1924
7. Sidorov, V. V.	1924
8. Belikov, V. A.	1925
9. Snetkov, B. V.	1925
10. Kapitanets, I. M.	1928
11. Rodin, V. S.	1928
12. Popov, N. I.	1930
13. Osipov, V. V.	1933
14. Shuralev, V. M.	1935
Auditors:	
1. Dragunskiy, D. A.	1910
2. Postnikov, S. I.	1928
3. Moiseyev, N. A.	1934

Analysis by Rank

	Rank
Full Members:	
1. Kulikov, V. G.	MSU
2. Ogarkov, N. V.	MSU
3. Sokolov, S. L.	MSU
4. Akhromeyev, S. F.	MSU
5. Kurkotkin, S. K.	MSU
6. Petrov, V. I.	MSU
7. Gorshkov, S. G.	AFSU
8. Koldunov, A. I.	CMAv
9. Tolubko, V. F.	CMAr
10. Ivanovskiy, Ye. F.	G/A
11. Gribkov, A. I.	G/A
12. Tret'yak, I. M.	G/A
13. Altunin, A. T.	G/A
14. Gerasimov, I. A.	G/A
15. Govorov, V. L.	G/A
16. Zaytsev, M. M.	G/A
17. Lushev, P. G.	G/A
18. Shabanov, V. M.	G/A
19. Maksimov, Yu. P.	G/A
20. Lizichev, A. D.	G/A
21. Yefimov, A. N.	M/Av
22. Chernavin, V. N.	A/F
23. Arkhipov, V. M.	G/C
Candidate Members:	
1. Varennikov, V. I.	G/A
2. Belikov, V. A.	G/A
3. Yazov, D. T.	G/A
4. Yegorov, G. M.	A/F
5. Konstantinov, A. U.	M/Av
6. Sidorov, V. V.	Adl
7. Sorokin, A. I.	Adl
8. Kapitanets, I. M.	Adl
9. Popkov, M. D.	G/C
10. Snetkov, B. V.	G/C
11. Popov, N. I.	G/C
12. Rodin, V. S.	G/C
13. Osipov, V. V.	G/C
14. Shuralev, V. M.	G/C
Auditors:	
1. Dragunskiy, D. A.	G/C
2. Postnikov, S. I.	G/C
3. Moiseyev, N. A.	G/L

Analysis by Nationality

	Nationality

Full Members:

1.	Altunin, A. T.	Russ
2.	Arkhipov, V. M.	Russ
3.	Akhromeyev, S. F.	Russ
4.	Gerasimov, I. A.	Russ
5.	Govorov, V. L.	Russ
6.	Gorshkov, S. G.	Russ
7.	Gribkov, A. I.	Russ
8.	Yefimov, A. N.	Russ
9.	Zaytsev, M. M.	Russ
10.	Koldunov, A. I.	Russ
11.	Kulikov, V. G.	Russ
12.	Kurkotkin, S. K.	Russ
13.	Lizichev, A. D.	Russ
14.	Lushev, P. G.	Russ
15.	Maksimov, Yu. P.	Russ
16.	Ogarkov, N. G.	Russ
17.	Petrov, V. I.	Russ
18.	Sokolov, S. L.	Russ
19.	Chernavin, V. N.	Russ
20.	Shabanov, V. M.	Russ
21.	Tolubko, V. F.	Ukr
22.	Tret'yak, I. M.	Ukr
23.	Ivanovskiy, Ye. F.	Belo

Candidate Members:

1.	Belikov, V. A.	Russ
2.	Varennikov, V. I.	Russ
3.	Yegorov, G. M.	Russ
4.	Kapitanets, I. M.	Russ
5.	Konstantinov, A. U.	Russ
6.	Popkov, M. D.	Russ
7.	Popov, N. I.	Russ
8.	Sidorov, V. V.	Russ
9.	Snetkov, B. V.	Russ
10.	Sorokin, A. I.	Russ
11.	Yazov, D. T.	Russ
12.	Osipov, V. V.	?
13.	Rodin, V. S.	?
14.	Shuralev, V. M.	?

Auditors:

1.	Postnikov, S. I.	Russ
2.	Dragunskiy, D. A.	Jewish
3.	Moiseyev, N. A.	?

Key to Abbreviations in Appendix A

A	Member Central Auditing Commission
A/F	Admiral of the Fleet
Adl	Admiral
AFSU	Admiral of the Fleet of the Soviet Union
Belo	Belorussian
C	Candidate Member Central Committee
C/S	Chief of Staff
Ch	Chief
Chmn	Chairman
CinC	Commander in Chief
CMAr	Chief Marshal of Artillery
CMAv	Chief Marshal of Aviation
Com Gen	Commanding General
CPSU	Communist Party of the Soviet Union
Def	Defense
Dep	Deputy
Dir	Directorate
Dis	District
DOSAAF	(Paramilitary Sports Organization)
G/A	General of the Army
G/C	General Colonel
G/L	General Lieutenant
G/S	General Staff
Gen	General
GSVG	Group of Soviet Forces, Germany
Insp	Inspector
M	Member of Central Committee
M/Av	Marshal of Aviation
MC	Military Council
MD	Military District
MoD	Minister of Defense
MSU	Marshal of the Soviet Union
Natl	Nationality
Pol	Political
Rear	Rear (Services)
Russ	Russian
Sov	Soviet
SRF	Strategic Rocket Forces
Tps	Troops
TVD	Theater of Military Actions
Ukr	Ukrainian
WTO	Warsaw Treaty Organization

Appendix B:
Official Military Holidays

February 23	Armed Forces Day
April 12	World Aviation and Cosmonauts Day
Second Sunday of April	Troops of Air Defense Day
May 28	Border Guards Day
First Sunday after July 22	Navy Day
Third Sunday of August	Air Force Day
Second Sunday of September	Tank Forces Day
November 10	Soviet Militia Day
November 19	Rocket Troops and Artillery Day

In addition military parades held in Moscow and the capitals of the republics that are also military district headquarters to celebrate the anniversary of the October Revolution on November 7, and ceremonies mark the end of the Great Patriotic War on May 9. Many of these holidays culminate in gigantic fireworks displays in Moscow, the capitals of the other republics, and "hero" cities. Main streets are closed to traffic so that people can stroll with their families.

Appendix C:
Official Books*

It is rare to find a list of books identified as official in a Soviet reference work. Below, for the use of students and researchers of Soviet military history, are the main titles that were listed:

Soviet Military Encyclopedia, A. A. Grechko, followed by N. V. Ogarkov, as editor-in-chief [Sovetskaya Voyennaya Entsiklopediya], published in eight volumes (Moscow: Voyendizdat, 1976–1980). 2nd edition announced in 1988.

Military Encyclopedia Dictionary, S. F. Akhromeyev, editor [Voyennyy Entsiklo-pedicheskiy Slovar'], 2nd edition (Moscow: Voyenizdat, 1986).

History of the Great Patriotic War of the Soviet Union 1941–1945, P. N. Pospelov, editor [Istoriya Velikoy Otechestvennoy Voyny Sovetskogo Soyuza 1941–1945] (Moscow: Voyenizdat, 1961–1965). Published in six volumes.

50 Years of the Armed Forces USSR, M. V. Zakharov, editor [50 Let Vooruzhennykh Sil SSSR] (Moscow: Voyenizdat, 1968).

Army of the Soviets, S. S. Lototskiy, editor [Armiya Sovetskaya] (Moscow: Politizdat, 1969).

Soviet Armed Forces, S. A. Tyushkevich, editor [Sovetskiye Vooruzhennyye Sily] (Moscow: Voyenizdat, 1978).

CPSU and the Development of the Soviet Armed Forces, N. M. Kiryayev, Ye. F. Nikitin and Yu. I. Korablev [KPSS i Stroitel'stvo Sovetskykh Vooruzhennykh Sil], 2nd edition (Moscow: Voyenizdat, 1967).

Party and the Army, A. A. Yepishev, editor [Partiya i Armiya], 2nd edition (Moscow: Politizdat, 1980).

Party-Political Work in the Soviet Armed Forces in the Great Patriotic War 1941–45, K. V. Kraynyukov, S. Ye. Zakharov and G. Ye. Shabayev, editors [Partiyno-Politicheskaya Rabota Sovetskikh Vooruzhennykh Sil v Gody Velikogo Otechestvennoy Voyny, 1941–1945], 2nd edition (Moscow: Voyenizdat, 1968).

History of the Second World War 1939–1945, A. A. Grechko, followed by D. F. Ustinov, editor-in-chief, published in 12 volumes [Istoriya Vtoroy Mirovoy Voyny, 1939–1945] (Moscow: Voyenizdat, 1973–1982).

---

*The complete list of seventy-five official books can be found in M. M. Kir'yan, *Velikaya Otechestvennaya Voyna 1941–1945* [Great Patriotic War, 1941–1945], a reference dictionary, published in Moscow by Voyenizdat in 1985, pp. 525–527.

Appendix D:
Original Plan of the Officer's Library Series

The 1950s (Gray) Officer's Library

Title	Date Published	Typeset	To Printer
1. *V. I. Lenin. On War, the Army and Military Science*[a]	1957	2-9-56	3-12-57
2. *F. Engels. Selected Military Works*[a]	1958	not given	2-24-58
3. *Marxism-Leninism on War and Army*[a]	1957	3-4-57	10-10-57
4. *M. I. Kalinin. On Communist and Military Education*[a]	1962	1-6-62	4-4-62
5. *Civil War and Foreign Military Intervention in the USSR*[b]	—	—	—
6. *A Short Outline on the History of The Great Patriotic War and World War Two* (published as *Second World War, 1939–45*)[a]	1958	5-29-58	11-26-58
7. *The Officer's Companion*	—	—	—
8. *The Air Forces*[a]	1959		
9. *The Navy*[a]	1959	7-23-58	2-26-59
10. *National PVO Troops*[a] (*Air Defense*)	1960	11-20-59	8-5-60
11. *The Physical Basis of Nuclear and Thermonuclear Weapons: Basis of Their Use and Protection from Them*	—	—	—
12. *Rocket Weapons*[a]	1960	2-1-59	4-26-60
13. *Radio and Radio-Locator Equipment and Its Use*[a]	1960	9-22-58	12-8-59
14. *Guide to the Armed Forces of Imperialist States*	—	—	—
15. *Atlas of the World*	—	—	—

[a]Published. Not all of the plan was carried out.
[b]A book of this title was published in 1958 but not in the Officer's Library series.

The 1960s (Blue) Officer's Library

Title	Date Published	Copies	Typeset	To Printer
1. *V. I. Lenin. On War, the Army and Military Science*	1965	29,000	2-8-65	2-28-65
2. *M. I. Kalinin. On Communist Indoctrination, Military Duty*	1967	32,000	2-9-66	11-1-66
3. *M. V. Frunze. Selection of Works*	1965	27,000	10-31-64	2-16-65
4. *Marxism-Leninism on War and Army*[a]	1965	50,000	4-29-65	9-14-65
5. *Party-Political Work in the Soviet Armed Forces*	1968	65,000	7-14-67	11-21-67
6. *History of Military Art*	1966	35,000	8-11-65	12-1-65
7. *Military Doctrine* (Never published)	—	—	—	—
8. *Military Strategy*[a]	1968	30,000	11-23-66	11-30-67
9. *Tactics*	1966	40,000	10-30-65	4-22-66
10. *Scientific-Technical Progress and Revolution in Military Affairs*[a]	1973	40,000	4-18-72	11-15-72
11. *Military Psychology*[a]	1967	50,000	10-4-66	9-14-67
12. *Military Pedagogics*[a]	1966	40,000	12-11-65	8-6-66
13. *Fundamentals of Soviet Military Law*	1966	40,000	1-30-65	11-23-65
14. *Organization and Armaments of Armies and Navies of Capitalist States*	1965	31,000	2-10-65	9-29-65
15. *Dictionary of Basic Military Terms*[a]	1965	27,000	4-20-65	7-14-65
16. *Officer's Guide for Quartermasters*	1968	32,000	4-24-67	11-28-67
17. *50 Years of the Armed Forces of the USSR*[b]	1968	100,000	1-4-67	11-6-67
18. *Officer's Handbook*[a]	1971	83,000	2-7-68	11-27-70
19. *Concept, Algorithm, Decision*[a]	1972	30,000	2-18-72	10-9-72

[a]These books are available in English translation.
[b]A book of this title was published but not in the Officer's Library series.

The 1980s (Red) Officer's Library

Title	Date Published	Copies	Typeset	To Printer
1. *V. I. Lenin and Soviet Armed Forces*	1980	75,000	9-26-79	12-29-79
2. *CPSU on Armed Forces of the Soviet Union*	1981	95,000	1-27-81	3-31-81
3. *L. I. Brezhnev. On Guard over Peace and Socialism*	1981	100,000	7-19-81	10-2-81
4. *Marxist-Leninist Teaching on War and Army*	1984	100,000	8-2-83	9-30-83
5. *Party-Political Work in the Soviet Army and Navy*	1982	100,000	6-24-82	7-30-82
6. *Fundamentals of Military Education*	—	—	—	—
7. *Fundamentals of Soviet Military Legislation* (Published as: *Military Legislation and Legal Education of Soldiers*)	1983	100,000	10-26-82	12-28-82
8. *Basic Methods of Combat Training*	—	—	—	—
9. *Tactics*	1984	55,000	6-26-84	7-25-84
10. *History of Military Art*	1986	90,000	3-29-84	1-23-85
11. *Armies of Warsaw Pact Countries*	1985	50,000	7-25-84	12-20-84
12. *Armed Forces of Capitalist States* (due in 1987)				

Announced later:

13. *M. V. Frunze. Collected Works*	1984	80,000	9-24-82	11-22-83
14. *Defense from Weapons of Mass Destruction*	1984	100,000	2-2-84	6-8-84
15. *Military Pedagogy and Psychology*	1986	100,000	8-22-85	10-17-85
16. *Officer's Handbook* (to be published in 1988)				

Appendix E: Winners of the Frunze Prize

1965

In March 1966, the Frunze Prize winners for 1965 were announced. The title of the work which won them the prize was not given. They were:[1]

Gen Col K. F. Skorobogatkin, chief, Military Science Directorate, General Staff
Gen Maj A. N. Strogiy, Military Science Directorate
*Gen Maj A. A. Prokhorov, Military Science Directorate
*Colonel V. V. Larionov, Military Science Directorate
*Colonel V. K. Denisenko, Military Science Directorate
Colonel V. V. Glazov
Colonel N. I. Kratinskiy
Capt 1st Rank Ye. N. Mamayev
Colonel I. M. Korzhov
Colonel S. V. Malyanchikov
Colonel A. S. Pekin

In addition, *Marxism-Leninism on War and Army* (4th edition), one of the books of the Officer's Library series, won gold watches for its editors:

Gen Maj N. Ya. Sushko, head, Department of Marxist-Leninist Philosophy, Lenin Military-Political Academy
Colonel S. A. Tyushkevich, instructor, Lenin Military-Political Academy
Colonel B. A. Belyy, assistant professor
Major D. A. Volkogonov, Department of Marxist-Leninist Philosophy
Colonel Ya. S. Dzyuba
Gen Maj S. N. Kozlov, editor, *Military Thought*

---

*Contributors to Sokolovskiy's *Military Strategy*.

Capt 1st Rank V. M. Kulakov, professor
Colonel Ye. V. Medvedev, assistant professor
Colonel K. V. Spirov, assistant professor, Department of Marxism-Leninism, Military
Academy of the General Staff
Colonel Ye. F. Sulimov, head, Department of Scientific Communism, Lenin Military-
Political Academy
Colonel Ye. A. Khomenko, assistant professor

A gold watch was awarded to General Major Engineer I. I. Anureyev, head of a department at the Academy of the General Staff, for research and writings on problems of military theory.
Certificates for writing valuable textbooks were given to:

Gen Col I. S. Glebov, head, Dept Operational Art, Academy of the General Staff
(G/S)
Gen Maj P. K. Altukhov, Dept Operational Art, Academy of G/S
Gen Maj B. M. Golovchiner, Dept Operational Art, Academy of G/S
Gen Maj V. I. Vol'khin, Dept Operational Art, Academy of G/S
Gen Maj L. M. Krylov, Dept Operational Art, Academy of G/S
Gen Maj B. G. Plashchin, Dept Operational Art, Academy of G/S
Gen Maj P. G. Yanovskiy, Dept Operational Art, Academy of G/S
Gen Maj D. K. Slepenkov, Dept Operational Art, Academy of G/S
Colonel S. F. Begunov, Dept Operational Art, Academy of G/S

1966

In 1967, the 1966 Frunze prize went to a group of authors representing the Frunze Military Academy "for elaborating the theoretical basis of combined arms battle." The title of the work was not given. The authors were:[2]

Gen of the Army P. A. Kurochkin, commandant, Frunze Military Academy
Gen Lieut V. Ya. Petrenko, Tactics Dept., Frunze Military Academy
Gen Maj R. G. Simonyan, Frunze Military Academy
Colonel P. V. Galochkin, Frunze Military Academy
Colonel L. M. Druzhinin, Frunze Military Academy
Colonel D. M. Milyutenkov, Frunze Military Academy
Colonel N. F. Miroshnichenko, Frunze Military Academy
Colonel P. M. Petrus, Frunze Military Academy
Colonel A. A. Sidorenko, Frunze Military Academy
Colonel P. V. Shemanskiy, Frunze Military Academy

Valuable prizes were also given to a group of authors for their work:

Gen Lieut Artillery S. A. Torkunov, dept head, Dzerzhinskiy Military Engineering
Academy
Gen Major D. I. Osadchiy
Gen Major N. S. Vasendin
Lieut Colonel K. A. Alekseyevskiy
Colonel A. M. Umanskiy
Colonel N. N. Kuznetsov
Colonel G. I. Il'in

Major I. P. Terekhov
Colonel A. I. Kuz'min
Colonel A. P. Gorbunov

A work on military art won honorable mention:

Gen Lieut P. V. Stepshin
Colonel N. G. Ganotskiy
Gen Major M. G. Titov
Colonel I. M. Bershadskiy

For a work valuable to the development of military science, honorable mention went to General Colonel M. I. Povaliy, deputy chief of the General Staff, and a group of authors from the Academy of the General Staff.

1967

In 1967, Marshal of the Soviet Union M. V. Zakharov, chief of the General Staff, chaired the Frunze Prize Commission, with Chief Marshal of Armored Troops P. A. Rotmistrov as his deputy. Three books edited by R. Ya. Malinovskiy were nominated for the 1967 Frunze Prize in late 1967. They were:[3]

The Yassy-Kishinev Cannae, Nauka, 1964
Budapest—Vienna—Prague, Nauka, 1965
Finale, Nauka, 1966

However, when the prizes were awarded in 1968, the 1967 prize went to *V. I. Lenin and the Soviet Armed Forces*, written by a group from the Lenin Military-Political Academy. The authors were:[4]

Gen Colonel A. S. Zheltov, commandant, Lenin Military-Political Academy
Gen Major A. A. Strokov, Dept History of Military Art
Colonel N. R. Pankratov, head, Dept History of the CPSU
Colonel V. A. Ustimenko, Dept History of the CPSU
Colonel Yu. I. Korablev
Colonel S. V. Baranov, Dept History of the CPSU
Colonel A. A. Babakov
Colonel P. S. Smirnov, Dept History of the CPSU
Colonel A. M. Iovlev
Colonel M. V. Vetrov, Dept Scientific Communism
Colonel A. D. Kiselev, Dept History of the CPSU
Colonel V. A. Matsulenko, Dept History of Military Art

This book came out in a second edition in 1969 and a third in 1980, as the first volume in the 1980s "red" Officer's Library series.

A number of other authors contributed to Soviet military science and received honorable mention:

Marshal of the Soviet Union I. Kh. Bagramyan, deputy Minister of Defense, chief, Rear Services
Gen of the Army V. F. Margelov, commander, Airborne Troops

Gen Col. F. M. Malykhin, 1st dep chief, Rear Services
Gen Major P. F. Pavlenko, C/S Airborne Troops
Gen Major I. M. Golushko, C/S, Rear Services
Colonel F. I. Patyk
Colonel V. A. Feklin
Colonel A. A. Bykov
Colonel Ya. P. Samoylenko
Colonel V. Ye. Kondrashev
Colonel I. N. Chaban
Colonel V. A. Bulatnikov
Colonel N. M. Sorokin

1968

In late December 1968, five books were nominated for the 1968 Frunze Prize. They were:[5]

1. *50 Years of the Armed Forces of the USSR* and *50 Years Soviet Armed Forces*, Voyenizdat, 1967, 1968, by General Colonel K. F. Skorobogatkin and K. V. Kraynyukov.
2. *Military Strategy*, Voyenizdat, 1968, edited by Marshal of the Soviet Union V. D. Sokolovskiy.**
3. *Tactics*, Voyenizdat, 1966, by General Major V. G. Reznichenko.**
4. *Order of Lenin Leningrad Military District*, Lenizdat, 1968, edited by General Colonel A. M. Parshikov.
5. *History of the Baltic Military District*, Za Rodinu Publishers, 1968, edited by General of the Army G. I. Khetagurov.

Two books were nominated in late 1969 for the 1969 Frunze Prize. They were:[6]

1. *Soviet Air Forces in the Great Patriotic War*, Voyenizdat, 1968, edited by Marshal of Aviation S. I. Rudenko.
2. *Aviation and Cosmonautics*, Voyenizdat, 1968, edited by Marshal of Aviation S. A. Krasovskiy.

1969

Krasnaya Zvezda announced that the Frunze Prize Commission awarded the 1969 prize to the book *50 Years of the Armed Forces USSR* at the Commission meeting of February 17, 1970.[7]

1970

In November 1970, *Krasnaya Zvezda* published the names of the books nominated for the 1970 Frunze Prize. They were as follows:[8]

1. *Party-Political Work in the Soviet Armed Forces in the Years of the Great Patriotic War*, Voyenizdat, 1968, edited by General Colonel K. V. Kraynyukov.

**Military Strategy* and *Tactics* were both part of the 1960s "blue" Officer's Library series. The winner of the Frunze Prize for 1968 was never announced.

2. *Kiev Red Banner,* Kiev Publishers, 1969, edited by General Lieutenant N. A. Soloveykin.
3. *Methodological Problems of Military Theory and Practice,* Voyenizdat, 1969, edited by General Colonel A. S. Zheltov.
4. *The Last Storm,* Voyenizdat, 1970, by General Major I. V. Parot'kin, Colonel A. N. Shimanskiy, and Colonel F. D. Vorob'yev.

1971

Regrettably, the prize winner for 1971 was never announced. Announcements of the Frunze Prize awards were drastically curtailed beginning in 1969. Marshal of the Soviet Union M. V. Zakharov, chief of the General Staff until September 1971, is believed to have been a moving force behind the introduction of the Frunze Prize.

1972

In November 1972, six books were nominated for the 1973 Frunze Prize:[9]

1. *Liberating Mission of the Soviet Armed Forces in the Second World War,* Politizdat, 1971, edited by Marshal of the Soviet Union A. A. Grechko.
2. *V. I. Lenin and Soviet Military Science,* Nauka, 1971, by Colonel N. N. Azovtsev.
3. *Philosophical Heritage of V. I. Lenin and Problems of Contemporary War,* Voyenizdat, 1972, edited by General Major A. S. Milovidov.
4. *Soviet Army,* Politizdat, 1969, edited by General Lieutenant S. S. Lototskiy.
5. *Heroic Defense of Sevastopol', 1941–1942,* Voyenizdat, 1969, Military Science Society of Sevastopol' Officer's Club.
6. *Questions of Strategy and Operational Art in Soviet Military Works, 1917–1940,* and *Questions of Tactics in Soviet Military Works, 1917–1940,* Voyenizdat, 1965 and 1970, sponsored by the Military Science Society of the Frunze Central Officer's Club.

According to one source, *Liberating Mission of the Soviet Armed Forces in the Second World War* won the prize.

1974

The winner of the 1974 Frunze Prize was *Methodological Bases for Determining Losses.*[10] Authors were:

Gen Lieut N. A. Sbytov, professor, head of Dept Strategy, Academy of G/S
Gen Maj K. K. Belokonov, professor, Academy of G/S
Rear Admiral V. I. Andreyev, professor, Academy of G/S

1975

Rear Services of the Armed Forces in the Great Patriotic War, 1941–1945 won the 1975 Frunze Prize. A three-volume work, *The Navy of the Soviet Union in the Great Patriotic War, 1941–1945* won a prize prior to 1975, but the year was not given.[11]

1982

In 1982, a series of five books entitled *Tactics in Combat Examples* won the prize.[12] In addition, books entitled *Mathematical Support of Usage of Automation Means and Automated Systems in the Process of Troop Control* and *The Rear of the Soviet Armed Forces in the Great Patriotic War, 1941–1945* won awards for their authors.

1984

An unnamed work on front operations won the Frunze Prize in 1984. The authors were affiliated with the Voroshilov Military Academy of the General Staff. They were:[13]

General Colonel F. F. Gayvoronskiy, professor
General Major B. A. Gusev
General Major A. Z. Yekimovskiy, candidate of military science, assistant professor
General Major N. G. Popov, doctor of military science, professor
General Major S. V. Shtrik, candidate of military science, assistant professor
General Major P. G. Yanovskiy, candidate of military science, assistant professor
Colonel V. G. Rog, doctor of military science, professor
Colonel N. V. Semenov, candidate of historical science, assistant professor
Colonel V. I. Spasov, doctor of military science, professor
Colonel I. A. Fedotov, doctor of military science, professor
Colonel T. S. Basiy
Colonel I. F. Pachok

1986

In March 1987, the 1986 Frunze Prize was awarded to a doctor of military science, General Colonel M. A. Gareyev, for his work *M. V. Frunze: Military Theoretician*. Another group of authors, headed by Marshal of Engineer Troops S. Kh. Aganov, was given awards for *Engineer Troops of the Soviet Army, 1918–1945*. A group headed by Rear Admiral N. S. Solomenko got honorable mention for its unnamed work.[14]

Many of the Frunze Prize winners have been affiliated with the Voroshilov Military Academy of the General Staff. In addition to those who won the 1984 prize listed above, the following authors from the Academy have won prizes:[15]

1974, Rear Admiral V. I. Andreyev, doctor of naval science, professor
1974, General K. K. Belokonov, candidate of military science, professor
1965, 1971, General Major V. V. Larionov, doctor of historical science, professor
1982, General I. S. Lyutov, doctor of military science, professor
1974, General Lieutenant N. A. Sbytov, candidate of military science

Notes

1. *Krasnaya Zvezda*, March 4, 1966.
2. *Krasnaya Zvezda*, March 2, 1967.
3. *Krasnaya Zvezda*, November 28, 1967.
4. *Krasnaya Zvezda*, February 21, 1968.
5. *Krasnaya Zvezda*, December 19, 1968.
6. *Krasnaya Zvezda*, November 23, 1969.
7. *Krasnaya Zvezda*, March 8, 1970.

8. *Krasnaya Zvezda,* November 28, 1970.
9. *Krasnaya Zvezda,* November 12, 1972.
10. *Akademiya Generalnogo Shtaba* [Academy of the General Staff] (Moscow: Voyenizdat, 1974), p. 207.
11. P. A. Zhilin, ed., *Problemy Voyennoy Istorii* [Problems of Military History] (Moscow: Voyenizdat, 1975), p. 376.
12. *Krasnaya Zvezda,* May 16, 1982.
13. M. M. Kozlov, *Akademiya Voyennogo Shtaba* [Academy of the General Staff], 2nd ed. (Moscow: Voyenizdat, 1987), p. 183.
14. *Krasnaya Zvezda,* March 4, 1987.
15. Kozlov, *Akademiya Voyennogo Shtaba,* p. 244.

Appendix F:
Warsaw Pact Military Doctrine

In the latter part of May 1987, General Secretary Mikhail S. Gorbachev met with his Warsaw Pact counterparts in Berlin. The Political Consultative Committee (PKK) of the Warsaw Pact discussed its disarmament proposals to that date and further steps to be taken. Accompanying Gorbachev were A. A. Gromyko, Politburo member and chairman of the Presidium of the Supreme Soviet, USSR; N. I. Ryzhkov, Politburo member and chairman of the Council of Ministers USSR; E. A. Shevardnadze, Politburo member and Minister of Foreign Affairs; Marshal of the Soviet Union S. L. Sokolov, candidate member of the Politburo and Minister of Defense USSR; and V. A. Medvedev, secretary of the CPSU Central Committee.

The meeting ended May 29 with the signing by all members of the document "On the Military Doctrine of the Warsaw Pact Member States." Such an agreement has never been published before. It should be remembered that they are talking about the military doctrine of the Warsaw Pact and not Soviet military doctrine. It may reflect that part of Soviet military doctrine that applies to the Warsaw Pact, but only, by the Soviet officials' own admission, the very basic provisions. The translation of the text of the document, as published in *Pravda* on May 30, 1987, is reprinted below.

In contemporary circumstances, the significance of the correct interpretation of the goals and intentions of states and military-political alliances in the military sphere, embodied in their military doctrines, is growing. Recognizing this and proceeding from the necessity for the final elimination of war from the life of mankind, for curtailing the arms race, for eliminating the use of military force, and for strengthening the peace and security and the implementation of general and complete disarmament, the states—members of the Warsaw Pact—have decided to set forth the *fundamental positions of their military doctrine which serves as a basis of the activities of the Warsaw Pact* and reflects the community of the defensive military-political goals of its member states and their national military doctrines. (Emphasis added.)

I

The military doctrine of the Warsaw Pact, just as that of each of its participants, is subordinated to the task of the preventing [*nedopushcheniya*] of war—both nuclear and conventional. By virtue of the very nature of the socialist social structure, these states have never tied and will not tie their future to military solutions of international problems. They advocate the solution of all disputed international problems only in peaceful ways, by political means.

In the nuclear-space age the world has become too fragile for war and power politics. Under conditions when colossal quantities of the most lethal armaments have been accumulated, mankind is faced with the problem of survival; world war, and even more so nuclear war, could have catastrophic consequences not only for the countries directly involved in the conflict, but also for life itself on Earth.

The military doctrine of Warsaw Pact member states is strictly defensive and proceeds from the fact that in today's circumstances the use of the military way for resolving any disputed question is inadmissible [*nedopustimo*]. Its essence is as follows:

Warsaw Pact member states will never, under any circumstances, begin military actions against any state or alliance of states whatsoever unless they themselves become the target of an armed attack.

They will never use nuclear weapons first.

They have no territorial claims to any state either in Europe or outside of Europe.

They do not treat [*otnosyatsya*] any state nor any people as their enemy; on the contrary, they are ready to build relationships with all countries of the world without exception on the basis of mutual regard for the interests of security and peaceful coexistence. The Warsaw Pact member states declare that their own international relations are firmly based on respect for the principles of independence and national sovereignty, the non-use of force or the threat of force, the inviolability of borders and territorial integrity, the resolution of conflicts in peaceful ways, noninterference in internal affairs, equal rights, and the other principles and goals envisaged by the United Nations Charter and the Helsinki Final Act and the generally recognized norms of international relations.

While advocating the carrying out of measures of disarmament, the Warsaw Pact member states are compelled to maintain their armed forces in such a strength and at such a level that would permit them to repulse any attack from outside against any member state.

The armed forces of the alliance states are maintained in combat readiness sufficient to not allow them to be taken by surprise; and in such a case, if an attack is nevertheless made upon them, they will give a crushing repulse [*sokrushitel'nyy otpor*] to the aggressor. The Warsaw Pact member states have never had and do not have an aspiration to have armed forces and armaments above what is necessary for these purposes. Thus, they strictly adhere to the limits of sufficiency for defense, for repulsing [*otrazhenya*] possible aggression.

II

The Warsaw Pact member states consider the primary obligation to their own people to be the reliable maintenance of their security. Allied socialist states do not aspire to greater security than other states have, but they will not accept less either. The existence at the present time of military strategic parity is a decisive factor of barring war. However, the further increase in the level of parity will not bring, as experience shows, greater security. Therefore they will continue to make efforts to preserve the balance of armed forces at an ever lower level. Under these conditions, curtailing the arms race and carrying out real measures of disarmament are acquiring genuinely historical significance. States in our time have no other way but to arrive at agreement on the radical lowering of military confrontation.

Warsaw Pact member states decisively adhere to these positions. In full correspondence with the defensive essence of their military doctrine, they consistently strive for the following basic goals:

FIRST: The earliest possible general and complete prohibition of nuclear testing as a primary measure in the matter of halting the development, production and improvement of nuclear weapons; their step by step reduction and complete elimination; and banning the spread of the arms race to outer space.

SECOND: Prohibition and elimination of chemical and other kinds of weapons of mass destruction.

THIRD: Reduction in Europe of armed forces and conventional armaments to a level at which neither side, while maintaining their own defense, would have means for a surprise attack on the other side, or for development of offensive operations in general.

FOURTH: Strict verification of all measures of disarmament, based on combining national technical means and international procedures, including the creation of corresponding international agencies, the exchange of military information, conducting on-site inspections.

FIFTH: The creation, in various regions of Europe and in other regions of the world, of zones free from nuclear and chemical weapons and also zones of lowered concentration of armaments, and increased confidence, carrying out military confidence-building measures on a mutual basis, and the achievement of agreement about such measures in other regions of the world, and also on seas and oceans. The mutual renunciation of Warsaw Pact member states and NATO members of the use of military force and the adoption of an obligation to maintain relationships of peace; the elimination of military bases on the territories of other states; the withdrawal of troops to within national borders; mutual withdrawal from zones of direct contact of the two military alliances of the most dangerous offensive kinds of weapons and also decreasing the concentration in these zones of armed forces and armaments to the minimum agreed levels.

SIXTH: Considering the continuing split of Europe into opposed military blocs as abnormal, the Warsaw Pact member states call for the simultaneous dissolution of NATO and the Warsaw Pact and, as a first step, the elimination of their military organizations, and the creation in the final count of a universal system of international security.

Warsaw Pact member states propose to NATO members to hold consultations for the purpose of comparing the military doctrines of both alliances, analysing their nature, and carrying out joint studies on the directions of their further evolution, with the idea in mind of removing the mutual suspiciousness and mistrust which has accumulated over the years, reaching a better understanding of each other's intentions, and ensuring that military concepts and doctrines of military blocs and their members are based on defensive principles.

Another subject for consultation might be the imbalances and asymmetries in individual kinds of armaments and armed forces and the search for ways to eliminate them on the basis of reductions by the side which is ahead, with the understanding that reductions will lead to the establishment of ever lower levels.

Socialist Pact member states propose to conduct such consultations on an authoritative expert level with the participation of military specialists of countries of both sides. They are ready to conduct such consultations in 1987. Consultations could be held in Warsaw or in Brussels, or in turn in each of these cities.

Todor ZHIVKOV, General Secretary of the Central Committee of the Bulgarian Communist Party, Chairman of the State Council of the People's Republic of Bulgaria.

Janos KADAR, General Secretary of the Hungarian Socialist Worker's Party.

Erich HONECKER, General Secretary of the Central Committee of the Socialist Unity Party of Germany, Chairman of the Council of State of the GDR.

Wojciech JARUZELSKI, 1st Secretary of the Central Committee of the Polish United Workers' Party, Chairman of the Council of State of the Polish People's Republic.

Nicolae CEAUSESCU, General Secretary of the Romanian Communist Party, President of the Socialist Republic of Romania.

Mikhail GORBACHEV, General Secretary of the Central Committee of the Communist Party of the Soviet Union.

Gustav HUSAK, General Secretary of the Central Committee of the Communist Party of Czechoslovakia, President of the Czechoslovak Socialist Republic.

Bibliography

Afanas'yev, V. G., *Marxist Philosophy*. Moscow: Foreign Languages Publishing House, 1962.

———, *Fundamentals of Scientific Communism*, 2nd ed. Moscow: Progress Publishers, 1977.

Akademiya General'nogo Shtaba [Academy of the General Staff], 1st and 2nd eds. Moscow: Voyenizdat, 1976, 1986.

Akademiya Imeni M. V. Frunze [Academy Named for M. V. Frunze]. Moscow: Voyenizdat, 1973.

Akhromeyev, S. F., ed., *Voyennyy Entsiklopedicheskiy Slovar'* [Military Encyclopedia Dictionary], 2nd ed. Moscow: Voyenizdat, 1986.

Andropov, Yuriy V., *Izbrannyye Rechi i Stat'i* [Selected Speeches and Articles]. Moscow: Politizdat, 1983.

———, *Sixtieth Anniversary of the USSR* (December 21, 1982). Moscow: Novosti, 1983.

Arbatov, A. G., *Voyenno-Strategicheskiy Paritet i Politika SShA* [Military-Strategic Parity and the Policies of the USA]. Moscow: Politizdat, 1984.

Astashenkov, P. T., *Sovetskiye Raketnyye Voyska* [Soviet Rocket Troops]. Moscow: Voyenizdat, 1967.

Azovtsev, N. N., *V. I. Lenin i Sovetskaya Voyennaya Nauka* [V. I. Lenin and Soviet Military Science]. Moscow: Nauka, 1971.

Bagramyan, I. Kh., ed., *Voyennaya Istoriya* [Military History]. Moscow: Voyenizdat, 1971.

Batitskiy, P. F., ed., *Voyska Protivovozdushnoy Oborony Strany* [National Air Defense Troops]. Moscow: Voyenizdat, 1968.

Bogdanov, R. G., M. A. Mil'shtein, and L. S. Semeyko, *SShA: Voyenno-Strategicheskiye Kontseptsii* [Military-Strategic Concepts]. Moscow: Nauka, 1980.

Bol'shaya Sovetskaya Entsiklopediya [Great Soviet Encyclopedia]. Moscow: Soviet Encyclopedia, 1970–1978.

Brezhnev, Leonid I., *Speech in the City of Tula*, January 18, 1977. Moscow: Novosti, 1977.

———, *Na Strazhe Mira i Sotsializma* [On Guard over Peace and Socialism]. Moscow: Politizdat, 1979.

Bublik, L. A., M. D. Popkov, N. S. Smorigo et al., *Partiyno-Politicheskaya Rabota v Sovetskoy Armii i Voyenno-Morskom Flote* [Party-Political Work in the Soviet Army and Navy]. Moscow: Voyenizdat, 1982.

Chernenko, K. U., *Safeguard Peace and Ensure the People's Well-Being*, March 2, 1984. Moscow: Novosti, 1984.

Chuvikov, P. A., *Kratkiy Ocherk Marksistsko-Leninskoy Teorii o Voyne i Armii* [A Short Essay on Marxist-Leninist Theory on War and Army], 1st ed. Moscow: Voyenizdat, 1949.

———, *Marksizm-Leninizm o Voyne i Armii* [Marxism-Leninism on War and Army], 2nd ed. Moscow: Voyenizdat, 1956.

von Clausewitz, Karl, *On War*, edited and translated by Michael Howard and Peter Paret. Princeton, New Jersey: Princeton University Press, 1976.

Constitution (Fundamental Law) of the Union of Soviet Socialist Republics. Moscow: Novosti, 1977.

Deputaty Verkhovnogo Soveta SSSR [Deputies of the Supreme Soviet USSR]. Moscow: Izvestia, 1984.

Derevyanko, P. M., *Problemy Revolyutsii v Voyennom Dele* [Problems of the Revolution in Military Affairs]. Moscow: Voyenizdat, 1965.

Dinerstein, H. S., *War and the Soviet Union*, rev. ed. New York: Praeger, 1962.

Douglass, Joseph D., Jr., and Amoretta M. Hoeber, *Selected Readings from Military Thought, 1963–1973* (English translations), vol. 5, Part 2. Washington, D.C.: US GPO, 1982.

Enthoven, Alain C., and K. Wayne Smith, *How Much is Enough?* New York: Harper and Row, 1971.

Fedorov, G. A., N. Ya. Sushko, B. A. Belyy, eds., *Marksizm-Leninizm o Voyne i Armii* [Marxism-Leninism on War and Army], 2nd ed. Moscow: Voyenizdat, 1961.

———, *Marksizm-Leninizm o Voyne i Armii* [Marxism-Leninism on War and Army], 3rd ed. Moscow: Voyenizdat, 1962.

Frunze, M. V., *Izbrannyye Proizvedeniya* [Selected Works]. Moscow: Voyenizdat, 1965.

Gareyev, M. A., *Takticheskiye Ucheniya i Manevry* [Tactical Training and Manuevers]. Moscow: Voyenizdat, 1977.

———, *M. V. Frunze—Voyennyy Teoretik* [M. V. Frunze—Military Theoretician]. Moscow: Voyenizdat, 1985.

Golubovich, V. S., *Marshal R. Ya. Malinovskiy*. Moscow: Voyenizdat, 1984.

Gorbachev, Mikhail S., *Perestroika: New Thinking for Our Country and the World*. New York: Harper and Row, 1987.

Gorshkov, S. G., *Morskaya Moshch Gosudarstva* [Seapower of a State]. Moscow: Voyenizdat, 1976.

Grazhdanskaya Voyna i Voyennaya Interventsiya v SSSR [The Civil War and Military Intervention in the USSR], encyclopedia. Moscow: Soviet Encyclopedia, 1983.

Grechko, A. A., *Na Strazhe Mira i Stroitel'stva Kommunizm* [On Guard over the Peace and the Building of Communism]. Moscow: Voyenizdat, 1972.

———, *Vooruzhennyye Sily Sovetskogo Gosudarstva* [Armed Forces of the Soviet State], 1st and 2nd eds. Moscow: Voyenizdat, 1974, 1975.

———, *Armed Forces of the Soviet State* (English translation), Soviet Military Thought Series, no. 12. Washington, D.C.: US GPO, 1975.

———, *Armed Forces of the Soviet Union*. Progress Publishers, 1977.

Grinishin, D. M., *O Voyennoy Deyatel'nosti V. I. Lenina* [On the Military Activities of V. I. Lenin]. Kiev: Kiev University Publishers, 1970.

Grudinin, I. A., *Dialektika i Sovremennoye Voyennoye Delo* [Dialectics and Contemporary Military Affairs]. Moscow: Voyenizdat, 1971.

How to Avert the Threat to Europe. Moscow: Progress Publishers, 1983.

Ivanov, S. P., *Leninskiye Osnovy Sovetskoy Voyennoy Nauki* [Leninist Basis of Soviet Military Science]. Moscow: Znaniye, 1970.

_____, *The Initial Period of War* (English translation), Soviet Military Thought Series, no. 20. Washington, D.C.: US GPO, 1974.

_____, *O Nauchnykh Osnovakh Upravleniya Voyskami* [On the Scientific Bases of Troop Control]. Moscow: Voyenizdat, 1975.

Jacobs, Walter Darnell, *Frunze: The Soviet Clausewitz, 1885–1925*. The Hague: Martinus Nijhoff, 1969.

Jones, Ellen, *Red Army and Society*. Boston: Allen & Unwin, 1985.

Khrushchev, N. S., *On Peaceful Coexistence*. Moscow: Foreign Languages Publishing House, 1961. "Report of the Central Committee CPSU to the Twentieth Party Congress," February 14, 1956.

_____, *Disarmament—The Way to a Sure Peace and Friendship Between Peoples*. Moscow: Gospolitizdat, 1960.

Kintner, W. R. and H. F. Scott, *Nuclear Revolution in Soviet Military Affairs*. Norman, Oklahoma: University of Oklahoma Press, 1968.

Kir'yan, M. M., ed., *Voyenno-Tekhnicheskiy Progress i Vooruzhennyye Sily SSSR* [Military-Technical Progress and the Armed Forces USSR]. Moscow: Voyenizdat, 1982.

_____, *Problemy Voyennoy Teorii v Sovetskikh Nauchno-Spravochnykh Izdaniyakh* [Problems of Military Theory in Soviet Scientific Reference Publications]. Moscow: Nauka, 1985.

_____, ed., *Velikaya Otechestvennaya Voyna, 1941–1945* [Great Patriotic War, 1941–1945], reference dictionary. Moscow: Politizdat, 1985.

Kiryayev, N. M., *KPSS i Stroitel'stvo Sovetskikh Vooruzhennykh Sil* [CPSU and the Structuring of the Soviet Armed Forces]. Moscow: Voyenizdat, 1967.

Kozlov, S. N., ed., *The Officer's Handbook* (English translation), Soviet Military Thought Series, no. 13. Washington, D.C.: US GPO, 1971.

_____, ed., *Spravochnik Ofitsera* [The Officer's Handbook]. Moscow: Voyenizdat, 1971.

Kozlov, S. N., M. V. Smirnov, I. S. Baz', and P. A. Sidorov, *O Sovetskoy Voyennoy Nauke* [On Soviet Military Science], 2nd ed. Moscow: Voyenizdat, 1964.

Kulish, V. M., ed., *Voyennaya Sila i Mezhdunarodnyye Otnosheniya* [Military Force and International Relations]. Moscow: International Relations Publishing House, 1972.

Kuusinen, O. V., sr. ed., *Fundamentals of Marxism-Leninism*. Moscow: Foreign Languages Publishing House, 1963.

Lee, William T., and Richard F. Staar, *Soviet Military Policy*. Stanford, California: Hoover Institution, 1987.

Levanov, I. N., B. A. Belyy, and A. P. Novoselov, *Markizm-Leninizm o Voyne i Armii* [Marxism-Leninism on War and Army], 1st ed. Moscow: Voyenizdat, 1957.

Lomov, N. A., *Sovetskaya Voyennaya Doktrina* [Soviet Military Doctrine]. Moscow: Znaniye, 1963.

_____, ed., *Nauchno-Tekhnicheskiy Progress i Razvitiye Voyennogo Dela* [Scientific-Technical Progress and Development of Military Affairs]. Moscow: Znaniye, 1970.

_____, ed., *Nauchno-Tekhnicheskiy Progress i Revolyutsiya v Voyennom Dele* [Scientific-Technical Progress and the Revolution in Military Affairs]. Moscow: Voyenizdat, 1973.

Lototskiy, S. S., ed., *Armiya Sovetskaya* [Army of the Soviets]. Moscow: Politizdat, 1969.

Malinovskiy, R. Ya., *Bditel'no Stoyat' na Strazhe Mira* [Vigilantly Stand Guard over the Peace]. Moscow: Voyenizdat, 1962.

Mal'tsev, Ye. Ye., *KPSS—Organizator Zashchity Sotsialisticheskogo Otechestva* [CPSU, Organizer of the Defense of the Socialist Fatherland], 1st ed. Moscow: Voyenizdat, 1974.

Materialy XXVII S"yezd KPSS [Materials of the 27th Congress of the CPSU]. Moscow: Politizdat, 1986.

Medvedev, Roy A., *Let History Judge.* New York: Alfred A. Knopf, 1972.

Milovidov, A. S., ed., *Voyenno-Teoreticheskoye Naslediye V. I. Lenina i Problemy Sovremennoy Voyny* [Military-Theoretical Heritage of V. I. Lenin and Problems of Contemporary War]. Moscow: Voyenizdat, 1987.

Milovidov, A. S., and V. G. Kozlov, eds., *Filosofskoye Naslediye V. I. Lenina i Problemy Sovremennoy Voyny* [Philosophical Heritage of V. I. Lenin and Problems of Contemporary War]. Moscow: Voyenizdat, 1972.

————, eds., *The Philosophical Heritage of V. I. Lenin and Problems of Contemporary War*, Soviet Military Thought Series, no. 5. Washington, D.C.: US GPO, 1972.

Newhouse, John, *Cold Dawn: The Story of SALT.* New York: Holt, Rinehart and Winston, 1973.

Ogarkov, N. V., *Vsegda v Gotovnosti k Zashchite Otechestva* [Always in Readiness to Defend the Fatherland]. Moscow: Voyenizdat, 1982.

————, *Istoriya Uchit Bditel'nosti* [History Teaches Vigilance]. Moscow: Voyenizdat, 1985.

Panov, B. V., ed., *Istoriya Voyennogo Iskusstva* [History of Military Art]. Moscow: Voyenizdat, 1984.

Perestroika: Views and Opinions. Moscow: Novosti, 1987.

Petrov, Yu. P., *Partiynoye Stroitel'stvo v Sovetskoy Armii i Flote, 1918–1961* [Party Structuring in the Soviet Army and Navy, 1918–1961]. Moscow: Voyenizdat, 1964.

————, *Stroitel'stvo Politorganov, Partiynykh i Komsomol'skikh Organizatsiy Armii i Flota* [Structuring of Politorgans, Party and Komsomol Organizations of the Army and Navy]. Moscow: Voyenizdat, 1968.

Petrovskiy, V. F., ed., *Doktrina "Natsional'noy Bezopasnosti" v Glogbal'noy Strategii SShA* [Doctrine of "National Security" in the Global Strategy of the USA]. Moscow: International Relations Publishing House, 1980.

Piterskiy, N. A., ed., *Boyevoy Put' Sovetskogo Voyenno-Morskogo Flota* [History of the Soviet Navy]. Moscow: Voyenizdat, 1967.

Political Report of the CPSU Central Committee to the 27th Party Congress. Moscow: Novosti, 1986.

Popov, M. V., *Sushchnost' Zakonov Vooruzhennoy Bor'by* [Essence of the Laws of Armed Conflict]. Moscow: Voyenizdat, 1964.

Pospelov, P. N., ed., *Istoriya Velikoy Otechestvennoy Voyny Sovetskogo Soyuza, 1941–1945* [History of the Great Patriotic War of the Soviet Union, 1941–1945]. Moscow: Voyenizdat, 1961–1965.

Problemy Revolutsii v Voyennom Dele [Problems of the Revolution in Military Affairs]. Moscow: Voyenizdat, 1965.

Programma Kommunisticheskoy Partii Sovetskogo Soyuza [Programme of the Communist Party of the Soviet Union]. Moscow: Pravda Publishers, 1961.

Programme of the Communist Party of the Soviet Union, a New Edition, approved March 1, 1986. Moscow: Novosti, 1986.

Prokop'yev, N. P., *O Voyne i Armii* [On War and Army]. Moscow: Voyenizdat, 1965.

Savkin, V. Ye., *Osnovnyye Printsipy Operativnogo Iskusstva i Taktiki* [Basic Principles of Operational Art and Tactics]. Moscow: Voyenizdat, 1972.

Scott, Harriet Fast, and William F. Scott, *The Soviet Art of War*, Boulder, Colorado: Westview Press, 1982.

————, *Soviet Control Structure.* New York: Crane, Russak and Company, Inc., 1983.

————, *The Armed Forces of the USSR*, 3rd ed., Boulder, Colorado: Westview Press, 1984.

Semmel, Bernard, *Marxism and the Science of War.* U.K.: Oxford University Press, 1981.

Serebryannikov, V. V., *Osnovy Marksistsko-Leninskogo Ucheniye o Voyne i Armii* [Basis of Marxist-Leninist Teachings on War and Army]. Moscow: Voyenizdat, 1982.

Shavrov, I. Ye., ed., *Lokal'nyye Voyny* [Local Wars]. Moscow: Voyenizdat, 1981.

Shtemenko, S. M., *General'nyy Shtab v Gody Voyny* [General Staff in the War Years]. Moscow: Voyenizdat, 1983.

Sibilev, M. U., *Armiya Strany Sovetov* [Army of the Land of the Soviets]. Moscow: Voyenizdat, 1985.

Skirdo, M. P., *Narod, Armiya, Polkovodets* [The People, the Army, the Commander]. Moscow: Voyenizdat, 1970.

————, *The People, the Army, the Commander* (English translation), Soviet Military Thought Series, no. 14. Washington, D.C.: US GPO, 1970.

Smirnov, M. V., I. S. Baz', S. N. Kozlov, and P. A. Sidorov, *O Sovetskoy Voyennoy Nauke* [On Soviet Military Science], 1st ed. Moscow: Voyenizdat, 1960.

Sobolev, M. G., ed., *Partiyno-Politicheskaya Rabota v Sovetskoy Armii i Flote* [Party-Political Work in the Soviet Army and Fleet]. Moscow: Voyenizdat, 1984.

Sokolovskiy, V. D., ed., *Voyennaya Strategiya* [Military Strategy], 1st, 2nd, and 3rd eds. Moscow: Voyenizdat, 1962, 1963, 1968.

————, ed., *Soviet Military Strategy*, 3rd ed., revised U.S. ed., edited, with analysis and commentary, by Harriet Fast Scott. New York: Crane, Russak & Company, Inc., 1984.

Sovetskaya Voyennaya Entsiklopediya [Soviet Military Encyclopedia]. Moscow: Voyenizdat, 1976–1980.

Sovetskoye Administrativnoye Pravo [Soviet Administrative Law]. Moscow: Legal Literature, 1981.

Soviet Military Power, Washington, D.C.: US GPO, 1987.

Spravochnik Partiynogo Rabotnika, 1986 [Party Worker's Handbook, 1986]. Moscow: Politizdat, 1986.

Sredin, G. V., *Na Strazhe Rodina* [On Guard over the Motherland]. Moscow: Voyenizdat, 1974.

Stalin, J. V., *O Velikoy Otechestvennoy Voyne Sovetskogo Soyuza* [On the Great Patriotic War of the Soviet Union], 5th ed. Moscow: Voyenizdat, 1949.

Strokov, A. A., *V. I. Lenin o Voyne i Voyennom Iskusstve* [V. I. Lenin on War and Military Art]. Moscow: Nauka, 1971.

Summer, Harry G., *On Strategy.* Novato, California: Presido Press, 1982.

Sushko, N. Ya., and T. R. Kondratkov, *Metodologicheskiye Problemy Voyennoy Teorii i Praktiki* [Methodological Problems of Military Theory and Practice], 1st ed. Moscow: Voyenizdat, 1966.

Svechin, A. A., *Strategiya* [Strategy], 1st and 2nd eds. Moscow: Voyenizdat, 1923 and 1927.

Sverdlov, F. D., *Takticheskiy Manevr* [Tactical Maneuver]. Moscow: Voyenizdat, 1982.

Tabunov, N. D. and V. A. Bokarev, eds., *Marksistsko-Leninskaya Filosofiya i Metodicheskiye Problemy Voyennoy Teorii i Praktiki* [Marxist-Leninist Philosophy and Methodological Problems of Military Theory and Practice]. Moscow: Voyenizdat, 1982.

Tolubko, V. F., *Raketnyye Voyska* [Rocket Troops]. Moscow: Znaniye, 1977.

Trifonenkov, P. I., *Ob Osnovnykh Zakonakh Khoda i Iskhoda Sovremennoy Voyny* [On the Basic Laws of the Course and Outcome of Modern War]. Moscow: Voyenizdat, 1962.

XXII S"yezd Kommunisticheskoy Partii Sovetskogo Soyuza [22nd Congress of the Communist Party of the Soviet Union], stenographic notes. Moscow: Politizdat, 1962.

XXIII S"yezd Kommunisticheskoy Partii Sovetskogo Soyuza [23rd Congress of the CPSU], stenographic notes. Moscow: Politizdat, 1966.

XXIV S"yezd Kommunisticheskoy Partii Sovetskogo Soyuza [24th Congress of the CPSU], stenographic notes. Moscow: Politizdat, 1971.

XXV S"yezd Kommunisticheskoy Partii Sovetskogo Soyuza [25th Congress of the CPSU], stenographic notes. Moscow: Politizdat, 1976.

XXVI S"yezd Kommunisticheskoy Partii Sovetskogo Soyuza [26th Congress of the CPSU], stenographic notes. Moscow: Politizdat, 1981.

XXVII S"yezd Kommunisticheskoy Partii Sovetskogo Soyuza [27th Congress of the CPSU], stenographic notes. Moscow: Politizdat, 1986.

Tyushkevich, S. A., *Sovetskiye Vooruzhennyye Sily* [Soviet Armed Forces]. Moscow: Voyenizdat, 1978.

———, *The Soviet Armed Forces: A History of Their Organizational Development* (English translation), Soviet Military Thought Series, no. 19. Washington, D.C.: US GPO, 1978.

Tyushkevich, S. A., N. Ya. Sushko, and Ya. S. Dzyuba, *Marksizm-Leninizm o Voyne i Armii* [Marxism-Leninism on War and Army], 5th ed. Moscow: Voyenizdat, 1968.

Tyushkevich, S. A., et al., *Marxism-Leninism on War and Army* (English translation), Soviet Military Thought Series, no. 2. Washington, D.C.: US GPO, 1972.

Upravleniye v Oblasti Administrativno-Politicheskoy Deyatel'nosti [Control in the Sphere of Administrative-Political Activity]. Moscow: Legal Literature, 1979.

Ustinov, D. F., *Izbrannyye Rechi i Stat'i* [Selected Speeches and Articles]. Moscow: Politizdat, 1979.

Vasilevskiy, A. M., *Delo Vsey Zhizni* [Business of a Whole Life]. Moscow, Politizdat, 1975.

Vneocherednoy XXI S"yezd Kommunisticheskoy Partii Sovetskogo Soyuza [Extraordinary XXI Congress of the Communist Party of the Soviet Union], stenographic notes. Moscow: Gospolitizdat, 1959.

Volkogonov, D. A., ed., *Marksistko-Leninskoye Ucheniye o Voyne i Armii* [Marxist-Leninist Teachings on War and Army]. Moscow: Voyenizdat, 1984.

Volkogonov, D. A., A. S. Milovidov, and S. A. Tyushkevich, *Voyna i Armiya* [War and Army]. Moscow: Voyenizdat, 1977.

Voprosy Strategii i Operativnogo Iskusstva v Sovetskikh Voyennykh Trudakh, 1917–1940 [Problems of Strategy and Operational Art in Soviet Military Works, 1917–1940]. Moscow: Voyenizdat, 1965.

Vorob'yev, K. A., *Vooruzhennyye Sily Razvitogo Sotsialisticheskogo Obshchestva* [Armed Forces of a Mature Socialist Society]. Moscow: Voyenizdat, 1980.

Voslensky, Michael S., *Nomenklatura*. Garden City, New York: Doubleday & Company, Inc., 1984.

Voyennaya Akademiya Imeni M. V. Frunze [Military Academy Named for M. V. Frunze], 2nd ed. Moscow: Voyenizdat, 1980.

Voyenno-Vozdushnaya Akademiya Imeni Yu. A. Gagarina [Military Air Academy Named for Yu. A. Gagarin]. Moscow: Voyenizdat, 1984.

Voyennyye Voprosy v Kurse Istorii SSSR [Military Questions in the Course of History of the USSR]. Moscow: Voyenizdat, 1986.

Yazov, D. T., *Na Strazhe Sotsializma i Mira* [On Guard over Socialism and Peace]. Moscow: Voyenizdat, 1987.

Yepishev, A. A., *Ideologicheskaya Bor'ba po Voyennym Voprosam* [Ideological Struggle on Military Questions]. Moscow: Voyenizdat, 1974.

────── , *KPSS i Voyennoye Stroitel'stvo* [CPSU and Military Development]. Moscow: Voyenizdat, 1982.

Yezhegodnik Bol'shoy Sovetskoy Entsiklopedii, 1986 [Annual of the Great Soviet Encyclopedia, 1986]. Moscow: Soviet Encyclopedia, 1986.

Zakharov, M. V., *O Nauchnom Podkhode k Rukovodstvu Voyskami* [On the Scientific Approach to the Leadership of Troops]. Moscow: Voyenizdat, 1967.

────── , *50 Let Vooruzhennykh Sil SSSR* [50 Years of the Armed Forces USSR]. Moscow: Voyenizdat, 1968.

Zheltov, A. S., ed., *V. I. Lenin i Sovetskiye Vooruzhennyye Sily* [V. I. Lenin and the Soviet Armed Forces], 1st ed. Moscow: Voyenizdat, 1967.

────── , ed., *Metodologicheskiye Problemy Voyennoy Teorii i Praktiki* [Methodological Problems of Military Theory and Practice], 2nd ed. Moscow: Voyenizdat, 1969.

────── , ed., *Soldat i Voyna* [Soldier and War]. Moscow: Voyenizdat, 1971.

Zhilin, P. A., *Problemy Voyennoy Istorii* [Problems of Military History]. Moscow: Voyenizdat, 1975.

────── , ed., *Zarozhdeniye i Razvitiye Sovetskiy Voyennoy Istoriografii, 1917–1941* [Origin and Development of Soviet Military Historiography, 1917–1941]. Moscow: Nauka, 1985.

────── , ed., *Istoriya Voyennogo Iskusstva* [History of Military Art]. Moscow: Voyenizdat, 1986.

Zhukov, G. K., *Vospominaniya i Razmyshleniya* [Reminiscences and Reflections]. Moscow: Novosti, 1975.

Zhukov, Ye. V., *XXVII S"yezd KPSS o Sovetskoy Voyennoy Doktrine* [27th Congress CPSU and Soviet Military Doctrine]. Moscow: Voyenizdat, 1987.

Name Index

Aganov, S. Kh., 242
Akhromeyev, S. F., 100, 120, 199, 217
Aliyev, G. A., 207
Alksnis, Ya. I., 13
Altunin, A. T., 177
Andropov, Yu. V., 70, 100, 101, 109,
    110, 124, 166–167, 230, 260, 263
Antonov, A. I., 214
Anureyev, I. I., 240
Arbatov, G. A., 222
Azovtsev, N. N., 235, 241

Bagramyan, I. Kh., 183
Baranov, P. I., 212
Batitskiy, P. F., 183
Baz', I. S., 42
Belikov, V. A., 185
Bel'tsin, B., 199
Beria, L., 71, 166, 188, 197, 237
Betekhtin, A. V., 168
Biryuzov, S. S., 44
Blyukher, V. K., 16, 213
Bovin, A., 249
Brezhnev, L. I., 19, 23, 32, 36, 44–48,
    53, 56, 60, 69, 72–73, 80, 92, 98–
    100, 109, 116, 124–125 150, 166–
    167, 194, 230, 253, 259–260, 263
Brokaw, Tom, 249
Brown, Harold, 259
Bubnov, A. A., 212
Budennyy, S. M., 212–214
Bulganin, N. A., 197, 214

Carter, Jimmy, 73, 92, 109
Chebrikov, V. M., 166, 199, 207, 209
Cherednichenko, M. I., 223
Chernavin, V. N., 185
Chernenko, K. U., 100, 101, 109, 166–
    167, 199, 230
Chou En-lai, 32
Chuvikov, P. A., 19, 137, 138

Chuykov, V. I., 166, 183
Clausewitz, Karl von, 3, 146, 218, 239

Demichev, P. N., 191
Denisenko, V. K., 218
Dobrynin, A. F., 192
Dolgikh, V. I., 191
Douhet, Giulio, 137
Dunayev, A. I., 222
Dybenko, P. Ye., 16

Eideman, R. P., 13, 16, 243
Eisenhower, Dwight D., 31
Engels, Friedrich, 20, 22, 28, 132

Fed'ko, I. F., 16, 213
Fedorchuk, V. V., 177
Flynn, Elizabeth Gurley, 32
Ford, Gerald, 69, 72
Frunze, M. V., 5–12, 14, 45, 171, 179,
    181, 212, 229, 243
Fuller, J.F.C., 137

Gagarin, Yu. A., 32
Gamarnik, Ya. B., 16
Gareyev, M. A., 103, 111, 113, 115, 124,
    170, 218, 242
Gastilovich, A. I., 36, 60
Gerasimov, I. A., 120, 168
Glazov, V. V., 218
Gomulka, Wladislaw, 32
Gorbachev, M. S., 32, 34, 97–98, 100–
    102, 109–110, 122, 159, 166–167,
    175, 189, 191, 198–199, 203, 209,
    223, 231, 233, 248, 253–254, 257,
    259–264
Gorshkov, S. G., 71, 176, 185
Grechko, A. A., 53, 57, 61, 71–72, 75–
    79, 80–83, 85–87, 104–105, 237,
    250, 257
Grinishin, D. M., 54

297

Subject Index

300